UNDERSTANDING FUNGI

By

Dr. Pooja

Deptt. of Botany
R.C.C. College
Ghaziabad (U.P.)
(India)

DISCOVERY PUBLISHING HOUSE PVT. LTD.
NEW DELHI-110 002

Published by:
Tilak Wasan
DISCOVERY PUBLISHING HOUSE PVT. LTD.
4831/24, Ansari Road, Prahlad Street
Darya Ganj, New Delhi-110002 (India)
Phone: +91-11-23279245, 43764432
Fax: +91-11-23253475
E-mail: parul.wasan@gmail.com
info@discoverypublishinggroup.com
discoverypublishinghouse@gmail.com
web: www.discoverypublishinggroup.com

First Edition: 2011
ISBN: 978-81-8356-858-6

Understanding Fungi

Printed at:
Mehra Offset Press
Delhi

UNDERSTANDING FUNGI

Preface

The present title "*Understanding Fungi*" provides a structured approach to learning by covering all the important topics in a uniform, systematic format. The book has been comprehensively designed incorporating recent advances in this fast moving field. It is written to provide accessible information on fungi in compact form for undergraduate students in biology and related life sciences. It will be useful for both beginning students and those who are more advanced. In addition, busy lecturers who require a quick reference compendium will find it useful, particularly for tutional planning. Simple, yet hopefully clear figures and tables are provided throughout the book.

The over-riding goal of this book, and indeed of the whole *Understanding series,* is to present the essential information concering microbiology in a compact, readily accessible form which leads itself to student learning and revision. The convergence of various approaches has generated a rich panorama of detail, the significance of which we are still attempting to unraval. The present text has been written as an introduction to this rapidly growing field.

To make the work more comprehensive and informative, the author has consulted many authoritative books, research journals, abstracts, monographs etc., so there can be no claim to originality except in the manner of treatment.

The author expresses his thanks to his friends and colleagues whose continue inspirations have initiated him to bring out this book.

The author expresses his gratitude to Mr. Wasan and staff of M/s Discovery Publishing House Pvt. Ltd. for their whole hearted co-operation in the publication of this book.

In the mean time, the author will remain sincerely responsible for any shortcomings of the book and be grateful to the readers for their suggestions and constructive criticism for the continuous betterment of the book. He takes this opportunity to appeal to the readers to send their suggestions straightaway to his Publisher.

Author

Contents

Gymnomycota: The Slime Molds

The slime molds, also known as Mycetozoa (fungus animals), have been comprehensively summarized by Olive (1975). They differ from the true fungi in their phagotrophic nutrition and in that their somatic parts lack cell walls, consisting only of protoplasts bounded by plasma membranes.

Their spores, however, are each enveloped by a rigid cell wall as are those of the true fungi. Three groups of slime molds are known: the cellular slime molds (Acrasiomycetes), the Protostelids (Protosteliom-ycetes), and the true, or plasmodial, slime molds (Myxomycetes).

Olive also includes the endoparasitic slime molds (Plasmodiopho-romycetes) and the net slime molds (Labryinthulales) in his discussion, but most mycologists believe these two groups to be more properly assigned to another division of fungi.

SUBDIVISION ACRASIOGYMNOMYCOTINA

Class Acrasiomycetes

The Acrasiomycetes (cellular slime molds) have the following characters:

1. They produce no flagellated cells.
2. Their *myxamoebae* (special types of amoebae formed

by slime molds) aggregate to form a pseudoplasmodium in which they do not fuse but retain their individuality.

3. The stalks of all but a few species consist of cells.
4. The spore walls contain cellulose.

Cellular slime molds have been discovered in all continents, occurring in cultivated as well as in native soils, but are most abundant in the upper layers of humus in well established deciduous forests.

They are important in human affairs only in that they provide excellent biological systems for the study of morphogenesis and molecular biology. The best-known system is *Dictyostelium* (Gr. *dictyon,* net + Gr. *stele,* a post) *discoideum* discovered by Dr. K. B. Raper in 1935.

The *sorocarps* (a special type of sporophore) of the Acrasiomycetes are delicate and ephemeral. As such, they are seldom encountered in nature and are known almost entirely from laboratory cultures. These organisms are easy to isolate.

If a suspension of finely divided surface humus is streaked onto a weak nutrient agar medium, such as glucose-peptone or hay-infusion agar, and cross-streaked with a suspension of the bacterium *Escherichia coli,* sorocarps often appear and may then be isolated and identified.

They can be recognized by their delicate, cellular stalks, which may be simple or branched and which may arise from a disc or a cramponlike base or just be plain without a differentiated basal structure. The stalk apex of each branch holds a droplet of mucus,. in which the spores are held.

There is no common envelope around all the spores as there is around the spores of the true slime molds.

Life Cycle

The spores of the cellular slime molds are generally ovoid, and each is enveloped by a cellulose wall. As the stalk that supports them bends over and falls, the droplet of spores at its apex is released and the spores eventually germinate, each producing a single, uninucleate, haploid myxamoeba.

The myxamoebae feed by engulfing bacteria and multiply by simple cell division until a large amoebal population results. Under unfavorable conditions, the

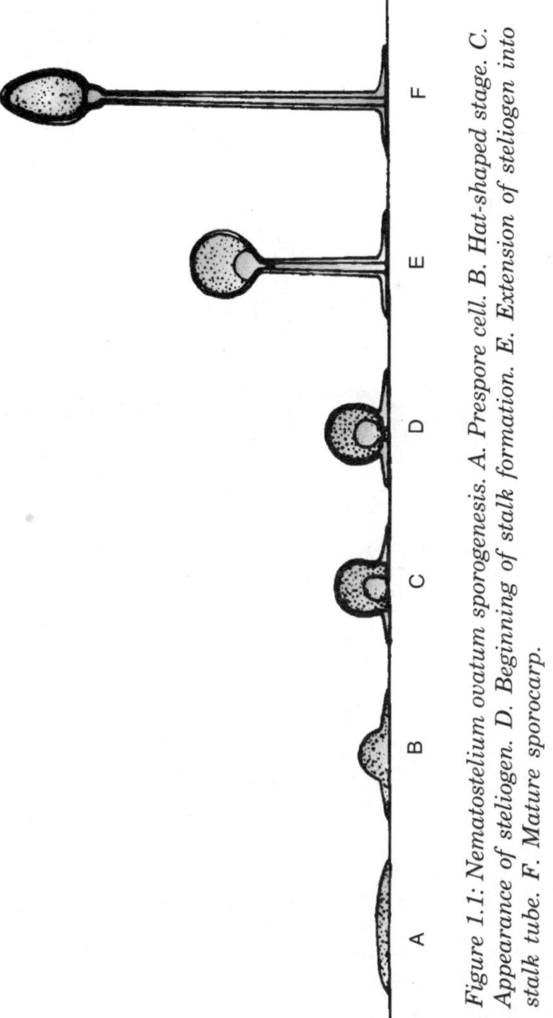

Figure 1.1: Nematostelium ovatum sporogenesis. A. Prespore cell. B. Hat-shaped stage. C. Appearance of steliogen. D. Beginning of stalk formation. E. Extension of steliogen into stalk tube. F. Mature sporocarp.

myxamoebae encyst, forming microcysts. A microcyst is an amoeba that has become rounded and has secreted a delicate but rigid cellulose wall around itself.

Upon return of favorable conditions the microcysts germinate, liberating myxamoebae that resume their normal activities. When the food supply is exhausted, an aggregation of myxamoebae begins. What triggers this stage is as yet unknown.

It is believed that a single cell in the population begins to secrete the attractant acrasin, recently identified as cyclic AMP in some species, toward which other myxamoebae migrate. These, in turn, develop the ability to secrete acrasin and so on down the stream, thus setting up a gradient of the attractant.

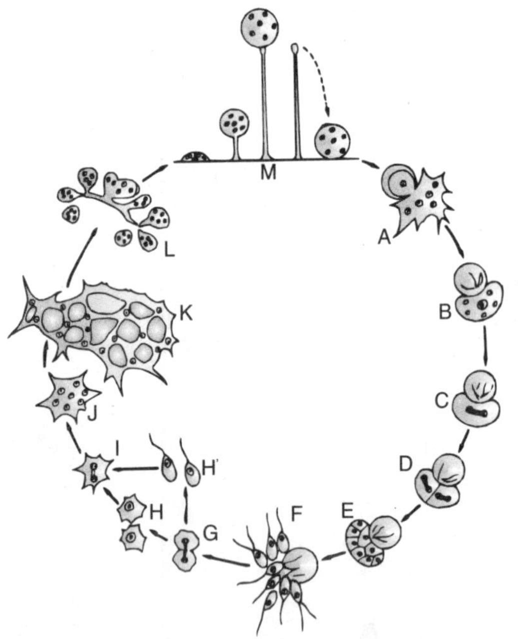

Figure 1.2: Life cycle of Ceratiomyxella tahitiensis. A. Germinating spore. B-F. Stages in zoocyst development. G, H, H. Proliferation of amoeboid and flagellate cells. I, J. Early stages in plasmodial development. K. Reticulate plasmodium. L. Prespore cell formation. M. Stages in sporogenesis.

As the myxamoebae reach the center of each aggregation, they come in intimate contact one with another and form a gelatinous unit commonly called the *slug* or grex but more technically known as the *pseudoplasmodium.*

This is a sausage-shaped mass of intimately associated amoebal cells, which, however, are not fused but retain their individuality and may be separated by mechanical means. Nevertheless, the amoebae in a pseudoplasmodium become differentiated.

Those in the front end of the slug become potential stalk cells, whereas those in the rear end will give rise to the spores of the sorocarp. In some species, such as *Dictyostelium discoideum,* the pseudoplasmodium migrates over the culture dish before it comes to rest in preparation for sporulation.

When it finally rests, it becomes flattened below but assumes a hemispherical shape above, with a papilla protruding from its center. As the mass of myxamoebae elongates vertically, certain of the cells at the apex migrate downward through the whole mass.

A cellulose cylinder is formed at this time, within which the cellular stalk of the sorocarp develops by the sacrifice of some of the amoebae, while the cells at the bottom migrate up the stalk to form the spores at the tip. This completes the life cycle.

Sexual Reproduction

For many years the matter of sexuality in the Acrasiomycetes was one of great controversy. In 1972, however, Erdos, Nickerson, and Raper found that the amoebae of *Polysphondylium* (Gr. *poly,* many, + *sphondylos,* vertebra) *violaceum* aggregate into large clumps, in the center of which a large cell originates, which engulfs the surrounding myxamoebae and secretes a thick wall around itself, thus becoming a *macrocyst.*

Macrocysts have also been found in *Dictyostelium mucoroides* and in other species. At first binucleate, the macrocyst becomes uninucleate probably through karyogamy. The evidence for karyogamy's taking place is derived from the discovery of structures resembling synaptonemal complexes at a somewhat later stage of development, which is followed by a multinucleate condition.

This is a strong indication that meiosis and several mitotic divisions have occurred. Erdos, Raper, and Vogen (1973) discovered that two mating types were necessary for macrocyst formation in Dictyostelium discoideum and later (1975) in Dictyostelium giganteum.

Sexuality and the existence of heterothallism in the Acrasiomycetes are thus well established, but the sexual cycle appears not to be necessary to the organism.

The fate of the macrocysts has been followed by Erdos, Nickerson, and Raper (1973), who found that they germinate, releasing myxamoebae, which then repeat the life cycle. The literature of the Acrasiomycetes consists of hundreds of research articles. It has been ably summarized by Bonner (1967), Raper (1973), and Olive (1975).

Classification

For an up-to-date classification of the Acrasiomycetes, see Raper (1973) and Olive (1975).

SUBDIVISIOIN PLASMODIOGYMNOMYCOTINA

In contrast to the Acrasiogymnomycotina, which form pseudoplas-modia by aggregation, many of the Plasmodiogymnomycotina form true plasmodia. There is no aggregation stage in this subdivision. The subdivision includes two classes, Protosteliomycetes and Myxomycetes.

Class Protosteliomycetes

The Protosteliomycetes are cosmopolitan, microscopic organisms invisible to the unaided human eye. They appear on dried leaves, flowers, fruits, and bark when these are wet and placed in moist chambers and may be observed under a stereomicroscope. Their sporophores produce from one to several spores, each of which, upon germination, gives rise to a single myxamoeba. In the simple genus Protostelium (Gr. protos, first, + stele, post), the sporophores produce only one or two spores each. The spore germinates to release a single myxamoeba, which feeds on bacteria and yeasts and eventually, after nuclear and cell division, forms a sporocarp (designation of the protostelid sporophore).

Nematostelium (Gr. *nema*, thread, + *stele*, post) is also a very simple organism. The more complex protostelids, such as Ceratiomyxella (diminutive of Ceratiomyxa), form flagellated cells that become converted into myxamoebae by withdrawing their flagella and by nuclear divisions develop into minute plasmodia (sing. plasmodium) in which protoplasmic streaming is unidirectional, as contrasted to the "shuttle streaming" of the myxomycete plasmodium.

A plasmodium is a multinucleate, creeping mass of protoplasm without cell walls, moving and feeding like a giant amoeba. In Ceratiomyxella the plasmodium eventually cleaves into prespore cells, each of which then develops a minute sporocarp with a single spore at its tip.

Such protostelids are believed by some to represent extant forms of types thought to be ancestral to the Myxomycetes, but this, of course, is only conjecture. No sexual reproduction has been found in any protostelid.

Class Myxomycetes

The true, or plasmodial, slime molds, Class Myxomycetes, have been treated in four comprehensive summaries in English recently: that of Gray and Alexopoulos (1968), a summary of their biology, and three taxonomic treatises, those of Martin and Alexopoulos (1969), Alexopoulos (1973), and Farr (1976).

There are about 450 known species of Myxomycetes. Most are widely distributed from the far north and far south regions to the tropics, but some are strictly tropical or subtropical and a few are strictly temperatezone forms.

Plasmodial slime molds occur mostly in regions of abundant rainfall but have also been found on desert plants.

Many of the smaller species develop on bark from living trees, or on plant debris, placed in moist chambers.

In nature, slime molds occur on various types of organic matter such as moist logs, dead leaves on the forest floor, city lawns, or sometimes living plants. A number of mountain species sporulate below the snow and appear as the snow melts in the spring. The Myxomycetes are characterized by a phagotrophic somatic phase, the plasmodium, a free-living, creeping, multinucleate mass of protoplasm usually enveloped by a slime sheath and totally devoid of cell walls, which becomes converted into one or more fruiting bodies, which bear the spores.

The protoplasm in the veins of a plasmodium exhibits reversible streaming. This is in contrast to the streaming in the plasmodium of the protostelids, which, as we have emphasized, is unidirectional. Morphologi-cally, there are three types of plasmodia recognized.

The type that most biologists are familiar with is the *phanerop-lasmodium*, characterized by conspicuous protopl-asmic veins in which shuttle streaming may be easily seen under the microscope. The phaneroplasmodium is granular and is quite conspicuous even when small. As it grows, it forms large, gelatinous, reticulate protoplasmic sheets that may cover an area as large as several feet square.

The phaneroplasmodium is enveloped by a slime sheath, which it leaves behind as a trace as the plasmodium creeps over the surface of the substratum feeding on various microorganisms such as bacteria and fungal spores. The *aphanoplasmodium* is nongranular and very transparent. Its veins are devoid of a slime sheath.

As such, it is, as its name indicates (Gr. *aphanes,* invisible), difficult to detect in nature. Both these types usually produce several sporophores from each plasmodium under conditions favorable for sporulation. The third type of plasmodium is the *protoplasmodium*, characteristic of the genus *Echinostelium* (Gr. *echinos,* hedgehog, + Gr. *stele,* post) and other minute Myxomycetes.

It is believed to be the most primitive type. A protoplasmodium never grows larger than 1 mm in diameter. It is granular in structure and has a slime sheath much like that of the phaneroplasmodium, but unlike the other two types, it is not differentiated into veins and its protoplasm streams irregularly.

Also, a protoplasmodium produces but a single sporophore when it fruits. The most commonly encountered plasmodia in nature are phaneroplasmodia. These are of various sizes and colors, ranging from minute, to large gelatinous sheets and from white to black through various hues such as cream, yellow, greenish, orange, red, brown, violet, and blue.

The plasmodia of most species are either white or yellow, but plasmodia of other colors are not rare. Plasmodia creep over organic matter, such as dead leaves or rotting logs, but may also appear, sometimes in massive quantities, on well-watered lawns and gardens, feeding on bacteria and other microorganisms.

Myxomycetes are not parasitic on plants, but sometimes their plasmodia may smother some plants such as strawberries. Many species of Myxomycetes can be grown easily in laboratory culture on agar, with *Escherichia coli, Enterobacter aerogenes,* or other bacteria that they use for food.

Large plasmodia are often developed in such cultures and can be easily propagated by cutting off small portions and transferring them to fresh media with a suitable bacterium, as shown in Figure elsewhere in this chapter.

The rhythmical shuttle streaming in the veins of such plasmodia is an unforgettable demonstration of protoplasmic streaming. Kamiya (1950), investigating the rate of flow in the plasmodium of *Physarum* (Gr. *physa,* bubble) *polycephalum,* the species commonly used in the laboratory, found that the maximum rate of flow in the plasmodial veins reached 1.45 mm per second, which, he stated, is the greatest velocity of protoplasmic flow recorded in any living organism. The motive force in plasmodium is generated by the interaction of ATP with two contractile proteins, actin and plasmodium-myosin A, in the plasmodial protoplasm.

Fibrils, which occur in the plasmodium, probably consist of these proteins, and it appears virtually certain that they are instrumental in generating the motive force required for protoplasmic streaming.

It has also been suggested that there is a primitive neuromotor system in the plasmodium that controls streaming. All pigmented and some white plasmodia require light in order to sporulate. Under the most favorable environmental conditions, the entire plasmodium is converted into a mass of sporophores, which may be stalked, sessile, or a mixture of both, depending on the species.

Under unfavorable conditions of moisture and nutrition, the plasmodium, instead of sporulating, changes into a hard, dormant body, the *sclerotium* (pl. *selerotia*; Gr. *skleros,* hard), composed of uninucleate or multinucleate round *spherules*, each enveloped by a cell wall.

Upon the return of a favorable environment the sclerotium again becomes plasmodial. When the plasmodium of *Physarum polycephalum* and other similar species reaches a certain stage of maturity, and when the food supply is nearly exhausted, under environmental conditions favorable for fruiting, it becomes concentrated at various points, forming small, papillalike mounds, which soon develop into sporophores, often objects of great and delicate beauty.

This has been appreciated by artistically inclined biologists, who have published beautiful paintings or color photographs of slime molds. Among the best of these are the paintings in Crowder's article in *the National Geographic Magazine* (April 1926), Lister (1925), Hattori (1935, 1964), Martin and Alexopoulos (1969), Emoto (1977), and the color photographs by Alexopoulos (1973).

Sporophores and spores. There are four main types of myxomycete sporophores: *sporangia*, *plasmodiocarps*, *aethalia*, and *pseudoaethalia*. *Sporangia* are simple fruiting

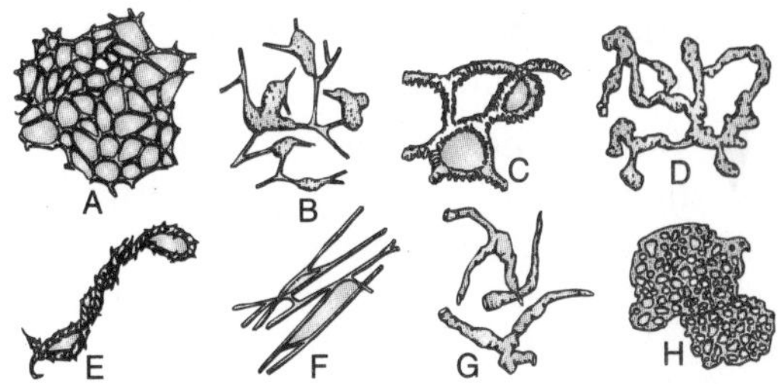

Figure 1.3: Several types of capillitium. A-F. True capillitium. A. Limeless surface net (Stemonitis, Stemonitales). B. Lime nodes connected by slender, tubular filaments (Physarum, Physarales). C. Spinulose network of tubular threads (Arcyria, Trichiales). D. Calcareous tubules (Badhamia, Physarales). E. Single, spiny elater (Trichia, Trichiales). F. Slender, branching, and anastomosing capillitial threads (Didymium, Physarales). G-H. Pseudocapillitium. G. Threadlike (Lycogala, Liceales). H. Platelike, perforated (Reticularia, Liceales).

bodies, which may be stalked or sessile. They vary in size from minute (less than 0.5 mm in diameter when sessile, as in *Licea tenera)* to as much as 25 mm tall, as in *Stemonitis splendens.*

Their stalks may be hollow or stuffed. Many are covered with lime ($CaCO_3$), which may be powdery or scaly or which may form a hard crust over the *peridium* (sporophore wall around the spores). In a few species, the peridium is composed of a number of ribs over which a fugacious membrane is spread.

When the membrane disappears, as in *Dictydium cancellatum,* the ribs remain and can easily be mistaken for capillitium by the inexperienced observer. *Physarum polycephalum* is an important slime mold, extensively used for research in molecular biology. This organism, as its name indicates (Gr. *poly,* many, + *kephale,* head), produces its spores in many heads on a single stalk. Its sporangium is, therefore, said to be lobed.

Plasmodiocarps are typically sessile. They are irregular in shape, varying from ovoid to elongated and even branched or netlike, as in *Hemitrichia serpula* (Gr. *hemi,* half + *Trichia).* They are formed by the secretion of a peridium around the veins or parts of the veins of a plasmodium just after it stops streaming and prepares to sporulate.

Aethalia (*sing. aethalium*) are relatively massive sporophores thought to have been formed by the complete fusion of large numbers of sporangia during their evolutionary development. If this is true, fusion is, indeed, complete, for no traces of individual sporangial walls are found in most aethalia, as those of the genus *Lycogala* (Gr. *lycos,* wolf, + Gr. *gala,* milk), for example. *Pseudoaethalia* (sing. *pseudoaethalium*) (false aethalia) on the other hand, are tight aggregations of sporangia, often on a single stalk or spongy hypothallus, which resemble single spore-bearing units.

The individual sporangia in a pseudoaethalium are, however, easily discernible. When the sporophore of a myxomycete has attained its maximum size, its multinucleate protoplast begins, in most species, to form a network of vacuoles, in which various substances are deposited to form the *capillitium*.

This is a mass of nonliving threads, variously sculptured and colored, depending on the species, which aid in the dissemination of the spores by absorbing water from a moist atmosphere or releasing it to a dry atmosphere.

This causes the capillitial threads to expand or contract and agitate the spores that cling to them. In some species, the capillitium is very elastic and expands greatly, bringing the spores with it as the peridium breaks.

The appearance of the capillitium varies greatly in different species, and capillitial structure and ornamentation are important taxonomic characters. Figure elsewhere in this chapter illustrates several types of capillitium and *pseudocapillitium*. The latter consists of irregular threads or of plates.

At the time of capillitial formation, the nuclei of the sporophore protoplasm undergo a single mitotic division, and the protoplast, by means of furrowing, cleaves progressively into uninucleate diploid segments, which become enveloped by cell walls and separate into spores. Myxomycete spores are typically globose but may be ovoid in a few species. They vary in size from 4 to 20 μm or more in diameter. Their walls are variously ornamented, ranging from smooth through spiny, verrucose (warty), and reticulate (bearing a network of ridges). In color they range from nearly colorless to yellow, reddish, violet, purple, brown, gray, or nearly black.

The chemical composition of the spore wall has not been determined, except in *Physarum polycephalum,* in which it is composed of 81% galactosamine polymer, 1.4% phosphate, 2.1% amino acids, and 15.44% melanin.

Soon after spore formation, meiosis takes place in the young spores. There is evidence that three of the four resultant nuclei disintegrate, so that the mature spore is usually uninucleate and haploid.

Life-cycle Pattern

When the spores are mature, they are released from the sporophores and are wind-borne. They eventually settle, and in the presence of water under favorable temperatures (around 20-25°C), they germinate, releasing usually one but up to four or more myxamoebae or flagellate, comma shaped, swarm cells.

Myxomycete spores are very resistant to desiccation and remain alive for long periods. Some have been germinated after 76 years' storage in a herbarium. It has been demonstrated that they occur in considerable numbers in the air, and those of *Fuligo (L. fuligo,* soot) *septica* at least, cause allergic reactions in susceptible individuals.

Myxamoebae feed on bacteria and yeasts, grow by mitosis, and divide. Thus a large population of myxamoebae results. When a critical mass has been reached, compatible myxamoebae fuse in pairs producing zygotes.

Swarmers, equipped with usually two anterior, whiplash flagella, may also behave as gametes, fusing by their posterior ends to form flagellate zygotes, which eventually withdraw their flagella. Sexual reproduction in the Myxomycetes takes place, therefore, by the fusion of two myxamoebae or two swarm cells. Some species are heterothallic, consisting of two mating types, (+) and (–), and only gametes of opposite mating type are able to fuse. In other species, all gametes appear to be compatible.

There is also evidence that in some strains the life cycle is completed without sexual fusions. Thus, in *Didymium* (Gr. *didymos,* double, twin) *iridis,* some strains are sexual, exhibiting mating types, some are sexual without mating types (homothallic), and some are asexual (apogamic). After the zygote has been formed, it feeds on bacteria or yeasts, creeps, and grows as successive, synchronous mitoses occur, thus developing into a plasmodium.

The nuclear divisions in the zygote and the plasmodium are intranuclear (closed), the spindle developing within the nuclear envelope, which breaks down only near the conclusion of nuclear division to form the envelopes of the daughter nuclei. Such intranuclear divisions are commonly found in the other divisions of fungi.

In contrast, nuclear divisions in the myxamoebae are centric (open), as they are in the majority of plants and animals. Swarm cells do not divide as such; they change into myxamoebae before they multiply.

The organisms mentioned or illustrated in this chapter may be classified as follows:

Division 1. Gymnomycota

- Subdivision 1. Acrasiogymnomycotina
  - Class 1. Acrasiomycetes
    - Order 1. Acrasiales
      - Family 1. Guttulinaceae
        - Genus: *Pocheina*
    - Order 2. Dictyosteliales
      - Family 1. Dictyosteliaceae
        - Genera: *Dictyostelium, Polysphondylium*
      - Family 2. Acytosteliaceae

Genus: *Acytostelium*

Subdivision 2. Plasmodiogymnomycotina

Class 1. Protosteliomycetes

Order 1. Protosteliales

Family 1. Protosteliaceae

Genera: *Protostelium, Nematostelium*

Family 2. Cavosteliaceae

Genus: *Ceratiomyxella*

Class 2. Myxomycetes

Subclass 1. Ceratiomyxomycetidae

Order 1. Ceratiomyxales

Family 1. Ceratiomyxaceae

Genus: *Ceratiomyxa*

Subclass 2. Myxogastromycetidae

Order 1. Liceales

Family 1. Liceaceae

Genus: *Licea*

Family 2. Reticulariaceae

Genera: *Tubifera, Lycogala*

Family 3. Cribrariaceae

Genus: *Dictydium*

Order 2. Trichiales

Family 1. Trichiaceae

Genera: *Arcyria, Hemitrichia*

Order 3. Echinosteliales

Family 1. Echinosteliaceae

Genus: *Echinostelium*

Order 4. Physarales

Family 1. Physaraceae

Genera: *Physarum, Fuligo*

Family 2. Didymiaceae

Genus: *Didymium*

Subclass 3. Stemonitomycetidae

Order 1. Stemonitales

Family 1. Stemonitaceae

Genus: *Stemonitis*

Chapter 2 Fungi with Absorptive Nutrition

In contrast to the Gymnomycota, other members of the Kingdom Myceteae, except for a few species, have definite cell walls. This is riot to say that many species do not produce unwalled cells such as zoospores or *planogametes* (flagellate gametes), but the somatic structures even of these have cell walls.

SOMATIC STRUCTURES

Some fungi with absorptive nutrition are unicellular, but the majority have a differentiated thallus consisting of threadlike, tubular filaments, the hyphae (sing. hypha). The network of hyphae constituting the body (thallus, soma) of a fungus is called the *mycelium*.

In the simpler fungi, the hyphae are coenocytic—i.e., they are long, tubular filaments filled or lined with cytoplasm in which many nuclei are embedded and are not separated into cells or compratments.

It was once believed that such fungi had originated from algal ancestors, and they were therefore given the name *Phycomycetes* (Gr. *phykos,* seaweed, i.e., alga, + *myketes,* fungi). Although this theory of their origin is no longer accepted, the term Phycomycetes is still used in a general way for them but without taxonomic significance.

In the more complex groups, the hyphae are *septate*—i.e., e divided into compartments or cells by cross walls we

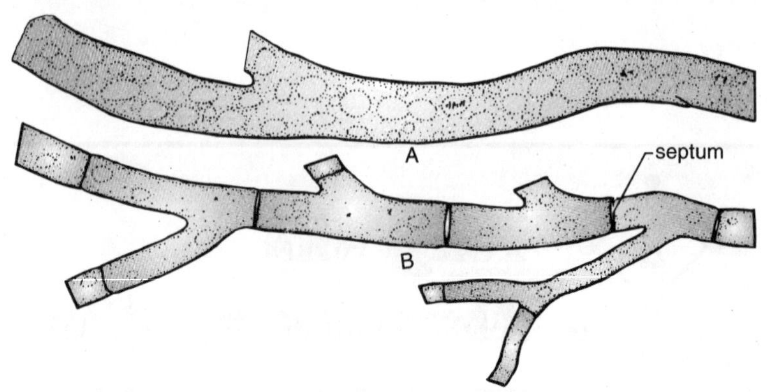

Figure 2.1: Somatic hyphae. A. Portion of a coenocytic (aseptate) hypha. B. Portion of a septate hypha.

call *septa* (sing. *septum*). In some of these, the septa are solid, whereas in others they are perforated and, in fact, may be very complex in structure.

The cells or compartments may be uninucleate, binucleate, or multinucleate, depending on the species. Perforated septa permit cytoplasmic strands to pass through them so that there is an organic connection of all parts of the mycelium.

Such septa also permit nuclei to travel through the mycelium from one cell to the other. Moving pictures have been taken of migrating nuclei, and Dowding (1958) has calculated that in *Gelasinospora* (Gr. *gelasinos,* dimple) *tetrasperma,* one of the Ascomycetes, streaming nuclei reach speeds of 40 mm per hour.

In the more complex fungi it is believed that septa may have the power to regulate the passage of nuclei or other organelles through them, but this has not been proved. The presence of plasmodesmata through the septa of fungi has been adequately demonstrated.

The cell walls of most fungi contain chitin and other complex carbohydrates but little or no cellulose except in one group, the Oomycetes, which appear to have had a different origin from all the other fungi.

NUCLEAR DIVISION

Nuclear division in the fungi has been studied for a very long time, and the type of division that occurs in this group of organisms was the subject of great controversy until the advent of the electron microscope.

Now it appears that mitosis in most fungi is typically intranuclear—i.e., the nuclear envelope remains intact through mitosis until late anaphase or telophase, when it breaks down and forms the nuclear envelopes of the daughter nuclei.

Associated with the mitotic process in fungi are *centrioles* in the aquatic fungi with motile cells (Mastigomycota) or small electron-opaque structures called "*spindle pole bodies*" (SPBs) in most other fungi. Otherwise, it appears that mitosis in most fungi is rather typical.

There are variations in different groups, to be sure. Two fine reviews of the whole subject of fungal nuclear division are by Heath (1978) and Fuller (1976). Meiotic divisions are also quite typical but also intranuclear.

The position of meiosis in the life cycle of the fungi has been pinpointed through the search for synaptonemal complexes and by measuring the amount of DNA in various stages of the life cycle by spectrophotometric analysis, in as much as chromosomes are too small to count accurately with the light microscope and do not show up clearly under the electron microscope.

REPORDUCTION

The chief method of fungal propagation is by means of spores, which may be motile (flagellate) or nonmotile and which are produced in various ways. Spores that are formed asexually are sometimes designated as *mitospores*.

If they are formed as a result of karyogamy and meiosis, they are *meiospores*. Most fungi reproduce both asexually and sexually. Asexual reproduction may take the form of spores, fission, budding, or fragmentation. Fission and budding are usually employed by unicellular fungi, such as the yeasts. Fragmentation occurs in mycelial fungi when the hyphae break into fragments accidentally in nature or are fragmented purposely in the laboratory, each fragment resuming growth and establishing a new colony. This is a common method of propagating fungi in the laboratory.

Sexual reproduction takes many forms in the fungi and it is better to discuss this topic in connection with various fungal groups. Suffice it to say here that fungi may be homothallic or heterothallic.

In the former all gametes are compatible; in the latter, gametes of different mating types are produced, which must meet before plasmogamy or karyogamy can occur. In heterothallic fungi two thalli must be present for sexual reproduction.

PHYSIOLOGY

Fungi obtain their food by secreting various enzymes outside their thalli and digesting the substratum on or in which they live so that nutriments in solution may pass through their cell walls and plasma membranes into their cells.

As we have already pointed out, fungi must have elaborated carbohydrate molecules inasmuch as they are unable to photosynthesize them. The various mineral elements, such as nitrogen, phosphorus, potassium, sulfur, iron, magnesium, manganese, and boron, are also essential to fungus nutrition.

These, too, are obtained from the substratum in the form of salts in solution. Various fungi differ in their ability to utilize certain sugars and salts. Thus, most species thrive on a substratum that contains glucose as a sugar, ammonium salts to provide nitrogen, and KH_2PO_4 for potassium and phosphorus.

Others, however, may be unable to utilize ammonium salts, preferring some other source of nitrogen, such as amino acids or perhaps nitrates. Most fungi seem to grow optimally in the laboratory at 20-25°C but can withstand considerably higher and very much lower temperatures.

Many fungi will grow slowly, to be sure-at 6°C, as evidenced by the growth of molds in household refrigerators. The fact that fungal cultures are often stored under liquid nitrogen at temperatures of –196°C shows how resistant some of them are to cold.

Of course at temperatures below freezing little or no growth takes place, the fungal structures remaining dormant. At the other end of the scale, there are some thermophilic fungi that will not grow when the temperature falls below 20°C and actually prefer temperatures in the upper 30s or in the 40s.

The role that these fungi play in composting and their economic importance in causing spontaneous combustion-which, measured in terms of U. S. dollars, exceeds $20 million a year in the United States alone-is discussed by Cooney and Emerson (1964), as is their importance in industrial processes, such as the fermentation of cacao, the sweating of tobacco, the composting of mushroom beds, and the disposal of refuse and sewage in large cities.

Fungi prefer an acid medium in which to grow, most of them thriving best at pH 6. Light is not required for the growth of fungi, but a few, such as *Blastocladiella* (dim in. of *Blastocladia) emersonii* (*Chytridiomycetes, Blastocladiales*), actually fix CO_2 in the presence of light.

Many species, too, require light for sporulation, but the stimulus does not appear to be transmitted from one portion of the mycelium to another. Many fungal *sporophores* are *phototropic*, *bending* and dispersing their spores toward the light.

For a detailed discussion of the physiology of fungi, see Hawker (1950, 1957, 1966) and Cochrane (1958) and the references therein. Growth of fungal hyphae is terminal, being confined at the very tip of each hyphal branch. Fungi, however, may be propagated by transferring a small section of the mycelium to new media. The cut areas regenerate new hyphal tips, which grow normally thereafter.

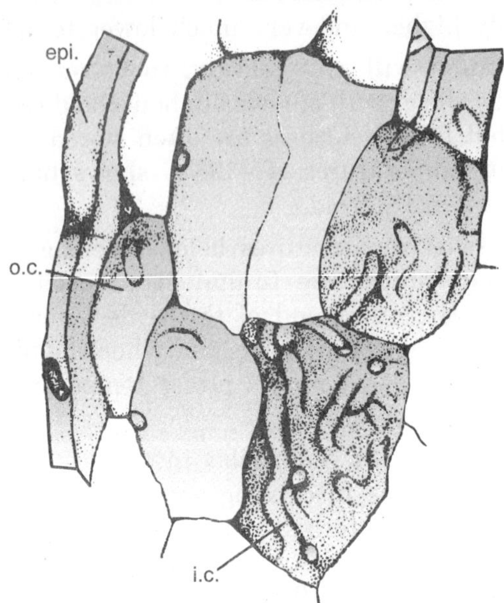

Figure 2.2: Fungus in rootlet of Amyelon radicans, Upper Carboniferous. epi., epidermis; i.c., inner cortex; o, c., outer cortex.

FOSSIL FUNGI

Although many fossil fungi have been found and more are being constantly discovered, we still do not know when the fungi originated or how they evolved in succeeding millennia. Fungal hyphae have been reported in *Precambrian strata* (along with *Cyanochloronta* and *green algae*), 900 million years old, but the supposed *fossil* fungi of the *Precambrian* cannot be unquestionably identified as such.

By the end of the Paleozoic, all the major groups of fungi are represented in the fossil record. In the stems and associated remains in an ancient bog at Rhynie, Scotland, which is of Lower Devonian age (inside front cover), very well-preserved fossil fungi are present. Mycorrhizal fungi were functioning in the superficial root cells of certain Carboniferous gymnosperms.

Andrews and Lenz (1943) illustrate a fungus within

the cells of a Carboniferous (inside front cover) rhizome. More recent fossil fungi from the Eocene appear to be closely related to modem genera, according to Dilcher (1965). Much work is being done, at present, on fossil fungal spores.

The following references summarize our present knowledge of fossil fungi admirably: Dilcher, 1965; Tiffney and Barghoorn, 1974; Elsik, 1976, 1977a,b; Pirozynski, 1976.

Summary and Classification

In the previous chapter we discussed a group of organisms with phagotrophic nutrition and without cell walls in their somatic structures. As we have, already said, the slime molds are regarded by many biologists as having their affinities with the Protozoa rather than with the fungi, but they have been studied almost exclusively by mycologists.

In this chapter we introduced the study of what might be called the true fungi, all of which have absorptive nutrition and almost all of which have cell walls.

Whether all these organisms, however, constitute a monophyletic series is highly controversial, as we shall see in the following chapters. In general, they are all considered to be fungi by most biologists, although there is considerable disagreement among phylogenists as to their origin and proper classification.

The points emphasized in this chapter are the presence of cell walls in and the hyphal structure of the soma; nutrition by absorption through the cell wall of simple organic molecules derived by the extracellular digestion of more complex carbohydrates and proteins in living or nonliving substrata; and *propagation* by spores.

The presence of both asexual and sexual reproduction in most fungi has also been brought out. As stated in the discussion of fossil algae, the fossil record of fungi, in part because of its *fragmentary* nature, has shed little light on fungal evolution.

Most ancient fungi seem to have been very similar to

extant forms, so that the fungi, like the algae, are a long-lived race and have been relatively little modified since they first evolved.

Classification of the fungi with absorptive nutrition is based on the structure of their hyphae; the chemical composition of their cell walls; the type of sexual reproduction; and the manner in which spores are borne. The fungi with *absorptive* nutrition may be classified as follows:

Division 1. Mastigomycota

Division 2. Amastigomycota

Subdivision 1. Zygomycotina

Subdivision 2. Ascomycotina

Subdivision 3. Basidiomycotina

Subdivision 4. Deuteromycotina

In the chapters that follow, we shall discuss each of these groups briefly. For a more complete discussion, read Alexopoulos and Mims (1979).

Mastigomycota: The Flagellate Fungi

The term Mastigomycota is derived from the Greek word *mastix* (*mastigos*),' which means "whip," combined with the Greek word for fungus, *mykes* (*myketos*). The group, therefore, contains all the fungi (exclusive of the slime molds) that produce flagellate cells in their life cycles, be these zoospores or planogametes.

There are two types of flagella produced by fungi: the whiplash and the tinsel. The whiplash flagellum is a long, relatively rigid filament with a flexible whip at the tip, which might be of considerable length also. The tinsel flagellum is long, bearing many filamentous extensions, the *masti-gonemes* (Gr. *mastix, mastigos,* whip + *nema,* thread, skein).

The presence of one or the other or both of these flagellar types and their position on the motile cells (zoospores or planogametes) is the basis for the classification of the Mastigomycota. One other important characteristic of this division is that *centrioles* are functional during cell division and in the formation of the flagella, for which they serve as basal bodies.

The Mastigomycota produce their spores in *sporangia* (sing. *sporangium*). These are saclike structures, the entire protoplast of which is cleaved into spores termed *sporangiospores*. Sporangiospores in this division are almost always motile-i.e., they are zoospores.

Sporangia release their spores through apical papillae or opercula, by bursting, or by deliquescing. Fungi that produce sporangia and have a coenocytic mycelium are often grouped under the general term Phycomycetes. Because they are regarded as primitive by most mycologists, they are also termed the "lower fungi."

These organisms are discussed in interesting detail in a recent book edited by M. L. Fuller (1978), *The Lower Fungi in the Laboratory*. The division Mastigomycota includes two subdivisions: the Haplomastigomycotina and the Diplomastigomycotina.

SUBDIVISION HAPLOMASTIGOMYCOTINA

In the subdivision Haplomastigomycotina meiosis is either zygotic or meiosporangial (sporic)—i. e., it takes place either during the germi-nation of the zygote or in special types of diploid sporangia, which, as a result, produce meiospores (haploid spores).

There are two types of life cycle in this subdivision, haplobiontic-haploid (H, h), or diplobiontic (D, h + d). The subdivision contains three classes of fungi—Chytridiomycetes, Hyphochytridiomycetes, and Plasmodiophoromycetes.

Class Chytridiomycetes

The motile cells of these fungi bear a single whiplash flagellum inserted posteriorly; the cell walls of those that have been examined in this regard contain chitin and glucans but no cellulose.

Sexual reproduction, when it has been found, takes place usually by the fusion of two planogametes or by the fusion of hyphalike, delicate filaments, the rhizoids (some other methods of plasmogamy have also been reported in a few special species), and results in the formation of a thick-walled resting body.

Meiosis, where it has been discovered, is either zygotic, or, in the case of a diplobiontic life cycle, takes place in special types of sporangia (meiosporangia), which release meiospores to start the haploid generation.

Order Chytridiales

The Chytridiales includes aquaticfreshwater or marine-fungi, commonly referred to as "*chytrids*." These may be *holocarpic*, converting their entire thallus into a reproductive organ, or *eucarpic*, with a portion of the thallus remaining trophic and supporting one or more reproductive organs.

Few chytrids are of great direct economic importance, but *Synchytrium endoboticum* does cause a serious disease of potatoes (potato wart) in all potato-growing regions of the world, and a disease of water cress, an important crop in Great Britain and other regions.

Members of the genera *Olpidium* and *Physoderma* also cause diseases of economic plants. Many chytrids are indirectly injurious to humans by parasitizing and destroying algae that form an important link in the food chain of aquatic animals.

The variety of fungi included in this order is so great that it is impossible to select any one organism to typify the order. We shall, therefore, discuss two species to illustrate some of the variation that exists.

Chytriomyces

The life cycle of *Chytriomyces* (Gr. *chytra,* jug) *hyalinus* has been thoroughly studied by its discoverer, Karling (1945), and subsequently by Miller and his coworkers. The posteriorly unifiagellate zoospore of this organism swims about for some time and eventually settles on some dead plant material or on exuviae of water insects.

There it germinates, producing a system of rhizoids. Rhizoids are not true hyphae but very delicate hyphalike filaments with protoplasm but without nuclei. Nuclei, however, travel through rhizoids to different parts of the thallus.

As the thallus develops, the main body of the zoospore becomes converted into a prosporangium in which nuclear divisions and protoplasmic synthesis occur, converting it into a sporangium. When a large number of nuclei have been formed, the multinucleate protoplasmic mass cleaves into posteriorly uniflagellate zoospores and is released into the sporangium through a hinged, caplike structure, the operculum.

The zoospores now separate and swim away, completing the asexual cycle of the organism. Some of the zoospores, however, develop into sexual thalli. They germinate, producing a rhizoidal system, but they themselves enlarge into a thin-walled cell in which nuclear divisions take place.

When the rhizoids of two compatible thalli come in contact, plasmogamy takes place, the protoplasm of each contributing thallus streaming toward the point of fusion, where a resting, thickwalled body is formed, receiving the protoplasts of the two contributing thalli, leaving them empty.

Karyogamy now occurs, converting the resting body into a zygote. Eventually, the resting body functions as a sporangium. Several nuclear divisions take place, two of which are presumed, but have not been proved, to be meiotic; zoospores are eventually delimited and the resting sporan-gium releases them into the water.

Note that the two contributing (sexual) thalli can in no way be morphologically distinguished as male and female and that neither receives the protoplasm of the other. Instead, they both contribute to a new structure, which becomes the resting sporangium.

In the next example to be discussed, *Polyphagus,* the beginnings of sexual differentiation in the chytrids may be noted.

Polyphagus

Polyphagus (Gr. *poly,* many, + Gr. *phagein,* to eat) is a chytrid genus with 10 or 11 species. *Polyphagus euglenae,* which attacks the green alga *Euglena*, is the best known of these through the work of Wager (1913). Its life cycle is illustrated in Figure elsewhere in this chapter.

The zoospore swims in the water together with the *Euglena* cells and eventually comes to rest, becomes rounded, and produces a number of delicate rhizoidal filaments.

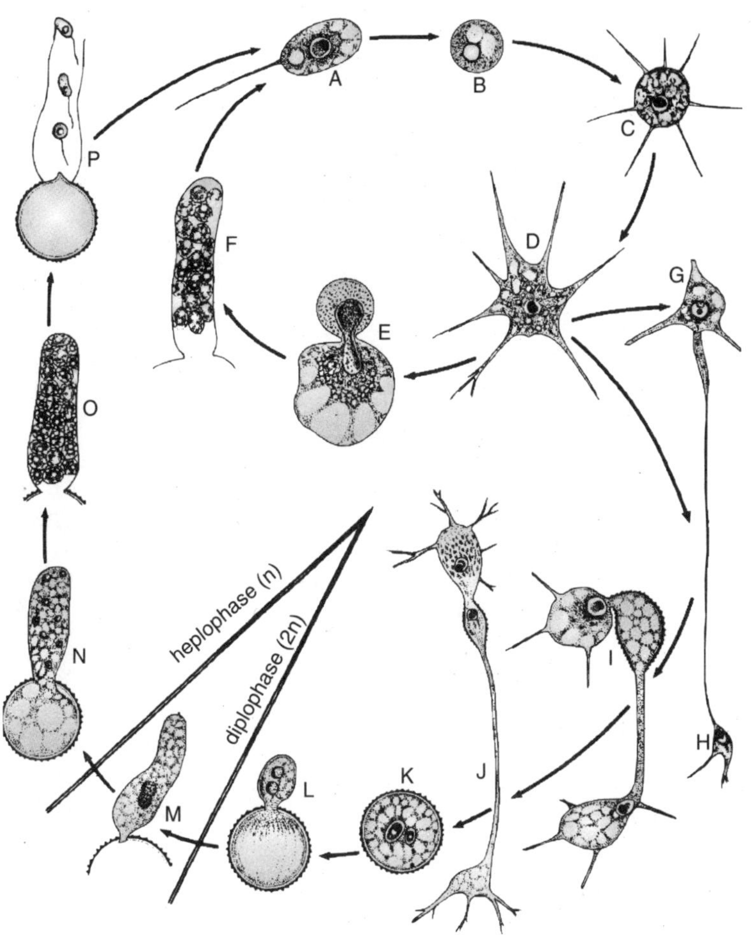

Figure 3.1: Life cycle diagram of Polyphagus euglenae. A. Zoospore. B. Encysted zoospore. C, D. Germinating zoospores. E. Formation of prosporangium. F. Sporangium. G. Large (female) thallus. H. Small (male) thallus with copulation tube already in contact with female thallus. I. Plasmogamy. J. Male nucleus in incipient zygote. K. "Zygote" with the two nuclei before fusion. L. Germination of "zygote." M. Karyogamy in prosporangium. N. Multinucleate, developing young sporangium. O. Mature sporangium with zoospores. P. Release of zoospores.

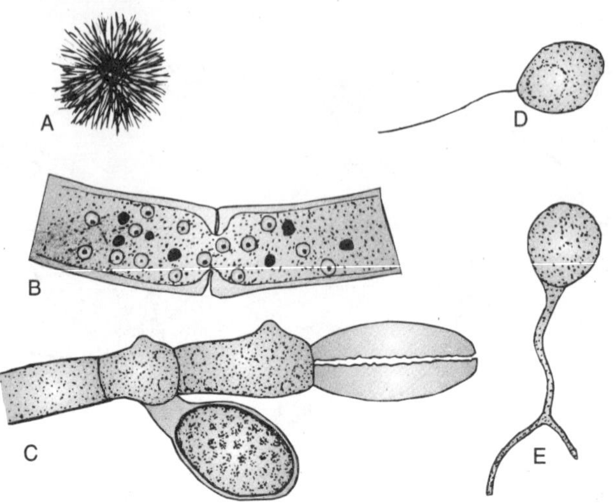

Figure 3.2: Allomyces macrogynus. A. Habit of growth on submerged hemp seed. B. Median longitudinal section of hypha; note multinucleate condition and partial septum. C. Three seriate, thin-walled mitosporangia (the apical one empty) and a thick-walled, lateral meiosporangium. D. Zoospore. E. Zoospore germination.

These become attached to a *Euglena* cell and penetrate it. The zoospore outside the cell develops into a sporangium, which becomes multinucleate by successive mitoses of its nucleus.

Its protoplasm now cleaves into zoospores, which are liberated in water. In sexual reproduction, some zoospores develop into small (male) thalli and others into larger (female) thalli. The small thallus produces a long, rhizoid-like copulation tube, which becomes attached to one of the larger thalli.

Just below the point of attachment a swelling develops, into which a nucleus from the male thallus enters, traveling through the copulation tube. The nucleus from the female thallus also enters the swelling, which eventually secretes a thick wall around itself and is termed a "zygote" even though no karyogamy has occurred as yet.

The "zygote" eventually produces a prosporangium, into

which the two nuclei pass and there fuse. The resulting diploid nucleus undergoes several divisions, the first two of which are presumed, but have not been proved, to be meiotic, and the prosporangium then develops into a sporangium in which the zoospores are delimited and from which they are released.

Here, then, seems to be the beginning of sexual differentiation, although it is represented only as a difference in size between the two contributing thalli and by the growth of a copulation tube from one (male) to the other (female).

The zoospores are eventually liberated, thus completing

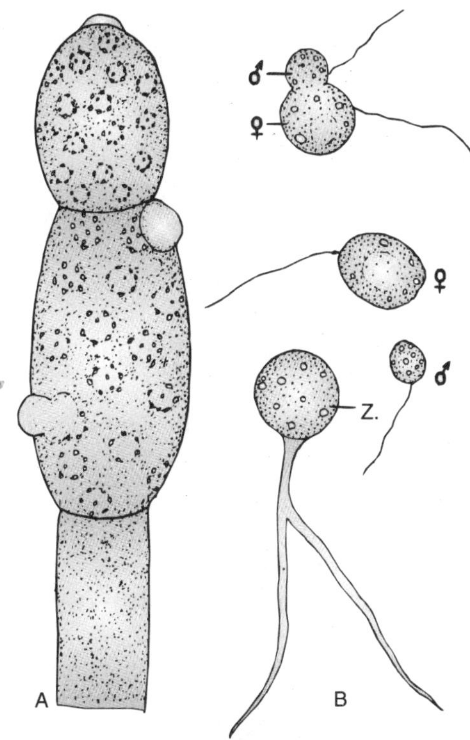

Figure 3.3: Allomyces macrogynus. A. Male (upper) and female gametangia; clusters of granules (mitochondria?) indicate nuclear position; note exit papillae. B. Heterogametes, gamete union and germinating zygote (z).

the life cycle. Whether a hormonal mechanism operates to attract the copulation tube from the small sexual thallus to the larger one is not known. Secretion of sex attractants will be mentioned in the next order to be discussed.

Order Blastocladiales

The characteristics of the fungi assigned to this order are (1) the presence of a nuclear cap in the zoospores, (2) sexual reproduction by fusion of anisogamous planogametes (motile gametes of different size), and (3) the production of characteristically pitted, thickwalled, resting sporangia (RS). Our example of this order will be *Allomyces macrogynus.*

Unlike the chytrids, which are either strictly unicellular or which have only rhizoidal processes, *Allomyces* (Gr. *allo,* other, + Gr. *mykes*) consists of a well-developed branching mycelium, anchored by rhizoidal absorptive branches that penetrate the substratum.

The organism, which occurs in moist soil and aquatic habitats, mostly in warmer climates, grows readily in laboratory cultures on split hemp seeds or other organic substrata.

Branching in *Allomyces* is typically dichotomous, and growth is apical. Superficially, the mycelium appears to be septate, but careful scrutiny of the septations indicates that they are incomplete and that the protoplasm is continuous throughout the plant.

The mycelium, with its many nuclei, is coenocytic. The cell walls contain chitin and glucan. After a period of vegetative growth, the mycelium enters the reproductive

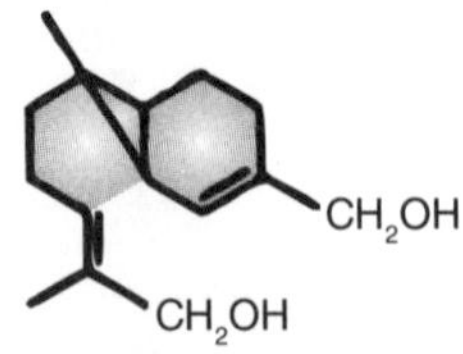

Figure 3.4: Chemical structure of sirenin.

phase. In *A. macrogynus,* the terminal portions of the mycelium of the sporothallus become delimited as zoosporangia (mitosporangia).

The portion of the hypha just below the sporangial septum may form a new branch; hence, the originally terminal sporangial initial becomes secondarily lateral in position. As development proceeds, it becomes apparent that two types of sporangia may be produced.

The first of these are thin-walled, ephemeral, and colorless *mitosporangia* and are produced early in development. The second type, the *meiosporangia*, are thick-walled, pitted, persistent, and brown and occur later.

Both types of sporangia contain a number of nuclei at the time of their formation; this number is increased by division as the sporangia mature. During development, the thin-walled mitosporangia undergo progressive cleavage to form a number of posteriorly uniflagellate zoospores. These are liberated at maturity through a pore in the sporangial wall.

The zoospores are attracted chemotactically by amino acids, a nutritional adaptation. The zoospores serve as agents for increasing the number of thalli, and under suitable conditions a large number of asexual generations is produced in this manner.

Only 30-48 hours are required for a mature thallus to develop from a zoospore. The thick-walled, resistant meiosporangia can withstand long periods of desiccation and temperatures up to 100°C for short periods and still retain their viability.

These meiosporangia also are multinucleate. It has been demonstrated that their nuclei persist for long periods in the prophase stages of meiosis, even when the sporangia have been dried. Transfer to water breaks their dormancy and stimulates further development.

This consists of the completion of the nuclear divisions, which are meiotic, and the formation of approximately 48 uniflagellate zoospores. The haploid chromosome number

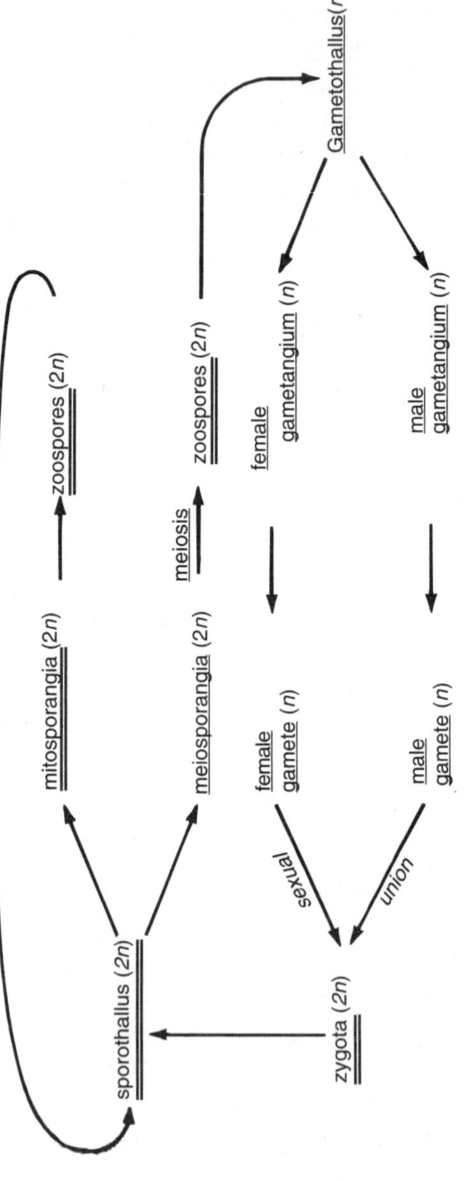

Figure 3.5: Life cycle of Allomyces macrogynus.

in *A. macrogynus* is 14, 28, or 56 (depending on the race); the haploid number in *A. arbuscula* is 8 or 16.

The zoospores from resistant sporangia settle on available substrata and develop into gametothalli that form only gametangia, not zoosporangia. The gametangia, as they first appear on the somatic branches of a clonal culture, occur in pairs, but those produced subsequently may be borne in chainlike series.

In their development the male gametangia produce an orange-red, carotenoid pigment, which is dissolved in droplets of oil in the gametes. The female gametangia remain colorless throughout their development. Both types of gametangia undergo progressive cleavage to form uninucleate gametes.

The male gametangia contain more nuclei than the female, and as a result the male gametes are considerably smaller than the female. Both are liberated through pores and unite in pairs under suitable environmental conditions. Mycelia of *A. macrogynus* derived from single zoospores are anisogamous and monoecious.

The female gametes secrete a hormone called *sirenin* (Gr. *seirin,* siren), which attracts the male gametes chemotactically. Sirenin, which is now available in pure form, was shown by its discoverer, Dr. Leonard Machlis (1958), and his coworkers to attract male gametes in concentrations as low as 10^{-10}M.

The chemical structure of sirenin was elucidated in 1968 by Nutting, Rapoport, and Machlis. Machlis (1972) has summarized the topic of plant hormones in algae and fungi. According to him, sirenin is an example of an *erotactin*, because it attracts male gametes.

The zygote settles on an available, nutriment-rich substratum and grows into a mycelium that develops only zoosporangia, not gametangia. Cultural and cytological studies have demonstrated the occurrence of isomorphic alternation of a diploid, asexual, zoospore-producing phase (*sporothallus*) with a haploid, sexual, gameteproducing phase (*gameto-thallus*) in *A. macrogynus*. Its life cycle may be summarized elsewhere in this chapter. The diplobiontic life cycle here is similar to that of *Cladophora* and *Ectocarpus* type D, h + d. Deviations from this life cycle may occur in certain strains.

Another interesting member of the Blastocladiales is *Coelomomyces* (Gr. *koeloma,* cavity, + Gr. *mykes*, fungus), a genus of fungi that parasitize mosquito larvae. Of interest is the fact that the hyphae of Coe*lomomyces* are unwalled. They do, however, develop septa to cut off the sporangia of the fungus.

These sporangia are brown,. thickwalled, and pitted, like those of *Allomyces*, and are one of the reasons for classifying *Coelomomyces* in the Blastocladiales. The life cycle of *Coelomomyces psorophorae* is of particular interest because it requires two entirely different species of hosts to come to completion.

This situation, known as *heteroecism***,** was hitherto known to exist only in the rust fungi (Uredinales, Basidiomycetes). *Coelonwmyces psorophorae* produces its spo-rothalli in the mosquito larvae and its gametothalli in the copepod *Cyclops vernalis*. Whether other species of *Coelomo-myces* are also *heteroecious* remains to be discovered.

Class Hyphochytridiomycetes

This is a small group of marine fungi with a single tinsel flagellum inserted anteriorly on the zoospores. Of particular interest is the fact that both cellulose and chitin occur in the cell walls of the few species that have been investigated in this regard.

The group is very thoroughly discussed by Sparrow (1960, 1973) and many fungi in this class have been meticulously illustrated by Karling (1977).

The best known species is *Rhizidiomyces* (Gr. *rhiza,* root, + Gr. ***mykes,*** fungus) *appophysatus* through the researches of Karling (1944), Fuller (1960, 1962), who grew the organism in pure culture, and Fuller and Reichle (1965).

Class Plasmodiophoromycetes

The Plasmodiophoromycetes, commonly known as the endoparasitic slime molds, differ from fungi other than slime molds in that their thalli are plasmodial. For this reason they have been classified by Ainsworth, Sparrow, and Sussman with the Myxomycota (our Gymnomycota), but neither Sparrow himself (1960) nor Waterhouse (1973) nor Alexopoulos and Mims (1979) subscribe to that view.

Two of these organisms are serious plant pathogens. *Plasmodiophora* (Gr. *plasmodium* + Gr. *phoreus,* bearer) *brassicae* causes club root of cabbage, and *Spongospora* (Gr. *spongos,* sponge, + Gr. *spora,* spore) *subterranea* is the cause of powdery scab of potatoes.

The zoospores of the Plasmodiophoromycetes are equipped with two anteriorly inserted whiplash flagella of unequal size. This character, together with their plasmodial thallus, links them to the Myxomycetes, but the fact that they produce spores in funguslike sporangia places them in the Mastigomycota.

An interesting character of this group is the so-called cruciform nuclear division in their sporangiogenous plasmodia. During nuclear division, the nucleolus elongates and assumes the shape of a dumbbell, around which the chromosomes become arranged in a ring formation at metaphase, so that the whole configuration, viewed from the side, resembles a cross-hence the name cruciform division. The life cycle of these organisms is not well known; it appears that it may be diplobiontic.

SUBDIVISION DIPLOMASTIGOMYCOTINA

In the Diplomastigomycotina, meiosis, wherever it has been investigated by modern methods, has been found to occur in the gametangia. The life cycle of these organisms is, therefore, haplobiontic-diploid (H, d), with the gametes as the only haploid cells. There is but a single class, the Oomycetes.

Class Oomycetes

This is a large class in which the organisms included differ so markedly from all other fungi that some mycologists do not include them in the fungi at all. The characteristics that set them apart are:

(1) the general absence of chitin and the presence of cellulose in their cell walls;

(2) biflagellate zoospores with two different flagella, one whiplash and one tinsel, anteriorly or laterally inserted on the zoospores;

(3) formation of two types of zoospores in some species, one pear-shaped (primary), the other reniform (secondary);

(4) oogamous sexual reproduction by the passage of gamete nuclei from a well-defined antheridium to a well-defined oogonium containing oospheres (eggs), thus resulting in thick-walled oospores; and

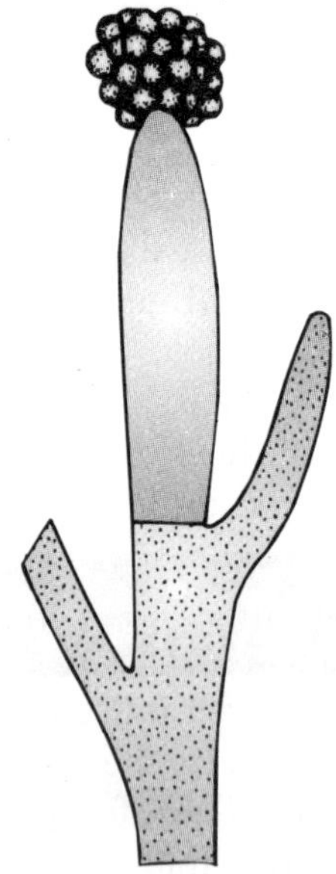

Figure 3.6: Sporangium of Achlya sp. showing encysted zoospores at the apical opening.

(5) gametangial instead of zygotic meiosis, rendering the thallus diploid. The first four of these characteristics have been well known for almost a century.

The fifth has been a matter of controversy ever since

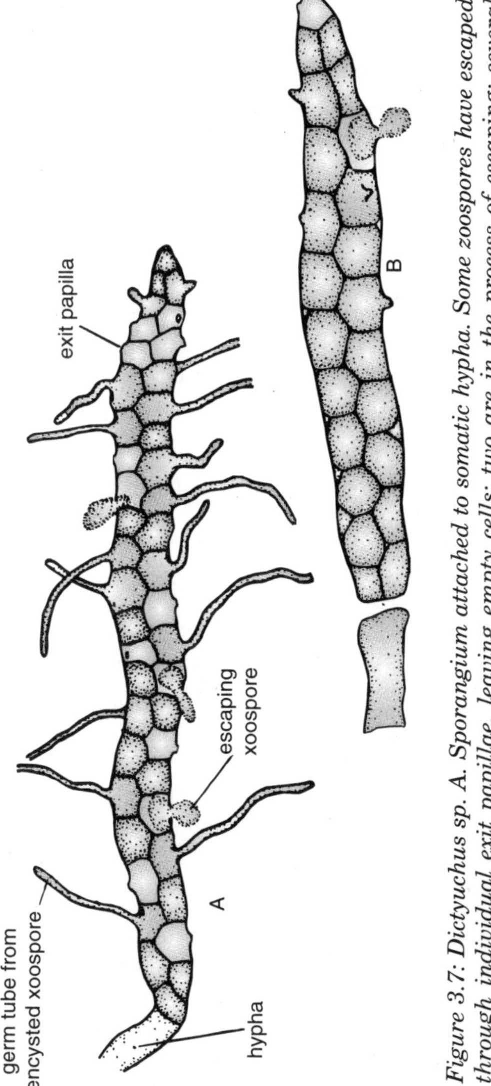

Figure 3.7: Dictyuchus sp. A. Sporangium attached to somatic hypha. Some zoospores have escaped through individual exit papillae, leaving empty cells; two are in the process of escaping; several have encysted within the sporangium and have produced germ tubes. B. Detached sporangium.

Stevens (1899), working with *Albugo,* one of the Peronosporales, found two nuclear divisions occurring in the gametangia and suggested that they represented meiosis.

This did not find general acceptance, however, and for the first sixty years of this century mycologists believed that the Oomycetes were haploid, like other fungi, and that meiosis occurred during the germination of the zygote.

There were, however, only a few researchers who claimed to have proof positive of zygotic meiosis. Since 1961, when Sansome published a paper claiming that gametangial meiosis occurs in *Pythium debaryanum,* a well-known member of the order Peronosporales of the Oomycetes, so many researchers have found gametangial meiosis in various Oomycetes that the evidence is now overwhelmingly convincing as summarized by Sansome (1966), Flanagan (1970), Dick and Win-Tin (1973, and WinTin and Dick (1975), and as referred to by Ellzey and Huizar (1977).

To be sure, there are some who still hold out for zygotic

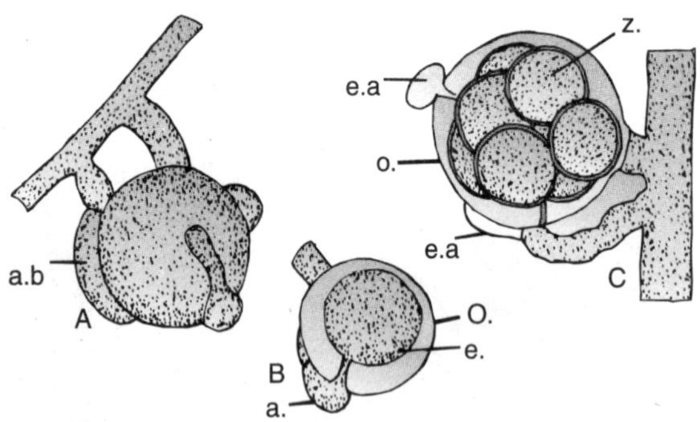

Figure 3.8: Achlya sp. Sexual reproduction, bisexual species. A. Immature antheridial and oogonial branches. B. Oogonium with single egg, antheridium, and fertilization tube. C. Oogonium containing dormant zygotes (oospores). a., antheridium; a.b., antheridial branch; e., egg; e.a., empty antheridium; o., oogonium; z., zygote.

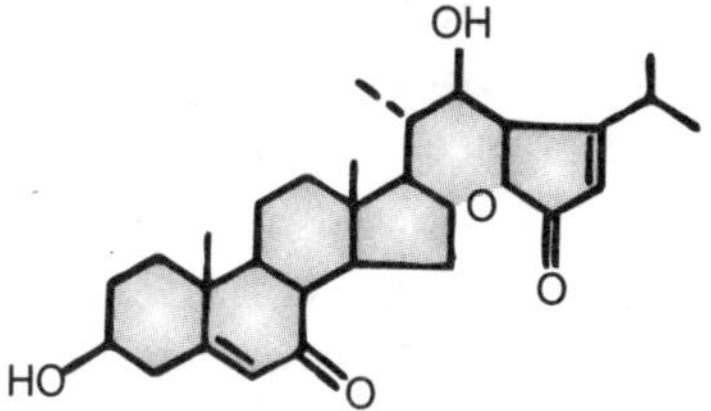

Figure 3.9: Chemical structure of antheridiol.

meiosis, but as Dick (1973) stated, if future research should show this to be the case in any family of the Oomycetes, its relationships will have to be reevaluated.

Classification

The class Oomycetes is usually divided into five orders:

Class Oomycetes

Order 1. Lagenidiales

Order 2. Thraustochytriales

Order 3. Saprolegniales

Order 4. Leptomitales

Order 5. Peronosporales

We shall discuss only two of these.

Order Saprolegniales

There are several families in the Saprolegniales, of which the Saprolegniaceae is the most typical and, by far, the best known. We shall confine our discussion to that family alone. The Saprolegniaceae are the classical "water molds," although that designation has also been given to the Blastocladiales.

The Saprolegniaceae are widespread, occurring in aquatic, mostly freshwater, habitats and also in the top layers of moist soils. A few have been found in brackish and salt waters. When the mycology of the oceans and seas is better known than it is at present, more Saprolegniaceous species may be found in that habitat.

These fungi are very easy to obtain for laboratory study by baiting pond water or aqueous soil suspensions with split hemp seed or sesame seed, around which they form fluffy colonies. Mostly saprobic, the Saprolegniaceae are of little economic importance.

A few, however, such as *Saprolegnia parasitica,* cause disease of fish and- destroy fish roe in commercial hatcheries. A few others, such as *Aphanomyces euteiches,* are parasitic on plants, causing root rot of beets and other crops. The coenocytic somatic hyphae of the Saprolegniaceae are large in diameter and easy to observe under the microscope.

They grow rapidly and branch profusely in a favorable nutrient medium. After a period of somatic development, the reproductive phases, asexual at first, are initiated by the development of hyphalike cylindrical zoosporangia, the cqntents of which become cleaved and differentiate into a considerable number of zoospores.

How the zoospores are liberated and how they behave, varies in different genera. The two most common genera of the Saprolegniaceae are *Saprolegnia* (Gr. *sapros,* rotten, + Gr. *legnon,* border), monographed by Seymour (1970), and *Achlya* (Gr. *achlys,* mist), monographed by Johnson (1956).

A still useful though outdated monograph of the family Saproleg-niaceae is the one by Coker (1923). A modern, updated treatment of this family is in preparation by Seymour and Johnson while these lines are being written (1979).

Two types of zoospores occur in the Saprolegniaceae: pyriform (primary) zoospores with two flagella, one whiplash, one tinsel, attached anteriorly; and reniform (secondary) zoospores with their two flagella, again one whiplash and one tinsel, attached at the concave side. Species that produce only one type of zoospore are *monomorphic*; those forming both types are *dimorphic.*

Life cycle

In the life cycle of *Saprolegnia* there are typically two swarming periods of the zoospores separated by an encystment stage. The occurrence of two motile periods is called *diplanetism*. The zoosporangia release their primary zoospores from their tips, one by one. After a period of motility these zoospores withdraw their flagella, come to rest, become spherical, and encyst by secreting walls around themselves. After a period of rest, the cysts germinate to form secondary zoospores, one from each cyst.

Thus, *Saprolegnia* is both *diplanetic* and dimorphic. The secondary zoospores also encyst after a period of motility. In germination to form a new thallus, the cysts produce delicate hyphae called *germ tubes*, which grow into the mycelium.

Achlya (note the spelling of this genus; it gives trouble to students) differs from *Saprolegnia* in releasing its primary zoospores rapidly and all at once. As soon as they strike the outside environment they encyst, forming a ball of spores that clings to the tip of the sporangium.

There, the cysts germinate and each liberates a secondary (reniform) zoospore, which continues the life cycle. In *Dictyuchus* (Gr. *dictyon,* net), another genus of the Saprolegniaceae, no primary, motile zoospores are formed.

Instead, the sporangium develops a network of walls, which are thought to be the walls of encysted primary zoospores. It is believed that such zoospores may actually be formed but encyst within the sporangium, their cysts being represented by the network of walls that divides the sporangium into a large number of small compartments. An ultrastructural study is needed here to elucidate the development of these stages. Be that as it may, the wall of each "cell" dissolves and a secondary zoospore emerges. These spores swim and encyst repeatedly, each new emerging zoospore being always reniform.

Thus, *Dictyuchus* has many swarming periods but only one type of zoospore. It is, therefore, *polyplanetic* but monomorphic. Following a series of asexual generations and when the food in the medium has been almost exhausted, the mycelium of the Saprolegniaceae initiates sexual reproduction.

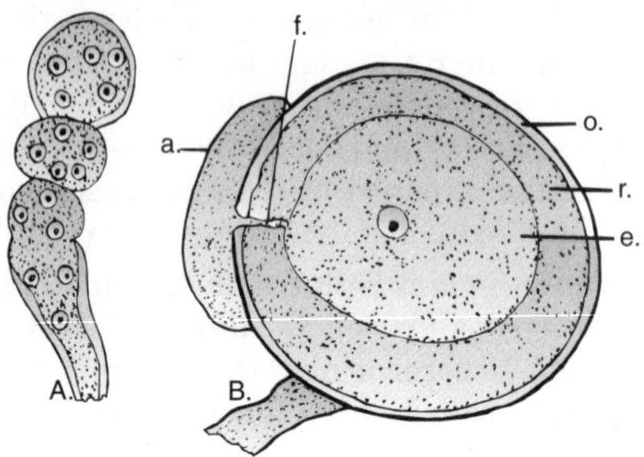

Figure 3.10: Albugo bliti. A. Sporangiophore and seriate sporangia. B. Mature sex organs at fertilization. a., antheridium; e., egg; f. , fertilization tube; o. , oogonium; r., residual cytoplasm.

The male and female gametangia (antheridia and oogonia) develop as lateral branches on the mycelium. Some clones are bisexual and others are unisexual. Careful study of the sex organs of *Achlya* has revealed a process of unsuspected complexity, involving the secretion of a number of complex chemicals that influence the course of development.

It has been demonstrated that the formation and maturation of the sex organs in *Achlya* are controlled by a hormonal system that operates when potentially male hyphae and female hyphae of *A. ambisexualis* are in close proximity in an aquatic environment.

The hormonal system is successively responsible for the proliferation of male somatic hyphae to form antheridial branches; the stimulation of the potentially female hyphae to form oogonial branches; the attraction of the antheridial branches toward the oogonial branches; the delimitation of the antheridia from their subtending branches; and finally, the septation of the oogonia from their stalks and the differentiation of the eggs.

This research of Dr. John R. Raper was summarized by him in 1957. One of these sequential stages in the sexual reproduction of *A. bisexualis,* the formation of antheridial branches on the male mycelium, has been studied by Barksdale.

As noted above, a substance secreted by the female filaments evoked the production of antheridial branches on the male mycelium. McMorris and Barksdale (1967) prepared a crystalline substance from the cultures of female thalli of *A. bisexualis* that could induce antheridium production and called it *antheridiol.*

The chemical structure of this compound was later ascertained, and antheridiol was later synthesized. As the antheridia become appressed to the oogonia, meiosis occurs within the gametangia, as a result of which oogonia produce haploid, nonmotile gametes, the oospheres (eggs), their number, from one to 20 or more in each oogonium, varying with the species.

Haploid gamete nuclei are also formed in the antheridia after meiosis, and these travel to the eggs through fertilization tubes that penetrate the oogonia. Karyogamy then occurs, reestablishing the diploid condition in the zygote. After fertilization, the zygotes rapidly develop thick walls, which obscure their contents.

The dormant zygotes are known as *oospores.* The oogonia eventually break down, releasing the thick-walled oospores into the water. After a period of rest the oospore germinates, giving rise to a diploid hypha, which establishes a new thallus. Accordingly, the life cycle of the Saprolegniaceae is haplobiontic, with the mycelium diploid and only the gamete nuclei haploid (H, d).

Order Peronosporales

In contrast to the Saprolegniales, the Peronosporales are of great economic importance, at least two of them having had a great impact on human affairs. Not long after the discovery of America by Columbus, the potato was introduced into Europe and eventually was established as an important food crop.

In some countries, such as Ireland, the potato was grown almost to the exclusion of other crops, and the Irish lived on the potato alone. In 1845, the fungus *Phytophthora* (Gr. *phyton,* plant, + Gr. *phthora,* destruction) *infestans,* one of the Peronosporales, invaded the island and spread like wildfire in the potato fields.

The destruction was enormous. Resulting in the complete failure of the potato crop, the fungus was directly responsible for the Irish famine of 1845 and 1846, during which over a million people died of starvation and more than that were forced to emigrate to foreign shores, notably those of the United States.

Because of the famine it caused, the fungus was also indirectly responsible for the repeal of the infamous corn laws of Great Britain which imposed heavy duty on imported grain to protect home farmers. In 1846, they were repealed so as to admit foreign grain into the country and so make it available to the starving population of Ireland.

Sometime during the latter part of the nineteenth century, *Phylloxera,* an aphid that attacks the roots of the grape, was accidentally introduced into southern France from the New World, where it is native. The European grapes (*Vitis vinifera*) proved to be extremely susceptible to it, and the whole French grape and wine industry was threatened when the vines began to die.

A French scientific mission, after studying *Phylloxera* in the United States, decided that the only solution to the problem was the introduction into France of resistant American stocks, on which the French wine grapes could be grafted. Large quantities of American grapevines were thus shipped to France, but while the *Phylloxera* problem was being solved, another equally severe one appeared.

It seems that some of the imported vines carried the spores of *Plasmopara* (*N. L. plasma,* mold, + *L. parere,* to bring), *viticola* another of the Peronosporales, and this destructive fungus, native to America, the cause of downy mildew of grapes, spread over the very susceptible European varieties.

The French wine industry appeared to be doomed. Fortunately, through a chance observation, Alexis Millardet, Professor of Botany at the University of Bordeaux, developed in 1885 Bordeaux mixture, the first fungicide to be discovered, and saved the grapes of France.

This introduced the era of plant disease control and the eventual development of a large number of different fungicides now used to combat plant diseases, of which Bordeaux mixture is still one of the most effective. These stories are related in detail by Large (1940) in his fascinating book *The Advance of the Fungi*.

The Peronosporales differ from the Saprolegniales in a number of important ways. Most, but not all, are terrestrial rather than aquatic fungi, although the genus *Pythium* (Gr. *pythein,* to cause to rot) does contain many aquatic species.

The terrestrial species produce their sporangia on special-ized, differentiated hyphae, the *sporangiophores*, rather than directly on the somatic hyphae as do the Saprolegniales; the Peronosporales are monoplanetic and produce only reniform (secondary) zoospores; the most complex Peronosporales (*Plasmopara, Peronospora* [*N. L. perono,* fibula, + Gr. *spora,* spore], *Albugo,* etc.) are obligate parasites, developing their entire life cycle on the living host, and cannot be grown in laboratory culture from spore to spore; with very few exceptions, only a single oosphere (egg) is formed within the oogonium, and this is surrounded by leftover cytoplasm (*periplasm*) rather than being free within the gametangium as in the Saprolegniaceae.

The genus *Albugo* will serve to illustrate the life cycle of the Peronosporales.

Albugo

Except for *Polyphagus* and a few species of the Saprolegniaceae, the fungi so far described are all similar in that they are saprobic. *Albugo* (*L. albus,* white), on the contrary, is a parasitic genus that occurs on a number of hosts. *Albugo candida* grows on certain mustards (Cruciferae).

Albugo impomeae-panduranae is widespread on sweet potatoes and certain morning glories, and *A. blitii* occurs on some species of *Amaranthus.* Leaves of infected plants become covered with conspicuous mealy white spots or patches, which are caused by eruptions of large numbers of sporelike sporangia below the epidermis.

Because of their lesions, infected plants are said to have white rust. The formation of the spores is preceded by the development of a vegetative mycelium, which spreads through the host tissues from the site of the primary infection; the mycelium is entirely intercellular.

The fungus obtains its metabolites by forming small, protuberant, papillate branches, haustoria (*sing. haustorium*; *L. haustor,* one who drinks), which penetrate some of the host cells. In sporangial formation, a number of multinucleate hyphal tips push out between the mesophyll cells, forming a bedlike mass, and enlarge terminally.

After several nuclei have migrated into the enlarged tip, the latter is delimited by an annular centripetal ingrowth of the wall. The tip of the hypha below the delimited sporangium now enlarges and is ultimately cut off like the first.

The sporangia thus are produced in chains in basipetal succession, the oldest being farthest from the sporangiophore. Continued sporangial production brings about a localized uplifting of the epidermis, which is finally ruptured, and the mature sporangia escape freely. The sporangia may function as zoosporangia, undergoing cleavage to form as many reniform zoospores as there are nuclei present. The sporangia are disseminated by wind, rain, or other agents, and if they settle on moist surfaces of leaves of the host species, they germinate either by germ tubes or by producing zoospores.

The biflagellate zoospores become spherical after a period of motility, encyst, and then develop delicate hyphal tubes, which usually enter the host through a stoma. The infection is spread in this way. Sexual reproduction may follow asexual later in the growing season.

The sex organs are produced from the tips of the hyphae among the mesophyll cells of the leaf and are suggestive of those of the water molds. After the hyphal tips have enlarged considerably, they are segregated from the remainder of the hyphae by cell walls.

The antheridia are smaller than the oogonia, but both are multinucleate. As the oogonium matures, the protoplasm becomes rather densely aggregated in the center, leaving a more watery, vacuolate peripiasm at the periphery.

After the antheridium comes in contact with the oogonium, meiosis occurs in both gametangia. By the time of fertilization, all but one of the nuclei of the oogonium disintegrate in certain species, notably *A. candida;* the remaining nucleus functions as the egg nucleus.

The egg is delimited from the peripheral cytoplasm by a delicate membrane. This type of cytokinesis, in which a cell is delimited within another, leaving residual cytoplasm (*periplasm*), is known as *free cell formation*.

The antheridium, which is appressed to the oogonium, now produces a small hyphal protuberance (fertilization tube) that penetrates the oogonial wall and grows through the periplasm, into the central dense cytoplasm containing the egg nucleus. After nuclear union, a multilayered wall is secreted by the zygote, the nucleus of which divides soon after fertilization, until about 32 nuclei are formed.

In the spring, further nuclear division and, finally, cleavage occur. Upon germination, usually in the spring after it is formed, the zygote forms numerous biflagellate, reniform, diploid zoospores, which renew the infection.

The sexual organs of *A. candida* are superficially similar to those of *Saprolegnia* and *Achlya*. The oogonia differ, however, in the production of a single egg, which is delimited from the periplasm by free cell formation. In *Saprolegnia* and *Achlya,* on the other hand, even in those cases when only one egg is developed, there is no residual cytoplasm.

Chapter 4 Amastigomycota I: Subdivision Zygomycotina

In contrast to the fungi we classify in the *Mastigomycota*, the *Amastigo-mycota* produce no flagellate cells whatsoever even in the aquatic species, and all but a few, therefore, have *spindle-pole* bodies (SPBs) instead of centrioles functioning in nuclear division.

Because these fungi are considerably more complex than those we have already discussed, they are often referred to as "higher fungi" to distinguish them from the so-called "*lower fungi*"designations we have *studiously* avoidedby those who believe them to have been evolved from the latter, and, therefore, more recently in the course of evolution.

Although such origin seems probable, it is merely conjecture. The division Amastigomycota contains four subdivisions: *Zygomycotina*, *Ascomycotina*, *Basidiomycotina*, and *Deuteromycotina*. In this chapter we shall deal with the first of these subdivisions.

SUBDIVISION ZYGOMYCOTINA: BREAD MOLDS, FLY FUNGI, AND ARTHROPOD COMMENSALS

The Zygomycotina reproduce sexually by the copulation of two usually equal gametangia, resulting in the formation of a *thickwalled zygosporangium* which contains a *zygospore*.

Two classes constitute this subdivision: the Zygomycetes

and the Trichomycetes. The former has been studied intensively for over 100 years. The latter is still not well known. We shall, therefore, devote most of our discussion to the Zygomycetes, which include the fungi commonly known as the bread molds and the fly fungi.

Class Zygomycetes

It will be recalled that in *Albugo* and the other Mastigomycota we have studied in the previous chapter, the asexual sporangia either produce zoospores upon germination or themselves germinate directly by germ tube. In the Zygomycotina, sporangia are still formed, but contain *nonmotile* spores called *aplanospores*.

These are released from the *sporangia* and *germinate* by germ tubes, which grow into mycelia. No flagellated cells are ever formed by any of these fungi, even though some live in aquatic or semiaquatic environments. About 600 species of *Zygomycetes* are known, which we classify in two orders: the Mucorales and the Entomophthorales.

Order Mucorales

Fungi in this order are mostly saprobes but may be weak parasites of flowers and fruits. Some are pathogenic to humans, causing a group of diseases known as *mucormycoses*. Perhaps the most familiar of all the Zygomycetes is *Rhizopus* (Gr. *rhiza,* root, + Gr. *pous,* foot), one of several genera in the family Mucoraceae.

Rhizopus stolonifer, commonly known as bread mold because of its occurrence on that substratum, frequently appears in damp, warm weather. It is also the chief cause of "*leak,*" a serious disease of *strawberries* while they are in transit to the market.

Its mycelium is nonseptate (coenocytic). *Rhizopus* and related genera may be present on all sorts of organic matter, including dung, fruit, and fleshy fungi, when there is sufficient moisture to support growth.

Its spores are almost always present in the atmosphere, as evidenced by the frequency with which it can be obtained

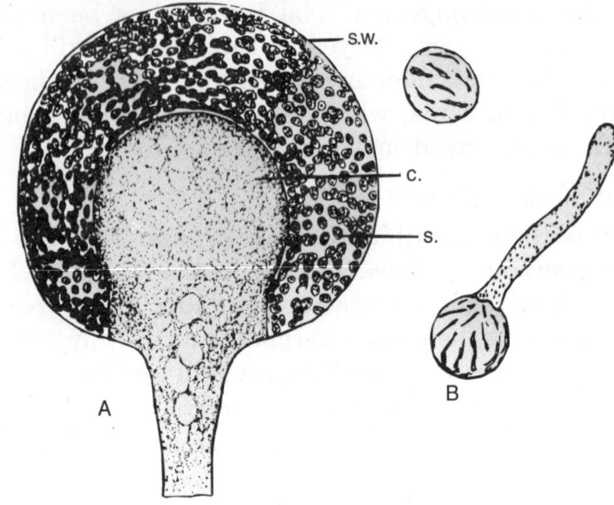

Figure 4.1: Rhizopus stolonifer. A. Median longitudinal section of mature sporangium. B. Spore and its germination. c., columella; s., spores; s.w., sporangial wall.

when moistened bread that does not contain preservatives, and other organic substances is exposed to air currents and then maintained in a humid atmosphere.

The mycelium of the *Mucorales* is a cottony white mass during the somatic phase but presents a sooty appearance at the time of *sporulation*. This is caused by the presence of large numbers of *black-walled* spores. Although the *mycelium* is coenocytic, it exhibits considerable differentiation.

Certain branches creep over the *substratum* much like stolons of strawberries, for example. Also like stolons, the portions of the horizontal hyphae that make contact with the substratum produce rhizoidal branches, which serve as absorptive organs and secrete *digestive* enzymes.

Asexual Reproduction

After a short period of somatic development in *Rhizopus,* groups of unbranched, elongate hyphae arise from the absorptive branches opposite a group of *rhizoids*, forming erect hyphae, the tips of which become enlarged with nuclei and cytoplasm as increase in length ceases.

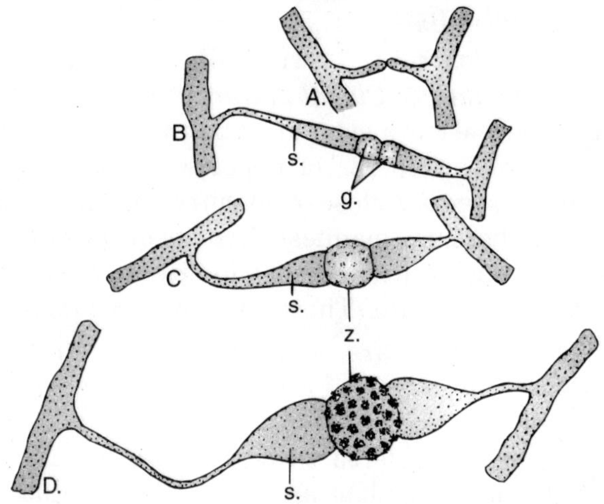

Figure 4.2: Rhizopus stolonifer. A-D. Stages in sexual reproduction. g., multinucleate gametes; s., suspensor; z. zygosporangium.

These sporangiophores bear single sporangia. The sporangia are formed in the following manner: As the enlarging tips of sporangiophores attain their *characteristic* size, the peripheral *cytoplasm* becomes dense and the central portion remains *vacuolate*.

The two regions are segregated from each other by the coalescence of a series of vacuoles present in a *domelike* arrangement.

A wall finally is secreted between the two portions of the protoplasm. The central sterile portion is called the *columella* (*L. columella*, dim. of column); the *peripheral* portion is fertile and sporogenous.

As the sporangium matures, the sporogenous *protoplasm* undergoes progressive cleavage, with the ultimate production of large numbers of minute spores, each of which contains several nuclei and develops a black wall.

The outer sporangial wall is extremely delicate and readily torn. When this occurs, the exposed spores are quickly carried away by air currents; the naked *columella* remains. The spores *germinate* readily on moist *substrates*.

Sexual Reproduction

Rhizopus stolonifer is heterothallic, consisting of two mating types (+ and -). *Clonal cultures* are, therefore, *self-sterile*. They are also considered to be isogamous in sexual *reproduction*. When spores of opposite mating types are planted in *reasonably* close *proximity* in agar cultures, sexuality soon becomes manifest. *Hyphae* of the two strains that approach each other increase in size at their tips and rise above the substrate. These are *progametangia*.

Transverse septa are soon laid down, so that the multinucleate tip of each branch is delimited from the remainder of the hypha. The delimited portions, called gametangia, are considered to be multinucleate gametes, and the subtending hyphae are known as *suspensors*.

After the *gametangia* have made contact, the walls between the tips of contiguous gametangia dissolve, with the result that the cytoplasm and *nuclei* then lie free within a single *lumen*.

During this period the nuclei in uniting gametangia increase in number; subsequently, many nuclei unite in pairs, but some supernumerary nuclei remain. A thick wall is secreted by the zygote. The supernumerary nuclei have been reported to disintegrate, so that the dormant zygote contains only diploid nuclei.

It has been recently shown that the thick-walled zygote is actually a sporangium, now called a zygosporangium, in which a zygospore is enclosed. Germination of zygospore when the zygosporangium splits open has been observed infrequently, but there is some *cytological* evidence that the nuclear divisions that occur during germination are

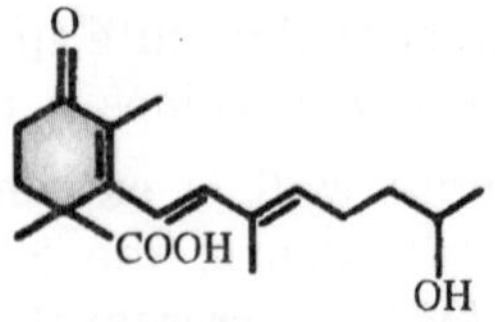

Figure 4.3: Trisporic acid C, chemical structure.

meiotic. This evidence is also supported by *genetic studies* of genera related to *Rhizopus.*

The spores from such a sporangium are either all (+) or all (–) or both (+) and (–) spores have been found. The cytological basis for this has not been elucidated with complete clarity, but it is thought that when all spores in a germ *sporangium* are of one mating type, all but one of the nuclei resulting from *meiosis disintegrate*, and all the spores, therefore, contain nuclei that are the progeny of the one surviving nucleus.

It was proved more than 70 years ago (for the first time in fungi) that the sexual process in *Rhizopus-like* molds (e.g., *Mucor mucedo* and *Blakeslea trispora*) is under chemical control. Van den Ende and Stegwee (1971) have summarized the literature on this subject. It has been shown that progametangia do not develop if the maturing types are grown separately.

It has been postulated that a "*progamone*" (not yet demonstrated to exist) "*informs*" the compatible mycelia of one another's proximity. This causes the *mycelium* to secrete trisporic acids, which evoke the differentiation of the progametangia in both the compatible strains.

Other, as yet chemically undefined, substances effect contact, gametangial union, and zygote formation. A number of genera similar to *Rhizopus* are widespread on organic substrata. *Mucor* (*L. muceo,* be moldy) is similar to *Rhizopus,* except that its sporangiophores arise from the main branches, rhizoids being absent at their bases, and its sporangiospores adhere closely one to another, forming a tight mass, and are therefore not windblown.

They are disseminated by splashing raindrops. *Phycomyces* (Gr. *phykos,* alga, + Gr. *mykes,* fungus) produces sporangiophores that may attain a length of 10 cm. Its zygosporangia are made conspicuous by the development of dark, branching projections on arched suspensors

The genus *Pilobolus* is an interesting dunginhabiting mold. Its resistant spores pass unharmed through the

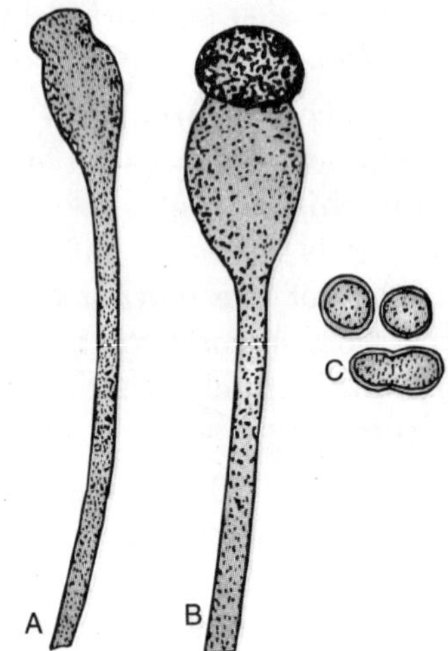

Figure 4.4: Pilobolus sp. A, B. Stages in sporangium development. C. Spores.

digestive tract of animals. Horse dung, if stored in a moist chamber, soon becomes covered with the positively *phototropic sporangiophores* of this organism. Each of them bears a terminal black sporangium.

Unlike that of *Rhizopus,* the sporangial wall of *Pilobolus* is firm, and the sporangium is abscised as a unit. The sporangiophores begin development early from the *mycelium* just below the surface of the *substratum*. In early evening their tips enlarge to form *sporangia*.

Shortly after midnight a subsporangial swelling appears, which explodes as a propulsive jet late the following morning because of excess *turgor* pressure. The sporangia and their spores thus are forcibly ejected for distances as great as 6 ft and at a rate of 16 m/sec. *Pilobolus* has an interesting mechanism that detects light and causes the sporangiophore to turn toward it.

When the sticky sporangia are ejected, they strike and adhere to the stem or leaf of a nearby plant and are then eaten by herbivorous animals. They are eventually voided, unharmed, in the excreta, where the sporangiospores germinate and repeat the life cycle.

Pilobolus, the hat thrower (Gr. *pilos,* hat, + *bole,* a throw), is often referred to as the fungus gun. Brodie (1978) in his book has an interesting short chapter on this fungus, entitled "Gunnery in the Fungus World."

Order Entomophthorales

These are the so-called fly fungi which attack flies on long-unwashed windows of garages and . . . university classrooms. The *Entomophthorales* shoot their one-spored *sporangia* off the tips of the *sporangiophores*. These propagative units are much like conidia in that in most instances they germinate directly by germ tube.

A dead fly stuck on a windowpane will usually be surrounded by a white, halolike zone on the glass. This white zone consists of thousands of "*conidia*" of *Entomophthora* (Gr. *entomon,* insect, + *phthora,* destruction), which have been forcibly expelled by the "*conidiophores*" issuing in large numbers from the infected body of the fly the fungus has killed and in which it is growing.

An interesting fungus in this order is *Basidiobolus ranarum,* abundant in soils, which grows on the dung of lizards and frogs and shoots off its sporangia. These are eaten by beetles, which in turn are eaten by frogs or lizards.

The beetles are digested in the *amphibian*'s stomach and the sporangia of the fungus are freed. There they divide internally to produce spores which multiply by budding in the body of the amphibian and are excreted with the dung. *Basidiobolus haptosporus* is pathogenic to animals and human beings, causing a disease generally known as *Entomophthor-omycosis*, or *Zygomycosis.*

Class Trichomycetes

The Trichomycetes are always found in association with *arthropods*, often attached to the gut of *centipedes* or *millipedes.* They do not seem to be parasitic, however, and are regarded as *commensals.*

Trichomycetes do not usually produce an extensive mycelium. The somatic stage of some species is confined to a foot cell or *holdfast*, from which a sporangium grows. In others, however, a limited *filamentous branched* or unbranched *mycelium* is produced.

The hyphae may be coenocytic or septate. Asexual reproduction takes place by amoeboid cells, *arthrospores*, or sporangiospores. All are aplanospores. No sexual reproduction is known in these organisms.

However, the production of structures resembling (and called) *zygospores*, in the order *Harpellales*, indicates that some sexual process probably occurs. Such *zygospores* are believed to be formed in the same manner as those of the Zygomycetes.

It is chiefly for this reason that the *Trichomycetes* are grouped with the Zygomycetes in the subdivision Zygomycotina. *Alexopoulos* and *Mims* (1979) discuss these organisms more fully.

Chapter 5 Amastigomycota II: Subdivision Ascomycotina

The three final subdivisions of the fungi the *Ascomycotina*, the *Basidiom-ycotina*, and the *Deuteromycotina* are structurally more complex than the *Mastigomycota* and the *Zygomycotina* and are thought to have originated more recently in *geologic* time.

These subdivisions share an important character with the *Zygomyc-otina*—that is, the complete absence of *flagellate* cells from their life cycles, and this is why they are grouped with them in the division *Amastigomycota*.

Even the aquatic and marine species among them lack such cells. *Denison* and *Carroll* (1965), among others, believe that the *Ascomycotina* originated in the sea from nonflagellate ancestors closely related to the red algae, but others favor a *zygomycetous ancestry* for them.

Many mycologists believe that the Basidiomycotina arose from *ascomycetous* ancestors for reasons that will become evident when we discuss the Basidiomycotina in other chapter of this book.

In both *Ascomycotina* and *Basidiomycotina* meiosis is *zygotic*, but in both subdivisions, as we shall see, a *dikaryotic* phase is interspersed between the haploid portions of the *thallus* and the *zygote*.

In a recent classification system these two groups are put together in a division *Dikaryomycota* to emphasize this point.

CLASS ASCOMYCETES

The subdivision Ascomycotina consists of the single class *Ascomycetes*, the chief characters of which are summarized below:

1. *Spores* resulting from *karyogamy* and *meiosis* are enclosed in an *ascus* (*pl. asci*), which is a saclike cell containing usually a definite number of *ascospores* (typically eight), developed by free cell formation. This is a process in which one or more cells are delimited within a cell in such a way as to leave residual *cytoplasm* (*epiplasm*) around the spores. It must be emphasized that if a fungus has asci, it is an ascomycete, regardless of other characters it may or may not have; if it does not, it cannot be placed in this class, again *regardless* of its other *characteristics*.
2. Absence of *flagellate* cells.
3. A septate *mycelium* (in *mycelial* forms) with centrally *perforated septa* that divide the hyphae into uninucleate, binucleate, or *multinucleate* segments and through which the protoplasm of adjacent cells is *continuous*. Nuclei and other organelles can pass through the septal *perforations* and travel through the mycelium.
4. Presence of *Woronin bodies* in the hyphal cells. These are ultrastructural elements of a crystalline nature but of unknown chemical composition.
5. Hyphal walls with a large proportion of chitin and, with very few exceptions, devoid of cellulose.
6. Asexual reproduction typically by means of *conidia* (sing. *conidium*), which are spores borne on specialized reproductive hyphae (*conidiophores*).
7. Formation by most species, as a result of sexual reproduction, of fruiting bodies (*ascocarps*) containing the asci.

There are a large number of fungi that closely resemble

the Ascomycetes except that they do not *reproduce sexually* and, therefore, form no asci.

Such fungi, classified in the form-class Deuteromycetes, are believed to be Ascomycetes, for the most part, which have lost their sexual (ascus) stages or whose asci are rarely formed and have not been discovered, or which, perhaps, never had a sexual stage. If and when, as often happens, a sexual stage is discovered, such a fungus is transferred to the proper genus of *Ascomycetes*.

Importance

Ascomycetes are *enormously* important in *human affairs*. A large number are parasitic on plants, causing the serious diseases apple scab, apple bitter rot, brown rot of *stone fruits*, stem rot of *strawberries*, and a large number of others.

Endothia (Gr. *endothen*, from within) *parasitica*, an ascomycete imported to the United States from Asia, which causes *chestnut* blight, has reduced the American *chestnut* (*Castanea dentata*) to a minor *understory shrub*.

The *Dutch elm* disease, caused by another ascomycete, was imported into the United States from Europe and is similarly threatening the American elm (*Ulmus americana*), which was once the dominant shade tree on "Main Street, U.S.A." *Oak wilt*, a very serious disease of various species of oak (*Quercus* spp.), is caused by still another destructive ascomycete.

In addition, most of the fungi that cause human diseases are Ascomycetes or related Deuteromycetes. On the other side of the coin, there are some very useful Ascomycetes. Yeasts are the basis of the baking and brewing industries.

Digesting sugar, they produce alcohol, important in the manufacture of beers and wines, and liberate CO_2, which causes the dough to rise in the baking of bread.

Morels and *truffles* are eagerly sought by "*mushroom hunters*" for their excellent flavors. Unfortunately, the former have not been grown to the ascocarp stage commercially.

The French, however, appear to have succeeded in cultivating truffles by inoculating the roots of seedling, symbiotic trees with the mycelium of the truffles and planting "truffle orchards," so to speak. This requires some explanation.

Many soil fungi, not only Ascomycetes, become associated with the roots of green plants, forming *mycorrhizae* (*sing. mycorrhiza*) (Gr. *mykes*, fungus, + *rhiza*, root) and living symbiotically with the plants, the fungus obtaining carbohydrates from the plant roots and the plant absorbing water with dissolved salts from the mantles of fungal hyphae that surround them and extend into the soil.

The truffle has long been known to be a mycorrhizal fungus living in association with oak and beech trees and producing its ascocarps (the truffles of commerce) below the ground. For an interesting discussion of how truffles are harvested in France and Italy, read Christensen's (1965) *The Molds and Man*.

Some Ascomycetes are both destructive and beneficial. *Claviceps* (*N.L. clavi*, club, + *L. ceps*, headed) *purpurea*, the ergot fungus, causes a destructive diesease of rye and other grasses by infecting their flower parts and replacing the grain with the sclerotia of the fungus.

Sclerotia (*sing. sclerotium*) are stony-hard bodies consisting of tightly cemented hyphae. When these bodies (known as ergot) are consumed by cattle grazing in infected fields, the alkaloids in the sclerotia cause abortion in cows and gangrene of the hooves and tails of the animals.

These same alkaloids are deadly to human beings, who contract a disease known as St. Anthony's Fire when they consume bread made with ergotized flour (flour made from grain that has not been thoroughly freed from ergot).

Yet some of these ergot alkaloids are eagerly sought by pharamaceutical companies for manufacturing drugs (which cannot as yet be economically synthesized in the laboratory) useful in inducing labor and preventing *post-partum* hemmorhage.

It is also of interest that ergot contains lysergic acid, from which LSD is easily synthesized. Although the ergot fungus can be grown in the laboratory on artificial media, no one has succeeded in inducing it to form sclerotia, in which the useful alkaloids are concentrated, apart from its natural hosts.

Pharmaceutical companies are, therefore, forced to purchase ergot from farmers who are willing to collect it before harvesting the grain. In some areas, rye and wheat fields are artificially inoculated with conidia of the fungus in order to increase ergot production.

Somatic Structures

Most species of Ascomycetes are mycelial, producing septate hyphae with perforated septa, with the perforations sometimes plugged and with Woronin bodies nearby. The hyphae originate by the germination of ascospores or conidia and grow and branch rapidly.

Asexual Reproduction

In the classical life-cycle pattern, the mycelium begins to produce conidiophores soon after it has attained some growth. Conidiophores are specialized, reproductive hyphae, usually with determinate growth, which produce conidia in various ways.

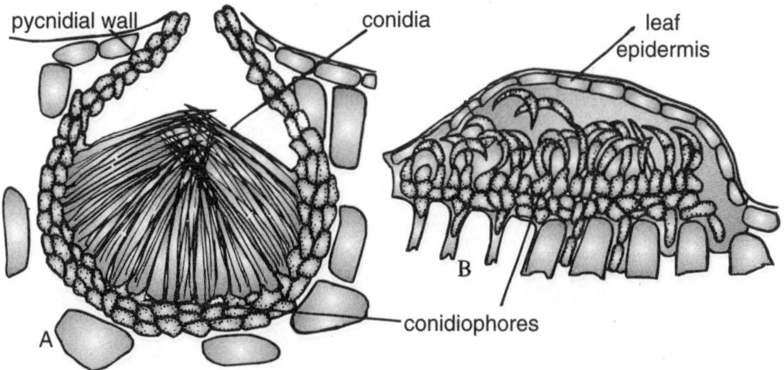

Figure 5.1: Asexual reproduction in Ascomycetes. A. Pycnidium B. Acervulus. Note the needle-shaped conidia in the pycnidium of this species.

Some species produce erect conidiophores from almost any hyphal cell without any seeming organization. These form conidia at their tips or sides, or the cells of the conidiophore may themselves become differentiated and be cut off as a chain of conidia.

In other Ascomycetes the conidiophores are organized in pycnidia (*sing. pycnidium*), which are generally flask-shaped bodies, their bases lined inside with short conidiophores, producing conidia (*pycnidiospores*) at their tips.

A pycnidium is usually provided with a pore at the top, the ostiole, through which conidia are exuded in a mucoid, tendril- or ribbonlike mass (*cirrhus*), much as toothpaste issues from a tube.

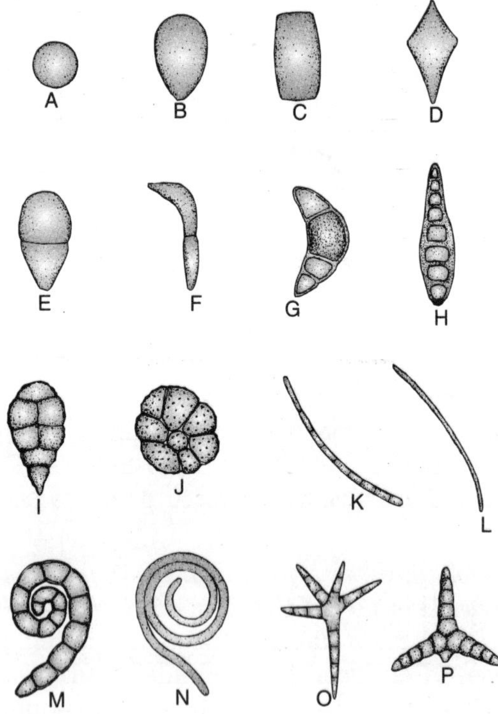

Figure 5.2: Various types of conidia. A-D. Nonseptate. E-H, K, M, P. Transversely septate. I, J. Muriform. K, L. Needle-shaped. M, N. Helical. O, P. Irregular.

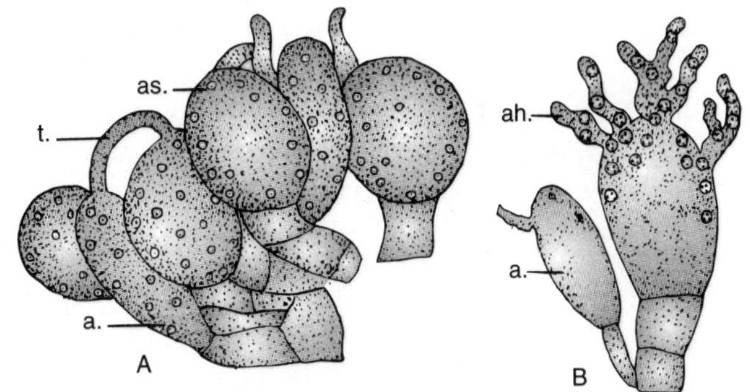

Figure 5.3: Pyronema omphalodes. Sexual reproduction. A. Sex organs at fertilization. B. Postfertilization. a., antheridium; a.h., ascogenoushyphae; as., ascogonium; t., trichogyne.

In other species, especially in the fungi that cause a disease of plants called anthracnose, the short conidiophores of the parasite form a bedlike mass (acervulus; pl. acervuli) under the epidermis or cuticle of the infected part (stem, leaf, or fruit), which breaks through to the surface much like the asexual stage of *Albugo.*

This produces enormous numbers of conidia, which are either splashed by raindrops or carried by insects or wind to other nearby susceptible plants. There are other ways, too, in which conidiophores are produced, but the three described above are probably the most common.

Conidia vary greatly as to size, shape, number of cells, and wall ornamentation. In general we recognize conidia as being hyaline (colorless) or brown. However, some are yellow, pink, or black. In shape, conidia vary from globose to needle-shaped straight or curved.

Some are cross- or star-shaped and some even resemble a tree or a pair of trousers. In size conidia vary from smaller than 2 µm to as much as 40 µm in length; in number of cells, from one to many. Some conidia are septate transversely, whereas others have both vertical and transverse septa, being muriform.

Sexual Reproduction

Plasmogamy in the Ascomycetes is accomplished by a

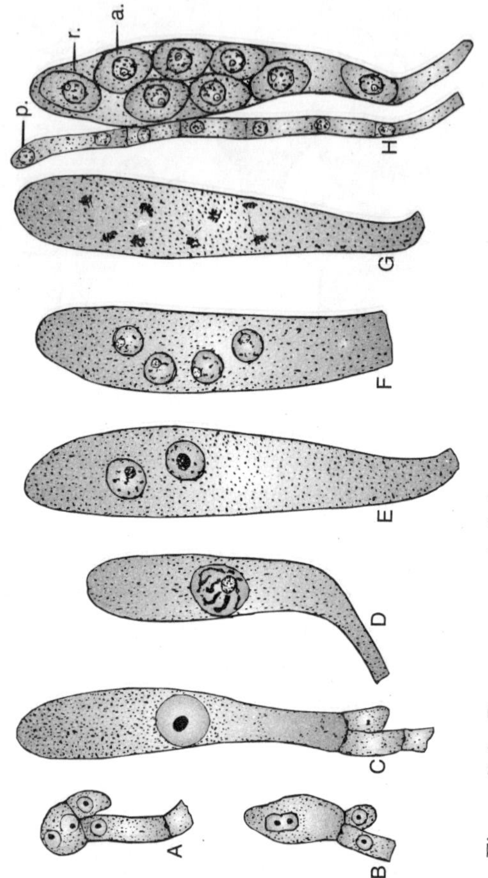

Figure 5.4: Pyronema omphalodes. Ascus and ascospore development. A-C. Origin of the ascus by crozier formation. D-G. Successive nuclear divisions in the ascus. H. Paraphysis and ascus. a., ascospore; p., paraphysis; r., residual cytoplasm (eninlasm).

variety of methods. In a typical species, the mycelium forms coiled *ascogonia* (female sex organs), each usually bearing a long, hairlike hypha, the *trichogyne*.

It also forms either club-shaped *antheridia* (sing. *antheridium*) or large numbers of very tiny sporelike *spermatia* (sing. spermatium) in various ways. Antheridia and spermatia are male sex organs. As is the case with the Zygomycetes, the Ascomycetes, too, may be homothallic or heterothallic.

In homothallic species there are no mating types and any male sex organ is compatible with any female sex organ of the same species, whether these are produced on the same or on different individual thalli. Heterothallic species consist of two mating types, designated (A) and (a) or A_1 and A_2. Both must be present so that the sex organs of opposite mating types may copulate.

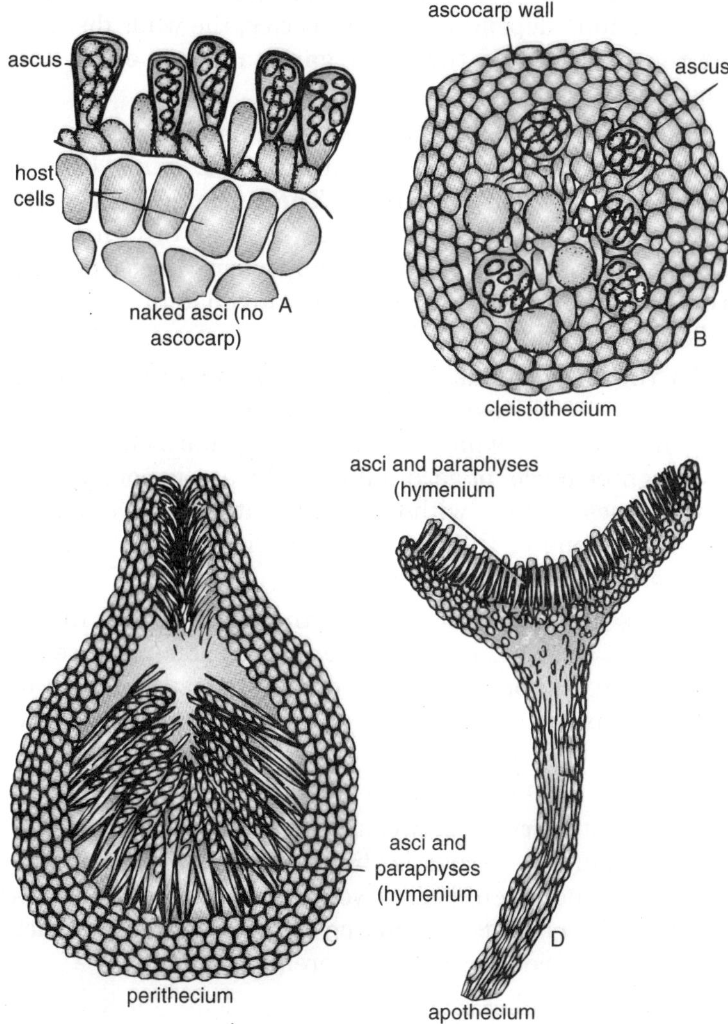

Figure 5.5: Four ways in which Ascomycetes bear their asci.

This implies, of course, that ascogonia and antheridia (or spermatizing cells) produced by the same mycelium are incompatible and that two individual thalli of opposite mating types are necessary for sexual reproduction to take place.

When a trichogyne contacts a compatible antheridium or spermatium, depending on the species, the walls dissolve and the contents of the male gametangium enter the ascogonium.

Nuclei of the male and female gametangia are thus brought together by plasmogamy in the, same cell in preparation for eventual fusion. The nuclei, however, do not fuse at this point. Instead, they appear to form pairs distributed under the oogonial wall, where the oogonium forms buds that grow into ascogenous hyphae in which the nuclear pairs migrate.

As the ascogenous hypha grows, the nuclei divide repeatedly by mitosis and become distributed in the ascogenous hypha, which produces a septum between the two daughter nuclei of each mitosis. The ascogenous hypha thus becomes septate, with each cell containing two nuclei, descendants one of the original antheridial and the other of the original ascogonial nucleus.

This is the dikaryotic phase of the Ascomycetes. In the majority of species, each ascogenous hypha produces a branch from one or more of its dikaryotic cells, the tip of which bends to form a hook (*crozier*), containing two compatible nuclei, which now proceed to divide so that the spindles are oriented perpendicularly.

With septa formed between the two daughter nuclei of each division, the crozier is divided into three cells. The penultimate (hook cell) is dikaryotic, containing one nucleus of each "sex," whereas the tip and basal cells of the crozier contain one nucleus each, of different origin.

Karyogamy takes place in the binucleate hook cell of the crozier, which is now termed the *ascus-mother-cell*, because as it elongates it will develop into the ascus. In

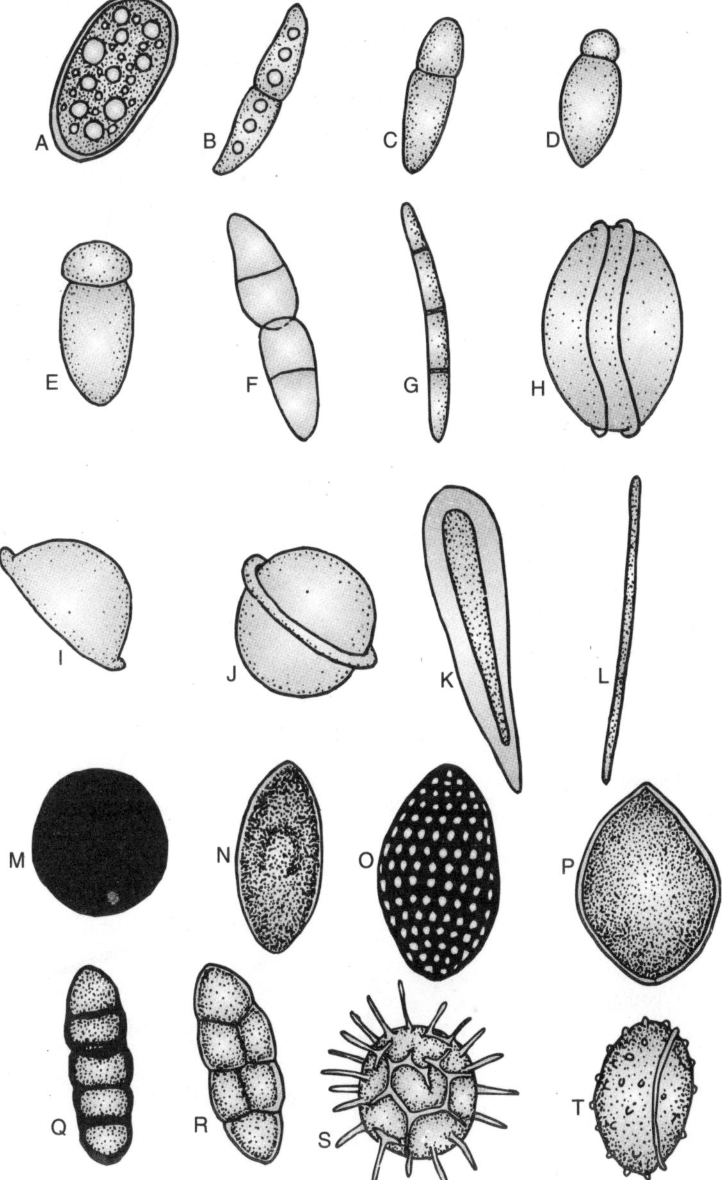

Figure 5.6: Various types of ascospores.

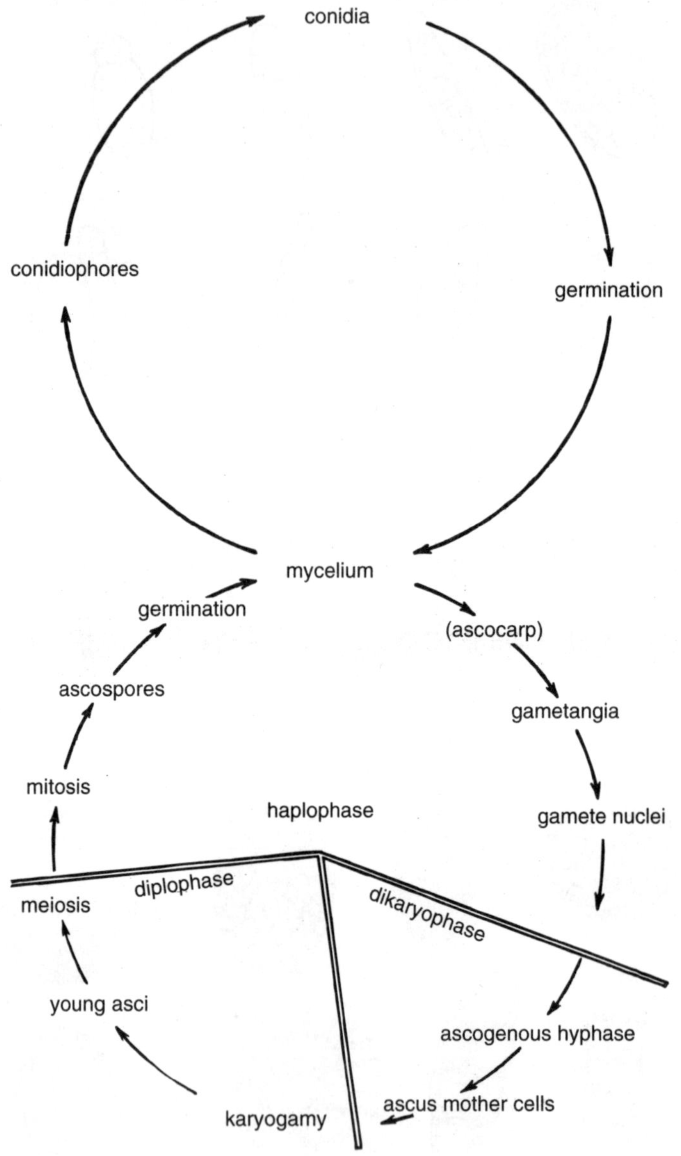

Figure 5.7: Life-cycle pattern of typical asocarpic Ascomycete.

fact, elongation often takes place first and karyogamy occurs in the young ascus.

As the ascus grows, the diploid nucleus undergoes meiosis, producing four haploid nuclei, which, in most species, divide once more by mitosis, resulting in an ascus with eight nuclei.

A system of membranes now results in an ascus vesicle, which surrounds all eight nuclei and which invaginates around the nuclei and, by the addition of new membrane, enfolds them and cuts them off from the surrounding cytoplasm.

A thicker wall then forms around each uninucleate unit, which then develops into an ascospore. The surrounding cytoplasm in which the spores are embedded is the *epiplasm*, and the whole process is called free cell formation.

In the meantime, the basal cell of the crozier fuses with the tip cell and then grows out into a new ascogenous hypha, wherein the history is repeated.

Thus, ascogenous hyphae proliferate so that many more asci are formed than there were ascogenous hyphae originally.

In fungi such as *Neurospora*, in which the asci are cylindrical and narrow, the arrangement of the spores (in pairs) represents the tetrad, and by dissecting and growing the ascospores in the order in which they were arranged in the ascus, it is possible to perform tetrad analysis and determine the way characters are inherited and segregated during meiosis.

This is one reason why *Neurospora crassa* has become such an important tool in the study of inheritance and has provided data on which the one-geneone-enzyme theory is based.

While this procedure is developing asci and ascospores, the stalk of the ascogonium and the hyphal cells below it are stimulated to proliferate and form a wall, which soon surrounds the sexual apparatus and forms an ascocarp.

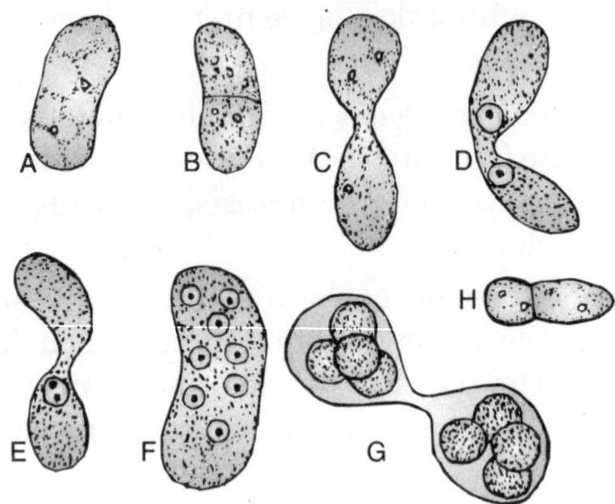

Figure 5.8: Schizosaccharomyces octosporus. A. Somatic cell. B. Cell division. C. Cell union (plasmogamy). D. Cell union stained; note nuclei. E. Zygote with diploid fusion nucleus. F. Free nuclei of ascus. G. Ascus with eight ascospores. H. Ascospore germination.

The Ascocarp

There are many kinds of ascocarps produced by the Ascomycotina but in general they may be organized into four main types: The cleistothecium,which is globose and has no opening, the *perithecium*, a flask-shaped body with an opening (ostiole) at the top, the *apothecium*, which assumes various forms but is always open with asci exposed, and the *ascostroma*, which is a cushion of somatic tissue (stroma, *pl. stromata*) in which one or more cavities are formed by the developing asci.

There are also some Ascomycetes that produce their asci naked, without forming ascocarps. Some methods in which Ascomycetes bear their asci are shown in Figures elsewhere in this chapter.

The Ascospores

As is true of conidia, ascospores, too, may be of an infinite variety of sizes, shapes, number of cells, colors, and wall ornamentations. As you might guess, these characters serve to distinguish genera and species within the group.

The release of the ascospores from the asci is apparently due to osmotic pressure that develops in the asci when the

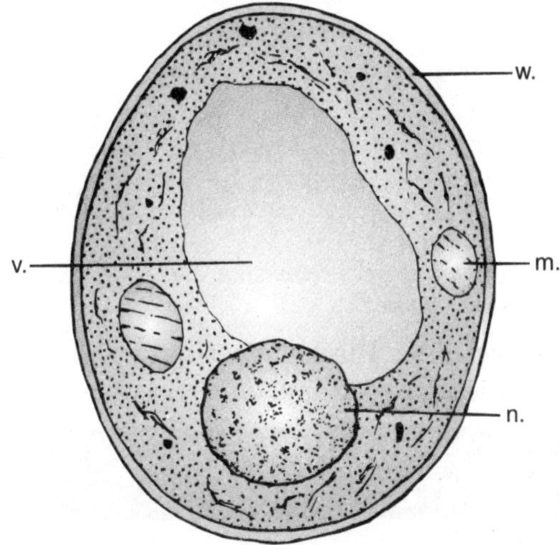

Figure 5.9: Saccharomyces cerevisiae. Cellular organization based on electron microscopy. m., mitochondrion; n., nucleus; v., vacuole; w., wall.

complex polysaccharides in the epiplasm are converted to osmotically active simpler sugars at the time the ascospores are mature and ready to be expelled.

Life Cycle

In nature many Ascomycetes produce several generations of d'onidia before sexual reproduction takes place. The asexual cycle is thus chiefly responsible for the propagation and dissemination of the fungus. Sexual reproduction takes place in many species in late summer or early fall, with the ascospores maturing at the end of the season or in very early spring. A typical life cycle diagram of the Ascomycetes is represented in Figure elsewhere in this chapter.

In spite of what we have said above, there is a group of Ascomycetes that form neither ascocarps nor ascogenous hyphae. These are the yeasts and their relatives, which we shall discuss presently.

Classification

The class Ascomycetes is divided into five subclasses on the basis of ascus and ascocarp characters. These are

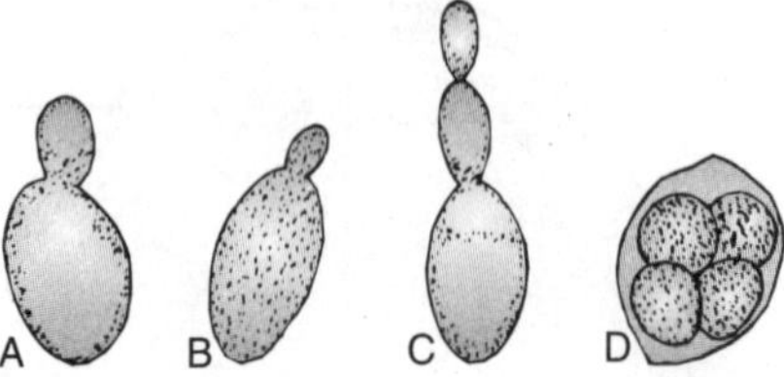

Figure 5.10: Saccharomyces cerevisiae. A-C. Budding somatic cells. D. Ascus with ascospores.

Hemiascomycetidae, Plectomycetidae, Hymenoascomycetidae, Laboulbeniomycetidae, and Loculoascomycetidae.

THE NONASCOCARPIC ASCOMYCETES

Subclass Hemiascomycetidae: The Yeasts and Leaf-Curl Fungi

The *Hemiascomycetidae* (Gr. *hemi*, half, + Ascomycetes) include the order Endomycetales, in which we classify the yeasts that produce ascospores (true or ascosporogenous yeasts), and the order Taphrinales (the leafcurl fungi), among others of less interest to the general student.

These fungi are morphologically simple; they produce no ascocarps or ascogenous hyphae, hence the name Hemiascomycetidae. The true yeasts are unicellular organisms that reproduce asexually either by binary fission or by budding.

Sexual reproduction occurs under conditions of reduced food supply and is accomplished by the fusion of two compatible cells to form a zygote, which develops directly into an ascus.

Order Endomycetales: The Ascosporogenous Yeasts

The ascosporogenous yeasts are classified in the family Saccharo-mycetaceae of the order Endomycetales but are sometimes placed in a separate order Saccharomycetales. *Schizosaccharomyces octosporus* (Gr. *schizo*, to cleave, + *saccharon*, sugar, + *mykes*, fungus; *okto*, eight, + *spora*,

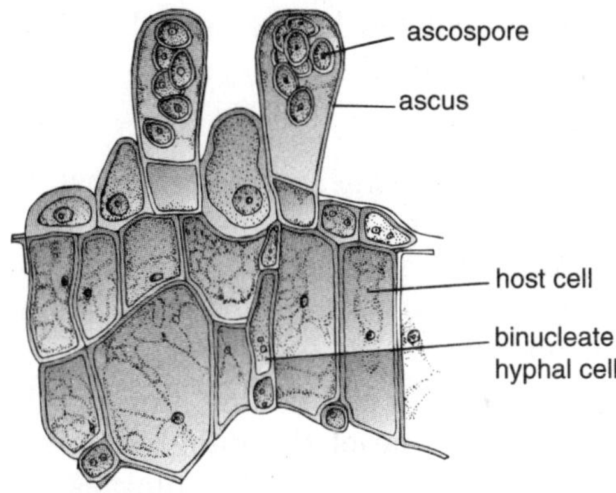

Figure 5.11: Taphrina deformans. Asci with ascospores on the surface of a host leaf.

spore) is the best known of the fission yeasts. It is a unicellular organism that occurs in nature on such fruits as grapes and figs. Certain species of the genus *Schizosaccharomyces* are the agents of fermentation in tropical beers. The cells of *S. octosporus* are spherical to ellipsoidal, vacuolate, and uninucleate.

Multiplication is effected by simple cell division, which follows nuclear division. Recently divided cells may remain adherent, or they may separate promptly. After several days' growth in laboratory cultures, sexuality occurs.

In this process two adjacent cells produce short protuberances that meet; their tips dissolve, and plasmogamy and karyogamy follow. The zygote nucleus soon undergoes three successive nuclear divisions, resulting in the formation of eight nuclei.

Two of these divisions constitute meiosis. An ascospore is delimited around each of the eight nuclei thus formed, leaving epiplasm around them. The zygote, thus, is transformed directly into a single ascus, which ultimately liberates the ascospores when its wall deliquesces. The ascospores contain abundant food reserves.

They produce new generations of cells asexually by nuclear and cell division. In the related *S. pombe*, it has been shown by Egel (1971) that the nitrogen of the culture medium must be depleted before sexual reproduction and ascus formation can occur.

Saccharomyces

Saccharomyces cerevisiae, a brewer's yeast, is representative of budding yeasts that occur in nature on various fruits. The ovoidal cells of *Saccharomyces* (Gr. *saccharon*, sugar, + *mykes*, fungus) contain a rather large vacuole and an excentric nucleus.

Multiplication occurs by budding, during which nuclear division takes place. One of the daughter nuclei migrates into the bud, which subsequently enlarges and becomes segregated from the parent cell.

Rapid budding may result in the formation of short chains of cells. Budding takes place in predetermined spots on the cell wall, which remain as bud scars after the buds have separated from the mother cell. *Saccharomyces cerevisiae* is heterothallic, consisting of two mating types, (A) and (a).

Under certain environmental conditions sexual reproduction results in the formation of asci, each of which usually produces four ascospores, two of each mating type. The ascospores from a single ascus, if isolated into individual culture vessels, will germinate to form spherical somatic cells, which will continue to reproduce by budding as long as the four cultures remain separated.

However, when cells of the two mating types are brought togetb'r into one culture, union of the haploid cells in compatible pairs forms diploid zygotes that multiply by budding and establish a diploid population.

In this process, the cells of one mating type elongate toward the cells of the other mating type when they are in proximity.

A diffusible sex substance (hormone) has been reported to be formed by cells of one mating type of *S. cerevisiae* by Duntze, MacKay, and Manney (1971). The diffusible substance stimulates the cells of the opposite mating type to elongate as they do in preparation for sexual union.

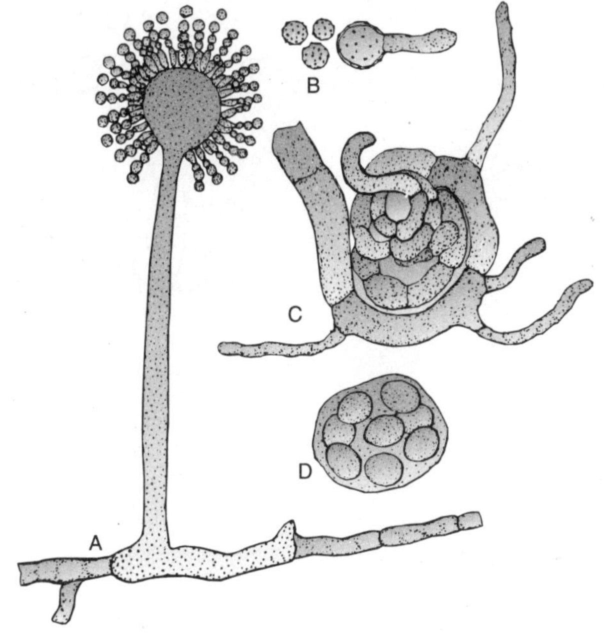

Figure 5.12: Aspergillus niger. A. Conidiophore on foot cell. B. Spores and spore germination. C. Eurotium chevalieri. Ascogonial coil. D. Ascus and ascospores.

Ascospores of different mating type may unite immediately (before undergoing asexual budding) to initiate the diploid phase. Ascosporo-genesis in yeasts differs some-what from that in other Ascomycetes in that a typical ascus vesicle is not formed. When the diploid nucleus divides, a nuclear plaque, functioning in the same manner as a centrosome in flagellate organisms, divides, and the daughter plaques migrate to opposite sides of the nucleus.

Microtubules that are formed become a part of the spindle, and the first meiotic division occurs, but without the nuclear envelope breaking up. Immediately after meiosis I, the two plaques divide again and migrate at an angle to the first spindle, so that the two parallel spindles are formed, while the original nucleus has now formed four lobes.

During meiosis II, a double membrane forms partially

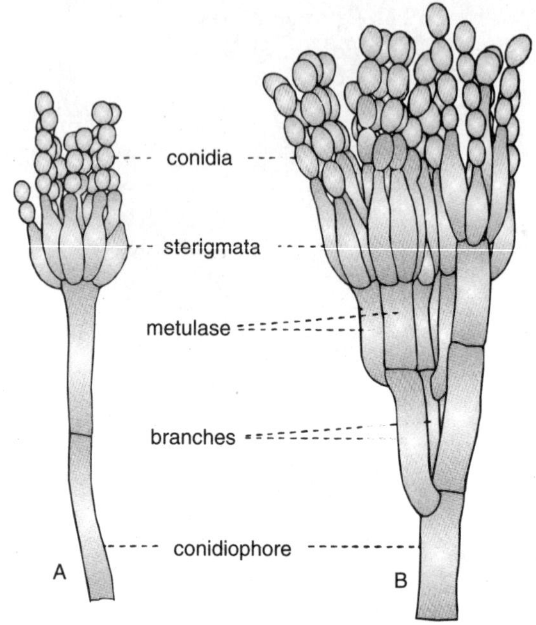

Figure 5.13: Morphology for the conidiophore (penicillus) of Penicillium. A. Single-branched penicillus as in P. frequentans. B. Asymmetric, branching type as in P. expansum.

around each nuclear lobe, and at the completion of meiosis II the membranes close around the nuclear lobes, thus cutting off four ascospores from the surrounding protoplasm (epiplasm).

The details of ascosporogenesis in *S. cerevisiae* are beautifully summarized by Tingle et al. (1973). The ascus wall of the yeasts is thin, and when the asci are mature it deliquesces and releases the ascospores. Although differing in detail, ascosporogenesis in the yeasts is the same in principle as that in other Ascomycetes.

With an alternation of haploid and diploid generations, the first through the budding of ascospores, the second through the budding of zygotes, the life cycle of *S. cerevisiae* is diplobiontic. This is reminiscent of the life cycle of *Allomyces* in the Chytridiomycetes.

The importance of various types of yeast to man,

because of their biochemical activities, can scarcely be summarized adequately in a short account. Yeasts are used as agents of alcoholic fermentation in brewing and as the leavening agent in baking, and for these reasons have been the subject of intensive cytological, genetic, and physiological investigations.

Order Taphrinales: The Leaf-Curl Fungi

The order Taphrinales includes simple Ascomycetes with a binucleate mycelium parasitic on flowering plants, causing puckering of the leaves, a disease known as leaf curl, and proliferation of small branches that characterize the disease called witches' broom.

The most important and best known species is *Taphrina* (*Gr. taphre*, trench or ditch) *deformans*, which causes peach and almond leaf curl. *Taphrina cerasi* causes witches' broom of cherry.

The ascospores of *T. deformans* are released from the asci, on the surface of the peach leaves, and bud like yeasts. Because of this behavior, they are called blastospores. This budding results in a population of free cells, which then germinate, producing germ tubes that penetrate into the peach leaf and form an intercellular mycelium.

At the time of germination, the nucleus divides, and the resultant pair of nuclei migrates into the germ tube. As the germ tube develops into a hypha, conjugate divisions of the nuclei perpetuate the binucleate condition of the hyphal cells.

The binucleate hyphae continue to grow and branch and eventually become massed just below the leaf cuticle; here they break up into their component binucleate cells. Karyogamy, followed by a single mitotic division and septum formation between the daughter nuclei, results in the formation of a diploid basal stalk cell and upper ascogenous cell.

The ascogenous cells continue to elongate and soon break through the leaf cuticle to the surface of the leaf. In the meantime, meiosis followed by a single mitosis occurs in the ascogenous cells. The ascus plasma membrane invaginates to cut off eight ascospores.

These are released through the ascus tip, which bursts open. Peach and almond leaf curl is worldwide in distribution and a serious disease in all peach- and almond-growing regions.

THE ASCOCARPIC ASCOMYCETES

Subclass Plectomycetidae: Blue Molds, Black Molds, and Human Pathogens

The Plectomycetidae produce their asci at various levels in a cleistothecium or more rarely a perithecium. The asci are thin and evanescent, releasing the ascospores within

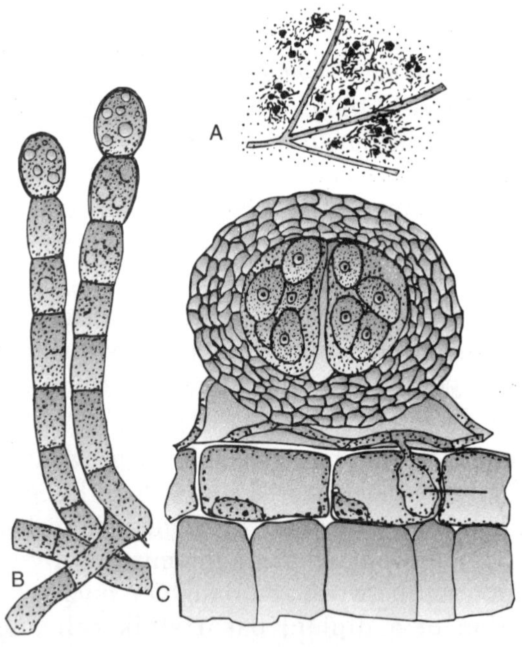

Figure 5.14: Microsphaera alni. A. Mycelium and cleistothecia on lower surface of lilac leaf. B. Conidiophore with seriate conidia. C. Stained section of cleistothecium on upper surface of lilac leaf. h., haustorium in epidermal cell.

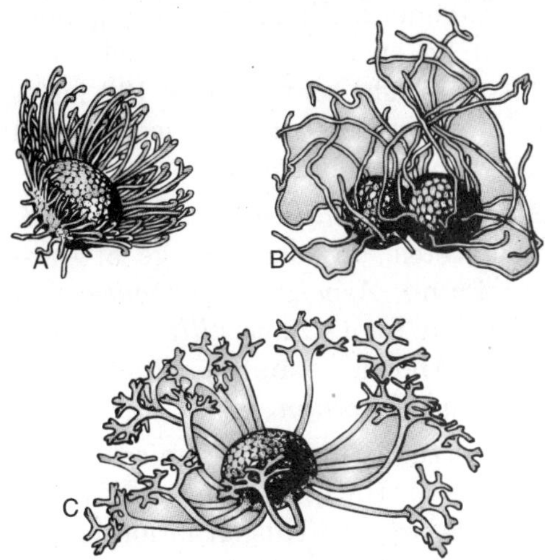

Figure 5.15: Cleistothecia of powdery mildews. A. Unicinula salicis. B. Sphaerotheca humuli. C. Microsphaera berberidis.

the ascocarp, from which they escape when the wall of the cleistothecium breaks or decays. The asci are usually formed from croziers on ascogenous hyphae.

Eurotiaceae

Most of these fungi are placed in the order Eurotiales, the two most important families of which are the Eurotiaceae and the Gymnoascaceae. In the Eurotiaceae, the genera *Eurotium* (Gr. *euros*, a mold) and *Emericella* have conidia that are classified in the formgenus *Aspergillus.*

Talaromyces and *Eupenicillium* have conidia that belong to the form-genus *Penicillium.* This requires some explanation. There are many fungi that reproduce solely by conidia and never-so far as is known-sexually. Such fungi are classified in the subdivision Deuteromycotina, form-class Deuteromycetes (*Fungi Imperfecti*).

At the same time, many common Ascomycetes are encountered in nature mostly in their conidial stages because they form their asci but once a year. The conidial stages of such Ascomycetes have the same characteristics as some Deuteromycetes and are conveniently classified in the same form-genera. Thus, the form-genera *Aspergillus* (*L. aspergillum, a* special type of brush) and *Penicillium* (*L. penicillus*, a brush) contain over 100 formspecies each, only a few of which also reproduce sexually and form cleistothecia with asci and ascospores.

For example, *Aspergillus niger* and *Penicillium notatum* are Deuteromycetes, no sexual stage of these fungi ever having been found; *Aspergillus chevalieri*, on the other hand, in addition to its *Aspergillus* conidial stage, also produces cleistothecia sexually, which we place in the ascomycete genus *Eurotium.*

Such fungi actually have two names, one for the ascocarp genus and one for the conidial *genus-Eurotium chevalieri* (= *Aspergillus chevalieri*). This situation is confusing to the beginning student but is very convenient for the mycologist, who can simply say that the ascomycete genus *Eurotium* produces *Aspergillus-type* conidia.

Returning to the Eurotiaceae, fungi in the genera *Eurotium*, and *Emericella*, as we have said, form conidiophores and conidia characteristic of the form-genus *Aspergillus*. Some species of *Aspergillus* form dark-brown almost black conidia, whereas in others the conidia are brightly colored in yellow or green hues.

The same is true of the genus *Emericella*, which differs from the other two in that its cleistothecia are covered with characteristic “hiille” cells, the function of which is not known. Hiille cells are able to germinate and form mycelium, but it is doubtful whether they are instrumental in propagating the fungus in nature.

The ascospores of *Emericella* are of interest in that they are brilliant red in color and have pointed ridges, which makes them appear starlike in side view. A similar relationship exists between the ascomycete genera *Talarornyces* and *Eupenicillium* (Gr. *eu*, well or good + *Penicillium*) and the deuteromycete formgenus *Penicillium.* All known species of *Talaromyces* and *Eupenicillium* form conidiophores and conidia characteristic of the formgenus *Penicillium*.

Of the four ascomycete genera listed *above-Eurotium*, *Emericella*, *Carpenteles*, and *Eupenicillium*—there are no species of importance to human beings. It is true that many species of *Aspergillus* and *Penicillium* are economically important, but none of these has a perfect stage of any kind. They will therefore be discussed in other chapter of this book with the Deuteromycetes.

Gymnoascaceae

Relatively few of the Eurotiaceae as such are of importance in human affairs. On the contrary, the *Gymnoascaceae*—the other family of the Eurotiales we have mentionedis of direct importance because it contains the ascus stages of all fungi that cause human skin diseases (ringworms) and of some that cause diseases of internal organs in humans.

The asci of the Gymnoascaceae are usually enveloped by a loose network of hyphae, sometimes ornamented with various types of appendages. This is the cleistothecium, which is sometimes nothing more than a loose cottony hyphal mass. The ringworm fungi-usually known as the dermatophytes—never form cleistothecia on the infected skin and seldom in nature, where they occur on such animal substrata as hair, feathers, and dung. Some are also found in the soil or even on plant debris.

The majority of the dermatophytes whose perfect stages have been discovered are heterothallic. It appears, however, that the ascospores are of little importance biologically and that these fungi depend for their multiplication on their conidia, most of which belong to the formgenera *Microsporum* (Gr. *mikron*, small) and *Trichophyton* (Gr. *thrix*, *trichos*, hair, + *phyton*, plant) of the Deuteromycetes.

The deuteromycete form-genus *Epidermophyton* (Gr. *epidermis*, skin, + *phyton*, plant) is also important in causing athlete's foot. No ascus stage has been discovered for this formgenus. There are two genera of Gymnoascaceae that are implicated in the causation of human skin diseases: *Arthroderma* (Gr. *arthron*, joint, + Gr. *derma*, skin) and

Nannizzia (after Nannizzi, an Italian mycologist). *Arthroderma* has *Trichophyton* conidia, and *Nannizzia* has *Microsporum* conidia. The various skin diseases caused by fungi are medically known as *Tineas.* Thus we have *Tinea barbae* (barber's itch), *Tinea corporis* (body ringworm), *Tinea pedis* (foot ringworm, or athlete's foot), *Tinea cruris* (ringworm of the groin), and others.

Up to recent years it was very difficult to treat these diseases, but with the discovery of griseofulvin, an antifungal antibiotic, treatment is now assured, even if long. More about griseofulvin when we discuss the Deuteromycetes.

In addition to the dermatophytes, the Gymnoascaceae include the perfect stages of at least two fungi that cause deep mycoses. Deep mycoses are fungal diseases that affect human internal organs such as lungs.

Ajellomyces dermatitidis (after Ajello, an American mycologist) is the perfect stage of the fungus that causes blastomycosis, a serious disease of the skin, lungs, and bones, and *Ajellomyces capsulatus* causes histoplasmosis, a widespread, serious respiratory disease.

SUBCLASS HYMENOASCOMYCETIDAE

The subclass Hymenoascomycetidae includes the powdery mildews, the perithecial fungi, and the cup fungi. Their chief characteristic is the formation of asci in a basal layer, the hymenium, inside an ascocarp, which may be globose and completely closed as in the powdery mildews (Erysiphaceae), flask-shaped and provided with an opening (ostiole) at its apex, as in *Neurospora* and *Sordaria*, or open from the beginning and variously shaped.

This is a very large subclass with several orders and many hundreds of species. We shall mention only a few forms as examples.

Order Erysiphales: Powdery Mildews

The powdery mildews are so called because they form

a mealy, powdery white stratum on the surfaces of leaves in a number of plants. Their mycelium is obligately parasitic on a specific host, because all attempts to grow them for prolonged periods in artificial culture have thus far failed.

Examples of powdery mildews that infect well-known plants are the following: *Microsphaera alni* (Gr. *mikro*, small, + *sphaera*, sphere) on lilacs and oaks, *Erysiphe cichoracearum* on garden plantain, *Sphaerotheca pannosa* (Gr. *sphaera*, sphere + *theke*, box, sheath) on roses and peaches, *Erysiphe* (Gr. *erys*, red, + Gr. *siphon*, tube) *graminis* on cereal grains, and *Uncinula* (L. *uncinus*, a hook) *necator* on grapes.

Ascocarps typical of the three genera are shown in Figure elsewhere in this chapter. The mycelium spreads over the leaf from the original point of infection and obtains nourishment by means of haustoria that penetrate into the epidermal cells.

The hyphal cells of most species are uninucleate. After a period of vegetative growth, certain hyphae in most species produce erect branches, which form conidia in

Figure 5.16: Humaria axillaris, a cup fungus (among plants of the moss Funaria).

chains. These are blown about by air currents and germinate, initiating new infections.

Unlike those of most other fungi, the conidia of many powdery mildews not only do not require free water for germination but are able to germinate in very dry air, even at 0% relative humidity. What it is that enables them to do this is not known.

The asexual cycle, frequently repeated, rapidly spreads the fungus. Sexual reproduction and ascocarp formation occur later in the growing season. About midsummer, in the temperate zones, the mycelium begins to form cleistothecia.

These first appear as minute white knots on the mycelium but soon grow and change color to cream, yellow, orange, and finally dark red to brown, nearly black. The sex organs, which precede the cleistothecium, are not highly differentiated but consist of short hyphae that curve around each other.

One has been identified as an antheridium and the other as the ascogonium. The walls between these dissolve at one point of contact, and the antheridial nucleus is reported to migrate into the ascogonium. Nuclear union is probably delayed, as in other Ascomycota. Descendants of the sexual nuclei are distributed among the cells of the ascogenous hyphae. The latter, depending on the genus, give rise to one or more asci. Soon after the sex organs have developed, somatic hyphae at their base form a sterile protective layer, which becomes the wall of the cleistothecium.

Three successive nuclear divisions occur in each ascus, so eight potential ascospore nuclei are developed. In some species each of these is delimited to form an ascospore by free cell formation. In others, fewer ascospores are produced, and the supernumerary nuclei disintegrate in the epiplasm.

The cleistothecia usually remain on the leaves when the latter are shed, and dissemination of the ascospores does not occur until the following growing season. In most localities in North America the ascospores do not mature until late fall or early winter, the fungi overwintering in the cleistothecial stage.

Ascospore discharge has been studied in *Podosphaera* (Gr. *pous*, *podos*, foot, + Gr. *sphaera*, sphere), which produces a single large globose ascus with eight spores in each cleistothecium. As the cleistothecium absorbs water in the spring, the ascus expands and the cleistothecium bursts, expelling the entire ascus forcibly. In flight, the ascus explodes and also releases its spores explosively.

These, in turn, germinate on the surface of a susceptible host and start the life cycle over again. Powdery mildews as a rule form no ascocarps in the tropics, where they reproduce entirely by conidia.

Cleistothecia of the powdery mildews bear appendages of different types, which are useful in anchoring the cleistothecium to the leaf surface. The type of appendage combined with the number of asci-one or many-within the cleistothecium are the characters on which the genera of the Erysiphaceae are separated.

Thus, *Erysiphe* and *Sphaerotheca* have mycelioid indefinite appendages. In *Microsphaera* and *Podosphaera* the tips of the appendages are dichotomously branched; *Phyllactinia* (*Gr. phyllon*, leaf, + Gr. *aktis*, ray) has appendages with bulbous bases and pointed tips, whereas *Uncinula* and *Pleochaeta* (Gr. *pleio*, more, + Gr. *chaete*, mane) have appendages with uncinoid (curled) , tips.

Of these genera-all that occur in North *America*-*Sphaerotheca* and *Podosphaera* produce only a single large ascus in each cleistothecium, whereas each cleistothecium of all the other genera mentioned contains many asci.

Perithecial Ascomycetes (Pyrenomycetes)

The genera *Sordaria* (*N.L. sordes*, dirt or filth) and *Neurospora* (Gr. *neuron*, nerve, + Gr. *spora*, seed, spore), both easily grown in the laboratory, are excellent for classroom demonstration of perithecial fungi.

Neurospora, you will remember, is the fungus that has been used so successfully by geneticists to elucidate the laws of heredity. It has become the *Drosophila* of the fungus world. In *Neurospora* and *Sordaria* the ascocarps are perithecia.

All species of these genera are easily grown on laboratory media. In addition, *Neurospora sitophila* and certain isolates of *Sordaria fimicola* are indispensable for demonstrating heterothallism and the segregation of characters in the ascus.

Neurospora

The conidiophores of *Neurospora* are not markedly differentiated from the multinucleate vegetative hyphae. Some species of this genus produce minute, uninucleate microconidia in addition to those of ordinary size; the latter are multinucleate and are called macroconidia.

The conidial walls are responsible for the pink color of the fungus. In *N. sitophila* the young ascogonium, a curved septate hypha with several nuclei in each cell, becomes covered with several layers of interwoven sterile hyphae.

This structure has been called a *protoperithecium*. Certain cells of the ascogonium produce long, tenuous, trichogynelike branches, which penetrate the sterile hyphal layers surrounding the ascogonium. It has been demonstrated that not only the microconidia but also the macroconidia and even vegetative hyphae and trichogynes of one strain may unite with the trichogynes and vegetative hyphae of another compatible strain.

Fusion of compatible vegetative hyphae is called *somatogamy*. Inasmuch as *Neurospora sitophila* is heterothallic, two different mating types are required for sexual reproduction to take place. Even though a mycelium derived from a single ascospore or conidium produces both ascogonia and microconidia (i.e., is monoecious), these sex organs are incompatible and cannot function among themselves to produce ascospores because they are of the same mating type.

In various ways cited above nuclei of the two mating types are brought together into the same mycelium and ultimately into the ascogonial cell. The latter now gives rise to ascogenous hyphae, the tips of which enlarge to form elongate asci.

Meanwhile, the sterile layer of the protoperithecium has increased in extent and organized itself into a perithecium, at the apex of which a small aperture, the ostiole, develops. The young asci of *Neurospora* are binucleate.

The two nuclei of each ascus represent descendants of nuclei of the two mating types originally brought together in trichogynal or other types of plasmogamy. In further development, nuclear fusion takes place in each young ascus.

This is soon followed by three successive nuclear divisions, during which meiosis is accomplished. The asci at this stage contain eight linearly arranged nuclei. These, with a portion of their surrounding cytoplasm, are finally segregated from the residual cytoplasm of the ascus by free cell formation.

The mature ascospores become binucleate as a result of mitosis within each spore. At maturity they are discharged from the perithecium through its ostiole. The mature spore walls are ribbed, an attribute that suggested the generic name.

The ascospores germinate in laboratory culture after suitable treatment (with heat or furfural), giving rise to a mycelium that produces only protoperithecia and conidia, unless contact is made with a mycelium or conidia of a compatible strain.

It has been shown experimentally that four of the eight ascospores of each ascus of *N. sitophila* give rise to one mating type and that the other four are of the opposite mating type. Various species and races of *Neurospora* have provided the basis for important genetic and biochemical studies.

It should be noted that the necessity for fusion between

two strains of *N. sitophila* for maturation of the perithecia is analogous to the selfincompatibility found in certain types of flowers. As in certain flowers, both types of reproductive organs are present but fail to function; the controlling factor here is apparently physiological.

Sordaria, *Gelasinospora*

Sordaria, an organism similar to *Neurospora*, differs from the latter, among other respects, in producing smooth-walled ascospores. *Sordaria fimicola* does not produce conidia or microconidia but reproduces solely by ascospores. The latter are surrounded by a gelatinous sheath.

The perithecial necks are positively phototropic, as they are in many ascocarpic Ascomycetes. As asci mature within, one of them at a time enlarges and protrudes through the ostiole. Its ascospores are violently discharged, the ascits collapses, and then, in turn, another protrudes to liberate its ascospores; such proliferation of asci is common in the ascocarpic Ascomycetes.

By subjecting cultures of *Sordaria fimicola*, to ultraviolet irradiation, Olive (1956) obtained ascospore color mutants. This is extremely useful for demonstrating segregation of characters in the ascus. By mating the wild type (brown ascospores) with the mutant (colorless or gray ascospores) and examining the hybrid asci produced, the student has a visual demonstration of how the color character segregates in the asci.

Gelasinospora, with pitted ascospores is another genus closely resembling *Sordaria* and *Neurospora.*

The Apothecial Ascomycetes (Discomycetes)

The Discomycetes are Ascomycetes that produce their asci in apothecia. An apothecium is an open ascocarp with its hymenium exposed from the time the ascospores are mature and in many species at an even earlier stage. Typically, paraphyses (sterile threads) are interspersed with the asci in the hymenium.

The apothecia of most Discomycetes are cup- or saucershaped, but in some groups they are clubshaped or tongue-shaped, or even mushroom-shaped. The morels, which also belong here, are spongelike, and the apothecia of the false morels are saddle-shaped or convoluted like brains perched on a stalk.

The bell-morels have bell-like apothecia. In some species the apothecia are funnel-shaped. The majority of Discomycetes are saprobic, but a few are parasitic, causing serious diseases of economic plants. Such is *Monilinia* (*L. monile*, necklace) *fructicola*, the cause of brown rot of stone fruits, probably the most serious disease of peaches.

The life history of this fungus is as follows: Ascospores are released from the apothecia in early spring when the peach trees are in bloom. Those that fall on the flowers germinate, and the mycelium invades the flowers and causes them to blight.

Conidia, produced in long chains on the flowers from conidiophores, are blown by the wind and spread the disease to other blossoms and eventually to the young peach leaves, causing leaf and twig blight.

The young fruit is not susceptible to the fungus, but when the fruit matures, the conidia germinate on the fruit surface and the germ tubes penetrate through insect punctures or other small wounds such as broken hairs.

The enzymes secreted by the hyphae dissolve the middle lamellae of the fruit cells and cause a softening of the invaded tissue, which turns brown. Eventually the fruit rots and shrivels, becoming a mummy. Some mummies remain on the trees after the ripe peaches are harvested, but many fall to the ground and are partially buried.

Before winter sets in, the mycelium in the mummies produces ascogonia and microconidia. The details of sexual reproduction have not been discovered, but it appears that plasmogamy takes place between trichogynes and microconidia, which results in the formation of apothecial primordia.

In early spring, these develop into funnel-shaped

apothecia on the surface of the mummies that have overwintered on the orchard floor. Weather conditions that bring about blossoming of peach trees also favor the maturing and release of the ascospores, which shoot up from the ground and are deposited by air currents on the peach blossoms, starting the cycle over once more.

It is of interest that mummies that hang on the trees through the winter do not produce apothecia but form new crops of conidia from the overwintered mycelium. The probable explanation for this is that conditions on the ground are favorable for spermatization but not so on the mummies hanging from the trees, which probably do not remain wet long enough for spermatia and ascogonia to be formed and spermatization to take place. This is only conjecture, however.

Many saprobic Discomycetes often produce brightly colored conspic-uous apothecia. An example is the scarlet cup fungus (*Sarcoscypha* [Gr. *sarx*, *sarkos*, flesh + Gr. *Kyphos*, crooked]) *coccinea*, a widely distributed fungus you can find in the spring growing on dead wood in the forests. Several other genera, among them *Pyronema* (Gr. *pyr*, fire, + *nema*, thread, skein, i.e., hypha), are inhabitants of burned-over or sterilized soil.

The apothecia of *Discomycetes* vary from a millimeter in diameter up to the size of small teacups. In some genera the apothecia are stalked. Although the fruiting body is somewhat ephemeral, its formation is in all cases preceded by an extended period of vegetative activity on the part of the mycelium, which ramifies in the substratum, absorbing nutriment.

In a few genera the vegetative mycelium reproduces itself asexually by conidia, but these are entirely absent in most others. There is good reason to believe that the apothecium typically arises as a result of sexuality, but the latter has been clearly demonstrated only in a few species, and even in these there is a difference of opinion regarding the cytological details of the process.

Pyronema has been investigated frequently regarding its cytological and sexual features. In this genus well-differentiated antheridia and ascogonia are developed. The inner surface of the apothecium in cup fungi, the hymenium, is composed of intermingled columnar asci and sterile paraphyses.

The remainder of the *apothecium* is made up of sterile *interwoven hyphae* that form pseudoparenchyma, as viewed in section. Spore discharge is explosive in many *species*, and large numbers of spores may be disseminated simultaneously in visible puffs.

The apothecia of *Pyronema* are relatively small and inconspicuous, and plane or almost convex. The apothecia of *Peziza* (Gr. *pezis*, puffball), *Humaria* (*L. humus*, earth), *Urnula* (*L. urnus*, pitcher jar), and *Sarcoscypha* are widely distributed, larger, and more conspicuous than those of *Pyronema;* they are flat or concave.

Unfortunately, however, their life cycles have not been worked out as completely as that of *Pyronema. Chorioactis* (Gr. *chori*, apart, distinct), with the single species *C. geaster*, is of interest because the apothecium, closed at first, splits open like an *earthstar* and because of its peculiar distribution: Texas and Japan!

Morels, False Morels, and Saddle Fungi

A word should be added about morels, saddle fungi, and false morels. Morels belong to the genus *Morchella* (Gr. *morchel*, morel), which includes several species. All morels have a stalked, spongelike apothecium. All are edible and delicious. Unfortunately, the morel season is short, not exceeding one month in the spring. They can be grown in culture from spores to the mycelial stage, but no one has succeeded in producing ascocarps on laboratory media.

It has been reported that in France morels have been grown by crumpling ascocarps over soil with which apple mash from nearby cider factories had been mixed, but apparently this method cannot be depended upon for commercial purposes because there is no morelgrowing industry anywhere in the world. Nevertheless, it is said that growing morels out of doors as a horticultural crop presents no problem. Such morels are harvested in the spring at the same time that wild morels appear. No one has succeeded in growing them commercially like other mushrooms, which are harvested at least twice a year.

The saddle fungi produce large apothecia that resemble saddles on a central stalk. There are a number of genera, among which are *Helvella* (*L. helvella*, a small pot herb) and *Discina* (Gr. *diskos*, disc, + *L. ina*, like).

Some of these are edible, but some are poisonous. The false morels are in the genus *Gyromitra* (Gr. *gyros*, rounded + Gr. *mitra*, girdle). The heads (pilei) of the apothecia of some species are highly convoluted, resembling brains on top of thick, ridged stalks.

Again, these may be eaten safely by some people but are poisonous to others and should therefore be avoided by mycophagists. The poison is gyromitrin, which is soluble in water and can enter the bloodstream easily.

Truffles

Truffles are mycorrhizal fungi that produce their ascocarps below the ground. Their spores are generally dispersed by animals digging up the truffles for food. Truffle ascocarps emit a strong odor, which enables animals to find them.

These fungi have been found in many parts of the world, but only the kinds native to southern France, northern Italy, and the shores of the Mediterrane an generally are edible and choice. Those in other areas, although not poisonous, are not worth hunting for the table.

The edible truffles belong chiefly to the genera *Tuber* (*L. tuber*, truffle) and *Terfezia* (Arabic *terfez*, truffle). The latter has been known since ancient times, when it was believed truffles were formed by thunderbolts striking the earth.

The Arabs of North Africa prize them as food. Most of

the truffles known from the United States were described from California and Oregon, chiefly because Dr. Helen Gilkey, who was interested in studying them and became an authority on this group, studied in California and later worked at Oregon State University.

It is axiomatic that the known distribution of living organisms coincides with the distribution and the activities of the biologists who hunt them! Truffle mycelium can be grown in artificial culture in the laboratory but does not produce ascocarps.

In recent years, Italian and French scientists have succeeded in artificially synthesizing truffle mycorrhizae by inoculating susceptible tree seedlings with the mycelium or spores of the edible truffles. This research was published in Italian with English summaries. The last comprehensive report on truffles in English is Singer's (1961) *Mushrooms and Truffles.*

SUBCLASS LABOULBENIOMYCETIDAE

This is a very large group of minute, very specialized fungi mostly on insects and some mites. A few are also known from marine red algae in the Southern Hemisphere. They seem to do no damage to their hosts and are of little interest to the general student although they are quite abundant.

SUBCLASS LOCULOASCOMYCETIDAE

The Loculoascomycetidae produce their asci in cavities (locules) in a stroma. A stroma is a cushion or mattress-shaped structure that bears reproductive organs. Often, only a single locule is produced in a stroma and is hard to distinguish from a perithecium. Such a stroma is called a *pseudothecium*.

There are a large number of Loculoascomycetidae that are of great economic importance. The most common perhaps is *Venturia inaequalis*, which causes the widespread apple scab, found everywhere apples are grown. In *Venturia* (after *A. Venturi*, nineteenth-century Italian botanist), sterile threads, the *pseudoparaphyses*, originate at the apex of the locule and grow down, anastomosing among the asci, which grow up from the base among them.

Pseudoparaphyses are produced by a number of other Loculoascom-ycetidae. Among the most economically important Loculoascomycetidae that form no sterile threads in their pseudothecia is *Guignardia bidwellii* (in honor of Guignard, a French mycologist). In addition to asci in *pseudothecia*, this fungus produces conidia in *pycnidia*.

Chapter 6: Amastigomycota III: Subdivision Basidiomycotina

The Basidiomycotina differ from the Ascomycotina chiefly in that they produce their meiospores externally on basidia instead of internally in asci. Other important characteristics of the Basidiomycotina, some of which they share with the Ascomycotina, are the following:

1. They produce no flagellate cells.
2. A dikaryotic phase is interspersed between plasmogamy and karyogamy. In the Basidiomycotina the dikaryotic phase is of long duration, being represented by the extensive dikaryotic mycelium, which produces the sporophores (*basidiocarps*).
3. The septa of most Basidiomycotina that have been investigated are swollen, more or less barrel-shaped, and centrally perforated. The pore is covered by a membranous pore cap. This is the *dolipore septum*.
4. The dikaryotic mycelium of many, but not all, Basidiomycotina has *clamp connections*.
5. No differentiated gametangia are produced except in the rusts (Uredinales), the sexual function having been relegated to less specialized structures, usually the somatic hyphae.

Of the above listed characteristics, the presence of the basidium is the *sine qua non* of the Basidiomycotina. It must be emphasized here that there are several types of basidia known, all of which are the organs in which karyogamy and meiosis take place.

The Dolipore Septum

This septum has been found in all groups of the Basidiomycotina except the subclass Teliomycetidae (the rusts and the smuts). It is a complex apparatus consisting of a central, perforated swelling over which there is a pore cap, sometimes referred to as the *parenthesome*.

This type of septum has also been found in some of the mycelial members of the subclass Hemiascomycetidae but is generally regarded as a typical basidiomycetous structure.

We know that nuclei and other cytoplasmic organelles can and do pass through the dolipore, and it has been suggested that this septum is able to regulate the passage of organelles from one cell to another, by opening and closing at the appropriate moment.

The Clamp Connections

Clamp connections have also been found in all groups of Basidiomy-cotina except for most Teliomycetidae. In many species they are restricted to the dikaryotic mycelium

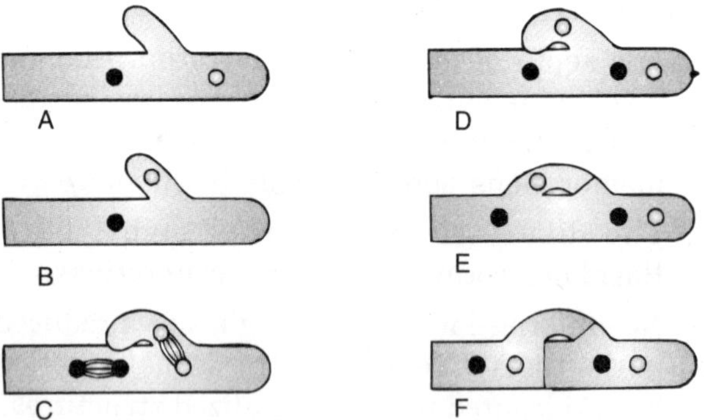

Figure 6.1: Stages in cell division and clamp connection formation in the mycelium of the Basidiomycetes, schematized; black nuclei represent one mating type and white nuclei the other. Successive stages show mechanism by which the dikaryotic condition is maintained.

and are often used in breeding experiments to indicate whether dikaryotization has actually occurred, because they are much easier to see than the nuclei in the hyphal cells.

A clamp connection begins as a short branch from an end cell of a growing hypha and forms a bent hook, the tip

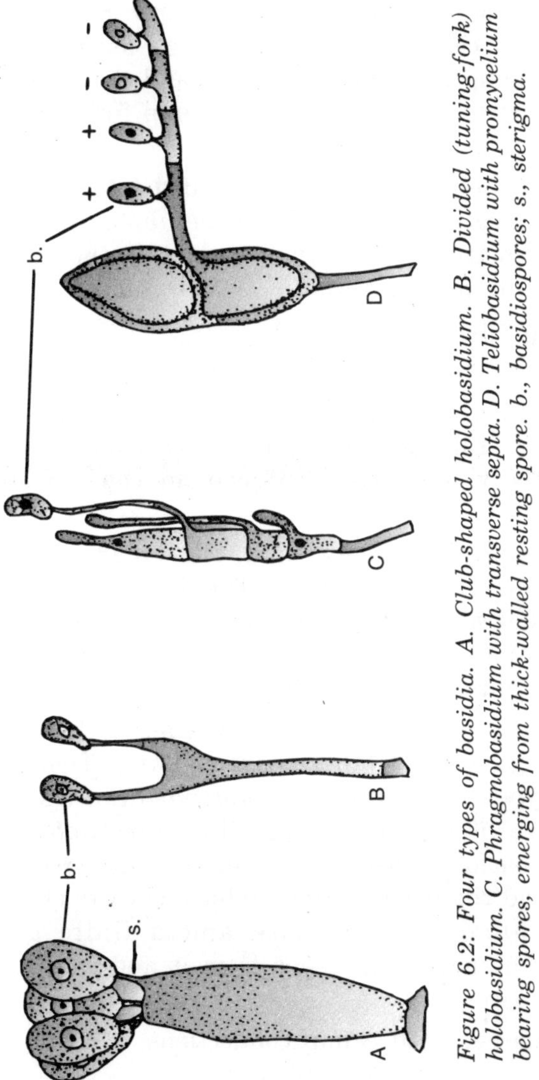

Figure 6.2: Four types of basidia. A. Club-shaped holobasidium. B. Divided (tuning-fork) holobasidium. C. Phragmobasidium with transverse septa. D. Teliobasidium with promycelium bearing spores, emerging from thick-walled resting spore. b., basidiospores; s., sterigma.

of which connects with the cell wall near the septum. As the walls between the clamp and the cell dissolve, the nuclei divide, one division so oriented that one of its daughter nuclei is formed in the clamp and the other in the mother cell. The other division is oriented horizontally in the mother cell.

The daughter nucleus in the clamp then migrates into the mother cell and the two septa are formed, one cutting off the clamp from its mother cell and the other vertically just below the point where the clamp fused with the cell wall of its mother cell.

Thus the mother cell has divided into two cells while the dikaryotic condition is perpetuated, with nuclei of different mating types always present in the newly formed cells as the hypha grows.

The Basidium

The basidium is the organ in which karyogamy and meiosis take place in the Basidiomycotina, as a result of which generally four meiospores, termed basidiospores in this subdivision, are produced on the surface of the basidium.

As we have already said, the basidium is the one characteristic structure of the Basidiomycotina that supersedes all others in importance. If a fungus produces its meiospores on basidia, it is placed in the Basidiomycotina regardless of its other characteristics.

If it does not, it cannot be classified in this subdivision, again regardless of other characteristics. There are three main types of basidia: the *holobasidium*, a one-celled structure of varying shape; the *phragmob-asidium*, a septate basidium with one or more transverse or vertical septa; and the *teliobasidium*, which consists of a generally thick-walled resting spore and a finite germ tube (promycelium), which issues from it and which bears the basidiospores.

In species with clamp connections, a clamp is always

formed at the base of a basidium. This has been likened to the crozier of the Ascomycetes and together with the dikaryotic phase in the two groups has been used as an indication of the origin of the Basidiomycetes from an ancestral ascomycete.

Classification

The subdivision Basidiomycotina consists of the single class Basidiomycetes, which we subdivide into three subclasses: Holobasidiomycetidae, Phragmobasidiomycetidae, and Teliomycetidae. We shall discuss each of these briefly.

SUBCLASS 1. HOLOBASIDIOMYCETIDAE

The Holobasidiomycetidae have onecelled, usually club-

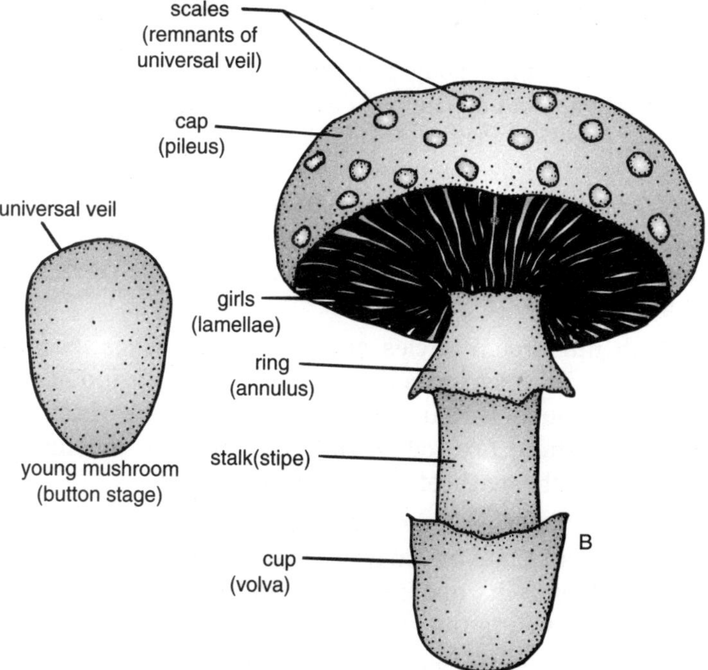

Figure 6.3: Schematic drawing of a basidiocarp of a mushroom (Amanita type). A. Immature (button) stage. B. Mature sporophore.

shaped basidia. This subclass consists of two large groups of fungi, Hymenoba-sidiomycetes and Gasteromycetes. These are convenient groupings without taxonomic rank.

Hymenobasidiomycetes

The Hymenobasidiomycetes produce their basidia in hymenial layers, reminiscent of those of the Hymenoascomycetidae. Their sporophores (basidiocarps) are either open from the beginning or they open, exposing their basidia, before the spores mature.

Familiar examples of Hymenobasidiomycetes are the mushrooms or toadstools, the boletes, and the shelf (bracket), coral, and toothfungi. The student must remember that these familiar structures are but the sporophores (basidiocarps) of the fungi that produce them, the most extensive portion of which is the mycelium from which the sporophores originate and which obtains nourishment from the substratum.

The mycelium of some mushrooms and some other large basidiocarps, such as the puffballs (in the Gasteromycetes), when it grows on the ground, particularly on lawns, golf courses, or other grassy places, forms a large, circular colony that continues growing year after year if undisturbed, producing a crop of basidiocarps at the periphery of the colony, with the grass much greener within the circle than outside.

Such mushroom circles are called *fairy rings*, because in the middle ages mycelium was unknown, and it was believed by superstitious people, of whom there were even more than there are today, that the circle of mushrooms represented the path of dancing fairies.

As the fairy ring grows, the older hyphae in the center die and disintegrate by bacterial action, which breaks down the fungal proteins and releases available nitrogen to the grass roots, causing the grass to have a brighter green color.

In some places it was considered bad luck to step inside a fairy ring; in other areas it was good luck to do so. No one ever reported seeing a dancing mushroom fairy except

Figure 6.4: Coprinus sp. Transection of pileus and gills; the dark margins of the latter constitute the hymenium.

in Walt Disney's Fantasia. Mushrooms are basidiocarps of fungi in the order Agaricales, which is subdivided into some 15 or more families. A mushroom consists of a stem (*stipe*), supporting a cap (*pileus*) and sometimes rising from a basal cup (volva).

Gills (*lamellae*), leaflike structures radiating from the edge inward toward the stem, under the pileus, are covered with basidia on both their surfaces, each basidium generally producing four spores, after karyogamy and meiosis have occurred.

In some mushrooms there is a ring (*annulus*) around the stem below the edge of the pileus. This represents the remnants of the *velum*, which covers the gills before the spores mature.

The pileus may also be covered with scalelike membranes, the remnants of the universal veil, a membrane that covered the entire sporophore in the young "button" stage, before its final expansion. In some mushrooms, also, a weblike membrane (cortina) hangs down from the edge of the pileus but soon wears off.

The rows of basidia on the membranelike lamellae

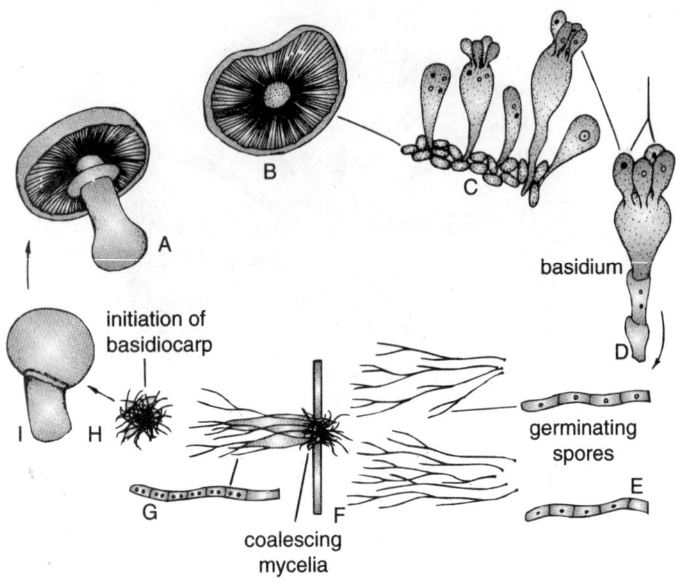

Figure 6.5: Life cycle of a mushroom.

represent the hymenium that gives this group its name. This is comparable to the hymenium of the Hymenoascomycetidae. We cannot overemphasize the fact, which many students find hard to believe, that a mushroom consists of tightly woven hyphae in its entirety.

Mounting a small piece of tissue from any part of the mushroom and examining it under the microscope will convince even the most skeptical. It cannot be otherwise, as the following short account of the mushroom life cycle indicates.

Life Cycle

Basidiospores are forcibly ejected from their basidia on the lamellae, to a distance of a millimeter or two, just far enough to free them from the basidia and propel them midway between two adjacent lamellae. By force of gravity they then fall on the substratum below, or, more likely, are carried by air currents to new sites, where they germinate and form a uninucleate mycelium. This stage is ephemeral because of the process of dikaryotization, which takes place soon. Most species of mushrooms are heterothallic and *tetrapolar*—that is, they consist of four mating types because there are four genes (A_1, A_2; B_1, B_2) on two chromosomes, controlling mating type. There are, therefore, four types of basidiospores on each basidium (A_1B_1), (A_1B_2), (A2B_1), (A_2, B2).

In order for sexual reproduction to take place, it is necessary for two compatible mating types to meet. Such a union must result in an $A_1B_1A_2B_2$ genotype for a sporulating mycelium to form.

When the uninucleate mycelia from two compatible basidiospores meet, the hyphal tips fuse (plasmogamy) and nuclei are exchanged, so that both mycelia behave both as donors and receptors of nuclei. The invading nuclei then multiply in the invaded mycelium in such a way so as to result in dikaryotization.

This means that all the cells of each mycelium will contain one nucleus of each mating type that engaged in plasmogamy. The details of exactly how this is done do not concern us here. They usually involve the presence of clamp connections.

For a detailed explanation of this process read Alexopoulos and Mims (1979) or any other general mycology book. Much work has been done on the genetics of the Basidiomycetes, particularly with regard to the incompatibility system, using *Schizophyllum commune* as the experim-ental organism. Some of this work is summarized by Raper and Flexer (1971). The dikaryotic hypha thus formed grows into a binucleate mycelium, the two nuclei in each cell dividing conjugately each time, forming new dikaryotic cells.

When the mycelium has stored sufficient food, small hyphal knots, the basidiocarp primordia, form on the periphery of the colony and develop into tiny sporophores (buttons), the tissues of which, in the presence of adequate moisture, expand rapidly into the familiar mushrooms.

As the binucleate basidia develop from hyphal tips on the lamellae, the two nuclei of opposite mating type in each

Figure 6.6: Hymenium of a polypore.

basidium fuse (karyogamy), and the zygote nucleus soon undergoes meiosis, during which the mating type genes, as well as those governing other characters, segregate into the resulting four daughter nuclei.

In the meantime, the tetranucleate basidium produces four stalklike, tubular extensions (sterigmata; sing. *sterigma*), the tips of which expand into spores. The haploid nuclei now migrate through the sterigmata into the basidiospores, thus completing the life cycle.

Identification of Mushrooms

Mushroom spores vary in color, shape, and markings in different species. Spore color is very important in identifying mushrooms.

However, looking at individual spores under the microscope is sometimes deceiving because the pigment is often very dilute and the spore color difficult to determine.

For this reason, a spore print is the first thing one needs in attempting to identify a mushroom. This is made by cutting the stem of the mushroom just below the cap, even with the edge of the gills, placing the cap—gills down—on a white piece of paper, and covering it with a bell jar or other convenient cover for a few hours.

The spores, forcibly expelled from the basidia, fall on the paper under the influence of gravity and pile up to form a spore print the same color as the pigment in the spores. Starting with spore color, one then identifies the mushroom by using any one of a number of available mushroom manuals, listed at the end of this chapter.

The student must be cautioned that mushroom identification is not a simple matter, and if the mushrooms are to be consumed, it is best to have the opinion of a mushroom specialist. There are many hundreds of mushroom species known.

The amateur collector cannot hope to learn all of them, nor is it necessary. He can learn a few edible, tasty species occurring in his region and leave the rest alone. It is of interest, however, to learn to recognize the genus *Amanita,* in which the most deadly of mushrooms belong.

The best advice we can give you here is: Don't touch any mushroom that has a volva (cup) at the base of the stem. Sometimes the volva is just below the surface of the ground and one must dig out the entire sporophore before he can be sure there is no volva.

If there is any doubt, do not take a chance. *Amanita phalloides* (the death cup) is present in the United States, particularly in the eastern states, but is not very common. *Amanita verna* and *Amanita virosa* (the destroying angel) are two very similar, very beautiful, and very deadly mushrooms.

They are almost pure white. *Amanita muscaria* (the fly agaric), the red form of which is spectacular, is hallucinogenic when eaten in small quantities but poisonous in larger doses. Wasson *(1968)* believes this mushroom to be the ancient Indian god Soma.

Polypores

In addition to mushrooms, other sporophores of the Hymenobasidi-omycetes are the so-called bracket, or shelf, fungi (Polyporaceae). These are also called *polypores* (Gr. *poly,* much, many, + *poros,* pore), because basidia line the inner surface of pores or tubes beneath the cap.

These basidiocarps may or may not have a stem, which, if present, may be centrally or laterally inserted. *Polyporus sulphureus,* the sulfur mushroom, growing on oaks and other trees, is easy to recognize and is said to be of excellent flavor when young, soft, and spongy. It becomes woody, however, with age.

Coral Fungi

Of the coral fungi (Clavariaceae) the famous funnel-shaped chanterelle *(Cantharellus cibarius),* which has shallow or deep ridges running from the underside of the funnel down onto the stem, is eminently edible. Many other coral fungi are beautiful, with their many upright branches and their colors ranging from white, through yellow, orange, and amethyst. Most are not poisonous.

Tooth Fungi and Boletes

The tooth fungi (Hydnaceae), too, contain a number of edible species. *Hericium coralloides,* with many-branched pendant teeth, resembling a large white coral, is one of these. It can attain a considerable size.

We must also mention the boletes (Boletaceae), which look like mushrooms but produce their basidia on the underside of the fleshy cap in pores or tubes instead of on gills.

Boletus edulis, as the name indicates, is edible and highly prized. It is often dried and pulverized and is offered for sale, particularly in central Europe (Switzerland and elsewhere), to flavor soups. Most species of boletes are not poisonous, but some have a disagreeable, bitter taste.

Cultivated Mushrooms

There are at least two species of mushrooms that form the basis of the everexpanding mushroom-growing industry throughout the world. *Agaricus* (Gr. *agarikon,* mushroom) *brunescens,* called until recently *Agaricus bisporus*, is extensively cultivated in Europe and the United States.

Lentinus edodes, the shiitake mushroom, is widely cultivated in the Orient-Japan and Taiwan chiefly. Needless to say, cultivated mushrooms offered for sale in reputable stores are safe to eat, if not as flavorful as some of the wild species. Wild mushrooms, offered for sale in farmer's and village markets in the United States, Mexico, and Central America, are not always reliably safe. In Latin American countries, hallucinogenic mushrooms can be bought on the streets and in some markets.

Hallucinogenic Mushrooms

Much interest has been aroused in recent years in hallucinogenic mushrooms, and much has been written about them ever since the distinguished French mycologist Roger Heim and his American sponsor, the ethnomycologist R. G. Wasson, visited Mexico and took part in the sacred mushroom rites of an Indian tribe conducted by the now famous curandera Maria Sabina.

Heim described the mushroom used in those rites as *Psilocybe mexicana,* and the Swiss chemist Hoffman isolated the hallucinogenic principles, *psilocybin* and *psylocin*. The writings by Heim and Wasson (1957), Wasson and Wasson (1957), and Wasson alone (1959, 1961, 1968) very well summarize our knowledge of hallucinogenic mushrooms.

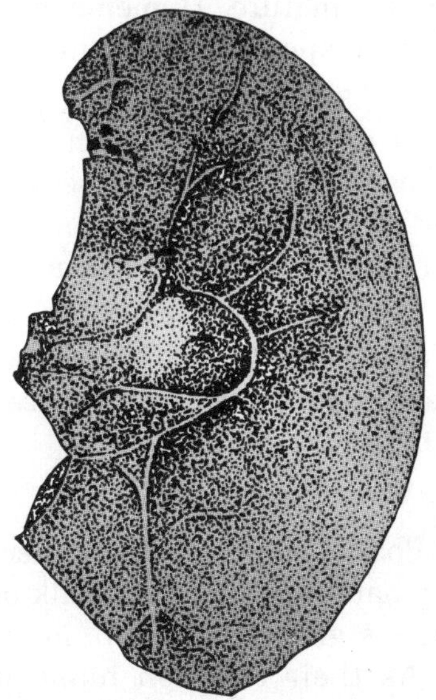

Figure 6.7: Auricularia sp.; an ear jelly fungus.

The more recent book by Wasson and coauthors (1974), entitled *Maria Sabina and Her Mazatec Mushroom Velada,* appears to be as complete an account of the use and effects of *Psilocybe mexicana* as anyone could wish for.

Gasteromycetes

These are the puffballs, the earthstars, the stinkhorns, and the bird's nest fungi and include some of the largest fungal sporophores known. The largest puffball of *L. calvus (L. calvus,* bald) *gigantea* on record was 1.6 m in length, 1.35 m in width and 24 cm in height.

Puffballs and Earthstars

The Gasteromycetes produce their spores in closed sporophores. In some groups, however, the sporophores do open and expose the spores but only after the latter are completely mature and ready for dispersal. Otherwise, the spores escape when the basidiocarp breaks or begins to disintegrate.

In these fungi, the basidia are not arranged in hymenia when the spores are mature. Hymenia may be present in the early stages of sporophore formation but become disrupted at a later stage.

Puffballs are so called because when the wall (peridium) of the mature basidiocarp breaks, the spores are puffed out by raindrops or when some object such as a twig falls on the sporophore or some animal touches it in an attempt to eat it.

Earthstars are puffballs with two or more peridia, the outer of which split open and turn over, resembling a star with a ball in the center.

Stinkhorns

Stinkhorns (Phallales) are egglike when immature. On maturity, the egg hatches and a long stalk usually expands, bearing a gelatinous gleba at the top, in which the spores are embedded. As their common name indicates, most stinkhorns emit an incredibly disagreeable odor, which, however, attracts flies and some other insects.

The insects fly to them and alight on the gleba to sip the sweet jelly and, in so doing, pick up the spores on their feet and mouthparts and so distribute them when they fly away.

Bird's Nest Fungi

The bird's nest fungi (Nidulariales) have developed an ingenious method for spore distribution, elegantly described by Brodie (1975, 1978) in his two books *The Bird's Nest Fungi* and *Fungi-Delight of Curiosity.* The sporophores of the bird's nest fungi are cups that contain small, waxy, hard peridioles, thus resembling birds' nests with eggs.

It is inside these peridioles that the basidia and basidiospores are formed. The cups are so shaped that when, during a driving rain, raindrops hit the peridioles with great force, those spore-containing bodies slide out of the cups, attaining a great velocity and traveling considerable distances.

In most species, peridioles are attached to their cups, each by a long cord neatly wound up under each peridiole, which becomes gelatinous and sticky when wet.

In flight, the cord trails behind and, striking a twig or other plant part nearby, adheres to it, causing the peridiole to wind itself around the object and hang down a few centimeters. There it is eventually devoured by some herbivorous animal and voided with excreta, where it releases the spores, which germinate to form mycelium.

Consequently, bird's nest fungi are usually found on horse or cow dung or in gardens fertilized with manure. The largest genus of the Nidulariales is *Cyathus.* Other genera are *Crucibulum, Nidula, Nidularia,* and *Mycocalia.* The fungus artillery *Sphaerobolus* also belongs here.

Jelly Fungi with Tuning-Fork Basidia

Mention must be made of those jelly fungi with holobasidia. These are the Dacrymycetales. Their basidia are deeply divided, resembling a tuning fork. Their basidiocarps are gelatinous and usually brightly colored,

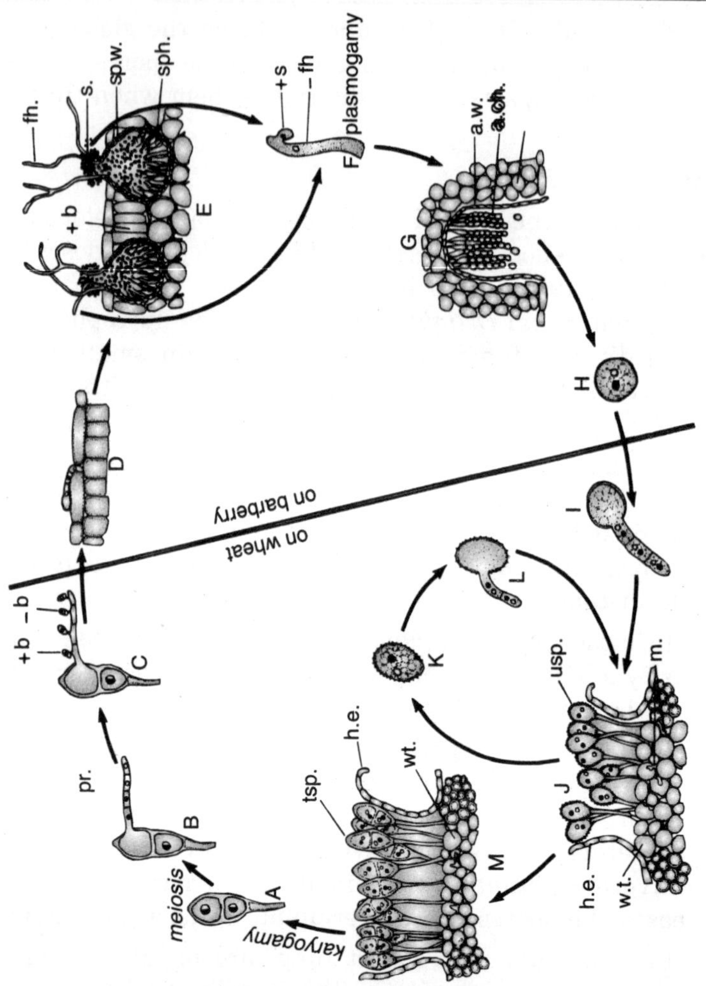

Figure 6.8: Life cycle of Puccinia graminis tritici (not to scale). A. Mature teliospore. B. Formation of promycelium. C. Formation of basidiospores of the two mating types, (+) and (-). D. Basidiospore germination and infection of barberry leaf. E. Spermogonia and flexuous (receptive) hyphae. F. Spermatization. G. Aecium with aeciospore chains. H. Mature, binucleate aeciospore. I. Germinating aeciospore. J. Uredinium with binucleate urediniospores. K. Mature urediniospore. L. Germination of urediniospore to form binucleate mycelium. M. Telium with binucleate, two-celled teliospores. pr., promycelium; +b., -b., basidiospores of two mating types; fl., flexuous (receptive) hypha; s., spermatia; sp.w., spermogonium wall; sph., spermatiophore; +s., -fh., spermatium and flexuous hypha of opposite mating types; a.w., aecium wall; a.ch., aeciospore chain; b.t., barberry tissue; m., mycelium; w.t., wheat tissue; h.e., host epidermis; usp., urediniospore; tsp., teliospore.

mostly yellow or orange.

They can be spotted easily on a rainy winter day in deciduous forests, where they contrast vividly with the dark tree branches devoid of leaves. *Dacrymyces* (Gr. *dakry,* tear, + *mykes,* fungus) forms cushion-shaped, gelatinous, orange masses several millimeters in diameter.

The very common *Calocera* (Gr. *kalos,* beautiful, + *keras,* horn) *cornea* grows on dead logs. It resembles tiny gelatinous horns 1-2 mm tall arising from the wet wood.

SUBCLASS 2. PHRAGMOBASIDIOMYCETIDAE

The Phragmobasidiomycetidae are also jelly fungi. Their chief distinguishing feature is that their basidia are septate, either transversely, as in *Auricularia (L. auricula,* ear), or longitudinally, as in *Exidia.* These fungi are saprobes on decaying logs in damp situations.

Their basidiocarps are most conspicuous after periods of prolonged rains, when they have absorbed water and

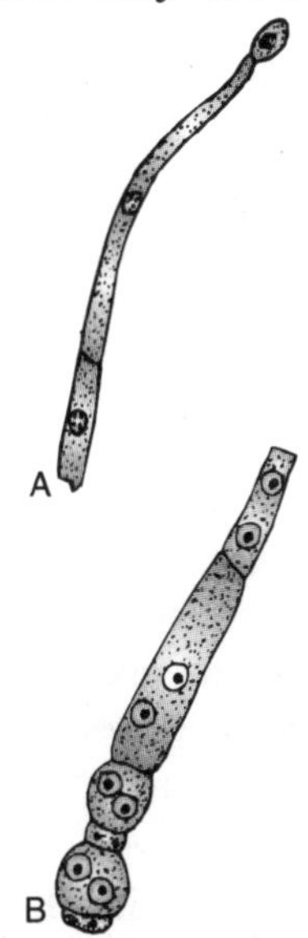

Figure 6.9: Puccinia Graminis. A. Spermatiophore bearing spermatium. B. Chain of binucleate aeciospores.

expand- L ed. When dry they form inconspicuous crusts. *Auricularia is* called the ear fungus because its basidiocarp somewhat resembles a human ear in shape.

There are several species, many tropical but some also in the temperate zones. *Auricularia auricula* is cultivated in the Orient and is almost indispensable in Chinese cuisine.

It is canned or dried and offered for sale in western markets, particularly in big cities with a large Chinese population. *Phlogiotis* (Gr. *phlox, phlogos,* flame) *helveloides,* a pink or rose funnel-shaped jelly fungus, is not uncommon in the United States. The white *Tremella* (Gr. *tremo,* tremble) *reticulata is* a showy, rather large jelly fungus.

SUBCLASS 3. TELIOMYCETIDAE

These are the rusts (order Uredinales) and the smuts (order Ustilaginales), the most economically important Basidiomycetes because of the serious diseases they cause on a large number of crops.

The chief characteristic of these fungi is the production of thickwalled resting spores (*teliospores*), in which karyogamy takes place. The teliospore is, therefore, a part of the basidial apparatus, which constitutes what we have called a *teliobasidium*.

Order Uredinales

It is impossible to do justice to this large and important group of fungi in the space we can devote to them in this book. We shall, therefore, do nothing more than to try to summarize some of the important facts concerning one or two species, to give you a general idea about the group.

Up to a few years ago the Uredinales were thought to be obligately parasitic on plants. We still believe that they do not grow outside their living hosts in nature, but now several species have been grown on artificial media in the laboratory and many more will undoubtedly be cultured in the future. For a discussion of axenic culture of rusts, see Cotley (1975).

The rusts, in general, differ from most other Basidiomycetes in a number of ways:

1. The mycelium bears no dolipore septa, nor does it produce clamp connections.
2. Many rusts are heteroecious—that is, they require two different species of plant host to complete their life cycle.' Incredibly, these hosts are usually very dissimilar, in some cases one an angio sperm and the other a gymnosperm or a fern; or, one a monocotyledon, the other a dicotyledon. Many rusts, however, are autoecious, completing their entire life cycle on a single species of host.
3. All rusts are heterothallic, as are many other Basidiomycetes, but in the rusts there are only two mating types for each species, (+) and (–). In this respect the rusts resemble the Ascomycetes and the Zygomycetes.
4. Sexual reproduction is accomplished by spermatization (the union of spermatia with receptive hyphae, similar to ascomycetous trichogynes), but somatogamy (hyphal fusion as in the mushrooms) also occurs.

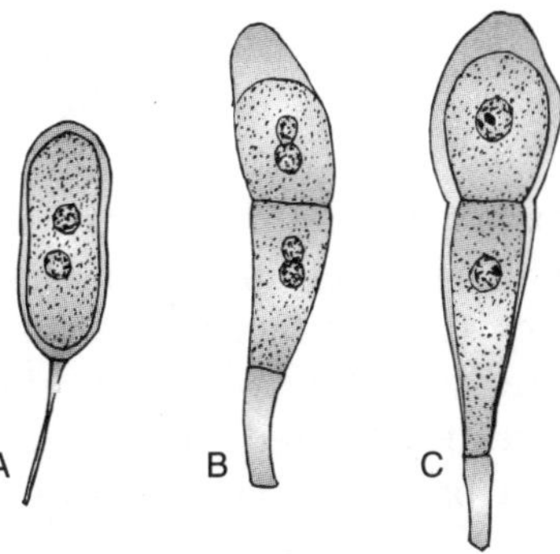

Figure 6.10: Puccinia graminis. A. Single urediniospore. B. Immature teliospore before karyogamy. C. Mature two-celled teliospore, each cell with a diploid nucleus.

5. The life cycle of most rusts is very complex, several types of spores being produced during its development.

Life Cycle

We have the space to consider only one life cycle, that of *Puccinia* (after *T. Puccini*, Italian anatomist) *graminis,* the cause of black stem rust of cereals. This species consists of several subspecies, or specialized forms," specialized in their parasitism of different groups of cereal crops.

All, however, require the common barberry *(Berberis vulgaris)* as the alternate host. Let us look at the life cycle of *Puccinia graminis* form spec.' *tritici,* which attacks wheat. The fungus overwinters on the wheat stubble in the form of thick-walled teliospores, each consisting of two binucleate cells.

Sometime during the winter, karyogamy takes place, rendering each cell uninucleate and diploid. In the spring the spore germinates, each cell producing a long, finite germ tube the promycelium (also called *metabasidium* or *epibasidium*), in which the diploid nucleus migrates and undergoes meiosis.

This makes the teliospore and the promycelium both parts of the basidial apparatus (teliobasidium). A septum is formed after each division of meiosis, separating the four nuclei into four cells, and a short sterigma develops from each cell of the promycelium, on the tip of which a small basidiospore is formed.

It is important to note that the genes controlling mating type segregate during meiosis so that two of the basidiospores carry the (+) factor and two carry the (–) factor. The basidiospores are forcibly ejected from the sterigmata and are distributed by the wind. Those that happen to fall on a barberry bush continue the life cycle; the others perish.

The importance of the barberry in the development of black stem rust of wheat had been noticed in the seventeenth century by French farmers, who, in 1660, persuaded the City Council of Rouen to enact a law ordering the eradication of all barberry bushes growing in the vicinity of wheat fields.

The reason for this was unknown and remained so until about two hundred years later, when Anton deBary, the great German mycologist, elucidated the complicated life cycle of *Puccinia graminis*. On the barberry, the basidiospores germinate and the germ tubes issuing from them invade the leaf, growing through the epidermal cells and then in between the mesophyll cells to the lower side of the leaf.

The uninucleate mycelium developing from the germination of the basidiospores now produces some important structures. Near the upper side of the barberry leaf, it forms the first of these, flaskshaped *spermogonia*, resembling pycnidia of Ascomycetes and Deuteromycetes, which are filled with long, fertile hyphae.

These are the *spermatiophores*, which cut off chains of minute uninucleate, conidiumlike spermatia mixed with a mucous jelly in the central cavity of the spermogonium. Eventually, they come out in fragrant droplets (nectar) from the necks of the spermogonia, which by now, protrude from the barberry leaf in pustules.

Other long hyphae, issuing from the spermogonia, and also pushing out from the leaf beside them, are the female receptive hyphae (also known as flexuous hyphae), on which the male spermatic from the *opposite mating type* are brought by flies or other insects that visit the fragrant pustules to sip the sweet nectar full of spermatia.

Thus spermatization is accomplished. It appears, however, that (+) and (–) mycelia from mixed infections also meet in the barberry leaf and exchange nuclei much as mushroom mycelia do. It is of interest to note that repeated attempts to germinate the conidiumlike spermatia have failed.

They appear to be specialized male reproductive cells. Other important structures formed by the uninucleate

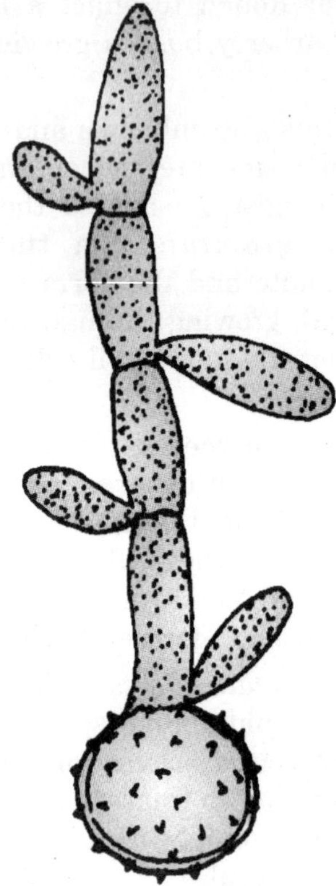

Figure 6.11: Ustilago zeae. Germinating teliospore with septate basidium and basidiospores (sporidia).

mycelium within the barberry leaf are knots of uninucleate cells, the aecial primordia. These become dikaryotized soon after spermatization of receptive hyphae has occurred.

It appears that the spermatial nuclei shed into the receptive hyphae, travel down the mycelial network in the barberry leaf, passing through the septal perforations, and enter the cells of the aecial primordia, which now become dikaryotic, each with one (+) and one (–) nucleus.

In a relatively short time, the aecial primordia develop into *aecia* (cluster cups) (sing. *aecium*), which contain chains of binucleate *aeciospores* when they break through the lower epidermis of the barberry leaf. When these spores are shed, they are distributed by the wind, and those that fall on wheat plants continue the life cycle of the fungus; all others perish.

Aeciospores germinating on wheat plants produce binucleate mycelium, which grows between the cells of the wheat and saps the strength out of the plant, severely reducing the yield of grain. In early summer, the mycelium in the wheat stalks and leaves produces lesions (*uredinia*) that produce relatively large binucleate, straw-colored spiny *urediniospores*, which, in mass, appear red.

This is the so-called red, or summer, stage of the rust, which gives it its name, because the wheat fields appear rusty. So great are the numbers of these spores in a heavily infected field that the author of these lines, walking across such a field in Illinois one summer, wearing a light-blue suit, came out the other side of the field in a red suit!

The urediniospores are windblown and have the ability to reinfect wheat plants. This is the repeating stage of the rust, which is responsible for spreading the disease from wheat plant to wheat plant; from wheat field to wheat field, from Texas to North Dakota, gradually but steadily.

When the wheat is nearing maturity, the pustules (uredinia) that produced the urediniospores now begin to produce teliosp"ores, the black stage of the rust. By the time wheat is harvested, the stalks are covered with long, black streaks (telia) composed of dark, reddish-brown teliospores, which appear black in mass and which give the disease its name, "black stem rust of wheat."

These spores overwinter on the straw and start the life cycle over again in the spring. Eradication of the barberry is the best and most economical way to control this disease, as the farmers of Rouen had discovered in the seventeenth century.

Yet, this has not eliminated the disease from the United States and Canada, where barberry eradication has been practiced for over half a century. The reason for this is the ability of the urediniospores to overwinter in the South.

Surviving until spring, they perpetuate the disease in the wheat fields the following year without needing the barberry. Nevertheless, barberry eradication has proved to be very important in reducing crop losses.

When this is coupled with early-maturing varieties in the northern wheat states, the onslaught from the southern urediniospores is greatly lessened.

Other Genera of Rust Fungi

Two other important genera of rusts are *Gymnospor-angium* and *Cronartium. Gymnosporangium* does not produce urediniospores and thus lacks a repeating stage. *Gymnospor-angium juniperi-virginianae,* the cause of apple and juniper rust, also infects the crab apple *(Crataegus),* as does *Gymnosporangium clavipes.*

Both produce their spermogonia and aecia on the angiosperm host *(Malus* or *Crataegus).* The *dikaryotic mycelium* in the junipers causes the formation of fairly large cells, galls, commonly known as "*cedar apples*" because the junipers are commonly but erroneously called "cedars."

In early spring after some good rains, the cedar apples, full of dikaryotic mycelium, produce long, gelatinous, orange-colored, fingerlike projections full of two-celled teliospores with long stalks. These germinate, producing promycelia and basidiospores, which are blown over to nearby apple or crab-apple trees and infect them.

Obviously if one grows apples, one should see that there are no junipers nearby. *Cronartium ribicola is* a very serious parasite of the white pine *(Pinus strobus);* it causes blister rust. The alternate hosts are species of *Ribes-currants* and gooseberries. Unlike *Gymnosporangium, Cronartium ribicola* has a complete life cycle.

The spermogonia and aecia are produced in blisters on large galls on the pine, and the aeciospores infect *Ribes,* where the *urediniospores* and *teliospores* are formed. The teliospores in *Cronartium* are sessile (*stalkless*) but are fused, forming fingerlike columns that protrude from the underside of *Ribes* leaves.

A campaign to eradicate wild *Ribes* has been in progress in the United States for many decades in an effort to save the white pine, which is an important forest tree. Fortunately, the repeating stage of this rust is produced on the less important host.

Another genus of rusts, *Phragmidium,* has many-celled teliospores on wide stalks. *Phragmidium disciflorum,* among other species, causes rust of roses.

Order Ustilaginales

These are the smut fungi. They resemble the rusts in producing teliospores that germinate to form promycelia and basidiospores. They differ from the rusts in that their life cycles are much simpler and in that none is heteroecious. The mycelium of some smuts has clamp connections.

Covered smut of wheat caused by *Tilletia caries* is a world problem. Maize (corn) smut, caused by *Ustilago zeae,* is very prevalent in the maize-growing regions of the world.

In addition to causing plant disease, smut spores, produced in enormous numbers, form explosive dusts in thrashing machines and storage bins.

Ustilago

Ustilago zeae, the corn smut, occurs in most spectacular fashion in the ears and tassels of the plant, where it causes immense, enlarged growths. These tumorlike galls of *Ustilago (L. ustus,* burned) are black at maturity.

The color results from the transformation of the mycelium in the swollen host tissue into a mass of countless dark-walled, globose teliospores, which are binucleate. The two nuclei in the young teliospore unite as the spore wall thickens.

The epidermis of the host, which at first covers the growing gall-like enlargement, is finally ruptured. The interior of the mass is composed of large numbers of teliospores, intermingled with the remains of sterile hyphae and host cells.

The spores are readily disseminated by air currents and

can germinate immediately, or they may undergo dormancy until the next growing season of the host. Upon germination, the thick spore wall is ruptured by the protrusion of a delicate promycelium, which becomes divided into four linearly arranged cells, each containing a single haploid nucleus.

The nucleus in each cell of the basidium divides mitotically to form two nuclei, one of which migrates into a thinwalled basidiospore (sporidium), which is budded off each basidial segment. Each of the latter may continue to produce additional basidiospores.

It has been demonstrated, by the technique of single-spore isolation and culture, that meiosis occurs during the division of the primary basidial nucleus-that is, the fusion nucleus of the teliospore. Therefore, the basidiospores are usually of two kinds, (+) and (–), in their sexual potentialities. Host plants innoculated with a single basidiospore fail to develop typical smut galls.

The basidiospores that chance to fall on the meristematic epidermis of young host tissues form delicate germination tubes, which penetrate it and develop an intercellular mycelium, nourished by intracellular haustorial branches.

The cells of this mycelium are uninucleate. The binucleate mycelium that produces the gall-like growth is initiated by somatogamy from basidiosporal infections of different mating type that chance to be in close proximity within the host. The infected region of the plant undergoes cell enlargement as a result of the presence of the fungus, and a new gall is ultimately produced. Other species of *Ustilago* cause smut diseases in different cereal grains. *Ustilago tritici* causes "loose smut" of wheat, and *U. avenae* causes a similar disease of oats.

In addition to the origin of the binucleate (dikaryotic) mycelium by somatogamy described above, other mechanisms occur among smuts to effect the same result. For example, the dikaryotic mycelium is initiated in some smuts by conjugation of compatible basidiospores, often called sporidia.

Once initiated, the binucleate condition of the mycelium of many smuts and other Basidiomycota is maintained by the formation of clamp connections, a phenomenon illustrated in figure elsewhere in this chapter and described in its legend. For a comprehensive discussion of the smut fungi, read Fischer and Holton (1957) and Duran (1973).

Chapter 7 Amastigomycota IV: Subdivision Deuteromycotina

The Deuteromycotina, all placed in the form-class *Deuteromycetes*, have no sexual reproduction and are consequently called the *Fungi Imperfecti,* because their life cycles are "*imperfect.*" Most reproduce by means of conidia.

The imperfect yeasts (those that form no ascospores) reproduce by budding. A few mycelial species of Deuteromycotina form no spores of any kind. They reproduce by other *asexual* methods such as sclerotia. We have already described *conidial* production in the *Ascomycetes.*

Most *Deuteromycetes* are so similar to the conidial stages of well-known Ascomycetes that they are believed to be Ascomycetes that have lost their ability to form asci through evolution, or whose ascus stages are *seldom* formed, under unknown conditions, and have not been discovered as yet.

When cultivated under *controlled* environmental conditions properly *manipulated*, a number of fungi once included in this alliance have been induced to undergo sexual reproduction and, thus, to complete their life cycles.

The spores produced as a result of sexual reproduction have been *ascospores* in a *majority* of species, but basidia and basidiospores have developed in a few. When the *ascosporic* or *basidiosporic* phase is known, the fungus can also be classified in the appropriate genus of *Ascomycetes* or *Basidiomycetes.*

It is probable that many Deuteromycetes never produce sexual stages, ascospores, or basidiospores. They are classified in what is called an artificial system, which emphasizes the location and manner of formation of the conidiogenous cells and the color and structure of the conidia.

Although a detailed consideration of this very large group of fungi is beyond the scope of the present volume, a short general discussion of their classification is certainly warranted. Because of the artificial nature of this classification, the designation of the taxa is often preceded by the *prefix "form"* as in *form-subclass*, *form-order*, *form-family*, *form-genus*, and *form-species*.

Many *mycologists*, however, do not use those designations. We place all the Deuteromycetes in three form-subclasses: *Coelomycetidae*, *Hyphomycetidae*, and *Agonomycetidae*.

COELOMYCETIDAE

The Coelomycetidae produce their conidiophores in pycnidia (sing. *pycnidium*) or in *acervuli* (sing. *acervulus*). Pycnidia are generally flask-shaped structures with an ostiole at the top through which the *conidia* escape.

Pycnidia of *Phyllosticta* (Gr. *phyllon,* leaf, + Gr. *stiktos,* spotted) *labruscae,* the imperfect stage of *Guignardia* (after Guignard, a French plant pathologist) *bidwellii* (one of the

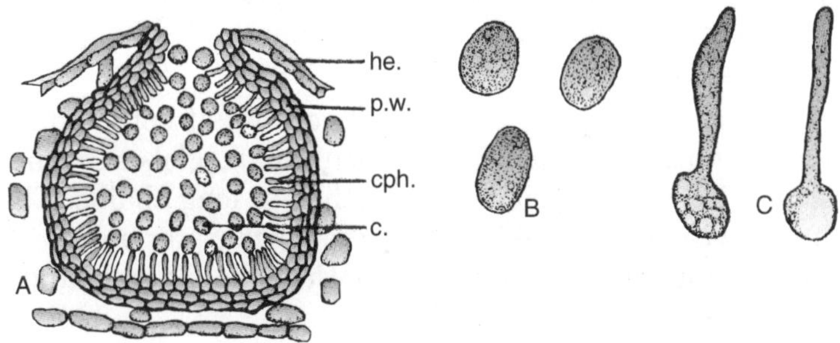

Figure 7.1: Guignardia bidwellii (Phylosticta labruscae). A. Longitudinal median section through a pycnidium. B. Conidia (pycnidiospores). C. Germinating conidia.

Loculoascomycetidae), are illustrated in figure elsewhere in this chapter.

Guignardia bidwellii (= Phyllosticta labruscae) is the cause of the serious black rot of grapes. An acervulus is a mass of hyphae (stroma) formed subepidermally or subcuticularly in an infected plant, which produces a bed of short *conidiophores* with one conidium at the tip of each.

The acervulr of some species produce *setae* among the conidiophores, as shown in figure elsewhere in this chapter. These are sterile, dark, bristle-shaped structures apparently induced by certain environmental conditions. Plant diseases caused by fungi with acervuli are called *anthracnoses*.

Hyphomycetidae

The Hyphomycetidae (commonly referred to as *Hyphomycetes*) is an enormous group of fungi that produce their conidia on conidiophores originating directly from the somatic hyphae and are more or less *unorganized*.

In our discussion of the Plectomycetidae (Ascomycetes), we mentioned the ascus stages of some species of *Aspergillus* (*L. Aspergillum,* brush) and *Penicillium* (*L. penicillus*) and pointed out that these are formgenera of Deuteromycetes.

Both, of great importance in human affairs, are classified as Hyphomycetidae. The conidiophores of *Aspergillus* originate from special mycelial cells called *foot cells*. They stand erect above the somatic hyphae and form globose swellings (vesicles) at their tips.

These are covered by one or two rows of bottle-shaped *phialides* (*sterigmata*), from which small, globose conidia issue forth adhering one to the other in long chains. Thus the *conidiophore* of *Aspergillus* somewhat resembles the aspergillum used in the Roman Catholic Church and is named after it.

As we have said before, the form-genus *Aspergillus* has over 100 species. It has been beautifully monographed by Raper and Fennell (1965). Many species are of economic

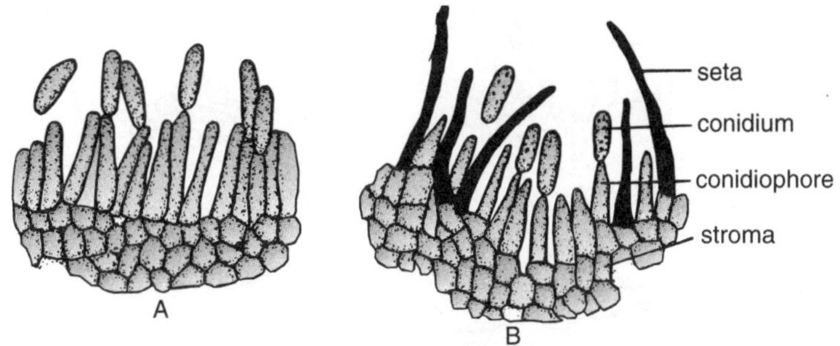

Figure 7.2: Two types of acervuli. A. Without setae. B. With setae.

importance but perhaps none more than *Aspergillus niger,* the very common black mold that is used for the *fermentative* manufacture of *citric acid*, the basis of the soft drink industry.

Citric acid used to be extracted from lemon juice, a rather expensive process, until it was discovered that *Aspergillus niger* can ferment sucrose and produce citric acid much more cheaply. Almost all the commercial citric acid is now produced by this process.

Aspergillus niger and some other species have been implicated in a human lung infection called *aspergillosis*, which resembles tuberculosis symptomatologically and which is difficult to diagnose.

The form-genus *Penicillium* produces its conidia in long chains on repeatedly branched, broomlike conidiophores called *penicilli* (sing. *penicillus*). Among the more than 100 form-species are several of economic importance.

Penicillium notatum is historically famous for being responsible for the discovery of penicillin when in 1928 it contaminated *a Staphylococcus* culture, with which Alexander Flemming was working in a London hospital, and inhibited the growth of the *Staphylococcus.*

Since then it has been discovered that *Penicillium chrysogenum* is much more productive and is now used exclusively for penicillin production.

Penicillium griseofulvum is another important species, used to produce the antifungal antibiotic griseofulvin, the

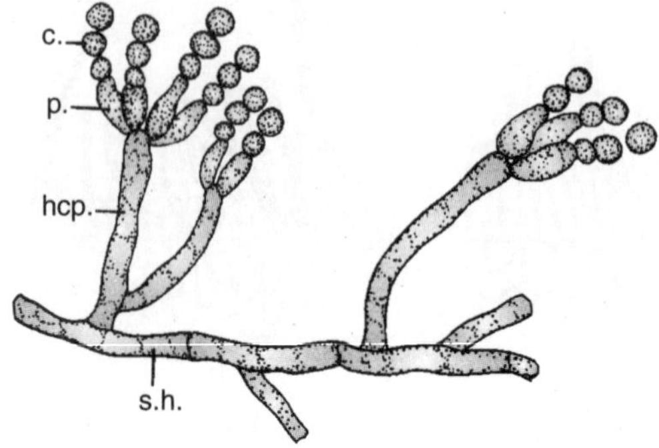

Figure 7.3: Penicillium notatum. Somatic hyphae bearing conidiophores (penicilli) with phialides and chains of conidia.

only effective treatment for ringworm diseases, including athlete's foot, the latter caused mostly by another hyphomycete *Epidermophyton* (Gr. *epidermis,* skin + *phyton,* plant) *floccosum.*

Penicillium roqueforti is used in the manufacture of various types of blue cheese such as Roquefort, Danish blue, and Gorgonzola, and *Penicillium camemberti is* the fungus used to impart its special flavor to Camembert cheese. It is quite probable that all these species are truly *Fungi Imperfecti.*

They have been studied and selected for so long that someone would have probably found their perfect stages if they existed. However, the form-genera *Microsporum* and *Trichophyton,* all known species of which cause ringworm of human beings and animals, were, as we have seen, also thought to be strictly deuteromycetous until recent years, when the ascus stages of all were discovered in relatively rapid succession.

A very large number of Hyphomycetidae cause serious plant diseases, but space does not permit us to discuss them here. We must, however, mention the ubiquitous *Alternaria (L. alternis,* interchangeable), a very large form-genus that produces easily recognized conidia. These are brown and many-septate, with some of the septa vertical.

Some species form their conidia singly, but many form them in long chains. *Alternaria* spores are common in house dust and are one of the primary fungal causes of allergy. Some species of *Alternaria* also cause plant disease.

It is among the Hyphomycetidae that we classify the asporogenous (imperfect) yeasts. They are of great significance to us because they are an important source of protein. As the world population increases and food supply becomes even more critical than it is today, food yeast may play an important role in feeding the human race.

Agonomycetidae

The form-subclass Agonomycetidae is a small group of fungi that produce no spores. They reproduce by fragmentation of the mycelium or by sclerotia. Some of these have proved to be Basidiomycetes when their sexual stages were discovered.

Parasexuality

One more point should be made. Many Deuteromycetes such as *Aspergillus fumigatus* exhibit what is known as *parasexuality*. This is a process in which a *heterokaryotic* condition is established in a mycelium through *hyphal anastomosis*.

Occasionally, two different nuclei fuse somewhere in that mycelium and perpetuate themselves through *mitosis*, spreading through the hyphae. Again *occasionally*, mitotic crossing over takes place and a mitotic reduction division occurs, resulting in daughter nuclei with new genetic *combinations*.

These nuclei propagate themselves by entering conidia and , establishing new genetic strains. Although anastomosis, nuclear fusion, and haplodization do occur, they do not take place at a specified place or time in the life cycle, which thus differs from a regularly occurring sexual cycle but provides some of the advantages of sexuality.

PREDACIOUS FUNGI

No account of the fungi, however necessarily abbreviated, should fail to present at least a brief discussion of a remarkable and miscellaneous group of organisms, nutrition of which, at least *facultatively*, is based on capture and *digestion* of *minute* animals.

The latter include amoebae, rotifers, nematodes, and springtails. The fungi involved are chiefly Zygomycetes and Deuteromycetes. Of especial interest are some nematoded-estroying organisms. *Nematodes* are minute (0.1-1.0 mm long), *wormlike* animals, many of which live in soil and are important enemies to *horticultural* and crop plants.

More than 50 species of *nematodedestroying* fungi are known. The *mechanisms* used by the fungi to trap the nematode are various and remarkable. In some species *undifferentiated* hyphae adhere to the animals, but in others special networks of adherent *branches, stalked adhesive knobs*, and nonconstricting and *constricting* rings occur.

The last are especially interesting, consisting of three curved cells in the form of a closed ring at the end of a short stalk. As the nematode enters the ring, the ring cells rapidly increase to three times their original size, thus constricting and holding the organism; this may occur in 0.1 sec.

After capture, *hyphae* of the fungus *penetrate* the animal and digest and absorb its substance. It is possible that the fungus produces a *toxin*. In writing of these *organisms, Duddington* has remarked *succinctly*:

It must be remembnered that nematodes are, for their size, powerful and enormously active; they move from place to place by means of a rapid thrashing of their bobies, so that a vigorous specimen will cross the vision field of a microscope witht he ferocious speed of a conger eel on the deck of a trawler. To capture such an anmimal is no mean task for a fungus that is itself composed of threads so delicate that the finest gossamer would by comparison be as a steel hawser to a piece of string, and the means by which this is accomplished by the predaceous fungi are as extraordinary as they are efficient.

For a modern, beautifully illustrated book on these fungi, see Barron's *Nematode Destroying Fungi (1977).*

Chapter 8 The Lichens

The organisms known as lichens, of which there are approximately 18,000-20,000 species, might be classified as a separate division of the plant kingdom were it not for the marked artificiality of such a grouping. Such a hypothetical division might be named the Mycophycophyta (Gr. *mykes,* fungus, + Gr. *phykos,* alga, + Gr. *phyton,* plant) or Phycomycophyta, names that emphasize that these organisms are dual in nature, consisting of a *phycobiont* (an *alga*) and a *mycobiont* (a *fungus*) growing together to form a plant body of consistently *recognizable* structure and appearance.

The most frequently encountered phycobiont is the unicellular green alga *Trebouxia*, which reproduces by *zoospores* and *aplanospores* when growing in liquid culture medium. *-Nostoc* is the most frequent blue-green-algal partner.

The lichen thallus is composed mostly of *interwoven* fungal hyphae, while the algae are usually limited to a subsurface layer and represent only about 5% of the dry weight of the lichen. Because the component organisms are members of other divisions-the *Cyanochloronta*, the *Chlorophycophyta*, and the *Eumycota* (*Ascomycetes*, *Basidiomycetes*, and *Deuteromycetes*)—the *lichens* usually are not classified as a separate division but are grouped with the fungi.

This probably stems from the circumstance that in a majority of lichens fungal morphology appears to determine the morphology of the lichen as a whole. This is suggested by the observation that a single algal species may reside in several *morphologically* distinct *lichen thalli*.

There appears to be limited evidence, however, that the phycobiont may play a morphogenetic role in the determination of the lichen growth form.

This is further supported by the fact that when the fungus is grown free from the alga in laboratory culture, its growth pattern is usually different from that assumed when it is associated with the lichen alga. In addition, the *phycobiont* may direct thallus morphology in many of the *gelatinous* lichens in which the fungus is loosely associated with the algal colony.

Lichens are *ubiquitous* plants that occur in a variety of habitats. One finds these organisms on the bare surfaces of exposed *desert rocks* or on the *frozen substrata* of polar regions. *Ahmadjian* reported that five species of lichens can survive a temperature of -198°C and that lichens can *photosynthesize* actively at -18.5°C in the Antarctic.

Lichens commonly colonize rocks (saxicolous-species) and *undisturbed soil* (*terricolous species*), and tree bark supports an extensive *lichen flora* (*corticolous species*). There are also reports of lichens growing on a number of unusual substrates, ranging from iron grave markers to the backs of large forest weevils.

A few species of lichens are submerged aquatics, both *freshwater* and *marine*, that are periodically exposed to the air, while others survive long periods of *desiccation*. Lichens can absorb water in both liquid and vapor form, and the absorption of water seems to be an entirely *physical* process.

In the desiccated state, they can survive with a water content of 2-15% of their dry weight; during a rain, they may contain 100-300% of their dry weight as water. *Rock-inhabiting* lichens have been implicated as agents initiating soil formation.

The underlying substrate is apparently chemically weathered by lichen *compounds* as well as subjected to mechanical destruction by the growing thallus. *Partially weathered* rock is then readily broken down by ice and other *physical* agents to form a primitive type of soil.

As organic remains from lichen vegetation become incorporated among the rock particles, other forms of vegetation become established in this primitive soil. Lichens are extremely slow-growing organisms, many increasing in size no more than 1 mm to 1 cm per year.

Accordingly, large plants are probably quite ancient. The age of some arctic lichens has been calculated to be 4500 years, and lichen growth rates are sometimes used to set approximate dates of glacial retreat in *arctic* and *alpine* regions. Their slow rate of growth is probably correlated with their lack of adaptations to conserve water. In the dry state their vital activities continue only at an *extremely* reduced rate. *Hydrated lichens*, however, have the capacity to absorb from their environment large quantities of solutes-for example, phosphate.

Lichens produce a variety of organic compounds, some of which occur as crystalline *encrustations* on the thallus surface. These are known as "*lichen acids*," although not all are acids, and the majority of these compounds are synthesized only by *lichenized fungi*.

These compounds have become increasingly useful in the identification and classification of *lichen taxa*. *Litmus* was prepared from lichen compounds until it was replaced by a *synthetic substitute*.

Usnic acid, one of these substances, has been shown to be antibiotic to Gram-positive bacteria and to inhibit the growth of *Trebouxia*, a common algal member of lichens. Culberson (1969) and *Huneck* (1973) have summarized our knowledge of these lichen compounds.

A number of electron *microscopic* studies of lichens have attempted to elucidate the relationships between the alga and fungus constituting various lichen thalli, the exact nature of which is only now beginning to be understood. Some view the lichen association as a fungus parasitizing an alga. Support for this view is afforded by lichens in which the fungal hyphae characteristically penetrate the algal protoplasts via specialized absorptive organs called *haustoria*. *Fungal haustoria penetrate* the algal cell walls, presumably by both mechanical and chemical (*enzymatic*) means.

However, this process occurs only to a limited extent, not to the point of complete elimination of the algal host. Webber and Webber (1970) suggested that this process represented a controlled "*harvesting*" of the *algal cells* by the *fungus*.

The fungus component of a number of lichens has been grown successfully in artificial culture media, so the supposed parasitism is not obligate or highly *specialized*. Furthermore, in spite of the inferred parasitism, the *algal cells* grow and multiply for long periods within the lichen thallus without apparent injurious effects from the fungus to most of the *algae*.

Other *investigators* interpret lichens as manifestations of a type of *symbiosis* (Gr. *sym*, together, + Gr. *bios,* life). *Symbiosis*, as originally defined by De Bary, meant the phenomenon of *dissimilar* organisms living together in a constant and *intimate association*.

This was a broad definition that included all types of association, including parasitism as well as associations in which the associated organisms benefit. Smith has suggested that such different types of association be designated, respectively, *parasitic symbiosis* and *mutualistic symbiosis*. Those proponents of the latter definition of the lichen association argue that the alga is surrounded and mechanically protected by the *meshwork* of *fungal hyphae*, which absorb and adsorb water, *mineral salts*, and *organic materials* from the *substrate*, thus extending the habitat range of the alga.

The fungus, presumably by means of *appressoria* or

haustoria, diffusion from the algal cells, or autolysis of the latter, is supplied with a source of carbohydrate, organic nitrogen compounds, and vitamins. Our knowledge of the physiological relations between fungi and algae in lichens has in the past been colored to some extent by *teleological* considerations and *speculation*.

It has been shown that in *Peltigera* (*N. L. pelta*, shield, + *L. genere*, to bear) *aphthosa*, which has two *phycobionts*-a green alga *(Coccomyxa)* and the cyanochloront *Nostoc*-*the* latter fixes nitrogen actively. Almost all of the fixed nitrogen is secreted into the *lichen plant* body, where it is used mostly by the *mycobiont*, the green *phycobiont* containing only 3% of it.

These *authors* state that normally only a small aliquot of the *nitrogen* compounds is released from the algal cells, further suggesting that the mycobiont controls the rate of secretion from the algal cells. Although *electron-microscopic examination* of this lichen revealed no haustorial penetration of the alga, or other evidences of parasitism, the authors nonetheless characterized this *association* as a more subtle type of "*controlled parasitism*" at the physiological level.

Richardson, Hill, and Smith (1968) demonstrated that a number of *phycobionts* excrete various sugar alcohols (*ribitol*, *sorbitol*, and *erythritol*) or glucose, which are used by the mycobiont. In the absence of the latter, this *excretion* ceases or is *markedly* reduced.

Cultured phycobionts also develop a pectic sheath, which is absent in the lichenized condition. Drew and Smith (1967), after exposing *P. polydactyla* to $^{14}CO_2$, detected ^{14}C-labeled compounds first in the algal cortex and later in the fungal medulla of that lichen.

More recently (1971), Jacobs and Ahmadjian have detected ^{14}C-labeled compounds in the chloroplast and pyrenoid of the green phycobiont in *Cladonia* (Gr. *klados,* branch or sprout) *cristatella* and also in the cell walls of the *mycobiont*.

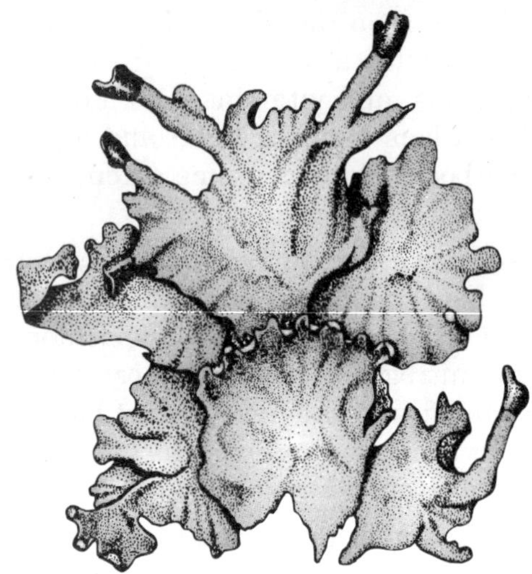

Figure 8.1: Peltigera rufescens. Portion of plant with fertile (ascospore-bearing) lobes.

In summary, it is difficult to generalize with assurance concerning the *physiological* relations between the component organisms of lichens. Further studies of these questions are now being carried on by a number of *investigators*. These are based on pure culture studies of the organisms grown separately and together, as well as on growth of lichens in field and in the *laboratory*.

The great majority of lichens have mycobionts that are ascomycetous, probably related to the cup fungi or to perithecium-forming genera. In a few lichens the fungus is one of the Basidiomycota. Their phycobionts are alternately cyanochlorontan organisms such as *Gloeocapsa, Nostoc,* and *Stigonema*, or Chlorophyceae such as *Trebouxia* (*a Chlorococcum-like* genus); in a few lichens *Cyanochloronta*, in addition to the *green algae*, are present *secondarily* in the fungal *fruiting body*.

The lichen thallus may be leaflike in organization, or *foliose*; crustlike, or *crustose*; or branching and cylindrical, or *fruticose*. Examples of foliose organization are *Peltigera* and *Parmelia* (*L. parma,* small shield). *Cladonia* and *Usnea* (Ar. *ushnea,* moss) are two *fruticose genera*.

A crustose lichen thallus may be seen in figure elsewhere in this chapter. In transverse sections of the typical stratified lichen thallus, the dense layer of surface hyphae, or *upper cortex*, may assume an epidermislike configuration and may have a colloidal, water-retaining *surface layer*.

The fungal hyphae of many lichens are densely *interwoven*, so that in section they seem to form a parenchyma. Lying just beneath the upper cortex is the *medulla*, or central portion of the *thallus*, below which a dense *lower cortex* may be present. The *medulla* is composed of a loose network of *hyphae* in which the alga is usually present in a *distinct zone*.

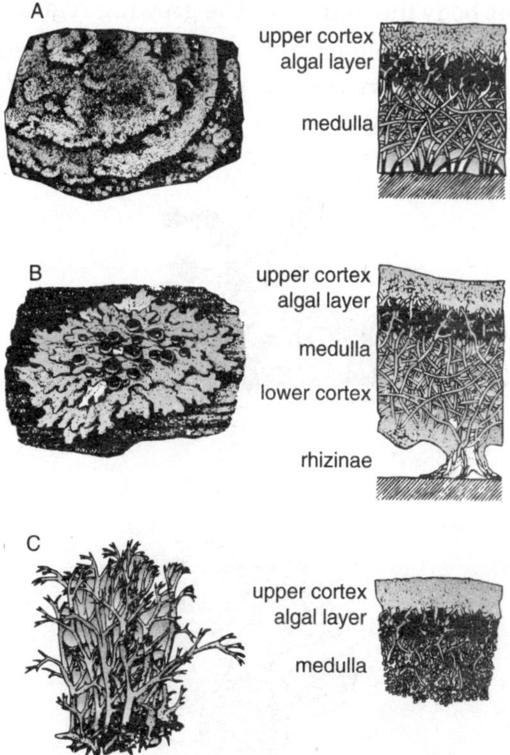

Figure 8.2: Growth habits of lichens, diagrammatic and transections thereof to the right. A. Crustose. B. Foliose, note apothecia; C. Fruticose.

The medullary hyphae are longitudinal in *orientation* in *Peltigera* and function in conduction. Special absorbing hyphae, the *rhizines*, enter the substratum from the lower surface of the thallus. Rhizines are complex bundles of *hyphae* that have *anastomosed* by fusion of young *hyphal tips*.

They conduct water rapidly in the capillary spaces among the component hyphae and also in their lumina, as demonstrated by experiments with watersoluble dyes. Rhizines also anchor the lichen to the substrate. Propagation of the usually slowly growing lichen thallus is generally effected by fragmentation as the older portions of the plant body die and leave the growing regions isolated.

A number of lichens also produce specialized asexual propagules called *soredia* (Gr. *soros,* heap) or *isidia* (origin uncertain). A soredium is an erumpent pustule in which the upper cortex is actually perforated, while in isidia the

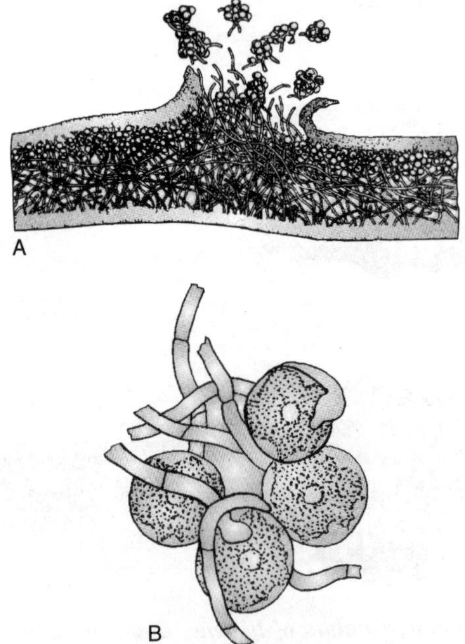

Figure 8.3: Lichen soredia. A. Release of soredia from a lichen, diagrammatic. B. Soredium of Parmelia sp.

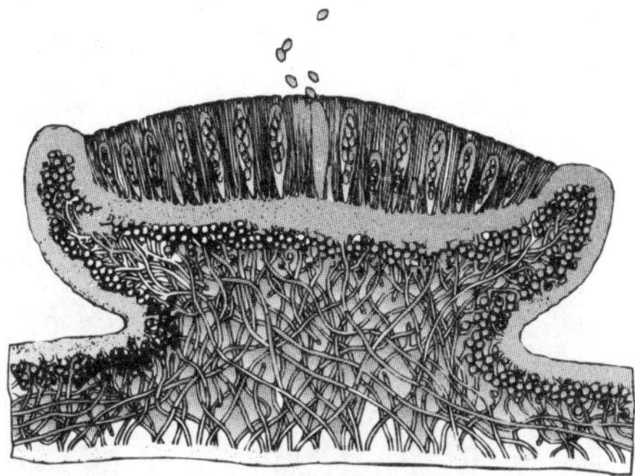

Figure 8.4: Section of the apothecium of a mycobiont of a lichen, digrammatic.

integrity of the upper cortex is maintained. These are small fragments of the thallus, consisting of one or more algal cells surrounded by fungal hyphae. These propagules are readily detached from the thallus and, when borne to suitable environments, by air currents or other dispersive agents, may develop into new lichen thalli.

In *Cladonia chlorophaea* the soredia are borne in goblet-like structures. It is probable that fragments containing both algal and fungal components are the primary agents of lichen dispersal and colonization. In addition to *multiplication* of the lichen as a unit, the component organisms also *reproduce* independently.

Under conditions of abundant *moisture* in the laboratory, the algal member may undergo rapid growth and cell division, thus outstripping the enveloping fungus; groups of algal cells are thus set free into the *substratum*. In many lichens the fungus regularly produces ascocarps and asci; the ascocarp may be a perithecium or an *apothecium*, or some modified form thereof.

The picturesque red tips of certain ascending branches of *Cladonia cristatella*, for example, are apothecia. It has been demonstrated in a number of genera that the formation of the ascocarp is preceded by the development of a coiled ascogonium, often with a trichogyne, which is probably fertilized by a spermatium.

Cytological details are unknown in most cases. *Lichen-*

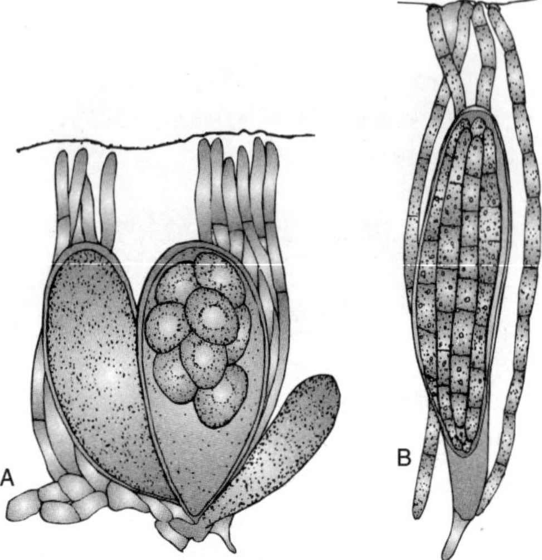

Figure 8.5: A. Parmelia sp. Asci and paraphyses. B. Peltigera sp. Ascus with septate ascospores and paraphyses.

ized fungi also produce asexual spores, *pycnospores*, in reproductive structures called *pycnidia*. It is believed that these spores may act as *spermatia* in the sexual *reproductive* process in some lichens.

In other lichens, they may function simply as conidia, as some pycnospores are capable of germination in culture. In general, our knowledge of *sexual reproduction* in lichenized fungi lags far behind that in other groups of *fungi*.

This situation is further complicated by the fact that isolated mycobionts in *axenic* culture exhibit an apparent loss of sexuality. The mature ascocarp may be elevated above the thallus on a stipelike structure called a *podetium*, or it may be sessile or even sunken. The *ascocarps* are *apparently perennial*.

The hymenial layer of the apothecium is composed of densely intermingled asci and paraphyses. The wall of the ascocarp may be composed only of fungal hyphae, or it may be overgrown by an alga-containing layer of the thallus.

The *ascospores* vary among the various genera in form

and number of component cells. They are *discharged explosively* from the apothecia and usually germinate readily if they fall on a favorable substratum.

It is clear that both the algal component and the spores of the fungus, once separated from the parent thallus, can initiate an independent existence. The synthesis of a new lichen thallus would then depend upon the fortuitous proximity of a germinating fungal spore and algal cells of the species with which the fungus had been associated in the parent *thallus*.

For this reason it has been suggested that ascospores do not play an important role in the multiplication of lichens as such. It is probable that *fragmentation* and asexual *propagule production* are more *efficacious* in this connection.

The researches of Ahmadjian have demonstrated clearly that assumption of the lichen relationship by an alga and a fungus depends on the existence of *minimal* nutrition for both organisms. Attempts to induce or initiate a lichen synthesis in culture media rich in *nutrients* are *consistently failures*.

However, in low-nutrient, minimal culture media, lichen synthesis has been *successfully* evoked in a few cases. Until recently, lichens have been neglected by most botanists, except for a few who have occupied themsleves almost exclusively with the taxonomy of these interesting composite organisms.

Careful *physiological* studies of the components, grown separately and together in laboratory culture under controlled conditions, are *augmenting* our *understanding* of these organisms.

It seems clear that the lichen association is in a delicate state of equilibrium in nature, a condition that is perhaps reflected by the sensitivity of these organisms to *sulfur dioxide* and other *gaseous pollutants*.

Lichens are becoming increasingly important as indicators of air pollution, being adversely affected or even eliminated following *prolonged* exposure to relatively low levels of pollution in urban areas. It is difficult to assign lichens a natural *position* in any plan of classification of the *plant kingdom*.

If they were classified with the group of ascomycetous or basidiomycetous fungi to which their fungus *component* is related, as is usually done, the *importance* of the algal component would be *minimized*. The opposite objection might be raised were they to be classified on the basis of their algal components.

In the present volume, therefore, they have been assigned no formal position in the *classification* of the plant kingdom but are treated separately in the present chapter.

However, the current prevailing consensus seems to be that these organisms are lichenized fungi. After all, the same phycobiont occurs in a great variety of different lichens that are seemingly not closely related.

Finally, the reader is referred to the publications of Smith (1962), Ahmadjian (1963, 1970b), Ahmadjian and Hale (1973), and Hale (1974) for further information on lichens.

Mycota

Hidebound for many years by the traditional idea that all life must be plant or animal, biologists were perplexed by the slime molds, which seemingly defied classification in either group because they exhibited some characteristics of both.

The acellular, creeping, somatic phase of the slime molds is definitely animal-like in its structure and in its physiology; the reproductive structures, however, are plant-like, producing spores covered by definite walls, probably containing cellulose.

De Bary (1887), one of the founders of the science of mycology, considered the slime *molds* to be animals and called them *Mycetozoa* (sing. mycetozoon; Gr. *mykes* = mushroom + *zoon* = animal). He believed that they originated independently from the bacteria, the Acrasiales, and the fungi, and treated them as a separate group.

Later, Lister (1925), Hagelstein (1944), Bessey (1950), and Kudo (1954), followed De Bary in the use of the name Mycetozoa, Bessey and Kudo actually classifying. the slime molds in the phylum Protozoa of the animal kingdom.

Thomas H. Macbride (1899), who was one of the first American monographers of this group, used the term Myxomycetes (Gr. *myxa* = slime + *myketes* = mushrooms, fungi), which Link had used in 1833 in accordance with his belief that the slime molds are fungi.

Professor G. W. Martin of the University of Iowa, who is the world authority on the taxonomy of the slime molds and who believes that the fungi have originated from protozoan-like ancestors, has put forth some very convincing arguments (1932, 1960/1961) for the fungal nature of the slime molds.

Nevertheless, because the Myxomycetes, a very old and relatively stable group, have become quite specialized in many ways, Martin considers that they have departed sufficiently from the main evolutionary line of the fungi to constitute a subdivision of their own, the *Myxomycotina*. This is the view we are adopting in this book.

Occurrence, and Importance to Man

Most slime molds live in cool, shady, moist places in the woods, on decaying logs, dead leaves, or other organic matter which holds abundant moisture. A few species occur in open spaces, creeping over vegetation, and these are especially conspicuous on the grass of city lawns.

Some species develop on pieces of bark taken from living trees and placed in a moist chamber for a few days. Moisture and temperature seem to be the factors most important in governing the distribution and abundance of slime molds. During a rainy season they begin, as a class, to appear in May, in the north temperate region, and continue to fruit through October.

However, not all species may be found at all times. Some are more abundant in the spring, some in the middle of the summer, others in early fall. Most of the 450 odd known species are universally distributed, but some are confined to the temperate regions, and others to the tropics.

Slime molds in general are of little direct economic importance. They feed on bacteria, protozoa, and other minute organisms. Occasionally slime molds creep over ornamentals, rendering them unsightly and, in rare instances, smothering them.

Physarum cinereum, one of the common Myxomycetes, may form colonies several feet in diameter on city lawns.

These colonies appear bluish and may be quite conspicuous. Lawn owners become disturbed about this "disease" of their lawns and write asking for advice concerning control methods. The cure is simple: mow the lawn!

In recent years, not only mycologists but also cytologists, biochemists, and biophysicists have become interested in the study of slime molds because these organisms are ideal tools for experimental studies on the mitotic cycle, morphogenesis, the chemical changes that govern reproduction, the structure and physiology of protoplasm, and a variety of other fundamental questions which challenge the scientist.

The slimy somatic phase of the slime molds, which has no cell walls, is considered the purest form of protoplasm encountered in nature in massive quantities. As such, it is frequently employed for laboratory studies on the chemical composition of protoplasm. Even so, it is actually far from being pure protoplasm, for it contains much non-living material such as food particles or other matter which is definitely not protoplasmic.

Plasmodia and fructifications of many species of slime molds are very colorful. In addition, fructifications of most species are delicately constructed, forming intricate designs. The artistic value of these organisms was recognized some years ago, when a series of paintings depicting slime mold fructifications appeared in full color in the *National Geographic Magazine.*

The fructifications of *Stemonitis,* one of the Myxomycetes, attained dubious fame at the Chicago World's Fair in 1933 when placed on exhibit at the "Believe It or Not" pavilion over the caption: "Hair growing on wood-Believe It or Not." Students of mycology did not!

Classification

Organisms included in the class Myxomycetes, which constitutes the sub-division Myxomycotina of the division Mycota, have a free-living, acellular, multinucleate somatic phase, the plasmodium, which behaves as a unit at all times and eventually gives rise to fructifications. Flagellated swarm cells are produced under proper conditions, probably by all species.

With the exception of the three species which are separated from all the others into a sub-class of their own (Ceratiomyxomycetidae), all others produce their spores inside a fructification which usually develops a peridium enclosing the spores.

The Myxomycetes are subdivided into six orders on the basis of method of spore production, spore color, type of fructification produced, and lime content of the fructification. These orders are Ceratiomyxales, Liceales, Trichiales, Echinosteliales, Stemonitales, and Physarales.

SUB-CLASS CERATIOMYXOMYCETIDAE (EXOSPOREAE)

This sub-class is a very small one consisting of but three species of the genus *Ceratiomyxa,* placed in the family Ceratiomyxaceae and the order Ceratiomyxales. *Ceratiomyxa fruticulosa* is one of the most common slime molds, world-wide in its distribution.

Its life history differs in many respects from those of

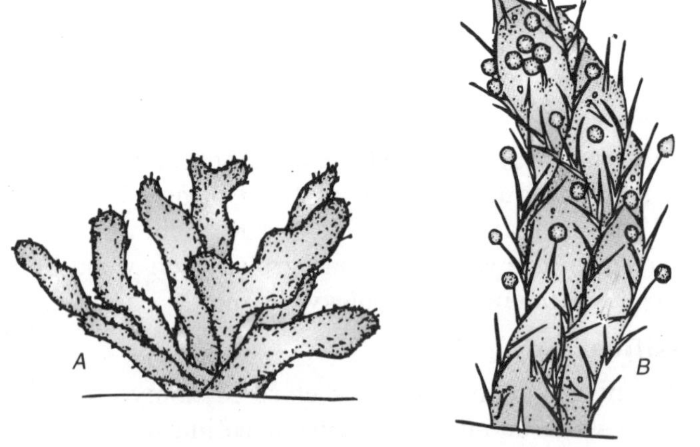

Figure 9.1 : Ceratiomyxa fruticulosa. A. Fruiting body. Habit. B. Detail of single column, showing attachment of spores.

Simple Key to the Sub-Classes and Orders fo the Class Myxomycetes

A.	Spores borne externally on individual stalks	Sub-class *Ceratiomyxomycetidae (Exosporeae)* *Ceratiomyxales*
AA.	Spores borne internally in fructifications	Sub-class *Myxogastromycetidae (Myxogastres)*
B.	Spores in mass pallid or brightly colored to dingy olivaceous	
C.	True capillitium and columella lacking	*Liceales*
CC.	Capillitium or columella characteristically present	
D.	Stalked, minute; columella present, rarely lacking	*Echinosteliales*
DD.	Stalked or sessile, larger; columella never present	*Trichiales*
BB.	Spores in mass black or deep violaceous to ferruginous	
E.	Neither peridium nor capillitium calcareous	*Stemonitales*
EE.	Peridium or capillitium or both calcareous	*Physarales*

other Myxom-ycetes. Its chief c aracteristic is that it produces its resting spores on the surface of any white, columnar structures which compose the fructification.

Although each resting spore has a cell wall of its own, there is no common membrane (peridium) enveloping all the spores as in the Myxogastromycetidae. Gilbert studied the life cycle of *Ceratiomyxa fruticulosa* in detail. His study indicated that the "spores" are actually one-spored sporangia, the walls of spore and sporangium being completely fused to form a single structure.

SUB-CLASS MYXOGASTROMYCETIDAE (MYXOGASTRES)

Martin (1949) recognizes 303 species of this sub-class in his taxonomic treatise on the North American Myxomycetes. Over 400 species have been described the world over, and many more probably await discovery.

Life History

The sequence of events in the life history of the Myxogastromycetidae is usually as follows. The spores germinate under favorable conditions and produce one to four flagellated swarm cells each. Either these swarm cells may behave as gametes and copulate in pairs soon after their formation, or they may first lose their flagella, undergo a number of divisions, and then copulate.

Plasmogamy is followed by karyogamy. The resulting zygote is either flagellate at first, later becoming amoeboid, or amoeboid from the start, depending on the nature of the gametes. Growth of the zygote is accompanied by a series of mitotic nuclear divisions resulting in a multinucleate plasmodium with diploid nuclei.

A plasmodium may also be formed by the coalescence of many zygotes, and may continue annexing zygotes and smaller plasmodia as it develops. At maturity, the plasmodium thickens and assumes the shape of the fructification typical of the species.

The nuclei now undergo meiosis with the accompanying reduction of the number of chromosomes. Each daughter nucleus, together with a portion of cytoplasm, is finally enveloped by a thick wall and develops into a spore. All this is summarized in the life history diagram in Figure elsewhere in this chapter.

There is a serious lack of life history data for the Myxo-

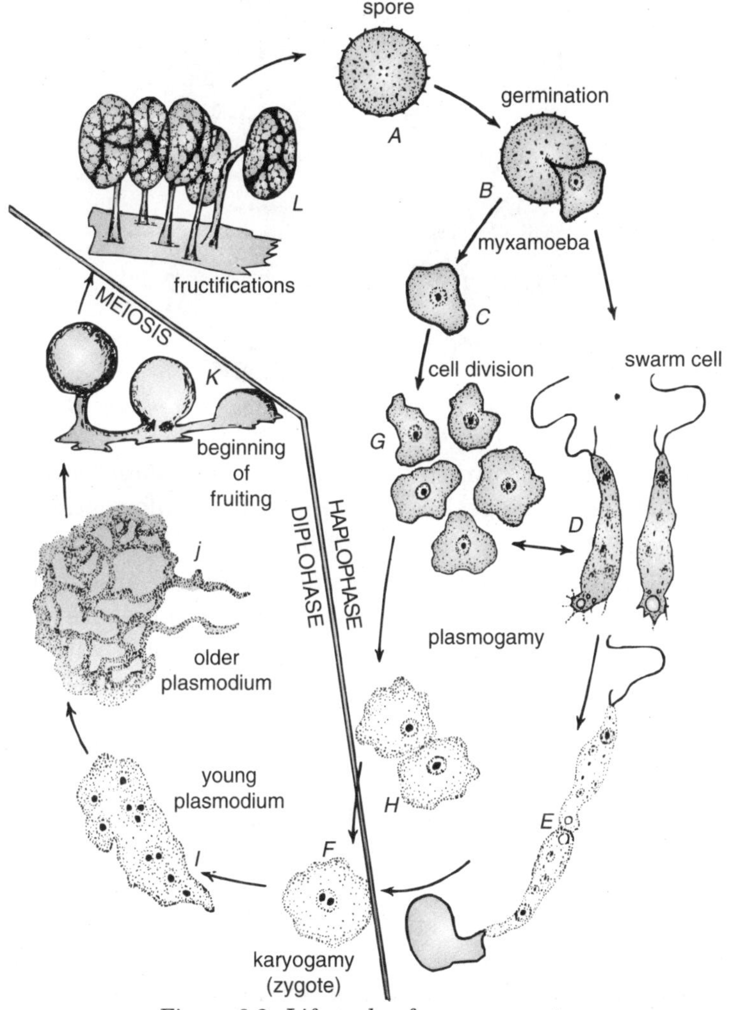

Figure 9.2: Life cycle of a myxomycete.

mycetes; as a whole, and the field is a very fertile and challenging one to the: research worker interested in this group.

The Spore

The Myxogastromycetidae bear their spores inside a fruiting structure covered by a peridium. The spores are generally globose, with a definite, rather thick cell wall

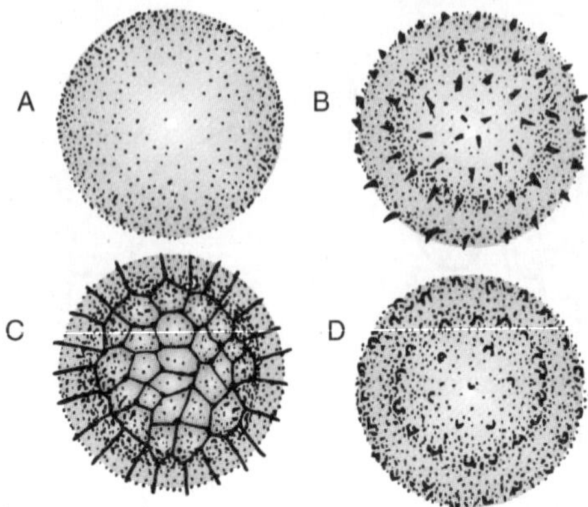

Figure 9.3: Four types of myxomycete spores. A. Smooth. B. Sp. Ridged (reticulate). D. Warty.

which can be smooth, spiny, warted or reticulate (covered by a network of ridges). We have very little information on the composition of the spore wall.

Cellulose is said to be present and chitin absent; but since no one has used modern methods for spore wall analysis, all such statements should be accepted with the greatest reservation. The color of the spores in mass may be pallid, yellow, purple, rosy, olivaceous, gray, deep violet, brown, or black. The pigments are dilute so that an individual spore, when viewed by itself under strong transmitted light, will not show the same color as the mass of spores. The spores are generally uninucleate and the nuclei typically haploid.

Spores of Myxomycetes are exceptionally resistant to unfavorable conditions, especially to prolonged periods of desiccation, which few other organisms are able to withstand. Such resistance is due to the thickness of the wall of the spore, and, no doubt, to the physicochemical structure of the protoplasm within it.

Elliott (1949) showed that spores of some species of Myxomycetes are capable of germinating after 61 years of storage in a herbarium, and if you have ever worked in a herbarium you will admit that that is quite a feat.

Factors affecting spore germination have been studied

rather extensively. The papers of Gilbert (1929a, b), Smith (1929), Smart (1937), and Elliott (1948, 1949) revealed that the spores of most species will germinate in water, especially if they are treated first with some wetting agent, such as one of the bile salts.

Weak decoctions of natural substrata such as wood, bark, and hay have been found to stimulate germination in a umber of species. As you would expect, temperature and pH of the medium are also factors which influence germination, as is the age of the spores.

The time required for germination differs with the species. The spores of *Reticularia lycoperdon,* on the one extreme, will germinate in as short a time as 15 minutes under favorable conditions, whereas those of *Oligonema flavidum,* on the other extreme, are said to require a minimum of 14 days.

Whether this behavior is due to a difference in thickness, penetrability, or chemical composition of the spore wall or to some other cause is yet to be discovered.

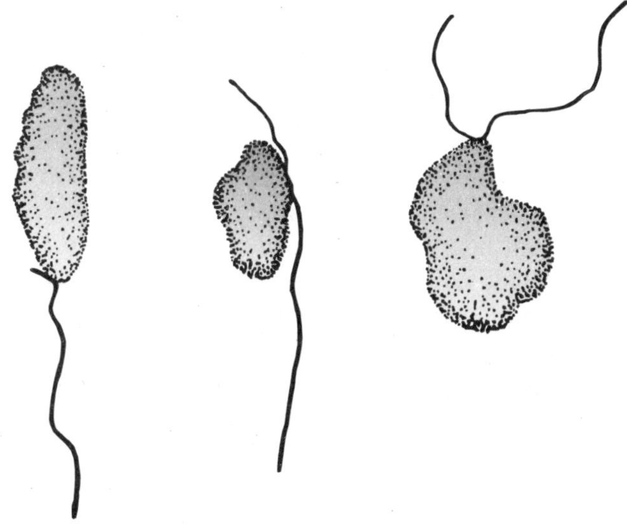

Figure 9.4: Swarm cells of Myxomycetes, showing variation in length of flagella.

Swarm Cells and Myxamoebae

In nature, spores of the Myxomycetes probably germinate in rain water which has formed a dilute solution with the substratum on which the spores happen to lie. A spore germinates by one of two methods. It either cracks open or germinates by means of a tiny pore through which the protoplast emerges.

The method seems to be specific for individual species. When a spore germinates, either a myxamoeba (pl. myxamoebae; Gr. *myxa* = slime + *amoeba)* or a flagellated swarm cell emerges. To a certain extent this depends on the environment.

If the spores are suspended in water, the emerging protoplasts are often, flagellated from the very beginning. Sometimes, however, an amoeba will issue from the spore, remain quiescent for a few minutes, and then develop flagella.

Echinostelium minutum, and perhaps other species whose spores germinate easily on the surface of moist agar in the absence of free water, is able to complete its entire life cycle without ever developing flagella. Flagellated cells, therefore, although characteristic of the Myxomycetes, are not necessary for the completion pletion of the life cycle, at least in some species.

For many years it was thought that the swarm cells of the Myxomycetes are typically uniflagellate with an occasional cell bearing two flagella. An extensive study by Elliott in 1948, however, showed that the swarm cells of some fifty-four species (all that he studied) are typically biflagellate.

In most of these one of the two flagella is shorter than the other. This short flagellum is often directed backward and furthermore may be appressed against the protoplasm of the swarm cell and be, "therefore, rather difficult to see.

Locquin (1949) arrived at the same conclusions independently. Ten years later, at the IXth International Botanical Congress, Cohen reopened the question by presenting electron micrographs showing uniflagellate swarm cells. University of Iowa films (1961) by Koevenig also show that uniflagellate swarm cells are not uncommon.

Similarly, Kole's electron micrograph demonstrates that the swarm cells of *Reticularia lycoperdon* are uniflagellate. The question of flagellation, therefore, cannot be regarded as settled. It is possible that some strains of a species produce mostly uniflagellate cells, other strains biflagellate.

It has been shown furthermore by both Cohen (1959) and Koevenig (1961) that swarm cells produce long, flagellum-like pseudopodia which originate at the anterior end of a swarm cell and migrate down the side, eventually becoming withdrawn or absorbed. It is possible that these have been mistaken for flagella.

Finally, Kerr (1960a) found that newly flagellated cells of *Didymium nigripes* are uniflagellate, but may become biflagellate after several hours. Perhaps the most accurate statement of the situation at present is that myxomycete swarm cells are potentially anteriorly biflagellate, but that uniflagellate cells are often produced.

More extensive studies with the electron microscope should clarify the situation. As for the structure of the mycete flagella, our present knowledge indicates that both flagella are whiplash. After the swarm cell escapes from the spore case, it swims about, with a rapid rotary movement which is combined with amoeboid of contractions.

At this stage it obtains nourishment by absorbing dissolved food material from the surrounding medium and by ingesting, at its posterior end, bacteria which it engulfs, by means of pseudopodia. The posterior end of a swarm cell is very sticky and appears to be quite important both in catching food and, as we shall see later, in reproduction.

Yeasts, fungal spores, and particles of organic matter which can serve as food are readily ingested, in addition to bacteria, upon contacting the d posterior end of the swarm cell. Food vacuoles are formed around such particles.

The fact that indigestible as well as digestible matter

is ingested-the former being eventually egested—may be an indication that the swarm cell does not have the power of selecting its food.

After a period of motility, the swarm cell eventually withdraws its flagella, thus changing into a myxamoeba. Under unfavorable conditions myxamoebae round up and encyst.

When favorable conditions return, the cysts germinate and a myxamoeba or swarm cell emerges from each. When food is abundant and environmental conditions are favorable, myxamoebae divide repeatedly, giving rise to a large population of haploid cells.

Sexual Fusions

Whether the term sexual should be applied to the fusions which take place between haploid cells of Myxomycetes is a matter of opinion. Martin (1940) has revived the term karyallagy (Gr. *karyon* = nut, nucleus + *allage* = change) to refer to fusions between morphologically similar cells, preferring to restrict the term sexual to the fusions between cells which can be differentiated into male and female.

In this book, however, we have adopted the view that any fusion of two haploid cells which results in the formation of a diploid zygote may be termed sexual. In the Myxomycetes which have been investigated, such fusions take place either between flagellated swarm cells or between myxamoebae into which swarm cells have changed after withdrawing their flagella.

Whether one and the same species may employ both of these methods, or whether some species employ the first and others the second, has been a matter of controversy. Kerr (1961) and Koevenig (1961) have settled this question for D*idymium nigripes* and *Physarum gyrosum,* respectively, by showing that fusions take place between both flagellated and non-flagellated cells in the two species.

In *Stemonitis fusca* it is said that copulation takes place only between a swarm cell and a myxamoeba, the latter flowing into the former and producing a flagellated zygote. These observations must be confirmed before they are accepted, in view of previous contradictory evidence.

A genetic explanation of gametic fusions in the Myxomycetes is just beginning to emerge. *Physarum polycephalum* is apparently eterothallic. Collins (1961) has shown that *Didymium iridis* is heterothallic and that *Fuligo cinerea* is homothallic. Certain interesting complexities in the heterothallic species, however, indicate that many more studies of monosporous cultures are needed before the situation is clarified.

The Zygote

The zygote of a myxomycete is thus formed by the union of two planogametes (swarm cells) or two myxamoebae. Contact of planogametes takes place at their posterior ends while they are swimming with a rotary movement, If the zygote is formed by the fusion of swarm cells, it is, of course, flagellate and swims for a time before retracting its flagella and changing into a myxamoeba.

As the zygote grows, its nucleus undergoes successive mitotic divisions and the zygote gradually becomes transformed into a multinucleate amoeboid structure, the plasmodium. It appears that in some species a plasmodium is formed by the coalescence of many zygotes.

Possibly the same species may form the plasmodium either by the growth of a single zygote or by the coalescence of many zygotes according to circumstances.

The Plasmodium

Being a mass of protoplasm, delimited only by a thin plasma membrane, the plasmodium does not have a definite size or shape. At one time it is globose, at another it is flat and sheet-like spreading over a large area in the form of a very thin network which is often brilliantly colored.

Ever changing, ever flowing, the plasmodium creeps over the surface of the substratum, engulfing particles of food in its way. Eventually it matures and changes into the fructification typical of the species. Camp (1937), who studied the formation and structure of plasmodia of *Physarum polycephalum,* concluded that the protoplasm of a plasmodium is an apparently structureless substance with granules, vacuoles, and various other bodies embedded within it.

He found that the viscosity of the protoplasm not only differs in various sections of the same plasmodium, but also changes constantly with modifications in the internal and external environments.

The protoplast is fluid in some portions and gelatinous in others, the two phases blending gradually. The fluid portion of the protoplast is usually in the form of an intricately branched network streaming through the gelatinous portion of the plasmodium.

The streaming of the protoplasm in the veins of a plasmodium is a fascinating process to watch under the microscope. If you will focus the low-power objective on one of the veins of a vigorously growing plasmodium, you will see the protoplasmic granules flowing in one direction at what appears to be a great speed.

And, actually, such streaming is comparatively rapid. Kamiya (1950b), investigating the rate of flow in *Physarum polycephalum,* reports that the maximum speed reached was 1.35 mm. per second which, he says, is "the greatest velocity of protoplasmic flow ever recorded."

But keep your eye on the ocular for 50 or 60 seconds, and you will see that the river of protoplasm slows down, comes to a momentary stop, and then begins to flow in the opposite direction for a certain length of tine, only to reverse itself again and again.

This more or less rhythmical reversal in the direction of protopla-smic flow within the veins of a plasmodium is a well-known phenomenon. Surprisingly enough, a study of the relation of this phenomenon to the direction in which the whole plasmodium is creeping reveals that the flow toward the direction of movement of the plasmodium does not necessarily last longer than the flow in the opposite direction.

As a matter of fact, the progressive flow in some cases lasts a shorter time than the regressive flow. There seems, therefore, to be no close correlation between the duration of flow in any direction and the protoplasmic volume transported in the same direction.

Among the most significant findings relative to the problem of the streaming of protoplasm in a plasmodium are those of Loewy (1952), Ts'O and his coworkers (1956, 1957), and Takeuchi and Hatano. These discoveries center around myxomyosin, a contractile protein which was found to be present in the plasmodium of *Physarum polycephalum.*

Myxomyosin is a rod-shaped molecule 4000-5000 A long with a molecular weight of *6* million. It behaves like actornyosin in animal muscle, changing its viscosity when ATP is added. Furthermore, the presence of ATP itself has been demonstrated in the plasmodium, and its effect on animal muscle is the same as that of muscle ATP.

At least three general types of plasmodia are now known. The most primitive type is the *protoplasmodium* (Gr. *protos* = first + plasmodium), characteristic of certain minute species *(Echinostelium minutum, Licea parasitica, Clasto= derma debaryanum,* etc.).

Such a plasmodium remains microscopic throughout its existence. It is more or less homogeneous, it forms no veins, and it exhibits a very slow, irregular streaming instead of the rapid, rhythmical, reversible streaming of the other plasmodial types. A protoplasmodium gives rise to but a single sporangium when it fruits. The *aphanoplasmodium* (Gr. *aphanes* = invisible + *plasmodium)* resembles a protoplasmodium in its initial stages, but soon elongates, branches, and becomes a network of very fine, transparent strands.

The protoplasm is not very granular, and the plasmodium is difficult to see. The veins are not conspicuously differentiated into gelified and fluid regions, and the streaming protoplasm seems to be confined by a very delicate membrane. Streaming is rapid and rhythmically reversible.

The *phaneroplasmodium* (Gr. *phaneros* = visible + *plasmodium),* characteristic of the Physarales, also resembles a protoplasmodium at first. Soon, however, it grows larger and becomes more massive. Its protoplasm is very granular, and the plasmodium is easily visible even at an early stage of development.

The gelified and fluid portions of the veins are easily distinguishable, and the rhythmic, reversible streaming is very conspicuous. Slime mold plasmodia are of various colors, ranging from colorless to white, gray, black, violet, blue, green, yellow, orange, and red, they color depending in part upon the species.

The yellow and the white plasmodia are probably the most commonly encountered. Color changes have been observed to occur in the same plasmodium under laboratory conditions and have also been induced artificially by various means.

We know, for example, that in some plasmodia the pigments responsible for the color are in the nature of chemical indicators and that their color changes with variations in the hydrogen ion concentration of the plasmodium.

Pigmented food particles may also be responsible for the color of a plasmodium. For example, it has been determined experimentally that the ingestion by plasmodia of cells of *Serratia marcescens—a* bacterium which possesses a red or pink pigment-imparts a reddish or pink color to the plasmodium.

Young plasmodia unite readily with other plasmodia or with zygotes of the same strain and thus increase in size. Such unions are probably somatic and are not followed by nuclear fusions.

That plasmodia of different species will not unite was

recognized by De Bary (1887) and has been confirmed so often that a fusion test had been used to determine the identity of species.

It was believed that non-fusion was proof that the species concerned were different. Skupienski (1934, 1939), however, showed that *Didymium iridis* and *Didymium squamulosum* consisted of physiological races whose plasmodia would not fuse one with another. Yet there was no doubt that all were somatic phases of the same morphological species. Gray (1945) later found that *Physarum polycephalum is* also composed of a number of physiological races.

When he placed plasmodia of this species, isolated from different localities, in contact with each other, some fused, but others did not. Such plasmodia were similar morphologically, but different physiolog-ically. Work in our own laboratory shows that many other species, perhaps all, are made up of physiological races.

Of considerable interest are some results which indicate that, whereas myxamoebae of two different races of the same species *(Didymium iridis)* unite to form zygotes, the plasmodia of the two parents will not fuse with each other. Haploid protoplasts thus appear to be compatible, whereas diploid protoplasts seem to be incompatible.

NUTRITION AND CULTURE

Growth of plasmodia necessarily involves the intake of food and the excretion of waste products. In nature plasmodia probably feed on bacteria, spores of fungi and green plants, and possibly on protozoa and even on bits of non-living organic matter. They also frequently envelop and consume the fruiting bodies of shelf fungi and mushrooms.

In the laboratory, the plasmodia of some species can be kept growing vigorously for a long time on a diet of finely ground oats, oatmeal, or oatmeal agar. Actually, very little is known about the nutrition of the Myxomycetes.

It-is well established that swarm cells and plasmodia

feed on microorganisms of various types and that they thrive better on some organisms than on others. Also, some species are known to survive on organic matter in the absence of living organisms. No extensive studies are extant, however, on the nutritive requirements of the slime molds.

The chief difficulty here lies in obtaining pure cultures of the Myxomycetes. A number of investigators have succeeded in culturing various species of Myxomycetes on artificial media and have induced them to complete their life cycles from resting spore to resting spore in culture.

Authentic reports of pure cultures of Myxomycetes, however, are rather rare in the literature, for it appears to be quite difficult to purify plasmodia from bacteria. Cohen (1939) was the first to apply rigid controls to test whether cultures which appeared to be pure were indeed so.

He succeeded in growing several species in pure culture in the absence of other living organisms, but had difficulty in maintaining the vigor of his cultures over a long period of time. Miss Johanna Sobels (1950), working in Holland with plasmodia isolated from natural substrata, concluded that some species of Myxomycetes are either parasitic or saprobic according to circumstances and can be purified and grown in pure culture with comparative ease.

Other species seem to be obligately parasitic and soon die in the absence of living microorganisms which they can utilize for food. Miss Sobels further discovered that the plasmodia of certain species produce soluble antibiotics which inhibit the growth of certain bacteria and yeasts in culture.

A great step in the study of the Myxomycetes was taken when Dr. H. P. Rusch and his associates at the University of Wisconsin succeeded in growing *Physarum polycephalum* in a chemically defined, liquid medium. This work made possible exact studies on the nutritive requirements of this organism.

Although, as mentioned above, we know that some

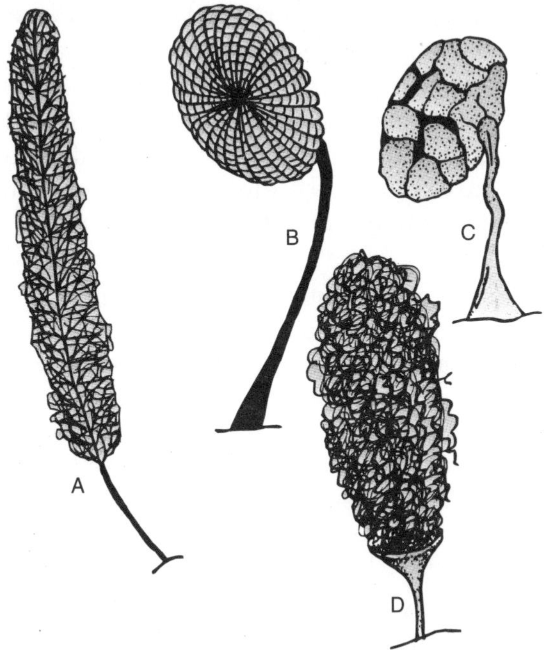

Figure 9.5: Four types of sporangia typical of four genera of Myxomycetes. A. Stemonitis. B. Dictydium. C. Physarum. D. Arcyria.

plasmodia may absorb food in the liquid state from their substratum, the ingestion of solid particles is probably the more usual method of food intake. The process of ingestion was described by Camp (1937) as follows: "When the plasmodium comes in contact with the food particle, the latter tends to. be pushed forward, away from the plasmodial margin.

However, that part of the plasmodium directly behind the food ceases its forward movement while . . on either side and above and below, the protoplasm flows out for a slight distance and tends to surround the food particle."

Thus, the plasmodium of the Myxomycetes ingests its food by the same method. which protozoa such as the amoeba employ. The protoplasm no doubt secretes enzymes into the food vacuole, and these convert the ingested food particle into simpler soluble materials which the protoplasm eventually absorbs and assimilates.

The plasmodium eliminates its waste products by depositing waste particles on the substratum and moving away from them. In some instances, according to Camp, the plasmodium forcibly ejects solid particles by a contractile movement, and throws them some distance away.

Assimilation of food into the plasmodium makes growth possible. Growth is accompanied by the successive division of the nuclei embedded in the cytoplasm. Howard (1931) found that, in growing plasmodia of *Physarum polycephalum,* nuclear division occurs almost simultaneously throughout the plasmodium and requires 20-40 minutes for completion. Centrosomes and astral rays are lacking. Each nucleus contains several nucleoli, and the nuclear membrane persists throughout nuclear division.

Under carefully controlled conditions, this same organism in pure, liquid, shake cultures forms many tiny plasmodia each of which has its own rhythm of synchronous mitoses. When two such plasmodia are permitted to fuse, all the nuclei in the resulting plasmodium divide synchronously after an adjustment period of about 7-8 hours.

Nuclear divisions are followed by a great increase in DNA synthesis . Since the plasmodium of the Myxomycetes develops from the growth of the zygote, or from the coalescence of many zygotes, all nuclei are diploid.

A mature plasmodium which is about to enter the fruiting stage contains from fewer than one hundred to many thousand nuclei, all of which may be derived from the successive mitoses of the original zygote nucleus and its progeny.

Sclerotia

In the normal course of events, the plasmodium gives rise to a fructification. Under certain conditions, however, the plasmodium becomes converted into an irregular hardened mass, the sclerotium, which can remain dormant for a

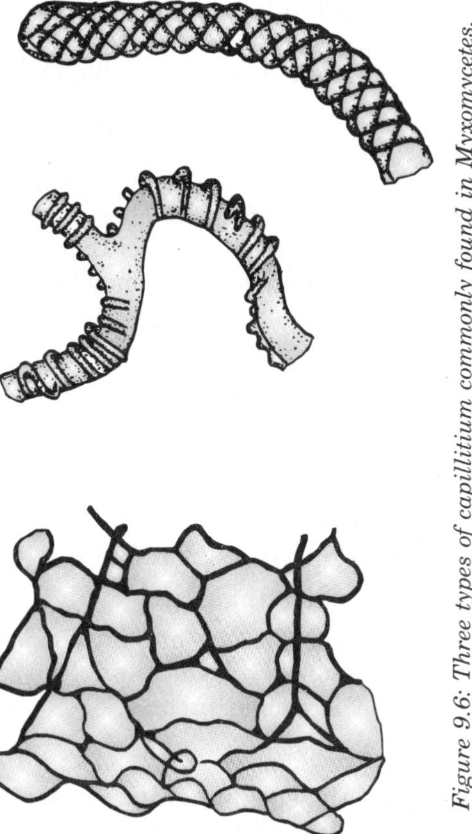

Figure 9.6: Three types of capillitium commonly found in Myxomycetes.

long time, but which grows out into a plasmodium again when conditions favorable for growth return.

Some Myxomycetes overwinter in the sclerotial condition, as evidenced by the fact that we can find their sclerotia in the soil, under fallen logs, or under tree stumps during warmer spells in the winter when the ground surface thaws sufficiently to permit observations.

In Michigan I have collected sclerotia of *Physarum polycephalum* during such thawing periods in January, and without difficulty have grown the plasmodia from them in the laboratory.

Sclerotia may be induced to form in the laboratory by

drying plasmodia gradually. They can be kept in the refrigerator or even at room temperature until needed, when they can again be placed on suitable moist media for growth.

Jump (1954), in what is probably the best study on sclerotization, found that all sclerotia are composed of small "cells" which he termed macrocysts. These vary in size from 10 to 25 µ and in the number of nuclei they contain (0-14). Each macrocyst is surrounded by a membrane. According to jump, the process of sclerotization goes through the following stages:

(1) cessation of streaming,

(2) gelation of the whole plasmodium,

(3) distribution of nuclei,

(4) depositing of macrocyst walls,

(5) completion of macrocyst formation,

(6) hardening of sclerotium, and

(7) shrinkage of nuclei to one-half diameter. The reconstitution of the plasmodium from a sclerotium reverses the foregoing process.

Sporulation

In passing from the somatic to the reproductive phase, the entire plasmodium of the Myxomycetes is usually converted into one or more fruiting bodies, so that the somatic and reproductive phases are seldom coexistent in the same individual.

The factors directly responsible for fructification in the Myxomycetes are not well understood. Moisture, light, temperature, and exhaustion of food supply have all been related to fruiting by some investigators and denied by others on the basis of contradictory laboratory experimental results.

Seifriz and Russell (1935) even postulated a reproductive rhythm independent of these factors for *Physarum polycephalum.* The work of Gray has shed some light on this subject. Dr. Gray (1939) found that the fruiting of *Physarum polycephalum is* influenced by both pH and temperature and that these two factors are closely related and interdependent.

Within certain limits, the higher the temperature at which a plasmodium is growing the greater the acidity required to induce fruiting. Gray (1938) also showed that light is necessary for the fruiting of *Physarum polycephalum* and certain other species with yellow plasmodia, and that this factor is independent of pH and temperature.

The work of Johanna Sobels and Henderica ·an der Brugge (1950) supports Gray's conclusions with respect to the effect of light on fruiting of pigmented plasmodia. A number of researchers have also shown that the shorter wave lengths of light are most effective.

Some of the pigments in a plasmodium appear to be photoreceptors which absorb large amounts of shortwave light at low pH values, thus explaining the effectiveness of both blue light and acidity for fruiting.

Of particular interest are the results obtained with *Physarum polycephalum* grown in bacteria-free culture. Plasmodia were grown in a liquid medium in the dark, harvested, and transferred to the surface of a filter paper in contact with a chemically defined liquid sporulation medium containing various inorganic salts, citric acid, niacin, and niacinamide.

The conditions which favored sporulation were an optimal age of the culture at harvest time, an additional dark incubation period, and a subsequent period of illumination. The presence of niacin, niacinamide, or tryptophan in the medium during the postgrowth period was necessary for sporulation. Light was indispensable.

The activating wave. lengths of light fell in the range of 310-500 mμ with the shorter wave lengths appearing to be more favorable. Whatever happens in a plasmodium that causes it to fruit appears to be irreversible, for once a plasmodium reaches the fruiting stage it cannot be induced to resume growth. Exactly what the changes are we do not know as yet, but a number of investigations are producing some interesting results.

The Fructification

Three types of fructifications are formed by Myxogastromycetidae. In the first of these, the plasmodium forms numerous individual sporangia, generally crowded together on the portion of the substratum formerly occupied by the plasmodium.

Each sporangium has a peridium of its own. There may also be a thin, cellophane-like base, the hypothallus (pl. hypothalli; Gr. *hypo* = under + *thallos* = shoot, thallus), from which the sporangia arise. Except for the hypothallus, which may serve as a common base for all sporangia, each of the latter is independent of all the others in the group.

Examples of slime molds which produce sporangia are *Hemitrichia clavata, Physarum globuliferum, Physarum viride,* and various species of *Stemonitis, Comatricha,* and *Arcyria.* The second type of fructification is called aethalium (pl. *aethalia*; Gr. *aethalos* = soot).

This is a fairly large, sometimes massive, generally cushion-shaped fructification which may represent a stage in the evolutionary development of the sporangia—a group of sporangia, so to speak, which have not separated into individual units.

In some aethalia the walls of the individual sporangia are quite evident; in others they are difficult to see; and in still others the aethalium shows no trace of sporangial walls. In all cases, the entire body is enclosed in a peridium which may or may not be an aggregate structure.

Some common examples of Myxomycetes whose fructifications are aethaloid are *Lycogala epidendrum*, *Tubifera ferruginosa,* and various species of *Fuligo.* The third type of fructification, the *plasmodiocarp (plasmodium* + Gr. *karpos* = fruit), is similar to a stalkless sporangium, but differs in that it retains, to a certain extent, the branching habit of the plasmodium.

In the formation of the plasmodiocarp, the protoplasm

concentrates around some of the main veins of the plasmodiurd and, secreting a membrane around itself, is converted into a fruiting structure which more or less retains the shape of the plasmodial venation at the time of fruiting.

It is very difficult to draw the line between the sessile (stalkless) types of sporangia and short plasmodiocarps. These two forms actually merge into one another and are found side by side in the same group of fructifications, developed from a single plasmodium.

In such mixed formations the plasmodiocarps are seldom branched. More often they are elongated, curved, or doughnut-shaped. An example of a truly plasmodiocarpous fructification is that of *Hemitrichia serpula*. A slime mold which often forms a mixture of sessile sporangia and plasmodiocarps is *Diderma testaceum.*

The type of fruiting body varies with the species and to some extent with environmental conditions prevailing during the development of the fructification. Light and moisture, for example, are known to influence the color of sporangia of *Physarum nutans.*

When subjected to different degrees of humidity and light experimentally, plasmodia of this species formed gray, gray-green, or bright yellow sporangia. In some species, however, the color of the sporangia appears to remain constant under different environmental conditions.

The sporangial type of fructification may be stalked or sessile. Stalks, when present, vary in length, thickness, color, consistency, and structure, according to species. If the stalks extend into the sporangium, the intrasporangial portion is known as the columella (pl. *columellae*; *L. columen* = column). However, many species with stalkless sporangia also possess a columella.

The Capillitium

The presence and type of capillitium (pl. capillitia; *L. capillus* = hair) are important characteristics in the 1
classification of the Myxomycetes. The capillitium is a group

of non-living, hair-like structures which may be united to form an intricate network attached to the columella or to the peridium, or which may consist of simple or branched filaments, unattached and independent of each other.

In the Trichiales and Physarales, when the sporangium is formed; but still immature, its protoplast becomes highly vacuolated. The vacuoles are probably formed by the liberation of water in which various materials are dissolved.

These materials furnish the substances for capillitium formation within the vacuoles. The appearance of the vacuolar system at the initiation of capillitium formation corresponds closely to the appearance of the capillitium in a mature sporangium.

Thus, if the capillitium is to be a network of filaments, the vacuolar system from which it will be formed develops into a tubular network; if the capillitium is to be composed of long threads, the vacuoles are elongated and possibly branched, but are scattered in the cytoplasm without coalescing.

In the Physarales the capillitial material is deposited within the vacuoles, whereas in the Trichiales it is deposited on the surface of the vacuoles. In the Stemonitales and the Echinosteliales the capillitium either forms as an out growth of the columella or is deposited in the cytoplasm without previous formation of a vacuolar system.

In many species the capillitium is an aid in the liberation of the spores. Forming a springy mat of threads, it expands when the peridium has disintegrated, and carries the spores with it to a considerable height above the base of the fructification.

The spores are then easily dispersed from this position by air currents. *Arcyria nutans, Arcyria incarnata,* and *Hemitrichia vesparium* are good examples of slime molds with greatly expanding capillitia.

Spore Formation

Soon after the formation of capillitium, the numerous

nuclei in the cytoplasm undergo division, which students of these organisms find to be meiotic. Uninucleate portions of the protoplast are now separated from each other by the formation of a system of furrows, and a thick wall eventually envelops each spore.

Thus, the entire protoplasm within the fructification is consumed in the development of the resting spores, which, in a mature fructification, occur closely packed in between the capillitial threads, but are in no way connected to them. The spores are loose within the fructification and are liberated upon the disintegration of the peridium.

ORDER LICEALES

The spores of the Liceales are typically light in color. The fructifications, which may be of any one of the various types described, do not contain true capillitium, but may or may not contain pseudocapillitium (pl. *pseudocapillitia*; Gr. *pseudo* = false + *capillitium)*.

This is composed of irregular threads or plates representing remnants of plasmodial membranes or walls of fused sporangia rather than new elements formed at or immediately before spore formation.

Martin (1949) lists three families and ten genera containing fortythree species. Some of the most common species are *Lycogala epidendrum*, *Tubifera ferruginosa,* and *Dictydium cancellatum*.

ORDER TRICHIALES

The spores of the Trichiales are also light in color. This order differs from the Liceales in that the fructifications contain abundant capillitium. Two families and ten genera with a total of fifty-'four species are listed by Martin. Representatives of the Trichiales are among the most ubiquitous of the Myxomycetes.

The genera *Hemitrichia, Trichia,* and *Arcyria* are well represented in the woods throughout the growing season. You can find *Hemitrichia clavata* on almost any fallen log that has retained some moisture, at almost any time from early spring to late fall.

Other prevalent species of *Hemitrichia* are *Hemitrichia vesparium* and *Hemitrichia serpula. Trichia scabra, Trichia persimilis,* and *Trichia varia* are frequently collected. In the genus *Arcyria, Arcyria denudata, Arcyria incarnata, Arcyria nutans,* and *Arcyia kcinerea* are commonly encountered.

ORDER ECHINOSTELIALES

A -small order with only four known species, the Echinosteliales contains the smallest of the Myxomycetes. The spores are colorless or lightly pigmented, rosy or golden yellow, and are characterized by thickenings in the wall at regular intervals.

The peridium as a general rule disappears early in the formation of the fruiting body so that the mature sporangium is almost always naked. Capillitium is absent in two species, rudimentary in a third, and well developed into a tiny network in the fourth.

Echinosteliumminutum develops abundantly on pieces of bark taken from living trees and placed in a moist chamber. Three of the four known species have been induced to develop plasmodia in culture. All three formed protoplasmodia.

ORDER STEMONITALES

This is the first order of the dark-spored Myxogastromycetidae. We have records of three families, twelve genera, and sixty-four species from North America. Lime is absent from the peridium and from the capillitium, but may be present on the stalk of the fructification.

The capillitium is usually abundant, thread-like, and dark. *Stemonitis fusca, Stemonitis splendens,* and *Stemonitis axifera* are perhaps the most commonly found species in this genus. *Comatricha typhoides* is one of the most prevalent species in the genus *Comatricha.*

Comatricha nigra, Comatricha laxa, Comatricha elegans, and *Comatricha cornea* are minute species which develop their fructifications on pieces of bark taken from living trees and placed in a moist chamber. *Lamproderma arcyrioides is* a beautiful species with a golden-blue iridescent peridium.

ORDER PHYSARALES

The last order of the Myxogastromycetidae is characterized by the usually abundant amount of lime present on the fructification. The order contains two families and twelve genera, with 142 species found on this continent. The genus *Physarum* with, sixty-eight species is the largest.

Physarum polycephalum, Physarum viride, Physarum leucophaeuin, and *Physarum leucopodium* are some of the most widely distributed species. *Fuligo septica* forms large plasmodia and some of the largest aethalia in the Myxomycetes.

It occurs on lawns, compost beds, and on growing plants over which the plasmodia creep in the summer. *Physarum nicaraguense* is mostly tropical. *Badhamia, Diderma,* and *Didymium* are three other common genera in the *Physarales*.

Eumycotina

The sub-division *Eumycotina* contains all organisms, other than the slime molds, which we include in our current concept of fungi. What has been said in other chapter of this book, therefore, refers more specifically to this group.

The *Eumycotina* consists of over 80,000 described species of true fungi. The great majority of fungi are filamentous organisms, their s*omatic thalli* consisting of *hyphae*. A few of the primitive forms, however, are unicellular.

All fungi have definite cell walls and definite *demonstrable nuclei*, similar to those of higher forms of life. How long fungi have inhabited the earth, or how they originated, are questions which have not been and may never be answered.

Some fossil remains of fungi have been discovered, but studies of fossil fungi are so few and fragmentary that it is impossible to draw any definite conclusions as to the phylogeny of the group. At the present state of our knowledge, the origin of the fungi is entirely a matter of speculation.

Some mycologists believe in a monophyletic origin from the green algae; others in a polyphyletic origin from various groups of algae; and still others in a monophyletic or polyphyletic *protozoan ancestry*. Opinions differ also concerning the evolution of the fungi.

In general, botanists consider the aquatic habitat more

primitive than the terrestrial. In keeping with this principle, we consider fungi producing motile structures (zoospores and planogametes) which depend on water for their function more primitive than those in which no motile structures are formed.

Within a morphological series, parasites are considered more advanced than saprobes, obligate parasites more advanced than facultative ones, and highly specialized obligate parasites more advanced than less specialized species.

In the development of fungal structures, the evolutionary curve which is thought to have taken place begins with simplicity, proceeds to complexity, and ends with degeneration and loss of structure. Obviously it is impossible in an introductory course, for which this book is intended, to discuss all the fungi, or even representatives of all the groups.

The examples chosen for discussion have been selected with the purpose of acquainting you with the basic structure of the fungi and of illustrating the evolutionary tendencies in this great group of organisms. The sub-division Eumycotina consists of eight classes and one form-class.

These are the Chytridiomycetes, Hyphochytridiomycetes, Plasmod-iophoromycetes, Oomycetes, Zygomycetes, Trichomycetes, Ascomycetes, Basidiomycetes, and the Deuteromycetes. The first six of the classes just listed, together with the Myxomycetes, are often referred to as the lower fungi.

The majority of these produce their spores in sporangia. Many produce motile spores or motile gametes. As we proceed from the more primitive to the more advanced forms, and from an aquatic to a terrestrial habitat, we find a tendency for the sporangium to behave as a conidium, and eventually we reach the higher forms in which sporangia have given way completely to conidia.

This transition will become apparent as you study the various forms in the discussions that follow. The rest of this chapter deals with the class Chytridiomycetes.

General Characteristics

The one characteristic which distinguishes the Chytridiomycetes from all other fungi is the production of motile cells (zoospores or planogametes), each with a single, posterior, whiplash flagellum. Other characters which Chytridiomycetes have in common but which other fungi may also exhibit are:

(1) the coenocytic structure of the thallus, be it a multinucleate globose or oval structure, an elongated simple hypha, or a well-developed mycelium, and

(2) the conversion of the zygote into a resting spore or a resting sporangium or, in one order, its growth into a diploid coenocytic thallus.

Mycologists who are interested in discovering relationships among fungi are paying increasing attention to physiological and microchemical evidence to supplement morphological observations.

The composition of the cell wall of fungi certainly is an important indication of relationships. From the evidence at hand it appears that chitin is the chief constituent of the cell walls of the Chytridiomycetes, but cellulose has also been reported from a number of species and is said in some forms to be masked by the chitin so that it is difficult to determine the presence of the cellulose.

Research along these lines with modern methods of analysis will show how farreaching are the relationships among the Chytridiomycetes now postulated almost entirely on the basis of morphological and life history data.

Occurrence, and Importance to Man

The Chytridiomycetes are typically found in aquatic habitats. Many of them, however, also inhabit the soil. Because of their microscopic size they cannot be observed in nature directly.

They can be detected only by microscopic examination of the tissues of living plants which some of them parasitize or of dead organic material on which they grow, or in artificial culture in which a number of them form colonies of considerable size.

Students of these organisms have devised special methods for trapping, collecting, and culturing them in the laboratory on artificial media. In his authoritative book on the aquatic species of the lower fungi, Professor Sparrow of the University of Michigan, an eminent student of these fungi, has brought together the important information we have on their collection and culture.

Dr. Ralph Emerson of the University of California, who has also done much work on the lower fungi, has recorded his methods for culturing many of these organisms for laboratory instruction.

Most Chytridiomycetes are of little direct economic importance. Some parasitize and destroy algae which form a link in the food chain of aquatic animals. They are thus indirectly injurious to man. Members of the genera *Synchytrium* and *Physoderma* are parasitic on economic plants.

In relatively recent years, mycologists have found various species of *Allomyces,* and *Blastocladiella* to be valuable research tools in the study of morphogenesis. As such, these fungi are certainly of considerable importance to the welfare of man.

SOMATIC STRUCTURES

The most primitive Chytridiomycetes are unicellular and holocarpic. Such organisms have no mycelium and, in the early stages of their development, may lack cell walls. These forms are sometimes separated into a distinct class, the Archimycetes.

In somewhat more advanced species, a few rhizoids (Gr. *rhiza* root + *-oeides* = like) are produced which serve to anchor the unicellular thallus to its substratum. Rhizoids are short, thin branches, superficially resembling a root system. Some species produce a many-branched rhizomycelium (Gr. *rhiza* = root + *mycelium).*

This is an extensive system of hypha-like filaments which usually do not contain nuclei. In still more advanced forms, a scanty mycelium, represented only by a few short hyphal branches, is produced. The most advanced of the Chytridiomycetes have a true mycelial thallus.

Although as previously mentioned, the hyphae of such species are typically coenocytic, a septum is regularly formed at the base of each reproductive organ. Such septa are solid plates.

In addition, the mycelium of the higher Chytridiomycetes may form pseudosepta (Gr. *pseudo* = false). These are septum-like partitions or plugs of a chemical composition different from that of the hyphal walls, which are deposited at intervals in the hyphae.

Asexual Reproduction

As it is in the majority of the lower fungi, the sporangium is the asexual reproductive structure of the Chytridiomycetes. In the young stage, sporangia are full of protoplasm containing many nuclei.

As the sporangium develops, the entire protoplast undergoes cleavage into numerous, minute sections each of which develops into a uninucleate zoospore. After discharge, the zoospore swims for a time, encysts, withdrawing or losing its flagellum in the process, and then germinates, usually after a short rest period.

Sexual Reproduction

Sexual reproduction in the Chytridiomycetes is accomplished by one of the following methods.

Planogametic Copulation

a. *Conjugation of isogamous plano-gametes.* The two gametes are morphologically similar, but physiologically different. They unite in water to form a motile zygote. In some species, gametes originating in the same gametangium will not copulate. Examples of fungi which produce isogamous planogametes are *Olpidium viciae* and *Synchytrium endobioticum.*

b. *Conjugation of anisogamous planogametes.* One planogamete is considerably larger than the other. Copulation takes place in water, and a motile zygote is formed. This type of sexual reproduction is found only in some species in the order Blastocladiales.

c. *Fertilization of a non-motile female gamete (egg) by a motile male gamete (antherozoid).* The male, motile gametes are released from the male gametangia (antheridia) into the water and swim away. Some of them reach the female gametangia (oogonia), whereupon one antherozoid enters each oogonium and unites with the egg within. This type of reproduction is found only in the order Monoblepharidales.

Gametangial Copulation

In the Chytridiomycetes this is accomplished by the transfer of the entire protoplast of one gametangium into the other.

Somatogamy

Fusion between rhizomycelial filaments is said to precede resting spore formation in some species of Chytridiomycetes, but this has not been confirmed.

Classification

The Chytridiomycetes are classified into three orders on the basis of their somatic and reproductive structures. In the order of their probable phylogenetic priority, they are the Chytridiales, the Blastocla-diales, and the Monoblepharidales.

Simple Key to the Orders of the Class Chytridiomycetes

A. True mycelium lacking; rhizomycelium present in some species *Chytridiales*

AA. True mycelium present

B. Sexual reproduction by fusion of planogametes; thick-walled, resistant sporangia characteristically formed

Blastocladiales

BB. Sexual reproduction by fusion of a male planogamete with a female aplanogamete; no resistant sporangia formed.

Monoblepharidales

ORDER CHYTRIDIALES

The organisms included in this order, often referred to as chytrids, are water- or soil-inhabiting species, many of the former parasitic on algae and water molds, many of the latter on vascular plants. There are only a few economically serious parasites in the entire order.

Synchytrium endobioticum causes the disease known as potato wart, which is widely distributed in the potato-growing regions of the world. This fungus causes hypertrophy and hyperplasia of the surface cell layers of the infected potato tubers, converting the latter into unsightly and useless masses of warty tissue.

Physoderma zeaemaydis causes *Physoderma* brown spot of corn. *Urophlyctis alfalfae* causes crown wart of alfalfa, which sometimes results in serious destruction of the crop. Many of the Chytridiales are saprobic and have been cultured on artificial media by special methods.

General Characteristics

The most primitive Chytridiales are endobiotic (Gr. *endos* = within + *bios* = life), living entirely within the cells of their hosts. The mature thallus is surrounded by a cell wall, although the early stages may be naked.

More advanced forms are epibiotic (Gr. *epi* = upon + *bios* = life), producing their reproductive organs on the surface of the host although their somatic structures may be sunken into the host tissues.

There is considerable variation within the group in the structure of the thallus and the reproductive organs. Primitive species are holocarpic, whereas the more advanced species are eucarpic. In the eucarpic forms a system of

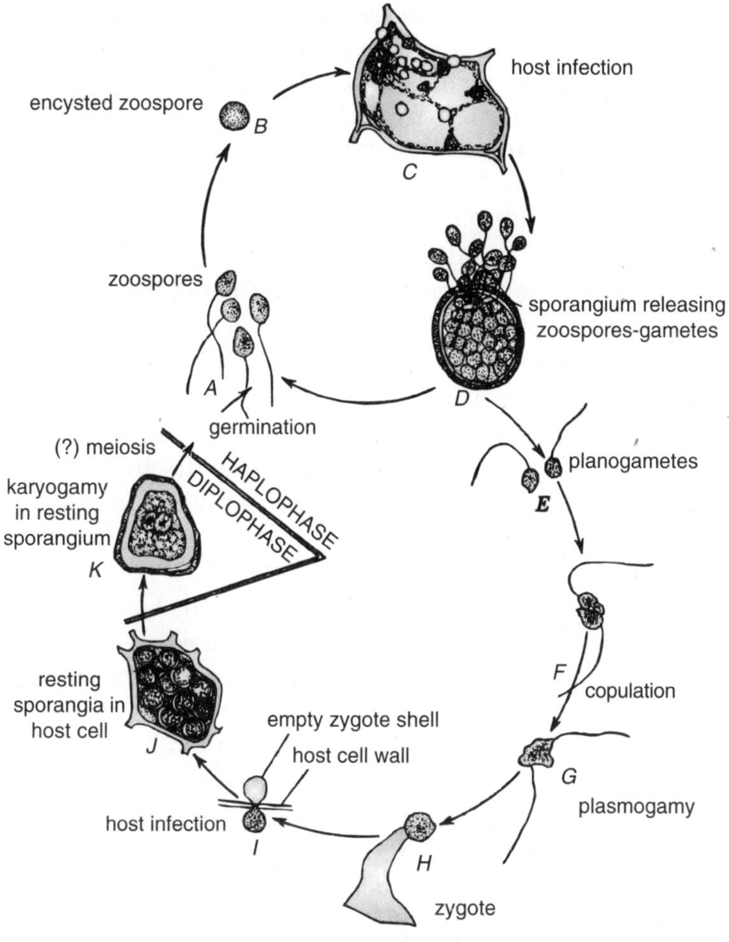

Figure 10.1: Life cycle of Olpidium viciae.

rhizoids is an integral part of the thallus. This system of rhizoids, which is the soma of the fungus as distinguished from the reproductive organs which it bears, may be very limited and inconspicuous or may be well developed. It serves to anchor the organism on its substratum and to absorb food.

If the rhizoidal system bears but a single reproductive structure, the thallus is *monocentric* (Gr. *monos* = alone, single + *kentron* = center); if it bears more than one reproductive structure, it is polycentric (Gr. *poly* = many + *kentron* = center), for such reproductive structures do not arise in tufts from a single point, but are scattered on the thallus, and are interconnected by an often extensive rhizomycelium. Asexual reproduction in the Chytridiales is by means of zoospores which are borne in sporangia and are discharged through one or more papillae.

A discharge papilla is formed on the wall of the sporangium or the tip of a tube issuing from it. Some species always form a well-defined circular cap at the tip of a discharge papilla.

This is the *operculum* (pl. opercula; *L. operculum* = lid). The species which form opercula we designate as operculate. Most species do not form opercula but discharge their zoospores through a pore in the wall of the sporangium or discharge tube formed when the discharge papilla dissolves away. We call such species inoperculate.

Sexual reproduction is accomplished by a variety of methods, some of which will be described in connection with the individual species whose life histories are discussed in the following sections. However, in the majority of species sexual reproduction has not been discovered.

When sexual reproduction occurs the result is a thickwalled resting spore or resting sporangium. Many species, however, are said to form resting spores asexually. Either sexual reproduction does not occur in such species, or it has not been observed.

The fact that some resting spores which had been described as asexually formed were later shown to result from sexual reproduction indicates that all reports of asexually formed resting spores should be carefully reinvestigated.

The order Chytridiales is subdivided into several families, distinguished chiefly on the basis of sporangial form and development. The life histories of the Chytridiales vary to such a degree that no typical example could be selected as a general illustration.

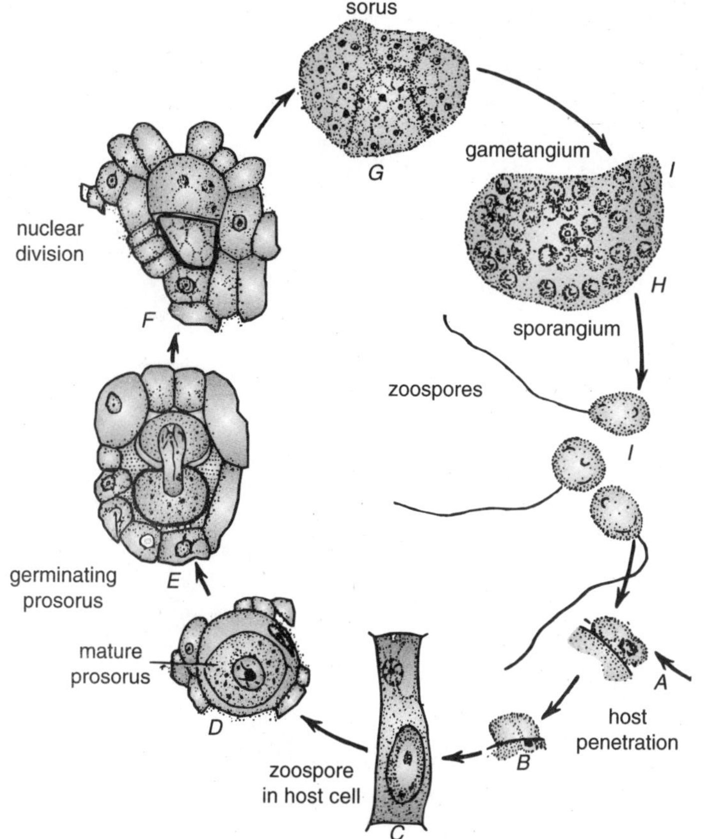

Figure 10.2: Life cycle of Synchytrium endobioticum. (Figure Contd.)

The four species discussed here-one from each of four families-will give you some idea of the diversity existing in this group and will illustrate different types of thalli, spore discharge mechanisms, and sexual reproduction,

FAMILY OLPIDIACEAE

The Olpidiaceae include holocarpic Chytridiales parasitic on algae, fungi, mosses, pollen grains, and flowering plants. The thallus is converted into a single sporangium or resting sporangium; sexual reproduction is by copulation of isoplanbgametes.

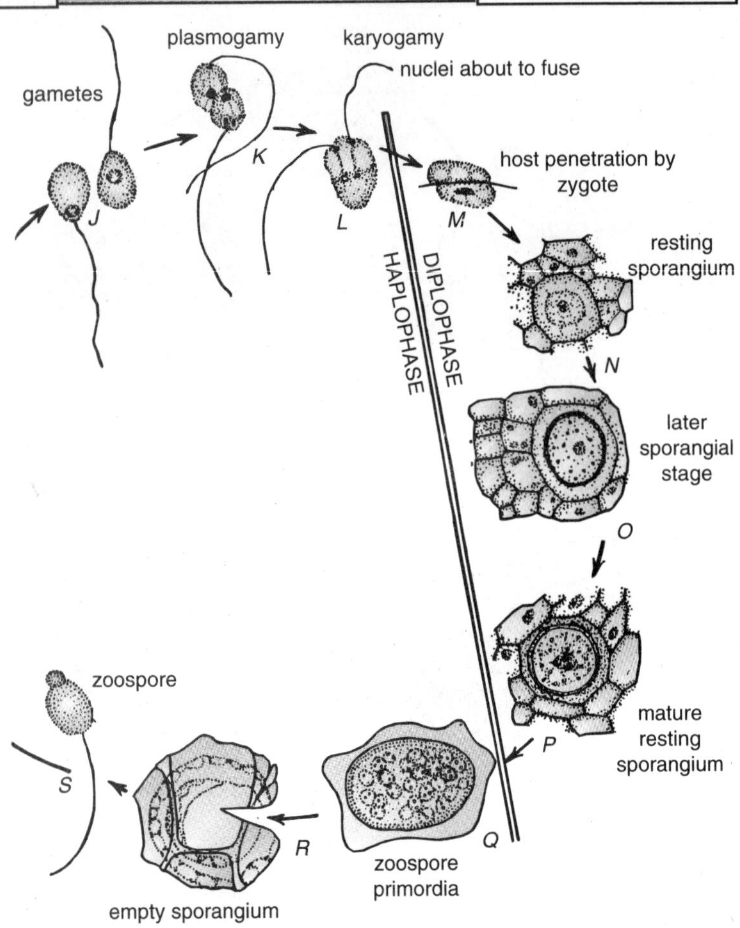

Figure 10.2 (Cont'd).

There are several genera in this family, of which *Olpidium* is probably the best known. *Olpidium viciae*, investigated by Shunsuke Kusano (1912), one of the foremost Japanese mycologists, is parasitic on the leaves and stems of *Vicia unijuga*. When the infected parts of the host are wet, the zoospores escape from the zoosporangium through an exit tube. After a period of swarming, they encyst on the surface of the host.

Infection takes place through a minute pore dissolved

in the host cell wall through which the protoplast of the parasite enters the host cell, leaving the cyst on the outside.

Within the host cell, the parasite becomes attached to the host nucleus, secretes a membrane around itself, and grows into a zoosporangium while its nuclei divide repeatedly.

Zoospores are soon formed which escape and repeat the asexual life cycle. The sexual phase is initiated when two zoospores, behaving as planogametes, copulate. Apparently, the swarm cells which issue from a zoosporangium may behave either as *zoo*spores or planogametes.

The copulating planogametes most frequently originate in different sporangia, but sister planogametes as well have been observed to fuse. Copulation of two gametes results in a motile zygote, but, according to Kusano, karyogamy is postponed for some time.

The zygote infects a host cell in the same manner as does a zoospore, but develops into a thick-walled resting sporangium which is capable of overwintering. The sporangium is binucleate at first, but, before germination, karyogamy takes place, probably followed, by meiosis.

Several nuclear divisions result in a multinucleate structure the protoplast of which eventually undergoes cleavage into presumably uninucleate zoospores. These escape and initiate a new life cycle.

FAMILY SYNCHYTRIACEAE

This is a family of parasitic, holocarpic Chytridiales in which the sporangia, as in the Olpidiaceae, are inoperculate. The thallus here, however, divides into several reproductive organs (sporangia or gametangia) which are enveloped in a common membrane and form a sorus. Sparrow (1960) recognizes three genera, of which *Synchytrium* is by far the largest.

Professor J. S. Karling of Purdue University, who has been studying this genus intensively for a number of years, subdivides it into seven sub-genera. Unfortunately the life cycles of only a few of the 200 or so species of *Synchytrium* are known in detail.

One of the best-known species is *Synchytrium endobioticum,* and a description of its life history, based on the excellent account given by Miss K. M. Curtis (1921), a British mycologist, will be described . As mentioned before, *Synchytrium endobioticum* is a serious parasite of potato tubers, causing black wart disease.

Infection of the potato tuber in the ground takes place in the spring when the zoospores, released in great numbers from infected parts of plants, swim in a film of water present in the soil. Under suitable conditions, the uniflagellate zoospore dissolves a minute pore in the epidermal wall of the host and penetrates, leaving its flagellum outside.

Once within the epidermal potato cell, the amoeboid spore sinks to the bottom of the cell or is carried there by protoplasmic streaming. Absorbing food from the surrounding protoplast, the parasite remains unicellular but grows in size, its nucleus becoming greatly enlarged. After reaching a certain size, it secretes a thick, golden-brown wall, and the structure is now the mature *prosorus* (pl. *prosori*; Gr. *pro* = before + *soros* = heap). Meanwhile, as the result of hypertrophy, the host cell has become greatly enlarged and pear-shaped.

The surrounding epidermal and cortical cells have been stimulated to divide, forming a tumor or wart-like tissue from which the disease gets its name. The infected cell is in the center and is surrounded by a rosette of more or less hardened epidermal cells.

The prosorus now occupies the lower half of the infected host cell, which, by this time, is dead. Soon after maturing, .the prosorus germinates within the host cell. Its wall ruptures, and the protoplast, surrounded by a very thin hyaline membrane, pushes out into the upper half of the host cell. Repeated mitotic divisions of the nucleus now take place.

The number of nuclei at this stage is in the neighbor-

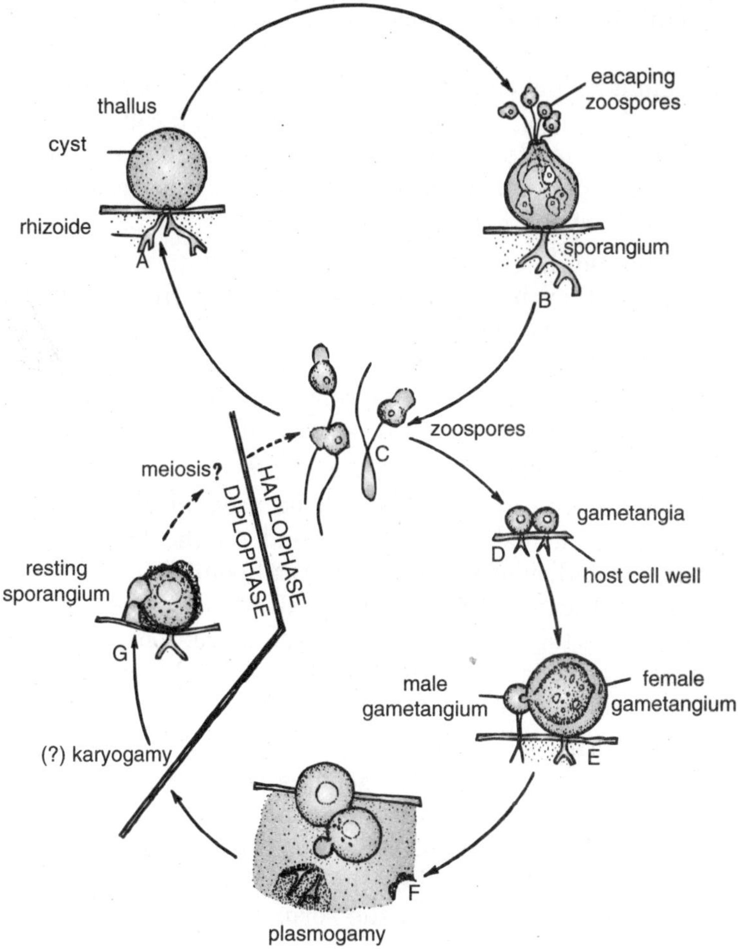

Figure 10.3: Life cycle of Rhizophidium couchii.

hood of thirty-two. A number of thin hyaline walls are now laid down in such a way as to divide the prosorus into from four to nine multinucleate segments. Repeated nuclear divisions increase the number of nuclei in each of these segments until from 200 to 300 have been formed.

Each prosoral portion thus develops into a sporangium or a gametangium, depending on the environment. This mass of sporangia is the sorus. If water is abundantly present, zoospores are formed. If, on the other hand, a period of drought sets in, the motile cells released are planogametes instead of zoospores, and fuse in pairs to form zygotes. According to Miss Curtis, lack of water at a certain period in the development of the fungus affords a maturation period between formation and release which is necessary for the formation of gametes.

If the motile cells are released immediately after their formation, they behave as zoospores. In either case, the cell in which they are formed is the same, and may be called a zoosporangium or a gametangium, depending on the behavior of the motile cells released. Here then is one example of the physiology of a structure being controlled by the environment.

Whether the motile cells will be asexual zoospores or sex cells (gametes) seems to depend on the presence or absence of sufficient water at a critical point in their development, and can be controlled at will by the experimenter, as Miss Curtis showed. In nature, more zoospores are formed at the beginning than at the end of the season, and the reverse is true for gametes.

The entire protoplast of each sporangium becomes segmented into as many portions as there are nuclei, and each minute portion, consisting of a nucleus with its surrounding cytoplasm, develops into a uninucleate, uniflagellate zoospore. When the zoospores are mature, the sporangia are forced out of the sorus on the surface of the host.

The zoospores now escape in the presence of a film of water and initiate a series of new infections, thus completing the asexual phase of the life cycle. This phase may he repeated several times during the season.

As mentioned above, under certain conditions the segments of the prosorus develop into gametangia. These are indistinguishable from zoosporangia except for the fact that they give rise to planogametes, which are somewhat smaller than the zoospores, and which copulate in pairs.

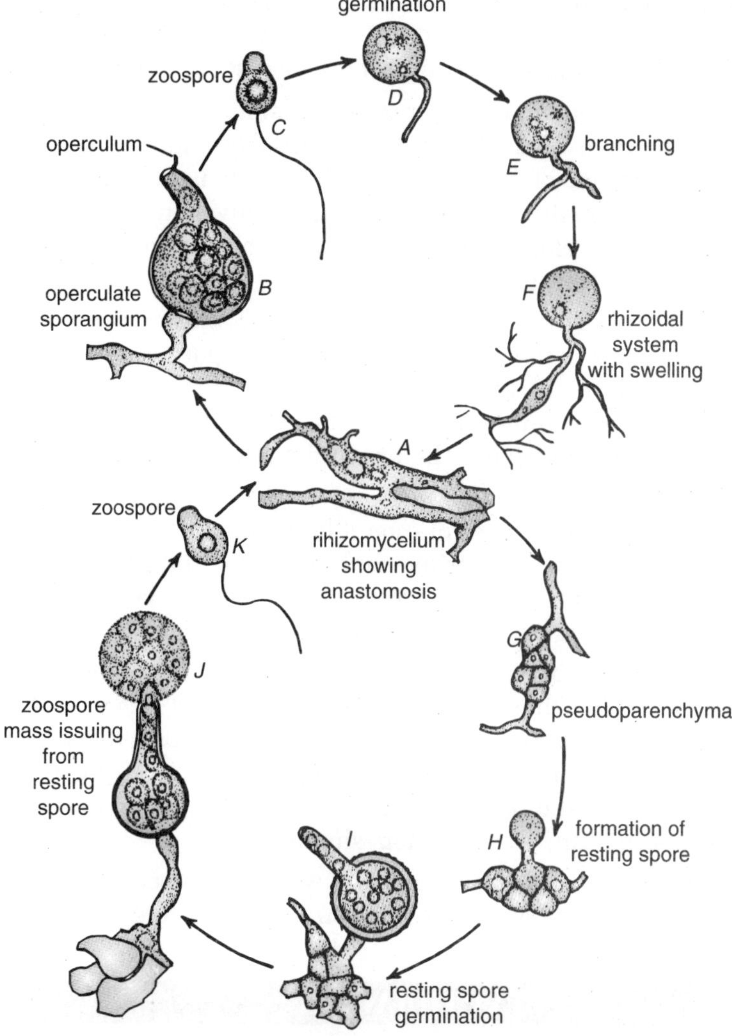

Figure 10.4: Life cycle of Nowakowskiella ramosa.

It appears that planogametes originating in the same gametangium do not copulate, but that planogametes from different gametangia in the same sorus may fuse. There seems to be, therefore, a physiological differentiation between gametes in different gametangia.

Copulation of gametes takes place in a film of water on

the surface of the host or in the soil; karyogamy follows plasmogamy, and the biflagellate zygote swims about for some time before it finally comes to rest on the host.

The zygote now penetrates an epidermal cell in the same manner as described for the zoospore, and soon sinks to the bottom of the infected cell, which is stimulated to divide repeatedly. As a result of these divisions and of the pressures developed, the infected cell is buried rather deeply within the tissues.

The parasite now enlarges, and the formation of a heavy wall around it converts it into a resting sporangium which remains dormant through the winter. The following spring a number of granules appear in the cytoplasm of the resting sporangium. These are the primordia of the zoospores being formed.

During zoospore formation a large amount of chromatin is extruded from the primordial granules, and Miss Curtis concluded that, since she was unable to observe meiosis, this chromatin extrusion may be the equivalent of meiosis.

However, in view of what happens in all other fungi whose cytology has been carefully investigated it is probable that meiosis does occur at this point. The zoospores which are liberated from the resting sporangium are larger than those released earlier in the life history from the zoosporangium, but function similarly.

Other species of *Synchytrium* which have been investigated in some detail are *Synchytrium fulgens* and *Synchytrium australe.*

FAMILY PHLYCTIDIACEAE–

The Phlyctidiaceae include about 100 species of eucarpic Chytridiales the thallus of which consists of a single cell (cyst) from which a haustorium or a group of rhizoids is developed. The cyst, which grows from a zoospore, is converted into a zoosporangium or a gametangium.

Sexual reproduction is by gametangial copulation, which results in the formation of a resting sporangium. *Rhizophid-*

ium 1 is the largest of the eighteen genera included in this family by Sparrow (1960). *Rhizophidium couchii* is one of the best-known species in this family.

It is named after Dr. J. N. Couch of the University of North Carolina, an eminent student of the lower fungi, who first discovered this species. *Rhizophidium couchii is* parasitic on *Spirogyra,* a green alga which you have undoubtedly studied in general botany, and has been reported from the United States and from Europe on that host.

According to Couch (1932), the zoospore settles on *a Spirogyra* filament and sends a rhizoidal process into the protoplast of the host through the wall. The zoospore, now in the form of a cyst, grows and develops into a sporangium in which a number of zoospores are delimited.

At maturity, a number of thin places develop in the wall and bulge out in the form of papillae because of internal pressure. Eventually the papillae burst and the spores emerge and swim away after first lingering near the mouth of the exit papilla. Sexual reproduction takes place by gametangial copulation.

The female gametangium (oogonium) develops from a zoospore in the same way as described for the sporangium except that no zoospores are formed. A second zoospore now attaches itself to the oogonium.

It does not enlarge, however, but remains small and behaves as an antheridium, emptying its contents into the oogonium through a pore or short fertilization tube. After receiving the male protoplast, the oogonium develops into a thick-walled resting spore. Sparrow (1933) found that in his material the two gametangia became initiated at about the same time as equal-sized zoospores, one enlarging, the other remaining small.

Germination of the resting spore of an unidentified species closely resembling *Rhizophidium couchii* takes place by the formation of a pore in the thick wall and the emergence of the protoplast, which develops into a sporangium. An apical exit papilla develops and deliquesces and the zoospores escape.

FAMILY MEGACHYTRIACEAE

This is a relatively small family which includes three genera of operculate, polycentric Chytridiales. There are eleven species altogether, all of them aquatic saprobes living on decaying plant materials.

Nowakowskiella ramosa, which will serve as our example of this type of chytrid, appears to be widely distributed. It was originally discovered in India in 1907 and has since been found in Europe, Africa, and North and South America. The fungus is saprobic, living in nature on plant debris.

The thallus consists of profuse, richly branched filaments which are occasionally septate and which bear terminal or intercallary sporangia and resting spores.

The zoospores are normally uniflagellate, although spores with two, three, and four flagella have also been seen. A crescent-shaped nuclear cap, which surrounds a third or more of the centrally located nucleus, is a conspicuous characteristic of the zoospore.

The nuclear cap disappears when the zoospore comes to rest before germination. The sessile zoospore now germinates by a single germ tube which begins to branch dichotomously.

Soon a swelling is formed. The nucleus may remain in the spore until a swelling occurs in the filament, and then divide, the daughter nuclei migrating into the swelling, or it may migrate into the germ tube which then swells around the nucleus.

As the thallus continues to grow, it branches dichotomously and produces more swellings. These are globose, spindleshaped, or irregular in shape. According to Roberts (1948), no crosswalls are formed in the extensions of the thallus.

Many-branched rhizoids, arising from various parts of the thallus, penetrate into the substratum and may expand into bladder-like structures. The nuclei are confined to the swellings. Neither the isthmuses which connect the swellings nor the rhizoids possess nuclei.

After the thallus has grown to some extent in the manner described above, filaments arise from the swellings or the isthmuses connecting them. These filaments, which Roberts calls flexuous filaments, branch repeatedly in a dichotomous manner and eventually form elongate, spindle-shaped swellings in which many nuclei may usually be seen.

Roberts believes that the flexuous filaments themselves are nucleated. Zoosporangia are now formed from the swellings of the flexuous filaments. These are terminal or intercallary. As the swelling increases in size and becomes globose, a septum is formed at its base.

Elongated, narrow vacuoles appearing in the cytoplasm cleave the contents of the zoosporangium into uninucleate portions which develop into zoospores. The wall now thickens, and an operculum forms in the shape of an arched dome at the tip of the sporangium.

The wall remains thin at the point of its attachment to the operculum. At the time of germination, the operculum dehisces and is either forced off the sporangium or is turned back by internal pressure as if it were on a hinge.

The zoospores escape individually. Anywhere from four to about forty zoospores may be formed in each sporangium. The average number has been determined by Roberts as about thirty-six. The resting spores or resting sporangia of *Nowakowskiella ramosa* develop from pseudoparenchymatous tissue, which is formed in various ways.

Several observers have described a fusion of cells which initiates the formation of the pseudoparenchyma, but no one has observed karyogamy, so that the significance of this fusion is not clear. The resting sporangia are therefore said to develop asexually, but the nuclear behavior which precedes their formation needs further investigation.

Resting bodies either germinate directly by releasing zoospores, and thus behave as resting sporangia, or produce a thin-walled sporangium which releases zoospores. *Nowak-*

owskiella ramosa may be cultivated in the laboratory on cellophane in sterilized river water. The optimum temperature for its development appears to be 16-18° C.

You have now studied the life histories of four of the chytrids. The first two are holocarpic and live inside the host, passing their entire life cycle within a single host cell. They represent the most primitive fungi known.

Their soma is unicellular-no mycelium; the *zoosporangium* is a simple structure which develops directly from the zoospore. In one case *(Olpidium) a singe sporangium is farmed* from each zoospore; in the other *(Synchytrium)* a whole sorus, of sporangia is developed. Sexual reproduction is by copulation of isoplanogametes released in water.

This is the most primitive method of sexual reproduction known. What is more, the behavior of the swarm cells as zoospores or gametes appears to be determined by the environment, and sex is not the definite phenomenon that it is in higher organisms.

A resting sporangium is formed in both species as a result of sexual reproduction. In the next example *(Rhizophidium) you* should note certain important differences. The thallus is eucarpic. It develops rhizoids which constitute the somatic phase of the fungus and which do not develop into any other structure.

They anchor the organism to the host and probably act as absorbing organs. The parasite is enabled to reproduce outside the host, sending only rhizoids into the host cells instead of being entirely immersed. This is the beginning of differentiation. Rhizoids are not hyphae, but a primitive type of soma.

The sporangium still develops directly from the zoospore. Sexual reproduction, however, is more advanced than in *Olpidium* or *Synchytrium.* Instead of motile gametes being released in the water and left to unite by chance, two gametangia contact each other and one sheds its contents into the other, sometimes through an especially developed fertilization tube. A resting structure again

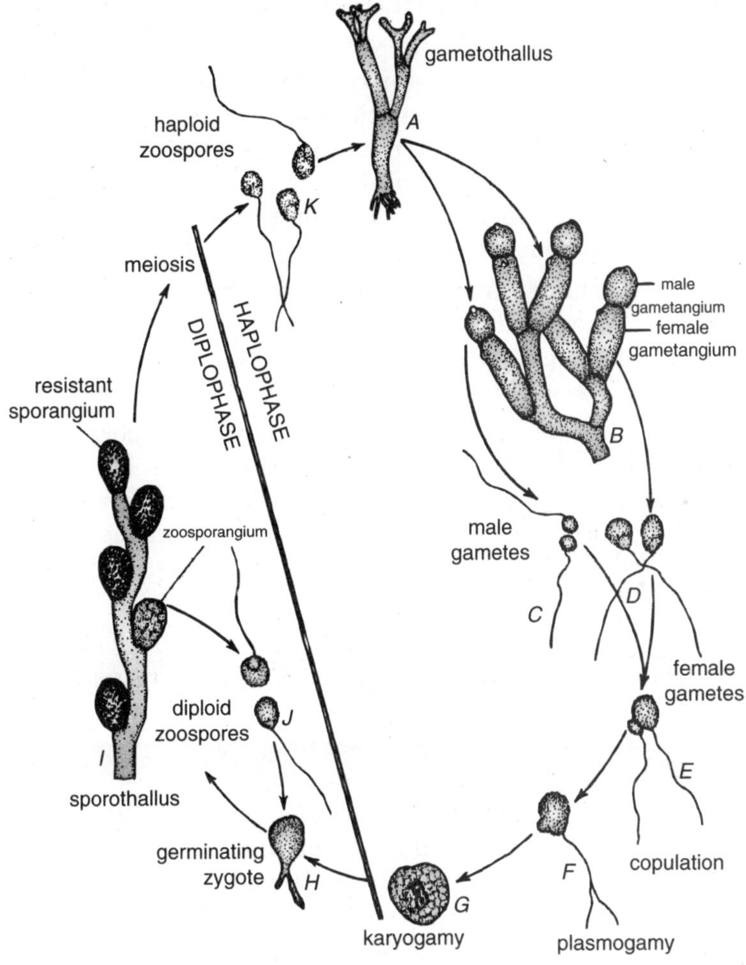

Figure 10.5: Life cycle of Allmyces macrogynus.

develops as a result of fertilization. This method of fertilization is sometimes called oiigamous or oomycetous, one of the gametes being non-motile, acting as an egg, the other flowing through the pore or tube and fusing with the egg.

Note that in none of these three fungi has meiosis actually been observed. Fungal chromosomes are very difficult to study because of their minute size. In

Nowakowskiella, the fourth chytrid studied, the thallus is not only eucarpic but also extensively developed.

Of interest is the apparent differentiation of the rhizomycelium into a somatic and a reproductive phase. Karling (1944) does not mention it, but Roberts (1948) makes a considerable point of this situation. Another interesting development is the presence of nuclei in the flexuous filaments of the "reproductive phase" of the thallus.

Such filaments certainly approach the structure of hyphae. Whether they are of significance in the evolutionary origin of fungal mycelium we cannot say. Sometimes superficial resemblances lead to erroneous conclusions.

The presence of an operculum in the zosporangia of *Nowakowskiella* should not go unnoticed. This is certainly a distinct structure which indicates some differentiation in the reproductive organ. No strong evidence can be presented at this time in favor of the existence of sexual reproduction in *Nowakowskiella.*

Fusion of cells, however, is undeniable. This may indicate that at least a parasexual cycle is in operation. We have much to learn about the chytrids!

ORDER BLASTOCLADIALES

The Blastocladiales are chiefly water molds or soil inhabitants, characterized by the production of thick-walled, resistant sporangia, usually with pitted walls. Another feature which links the members of this order is a prominent structure, the nuclear cap, located near the center of the zoospore or planogamete.

The characters of the thallus, of the sporangia, and of the sex organs, where known, vary greatly and can be discussed only in connection with individual groups.

Three families are now recognized: Coelomomycetaceae, Catenariaceae, and Blastocladiaceae. Of these, the last is the best known. The Coelomomycetaceae are obligately parasitic in the body cavities of mosquito larvae.

They are of particular interest mycologically because

their hyphae are naked, and somewhat resemble the strands of a myxomycete plasmodium. The entire mycelium is converted into thick-walled resistant sporangia which germinate, releasing a mass of zoospores.

Sexual reproduction is unknown in this family. The Catenariaceae are a small family of parasitic or saprobic fungi. Some species are parasitic on microscopic animals, others on fungi; some are saprobic on plant and animal debris.

The thallus is tubular, walled, and septate. It bears numerous rhizoids. The Catenariaceae reproduce both asexually and sexually. Sexual reproduction is by means of isogamous planogametes.

FAMILY BLASTOCLADIACEAE

The soma of the Blastocladiaceae is well developed, usually consisting of (1) a group of well-formed, branched rhizoids by means of which the fungus attaches itself to the substratum; (2) a stout or . slender trunk-like body; and (3) numerous side branches, usually dichotomously branched, on which the reproductive organs are formed.

In some species, the thallus is simple rather than branched. The walls of the hyphae give a chitin reaction. The hyphae are non-septate, but pseudosepta, in the form of thickened rings, are present in some species.

In species known to reproduce sexually, two types of thalli are produced: gametothalli (haploid thalli) and sporothalli (diploid thalli).

These two types, however, are distinguishable only by the types of reproductive organs they bear; the gametothalli normally produce gametangia, the sporothalli sporangia.

Sexual reproduction takes place by planogametic copulation. The copulating swarmers are either isogametes or anisogametes, depending on the species.

The Blastocladiaceae are subdivided into four genera of which *Allomyces* and *Blastocladiella are* the best known.

GENUS ALLOMYCES

Chiefly because of the early work of Hans Kniep, followed by the researches of Winslow Hatch, Ralph Emerson, Charles Wilson, Leonard Machlis, Gilbert Turian, and others, we now pbssess a great deal of information on the life cycles, cytology, genetics, and physiology of at least some members of this interesting genus, first discovered in India in 1911 by E. J. Butler, the distinguished British mycologist, and subsequently found to be widely distributed over the globe.

Three types of life cycle have been discovered in *Allomyces,* and on that basis Emerson (1941) established three sub-genera: *Euallomyces, Cystogenes,* and *Brachyallomyces.* The following discussion refers to *Euallomyces.*

Species of the sub-genus *Euallomyces* exhibit a definite alternation of generations, haploid gametothalli alternating with diploid sporothalli. The two types of thalli are indistinguishable until they begin to form reproductive organs.

The well-developed hyphae are dichotomously branched. Their walls consist chiefly of chitin, glucan, and ash. Gametothalli and sporothalli of the same strain have the same general nutritional requirements. When they reach a certain stage of maturity, the gametothalli produce colorless female gametangia and orange male gametangia in close proximity to one another and usually in a 1:1 ratio.

The orange pigment is in the cytoplasm which eventually becomes differentiated into male gametes, and is due to y-carotene synthesized by the fungus. The male gametangia are noticeably smaller than the female and may be borne on the latter *(Allomyces macrogynus)* or below them *(Allomyces arbuscula).*

Both types of gametangia release motile gametes (planogametes) in the water. The gametes are posteriorly uniflagellate and of the same general structure as zoospores typical of the Blastocladiales in general. Each exhibits, as do the zoospores, a prominent nuclear cap consisting chiefly of RNA.

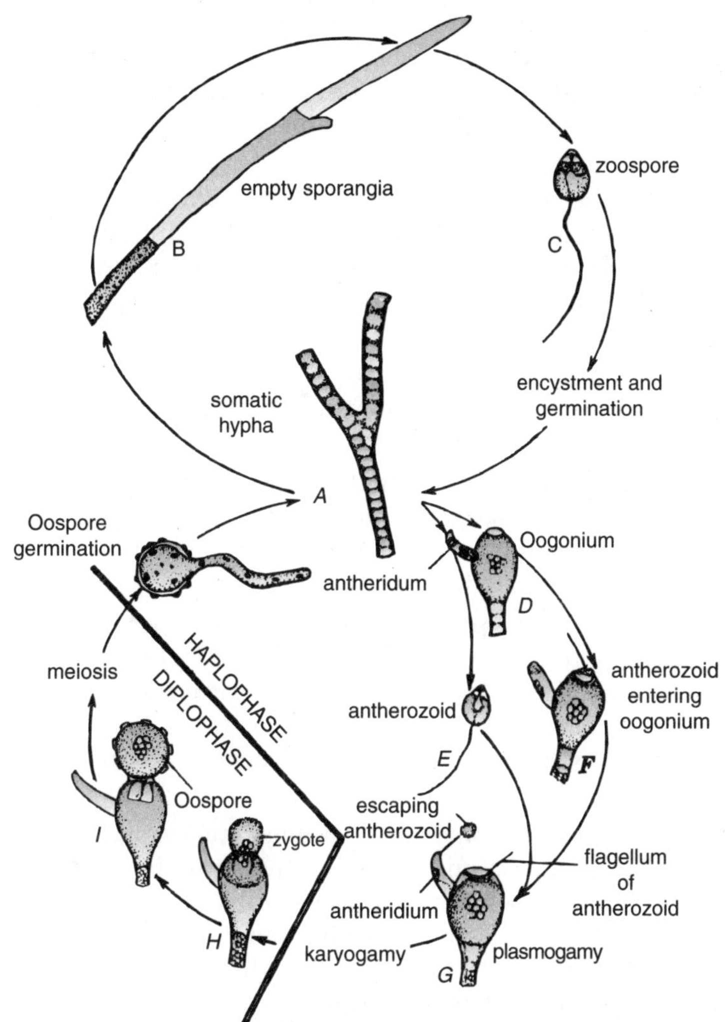

Figure 10.6: Life cycle of Monoblepharis polymorpha.

The male gametes are orange and about half the size of the female gametes. Attracted by the sexual hormone sirenin (Gr. *seirin* = siren) produced by the female gametes, the male gametes copulate with the latter in pairs very soon after their release from the gametangia.

Copulation, however, may be completely prevented in culture by the addition of boric acid (dose of 1/15,000) to the water in which the gametothalli are growing. Karyogamy follows plasmogamy, and the motile zygote comes to rest, loses its flagella, rounds up, and soon germinates. First a germ tube is produced which develops into rhizoids.

Then the main body of the zygote enlarges and gives rise to the first hyphal tube, which elongates, branches dichotomously, and develops into a diploid sporothallus.

At maturity, the sporothalli form two types of sporangia: thinwalled, elongated, colorless zoosporangia (mitosporangia), and oval, thick-walled, pitted, resistant sporangia (meiosporangia) which contain melanin pigments and appear reddish brown.

The zoosporangia germinate soon after their formation, releasing diploid zoospores (mitospores) which swim; about for a time, round up, and give rise to sporothalli, thus repeating the diploid generation.

The resistant sporangia require a rest period. of 2-8 weeks or more before they germinate, but Machlis and Ossia (1953) have been able to reduce the maturation period of certain strains of *Allomyces arbuscula* to as short a time as 2 days by changing the culture medium at the proper stage of development.

Meiosis in the resistant sporangia takes place at the time of germination and results in the formation of haploid zoospores (meiospores) which are slightly smaller than the diploid zoospores. Upon germination, meiospores, being haploid, give rise to gametothalli, which produce gametangia instead of sporangia.

Cytological investigations which established that meiosis takes place in the resistant sporangia also revealed two general series of strains in *Euallomyces*. The basic haploid chromosome number in one series is 8. Strains with 16, 24, and 32 chromosomes have also been found, indicating that polyploidy has occurred.

This is the *Allomyces arbuscula* series in which the male gametangia are hypogynous (located below the female). In the other series the basic chromosome number is 14, and strains have been found which appear to be polyploids with 28 and 56 (?) chromosomes.

This is the *Allomyces macrogynus* series in which the male gametangia are epigynous (located terminally, above the female). Natural hybrids with other chromosome numbers have also been found. Interspecific hybrids, different from both parent types, have been obtained artificially.

One interesting variation is represented by gametothalli which are nearly all (99+ per cent) female or nearly all male. Inasmuch as no sex chromosomes are involved here, sex determination is not genetically controlled-in the usual sense of the terms-and the explanation must be sought elsewhere.

Turian (1960) induced female strains to revert partially to maleness by growing them on a synthetic medium with acetate as the single source of carbon and traces of coenzyme A, or with glucose as the carbon source enriched with glycine and folic acid.

The same media induced a high degree of maleness (80-90 per cent) in a normally bisexual strain with a 1: 1 male : female ratio. Thus we are approaching a physiological explanation for the morphological differentiation of sex in this fungus.

Another interesting result of genetic experiments was proof that *Allomyces javanicus,* originally discovered in Java and subsequently in several other widely separated localities, is a natural hybrid between *Allomyces arbuscula* and *Allomyces macrogynus.* By experimentally hybridizing these two species in the laboratory, Emerson and Wilson, (1954) obtained *Allomyces javanicu s*

GENUS BLASTOCLADIELLA

This genus differs from *Allomyces* in that its thalli are minute, consisting in most species of a short unbranched hypha bearing a system of rhizoids at the lower end and a single reproductive organ at the tip. *Blastocladiella variabilis,* with a *E.uallornyces* life cycle, consists of four types of thalli, each bearing a zoi sporangium, a resistant sporangium, a male gametangium, or a female gametangium. The planogametes in this genus are isogamous.

If you know the life cycle of *Euallomyces, you* should be able to construct an illustrated life cycle of *Blastocladiella variabilis.* Try it and then check your results with Figure 3 in Emerson's "The Biology of the Water Molds" (1955).

Blastocladiella emersonii, another species in this genus, has been studied intensively by Cantino and his associates. The organism consists of three kinds of morphologically distinct thalli bearing a thin-walled colorless sporangium, a thin-walled orange sporangium, or a thick-walled resistant sporangium.

All sporangia produce posteriorly uniflagellate swarmers, the first two colorless ones, the last orange-colored. No one type of swarmer is capable of fusing with any other in the usual sense, but there is good reason to believe that cytoplasmic exchange may take place when a colorless warmer and an orange swarmer of certain strains remain in contact for some time.

Cytoplasmic bridges temporarily formed between contacting swarmers have been observed. Studies on the morphogenesis of *Blastocladiella emersonii* have shown that CO_2 plays an important role in determining whether a sporeling will develop into a thallus bearing a resistant sporangium or a thallus bearing a zoosporangium. Essentially all sporelings exposed to $NaHCO_3$ develop into thalli bearing resistant sporangia, whereas ordinarily none does.

Another important discovery concerned the effect of light on growth of *Blastocladiella emersonii.* It is now known that the organism grows better in light than in darkness and that the stimulatory effect involves increased CO_2 fixation under the influence of lights Further studies are linking biochemical changes with morphological development so that little by little we are beginning to understand the physicochemical basis of structure in this fungus.

There are some important advancements which you should note in the Blastocladiales. First of all, the thallus is now large enough to be seen with the unaided eye. This increase in "size over the microscopic chytrids is in itself notable, for it permits considerable differentiation.

The soma is now composed of true 'hyphae which carry on the metabolism of the fungus and form reproductive organs on their branches. No striking evolutionary advance is to be noted in the sporangia or zoospores, except, of course, for the occurrence of diploid zoospores which reproduce the sporothallus.

In sexual reproduction we find these fungi employing the primitive method of planogametic copulation which we observed in the simpler chytrids, but in *Allomyces* the planogametes have become unequal in size (anisogametes) and the two types are borne in separate, distinguishable gametangia.

This differentiation represents an advancement over isoplanogametes and the method by which the latter are produced. Another important fact is the lack of a sexual resting spore in this group. Its function has been taken over by the resistant sporangia.

The definite alternation of generations that occurs in *Allomyces* and *Blastocladiella is* another interesting phenomenon that sets these fungi apart from all others.

ORDER MONOBLEPHARIDALES

The Monoblepharidales, closely related to the Blastocladiales, represent the culmination of the Chytridiomycetes. Only a few species are known, most of them aquatic. These are distributed among the genera *Monoblepharis, Monoblepharella,* and *Gonapodya.*

The first of these is placed in the family Monoblepharidaceae. The other two genera constitute the family Gonapodyaceae. Of no direct economic importance, these fungi are nevertheless of interest because of their method of sexual reproduction, found nowhere else among the fungi.

FAMILY MONOBLEPHARIDACEAE

Monoblepharis polymorpha Cornu

In *Monoblepharis polymorpha* the somatic thallus consists of hyphae whose protoplasm, which is highly vacuolated, appears foamy. This foamy appearance is characteristic of the entire order. The hyphae are well developed with many branches. Elongated sporangia are borne singly at the hyphal tips.

They are generally no larger in diameter than the somatic hyphae. The sporangia are subtended by a septum. Multinucleate from the first, the sporangial protop ast becomes divided into many uninucleate portions, each of which develops into a posteriorly uniflagellate zoospore.

The zoospores are released from the tip of the sporangium, swim for a time, become rounded, and germinate, each by a germ tube, forming a new mycelium. The same thallus which produces the sporangia produces gametangia when subjected to higher temperatures.

The gametangia are easily distinguishable as male and female, the narrow, elongated antheridia being borne on the rounded, larger oogonia. A number of uniflagellate gametes, called antherozoids, are formed within and released from each antheridium.

The protoplast of the oogonium becomes rounded and forms a uninucleate *oosphere* (Gr. *oon* = egg + *sphaera* = sphere). An oosphere is defined by Fitzpatrick (1930) as "a single, large, spherical, naked, non-ciliate, and practically non-motile gamete."

This is the egg. In *Monoblepharis* it is uninucleate. After the antherozoids (sperms) are released from the antheridia, they swim or creep over to the oogonia. A single sperm enters the oogonium through a papilla present in the oogonial wall, penetrates the oosphere, and fuses with it (plasmogamy).

The fertilized egg soon emerges from the oogonium, and, while still attached to the oogonial wall by a hyaline collar, secretes a thick wall around itself and develops into an *oospore* (Gr. *oon* = egg + *sporos* = seed, spore).

An oospore is a thickwalled spore which develops from an oosphere either through fertilization or parthenogenesis (Gr. *parthenos* = virgin ± *genesis* = birth). Karyogarny is delayed until the oospore wall is partially formed. The oospore germinates under favorable conditions by producing a hypha which develops into a new thallus. Meiosis probably takes place during the germination of the oospore, when the zygote nucleus first divides.

FAMILY GONAPODYACEAE

This family differs from the Monoblepharidaceae chiefly in the behavior of the zygote. In *Monoblepharella* fertilization of the oosphere occurs in the oogonium as in *Monoblepharis,* but the male gamete is only partially engulfed by the female, its flagellum remaining outside. The zygote now issues from the oogonium and swims free in the water, propelled by the flagellum of the antherozoid.

In *Gonapodya* the female gametangium may form more than one gamete. The eggs are fertilized either within the oogonium or after being discharged. The zygotes behave as in *Monoblepharella,* using the flagellum of the antherozoid to propel themselves through the water. The oospores develop a thick, smooth wall.

The following then are the important changes which have occurred in the Monoblepharidales from previous orders studied. The, mycelial type of soma, which consists of well-developed hyphae, and which is characteristic of the vast. majority of fungi, is now well established.

The elongated hypha-like sporangium, characteristic of a great many water molds, is found here for the first time. Sexual reproduction as it occurs in the Monoblepharidales is found nowhere else in the fungous world.

However, the important development in this order is

the first appearance of the definite oosphere which, upon fertilization, develops into a definite oospore. The oospore germinates by germ tube instead of forming zoospores as do the resting sporangia of the Chytridiales.

Hyphochytridiomycetes

The *Hyphochytridiomycetes* are aquatic, freshwater or marine chytrid-like fungi whose motile cells are *anteriorly* uniflagellate, possessing a flagellum of the tinsel type. They are parasitic on algae and fungi or saprobic on plant and insect debris in the waters in which they live. All are included in the single order *Hyphochytriales*.

As compared to the *Chytridiomycetes*, the class *Hyphochytridiomycetes* is very small, consisting of about fifteen known species. There is, however, considerable variation among these fungi, reflected in their classification into six (or seven) genera which have been placed in three families: *Anisolpidiaceae*, *Rhizidiomycetaceae*, and *Hyphochytriaceae*.

The resemblance of the Hyphochytriales to the chytrids is so great that for many years the few known species were included in the *Chytridiales* in spite of the difference in the structure of the flagellum and its position on the *zoospore*.

As more species were discovered, greater attention was paid to their classification, and it was eventually recognized that these fungi should be treated as a group separate from the *Chytridiales*. The walls of all species which have been investigated contain chitin. In addition, cellulose is present in some.

The thallus, which may be *holocarpic* or *eucarpic*, shows an evolution which parallels that of the *chytridiaceous thallus*. In the holocarpic species the thallus is *endobiotic* and is converted into a *zoosporangium*. In the eucarpic forms the thallus may consist of a single reproductive organ bearing a branched rhizoidal system, or may be *polycentric* and consist of *branched hyphae* with some septa.

The zoosporangia are *inoperculate* and release their zoospores through discharge tubes. The zoospores germinate and reproduce the thallus. Sexual reproduction is known only in the genus *Reessia*, whose systematic position is still uncertain and whose morphology requires reinvestigation.

Rhizidiomyces apophysatus, one of the better-known Hyphochytriales, will serve as our example of this small class of fungi. The following account is based on *Karling's* discussion (1944).

FAMILY RHIZIDIOMYCETACEAE

The Rhizidiomycetaceae include three small *genera*, the largest of which is *Rhizidiomyces* with five species. The thallus is *monocentric*, consisting of a single cell which bears a system of branched rhizoids sunken into the *substratum*, and which becomes converted into a *sporangium*. Sexual reproduction has not been observed.

Resting spores are known only in the monotypic genus *Latrostium. Rhizidiomyces apophysatus* is parasitic on the oogonia of water molds of the family Saprolegniaceae and on the green alga *Vaucheria*. It has also been isolated from soil and pine pollen.

Mycologists have found this fungus in Europe, North and South America, Asia, and Africa. It probably occurs all over the world. *Karling* (1944) gives a full account of the life cycle in his studies of the fungus which he isolated from river water collected in the Amazon Valley of *Brazil*.

The zoospores swim for a time (25-90 minutes), before coming to rest on the host. They round up and soon *germinate*, producing a germ tube which penetrates the

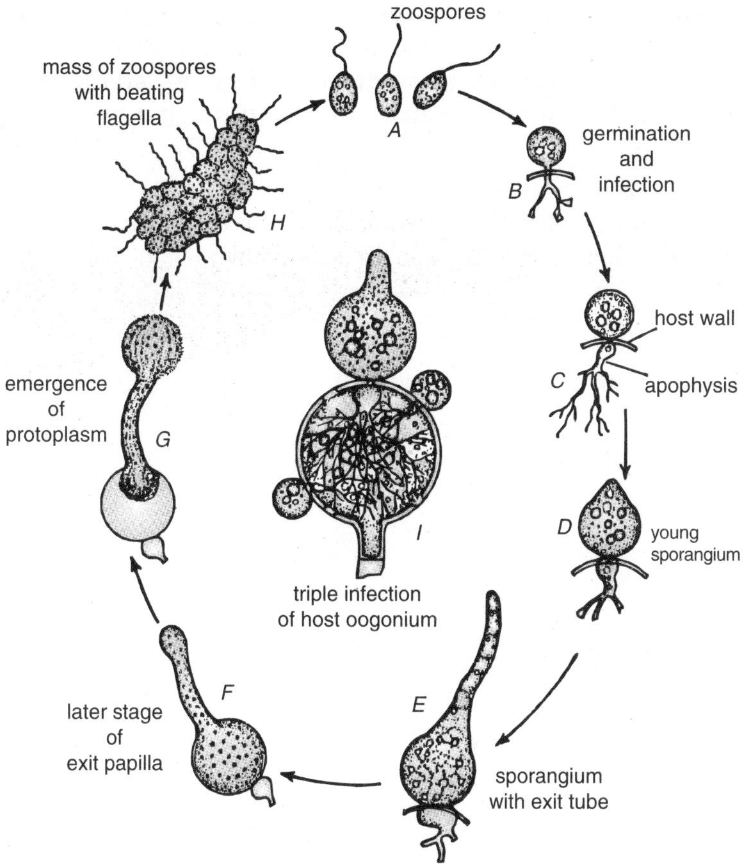

Figure 11.1: Life cycle of Rhizidiomyces apophysatus.

oogonial wall of the host and begins to branch. At this time, a *swelling* is formed on the germ tube just inside the oogonial wall.

As the rhizoidal system develops, the swelling enlarges and becomes an *apophysis* (Gr. *apo* = from + *physis* growth) of the sporangium, which *synchronously* develops from the main part of the zoospore on the surface of the host. As the *sporangium* matures, it develops an exit *papilla* which elongates and forms the discharge tube.

Nuclear divisions have probably taken place in the meantime, and by this time the sporangial protoplast must be *multinucleate*. The *protoplast* now moves up and slowly emerges from the *discharge* tube as a naked *protoplasmic mass* which almost immediately changes shape and becomes cleaved into zoospore initials through a process of *furrowing*.

The zoospores soon become differentiated, the flagella are formed, and the *zoospores* swim away. No sexual reproduction or resting spores are known.

Oomycetes

The class Oomycetes consists of fungi which reproduce asexually by means of biflagellate zoospores, each bearing one tinsel flagellum directed forward and one whiplash flagellum directed backward. Zoospores are borne in sporangia of various types.

The most advanced of the Oomycetes are terrestrial obligate parasites passing their entire life history in the host, and depending on the wind for the dissemination of their spores or spore-like sporangia. Even in these, however, the production of zoospores continues to be common, a strong indication of their aquatic ancestral life.

The somatic structures of the fungi in this class range from a primitive unicellular thallus to a profusely branched, copious, filamentous mycelium, which grows abundantly in the substratum or in the surrounding medium.

The majority of the Oomycetes are eucarpic. Both asexual and sexual reproductive structures occur in most species, but there are considerable gaps in our knowledge of - many life histories in the group.

In the highest forms, which are specialized parasites on plants, the tendency to produce several asexual generations during the growing season, but only one sexual generation, has become firmly established. Zoospores are produced throughout the class except in the most advanced species, in which the sporangium itself assumes the function of a spore and germinates directly by a germ tube which gives rise to the mycelium.

Sexual reproduction is almost always heterogametangic. In the more primitive forms, the entire thallus acts as a gametangium. The formation of oospores is characteristic of all but the most primitive species. oospores originate in the oogonia and mature within them. The central part of the oogonium is differentiated into one or more oospheres. These are typically uninucleate when mature. In some forms they are multinucleate, and the oosphere is then called a *compound oosphere*.

Classification

As considered here, the Oomycetes consist of four orders: Saprolegniales, Leptomitales, Lagenidiales, and Peronosporales. A simplified form of Sparrow's key to these orders is presented below.

Key to the Orders of the Class Oomycetes

A.	Zoospores always formed within the sporangium, diplanetic, monoplanetic, or, rarely, aplanetic	
B.	Holocarpic or eucarpic; hyphae when present without constrictions	*Saprolegniales*
BB.	Eucarpic; hyphae constricted	*Leptomitales*
AA.	Zoospores formed within the sporangium or, if not, then usually within an evanescent vesicle arising from the sporangium; monoplanetic, reniform	
C.	Holocarpic	
CC.	Eucarpic	*Peronosporales*

Importance to Man

Of the four orders in this class, only the Peronosporales affect man's welfare to a great extent. A few species in the Saprolegniales attack economically. important plants, and a few others cause serious diseases of fish, but taken as a whole they are of no great significance. The Peronosporales, on the other hand, include some of the most destructive parasites known, and at least two of them have had a hand-or should we say a hypha!—in shaping the economic history of an important portion of mankind.

These are *Phytophthora infestans,* the cause of late blight of potatoes, and *Plasmopara viticola,* the cause of downy mildew of grapes.

ORDER LAGENIDIALES

General Characteristics

Our modern concept of the Lagenidiales encompasses a rather small group of aquatic fungi parasitic on algae, water molds, small animals, and other forms of aquatic or semiaquatic life. The somatic structure of these fungi is either a simple cell or a very short, unbranched or sparingly branched filament. Sexual reproduction takes place by gametangial copulation, with or without a fertilization tube, and results in the formation of a thickwalled resting spore.

In unicellular species *(Olpidiopsis) the* entire thallus acts as a gametangium. In filamentous species *(Lagenidium)* the filament first becomes divided into cells by the formation of septa, and then some or all of these cells change into gametangia or sporangia.

Sparrow (1960) divides the Lagenidiales into three families the *Olpidiopsidaceae*, the *Sirolpidiaceae*, and the *Lagenidiaceae*. The *Olpidiopsidaceae* have a unicellular thallus.

The two other families, especially the Lagenidiaceae, are more typical of the order. We shall, therefore, discuss only the Lagenidiaceae in this book to give you a general idea of the morphology and life cycle of these fungi.

FAMILY LAGENIDIACEAE

Life History

Although I can discuss with you a general life history for the Lagenidiaceae, the truth is that the life history of

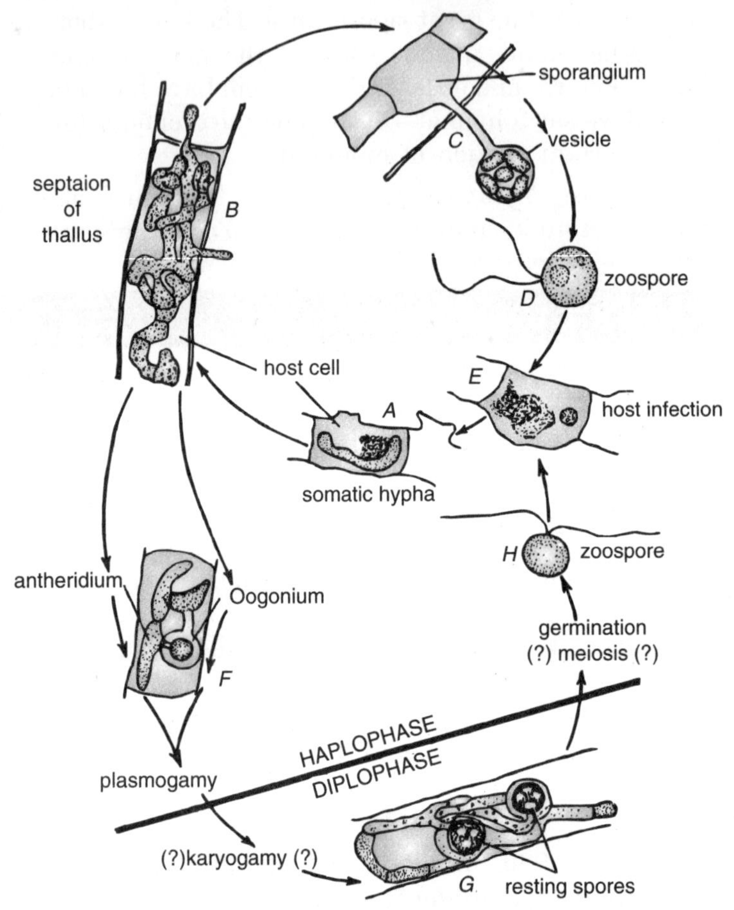

Figure 12.1: Life cycle of Lagenidium rabenhorstii.

not a single species has been worked out completely. This remark implies no lack of appreciation for the splendid work of such men as Zopf, Scherffel, Cook, Couch, Dangeard, and Sparrow, who have studied these organisms; it merely indicates the difficulty of such an undertaking.

These fungi are not easy to find, and most of them will not grow in culture under any known conditions. Furthe-rmore, their nuclei are so minute that cytological studies are extremely difficult. Here are some things we know about the Lagenidiaceae.

The thallus of most is filamentous, but not well developed. There is no extensive mycelium to be found, only a small filament which may or may not be branched, growing in a cell of an alga or the body of some unfortunate microscopic animal that has been attacked.

After the thallus reaches a certain stage of maturity, septa are formed which divide the tubular thallus into a few cells. Each of these Bells now changes into a reproductive organ-a sporangium or gametangium.

The protoplast of a sporangium divides itself into a number of zoospores, probably as many as there are nuclei in the sporangium, and the zoospores escape through one or more exit tubes formed in the sporangial wall and penetrating through the host cell wall (if any) to the outside.

In the genus *Lagenidium* a thin, bubble-like *vesicle (L. vesicala* = small bladder) develops at the mouth of the exit tube and makes the sporangium appear to be blowing a soap bubble.

The sporangial protoplast moves through the exit tube into the vesicle, and the zoospores become differentiated therein. They then become liberated into the surrounding water when the bubble bursts. The zoospores swim around in the water for some time.

Eventually they come to rest on a susceptible host and penetrate the wall or membrane. Inside the host the zoospore gives rise to the thallus typical of the species.

Cook, Couch, Sparrow, and others have observed sexual reproduction in a number of species in the Lagenidiaceae. In all cases, they have found that this takes place by the copulation of two gametangia and the passing of the protoplast of one gametangium into the other through a pore or a tube.

The contacting gametangia, in some species, are formed from adjacent cells of the same thallus. In other species, gametangia from two thalli lying side by side come in contact. Dangeard (1903) found that the gametangia of *Myzocytium vermicolum* are multinucleate, but that only one nucleus in each is actually functional; the others disintegrate.

He observed that a thin wall is formed around the combined protoplasts and that karyogamy takes place soon after. The zygote is eventually transformed into a resting spore by the formation of a thick wall. These observations, made in 1903 by this French investigator, still remain unique in the cytology of the Lagenidiaceae.

Germination of the resting spore has been observed in only two species, according to Sparrow (1960). Meiosis presumably takes place-but has not been observed—when the oospore germinates. In *Myzocytium vermicolum* the "resting spore" releases zoospores upon germination, i.e.; it acts as a zoosporangium.

Lagenidium rabenhorstii Zopf is one of the best-known species, although its cytology has not been worked out. Figure 48, constructed from the drawings which W. R. I. Cook published in 1935, will give‘ you a clear idea of the life cycle of this species, which in many respects may be considered representative of the family.

ORDER SAPROLEGNIALES

The term water mold, though applicable to a number of other fungal groups as well, is customarily used to designate the Saprolegniales, for most of them occur abundantly in clear waters and are easily isolated. Many species are, however, soil-inhabiting.

The majority of species in this order are saprobic and are of little direct economic importance. A few of them, however, are important parasites.

Some species of *Saprolegnia,* as *Saprolegnia parasitica,* cause diseases of fish and fish eggs, and may do significant damage to commercial or government fish hatcheries.

The genus *Aphanomyces* contains several destructive parasites of the roots of vascular plants, causing serious diseases of sugar beets, peas, and other crops. *Aphanomyces euteiches,* which attacks a number of economically important hosts, is particularly prevalent.

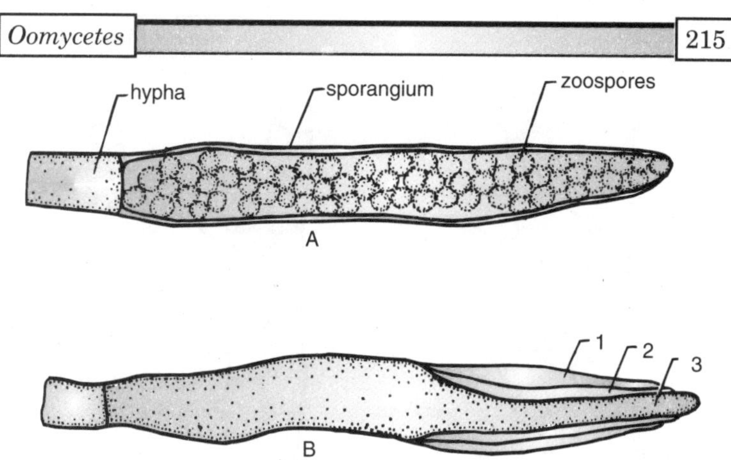

Figure 12.2: A. Mature sporangium of Saprolegnia sp. B. Internal proliferation. 1, 2. Empty sporangial cases. 3. Developing sporangium.

Classification

The order Saprolegniales is divided into three families by Sparrow: the Ectrogellaceae, the Thraustochytriaceae, and the Saprolegniaceae. The Ectrogellaceae include one-celled, holocarpic organisms parasitic on algae.

The Thraustochytriaceae, consisting of four species parasitic on marine algae, have a rhizoidal system which anchors the minute thallus to the host. No mycelium is developed by any species in either of these families.

The Saprolegniaceae are considerably more advanced than either of the other two families and contain a much larger number of species. They may be regarded as typical of the order and are the only ones to be discussed here.

FAMILY SAPROLEGNIACEAE

Occurrence, Isolation, and Laboratory Cultivation

The Saprolegniaceae are among the most ubiquitous of aquatic fungi. They are present in most bodies of fresh water. Some species, able to withstand a certain degree of salinity, live in brackish waters of estuaries as well, when salinity does not exceed 2.8 per cent.

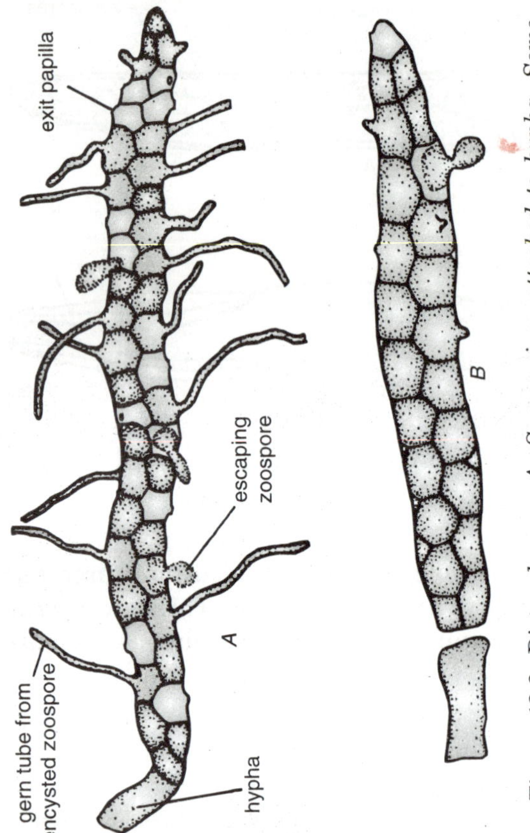

Figure 12.3: Dictyuchus sp. A. Sporangium attached to hypha. Some zoospores have escaped through individual exit papillae, leaving empty cells; two are in the process of escaping; several have encysted within the sporangium and have produced germ tubes. B. Detached sporangium.

Higher salinities limit the distribution of these fungi. Saprolegniaceae are also abundant in moist soils. Although they have not been reported from all parts of the world, there is little doubt that they are universally distributed and that we need only look for them in order to find them.

In addition to being widely distributed, the Saprro legniaceae are among the easiest fungi to isolate and cultivate in the laboratory. To isolate the Saprolegniaceae, go to the nearest pond and fill a quart jar half full of water.

Add some bait in the form of three or four dead flies, split boiled hemp seeds, split boiled wheat, or corn grains. In a few days you should have good colonies which may then be transferred to sterile culture dishes, each containing 25 ml. of half and half autoclaved tap water and sterile distilled water.

If no ponds are near by, some soil collected 1 or 2 inches below the surface and poured into a quart jar half full of autoclaved water should give good results when properly baited. Pure cultures are more difficult to obtain and require special techniques.

Somatic Structures

The Saprolegniaceae are characterized by a profusely branched, coenocytic mycelium easily visible as it forms, a colony around some bit of decaying plant or animal tissue in water.

The hyphal walls contain cellulose. Septa are formed in the mycelium just below the reproductive organs, separating them from the somatic hyphae, which generally remain aseptate.

The hyphae vary considerably in diameter. In some species they are very wide; in others they are characteristically fine.

The nutritive requirements for growth of some of the Saprolegniaceae have been investigated, and a general picture is beginning to appear.

Glucose seems to be the best source of carbon for most species; maltose, starch, and glycogen are available to several; fructose, mannose, sucrose, and ethanol are utilized by some.

In general the Saprolegniaceae appear unable to utilize nitrates, but grow well on media containing organic N in the form of peptone or any one of a number of amino acids. Whether ammonium salts can serve as the sole source of N is controversial, but the evidence seems to indicate this is true for certain species and under some conditions.

Most species investigated are able to synthesize all the vitamins required for growth. Inorganic growth requirements include Mg, Ca, Zn, Mn, Fe, and S. Sulphates apparently cannot be utilized, but S may be conveniently supplied in organic form as cysteine, cystine, glutathione, or methionine. A pH range from 4.0 to 6.0 has. been found to be optimal- for the growth of five species.

Asexual Reproduction

Long, cylindrical, terminal zoosporangia are typically produced by members of this family, In general the sporangia are somewhat greater in diameter than the hyphae on which they are produced. The young sporangia are full of dense, granular protoplasm which gives them a somewhat brownish appearance by transmitted light under the microscope. Sporangia are usually terminal.

The exact conditions which induce the mycelium of the Saprolegni-aceae to sporulate have not been studied in detail, little knowledge having been added since the classic experiments of Klebs (1898-1900).

Klebs found that he could maintain *Saprolegnia cultures* in the assimilative stage for 2½ years if he provided them with fresh supplies of nutrients. To induce sporangial formation the cultures were transferred to water.

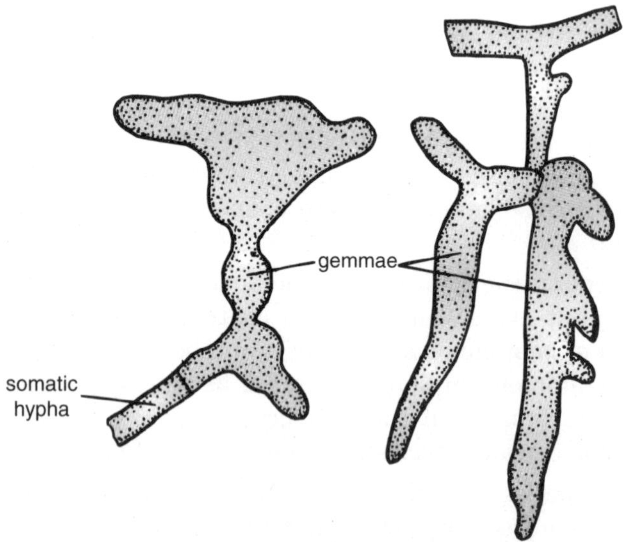

Figure 12.4: Gemmae of Saprolegnia.

Sporangial proliferation is an interesting phenomenon in the Saprolegniaceae. It may occur in various ways. In the genus *Saprolegnia* it takes place as follows. When a sporangium has emptied its contents of spores, another or secondary sporangium often is initiated at the basal septum, and grows through the first sporangium, maturing within it or beyond it.

Several sporangia may thus be formed one within the other, each maturing and shedding its spores before the next one is formed, As a general rule, the sporangia of the Saprolegniaceae remain attached to the somatic hyphae throughout their lives, and even after they have discharged their spores. The genus *Dictyuchus* is an exception, the sporangia commonly falling off the hyphae at maturity.

Zoospores and Zoospore Behavior

Two types of zoospores occur in the Saprolegniaceae. The primary zoospores are pear-shaped and bear their two flagella at the apex; the secondary zoospores are kidney-shaped and bear two oppositely directed flagella at the concave side of the zoospore.

Species which produce only one type of zoospore are monomorphic (Gr. *monos* = alone, one + *morphe* = shape, form). Species which produce both types of zoospores are dimorphic (Gr. dis = twice +*morphe* = shape, form).

The behavior of the zoospores differs in different genera and is an important taxonomic character. The several types of zoospore behavior may be illustrated by the following examples.

In the genus *Pythiopsis,* the zoospores released from the zoosporangium are primary zoospores. They swarm for some time, then come to rest, become rounded, encyst, and eventually germinate, each putting forth a germ tube which grows into a hypha.

There is thus typically only one swarming period and only one type of zoospore produced. Such behavior is called monoplanetism, and the species behaving thus are called monoplanetic (Gr. *monos* = alone, only *planetes* = wanderer).

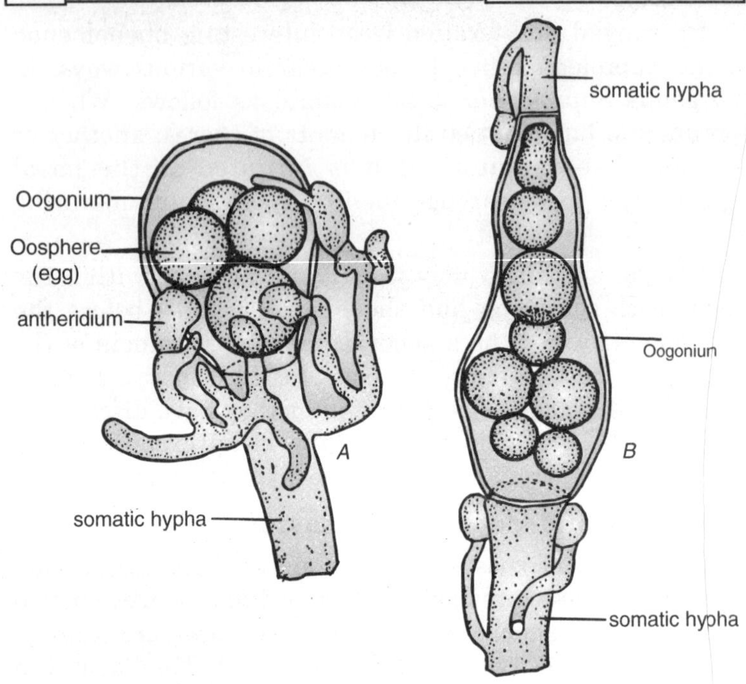

Figure 12.5: Saprolegnia litoralis. A. Terminal pogonium with antheridia. B. Intercalary oogonium.

The genera *Saprolegnia, Isoachlya, Leptolegnia,* and *Leptolegniella* produce both types of zoospores in succession. The primary zoospores are released from the sporangium, and after a period of swarming encyst. Instead of germinating by germ tube, however, each cyst gives rise to a secondary zoospore which embarks upon a second swarming period.

Encystment and germination by germ tube follow. Species in which two swarming periods occur, involving two types of zoospores, we call diplanetic, and the phenomenon diplanetism (Gr. *dis* = twice + *planetes* = wanderer). In *Saprolegnia,* both swarming periods are of considerable duration. *In Achlya,* the primary zoospores encyst just outside the mouth of the sporangium as soon as they are released.

Eventually they germinate and release secondary

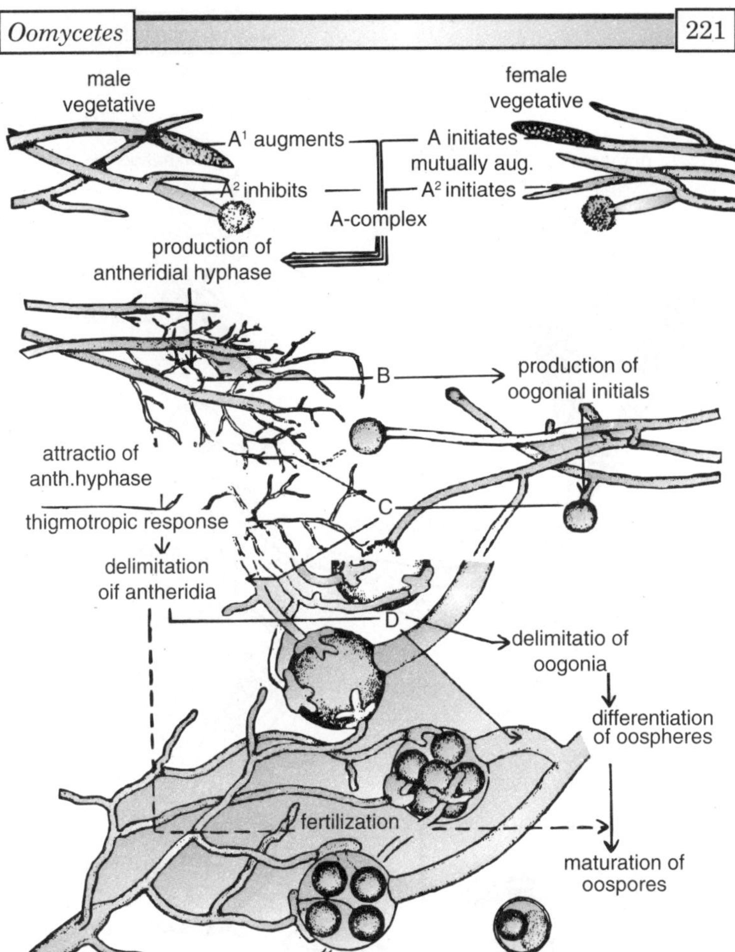

Figure 12.6: A semidiagrammatic representation of the sexual progression in heterothallic species of Achlya *relating the sequence of morphological developments to the origins and specific activities of the several sexual hormones.*

zoospores. *Achlya* thus exhibits a strong tendency to suppress the first swarming period. In the genus *Dictyuchus* no primary zoospores are liberated. Instead, they encyst within the sporangium and each releases a secondary zoospore which escapes from the sporangium, swarms for a time, and encysts.

After a resting period each of these cysts releases

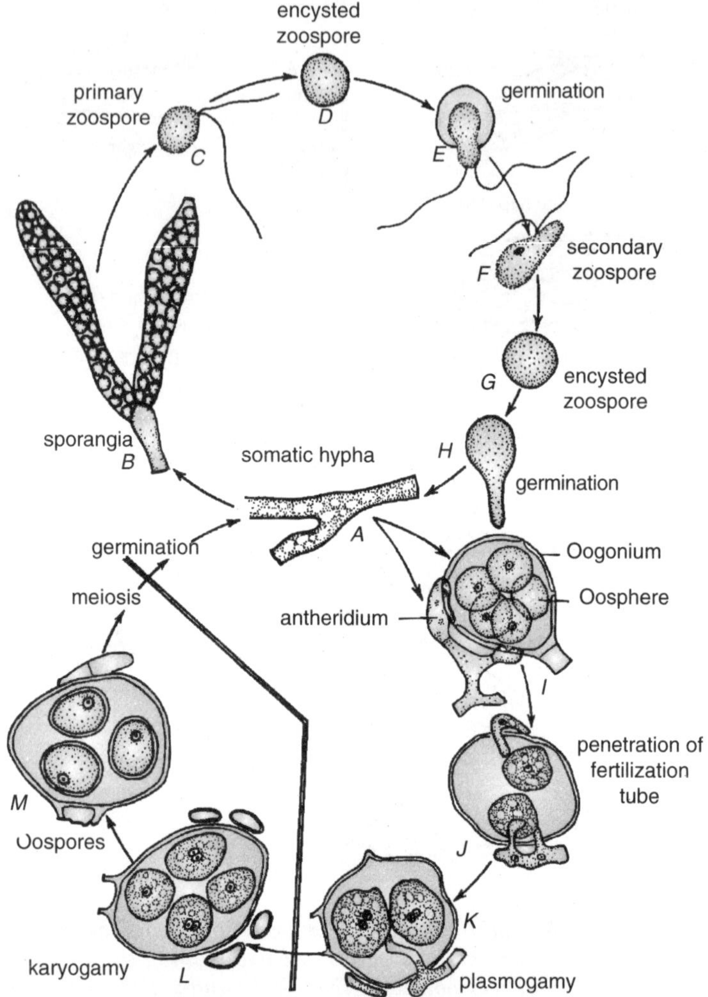

Figure 12.7: Life cycle of Saprolegnia sp.

another secondary zoospore which in turn swarms and encysts. This process may be repeated several times, all swarming zoospores being of the secondary type. Such a phenomenon is called *repeated zoospore emergence*, or *polyplanetism* (Gr. *poly* = much + *planetes* = wanderer).

In the genus *Thraustotheca,* the primary zoospores encyst within the sporangium and eventually liberate secondary zoospores which swarm but once. In *Geolegnia, which* possibly represents the culmination of this evolutionary series, both swarm periods have been suppressed and no zoospores are formed. Each of the aplanospores which escape from the sporangium germinates by a germ tube. *Geolegnia* is thus *aplanetic* (Gr. a = not + *planetes* = wanderer).

It is thought that an ancestral type resembling *Geolegnia* may have given rise to the fungi of the class Zygomycetes, which we shall discuss in other chapter of this book. It is important to remember at this point that organisms do not behave in the same way under all conditions.

Thus, an organism which is usually monoplanetic or usually diplanetic may at times exhibit polyplanetism, as has been shown with *Pythiopsis* and *Achlya,* respectively. What causes this behavior is not known.

Chlamydospores

Another method of asexual reproduction in the Saprolegniaceae, in addition to the production of sporangia and sporangiospores, is by means of chlamydospores, sometimes called *gemmae* (sing. gemma; *L. gemma* = bud).

These are generally borne terminally, either singly or in chains. In the latter event, they become separated after maturing. Gemmae germinate by means of germ tubes which either grow into hyphae or develop into short-stalked sporangia typical of the species.

Sexual Reproduction

Sexual reproduction in the Saprolegniaceae is by means of gameta-ngial contact, the passage of the male gametes into the female gametangium taking place through a fertilization tube. The sex organs are generally terminal, but intercalary oogonia also may be formed.

The oogonium is usually g'obose, its entire contents differentiating into one or more globular, finally uninucleate oospheres. The elongated and multinucleate antheridia originate either on the same hyphal branch on which the oogonium is attached, on a different branch, or on an entirely different thallus.

One or more antheridia become attached to the oogonium, pierce it, and branch out, sending one branch to each oosphere within the oogonium. One nucleus of the antheridium now passes through each fertilization tube into each oosphere and fuses with the egg nucleus therein.

Fertilized oospheres develop thick walls and are converted into oospores. In the mature oospores of the Saprolegniaceae the fatty reserve is stored in the form of oil droplets characteristically arranged in different species. These arrangements are of considerable taxonomic value.

After a period of rest, the oospore germinates by means of a hyphal tube which shortly afterwards gives rise to a zoosporangium typical of the species. Although karyogamy has been demonstrated in a considerable number of species, in others the oospores develop parthenogenetically. In some species, no antheridia are known to be formed.

The majority of the Saprolegniaceae are hermaphroditic and homo-thallic, producing compatible antheridia and oogonia on the same thallus. However, some dioecious species are also known, which require two individuals for sexual reproduction, one male, one ferhale.

Achlya bisexualis and *Achlya ambisexualis,* which are dioecious, were used by Dr. John R. Raper (1939-1951) in his now classic investigations on the sexual mechanism involved. Raper demonstrated conclusively that, when potentially male and female thalli grow in close proximity, a system involving at least four distinct hormones becomes operative and initiates the sexual process.

Hormone A (actually consisting of several entities) is liberated by the somatic hyphae of the female thallus and induces the formation of antheridia by the hyphae of the male thallus. The antheridial branches now produce hormone B, which induces the formation of oogonial initials by the female thallus.

These oogonial initials produce hormone C, which

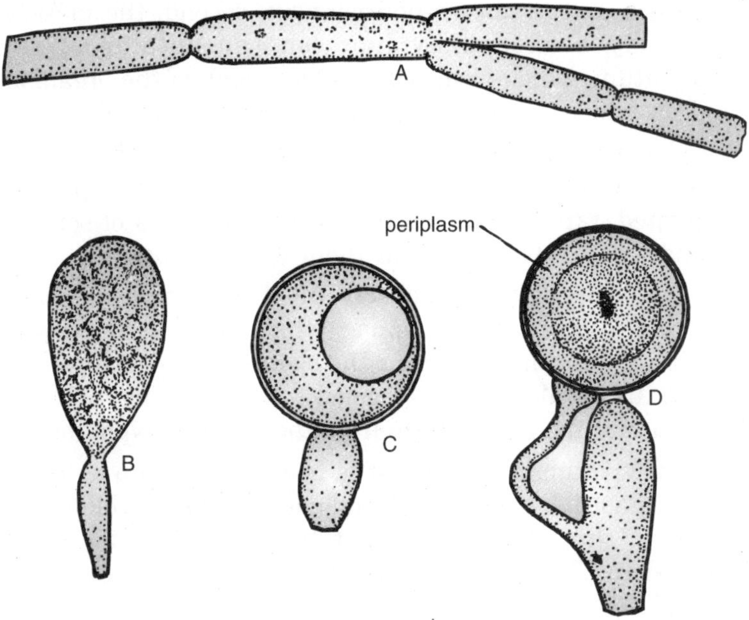

Figure 12.8: Leptomitales. A-C. Apodachlya pyrifera. A. Somatic hypha showing constrictions. B. Sporangium. C. Oospore. D. Rhipidium americanum. Periplasm depositing wall of oospore.

attracts the antheridial branches of the male thallus to the oogonial initials of the female thallus. Upon contact, the delimitation of antheridia is induced. The antheridia finally produce hormone *D,* which induces the formation of a wall at the base of each oogonium, thus delimiting the female sex organs. These processes are illustrated in Figure elsewhere in this chapter.

Life History

Several genera of water molds belong to the Saprolegniaceae. The most common are *Saprolegnia, Achlya,* and *Dictyuchus.* The genus *Saprolegnia will* be taken as an example of the general life history of members of this family.

The somatic portion of the thallus is composed of two types of hyphae: first, the rhizoidal hyphae, which enter the substratum, be it the body of a dead fly or a dead seed of some flowering plant, and which serve to anchor the organism and to absorb nourishment; second, the mass of profusely branched hyphae on the outside of the substratum, which forms the visible colony of the organism and on which the reproductive organs are formed.

Under the proper environmental conditions, the hyphae give rise to sporangia. Typically, the sporangia are elongated, tapering structures borne at the tips of somatic hyphae, and separated from them by a septum.

The sporangia are densely filled with protoplasm in contrast to the somatic hyphae, which are only lined with a thin protoplasmic layer. As the sporangium develops, and before the basal septum is formed, a large number of nuclei stream into the sporangium from the somatic hypha below.

The sporangial protoplast is now divided into as many portions as there are nuclei, and each portion develops into a spore, the whole protoplast being utilized for spore formation. The method of escape of the zoospores varies with different genera.

In *Saprolegnia,* an opening develops at the tip of the sporangium, and the primary zoospores escape into the surrounding water. Here they swim about for some time, come to rest, and encyst. After a short resting period, a thin papilla develops on the cyst, its tip dissolves, and a reniform zoospore with two lateral flagella creeps out.

After a short swarming period, encystment follows. The encysted spore now germinates by a germ tube which develops into a hypha and initiates a new colony. Diplanetism is the rule in *Saprolegnia* . By proliferation or branching, sporangia continue to be formed, several asexual generations following one another.

When conditions favorable to sexual reproduction appear, the somatic hyphae give rise to oogonia and antheridia. Oogonia range from globose to oblong in shape, the globose type predominating. They have relatively thick walls as compared with the walls of somatic hyphae, and each when mature contains from one to many free oospheres, most species producing several.

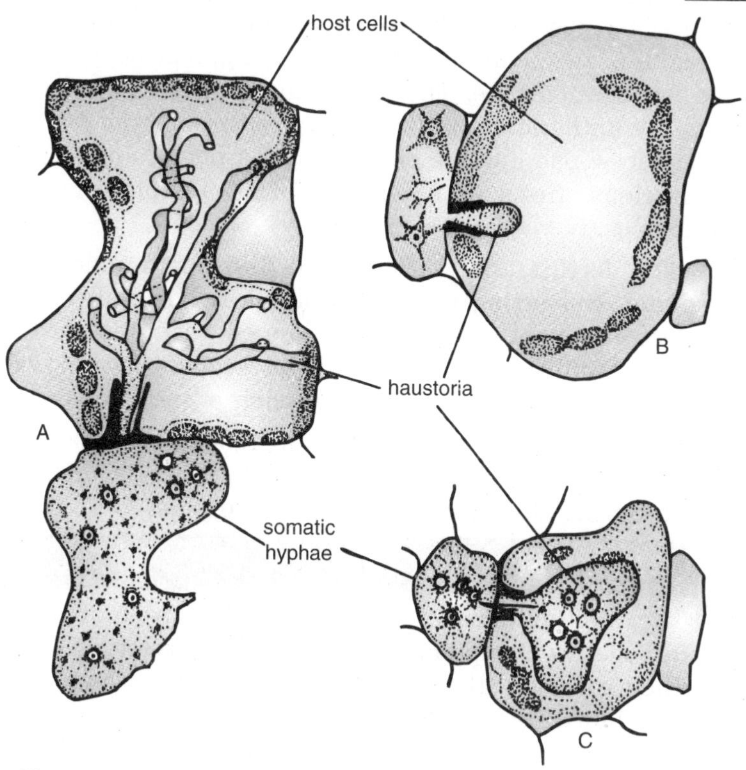

Figure 12.9: Haustoria of the Peronosporaceae. A. Peronospora ficariae. B. Plasmopara pygmaea. C. Peronospora parasitica.

A single nucleus is present in each mature oosphere. The antheridia are much smaller than the oogonia. They are multinucleate, elongated bodies borne terminally on slender branches of the somatic hyphae.

They are often borne on the same hypha which bears the oogonium, and arise immediately below it, but in some species they are formed on different hyphae.

The antheridia, when fully formed, become attached to the oogonia, one or more for each oogonium. Fertilization tubes originating in the antheridium penetrate the oogonial wall and reach the oospheres. Upon entering the oogonium, a fertilization tube may branch out and send one branch to each oosphere.

Even when more than one antheridium contacts the oogonium, an oosphere is, as a rule, approached by only one fertilization tube. The antheridial nuclei now migrate from the antheridium to the oospheres through the fertilization tubes; one nucleus enters each oosphere, approaches its nucleus, fuses with it, and forms a diploid zygote nucleus.

After fertilization, a thick wall develops around each oosphere, converting it into an oospore. The wall of the oospore is smooth. After a prolonged rest period, the oospores are liberated from the disintegrated oogonial wall and germinate, each oospore producing a germ tube.

Shortly thereafter, a sporangium generally develops at the tip of this hypha, completing the life cycle. Meiosis occurs during the germination of the oospore.

ORDER LEPTOMITALES

The Leptomitales constitute a small order of about twenty species of saprobic, aquatic Phycomycetes. In general they resemble the Saprolegniales, under which they were included as the family Leptomitaceae until 1927, at which time, as a result of her extensive studies, Dr. Bessie B. Kanouse of the University of Michigan established the order Leptomitales.

The somatic hyphae of the Leptomitales, though truly aseptate, are nevertheless constricted at intervals, and the constrictions are sometimes plugged with granules of cellulin, giving the appearance of septa. This is the outstanding morphological characteristic of the order which distinguishes it from the Saprolegniales.

Some interesting differences in S and N nutrition between the Saprolegniaceae and the Leptomitales have also been discovered. Whereas the Saprolegniaceae, you will remember, appear unable to utilize sulfates, the Leptomitales reduce sulfates and utilize the S in their metabolism.

Members of both families appear unable to utilize nitrate N, but some Saprolegniaceae can probably use ammonium N, whereas the Leptomitaceae seem unable to do so. Asexual reproduction takes place by means of terminal zoosporangia from which biflagellate zoospores are released.

The species may be diplanetic or monoplanetic. The sporangia of some species are elongated and of the same diameter as the somatic hyphae. Many species, however, produce pyriform sporangia.

This is an important detail, for, as we shall see presently, the oval or round shape represents an advanced development in the evolution of the sporangium, and the presence of pyriform sporangia in this order, together with other factors, may be an indication that the Leptomitales are intermediate between the Saprolegniales and the Peronosporales. Although oval sporangia are not unknown in the Saprolegniales, their sporangia are typically elongated.

The opposite is true of the Peronosporales. Sexual reproduction takes place as in the Saprolegniales, by gametangial contact. In most Leptomitales, however, each oogonium contains but a single oosphere.

In most species the oosphere does not lie free within the oogonium, but is surrounded by a rather thick layer of protoplasm, the periplasm (Gr. *peri* = around + *plasma* = *a* molded structure). This is the first time we have encountered periplasm in the Oomycetes.1 We shall see that it becomes well established in the Peronosporales.

Two families, the Leptomitaceae and the Rhipidiaceae, with seven genera are now recognized. For further details consult Sparrow (1960).

ORDER PERONOSPORALES

The Peronosporales represent the highest development of the class Oomycetes. This large order of fungi includes aquatic, amphibious, and terrestrial species, culminating in a group of highly specialized obligate parasites. Many species in this order are destructive parasites of economic plants, frequently causing epiphytotics with tremendous losses to crops. The damping-off fungi, the white rusts, and the downy mildews all belong to this order, which includes several hundred species.

Somatic Structures

The mycelium of the Peronosporales is well developed, consisting of coenocytic, stout hyphae which branch freely. A large number of species in this order produce haustoria by means of which the hyphae obtain nourishment from the host cells.

The haustoria may be knob-like, elongated, or branched within the host cells. The hyphae of the parasitic species are intercellular or intracellular, those of the most speciali-zed parasites growing between the cells.

Asexual Reproduction

Asexual reproduction is in principle the same as in the Saprolegn-iaceae and the Leptomitales, but differs' in detail. Thus, although a sporangium is formed which typically produces zoospores, the typical sporangium is strikingly different from that in the previous orders, being oval or lemon-shaped in most species, rather than elongated.

Although in the lower Peronosporales the sporangia are borne on ordinary somatic hyphae and remain attached even after the zoospores have been released as in the Saprolegniaceae, in the more advanced types the sporangia are borne on sporangiophores and are deciduous upon maturity, depending on the wind for dissemination.

In this respect, the whole sporangium acts as a spore, and in the highest forms actually germinates by a germ tube instead of producing zoospores. The majority of species, however, produce zoospores, which are reniform, biflage-llate, and monoplanetic.

Diplanetism and polyplanetism occur in a very few species. Upon their release from the sporangium, the zoospores swarm for some time, come to rest, encyst, and germinate each by a germ tube which develops into the mycelium.

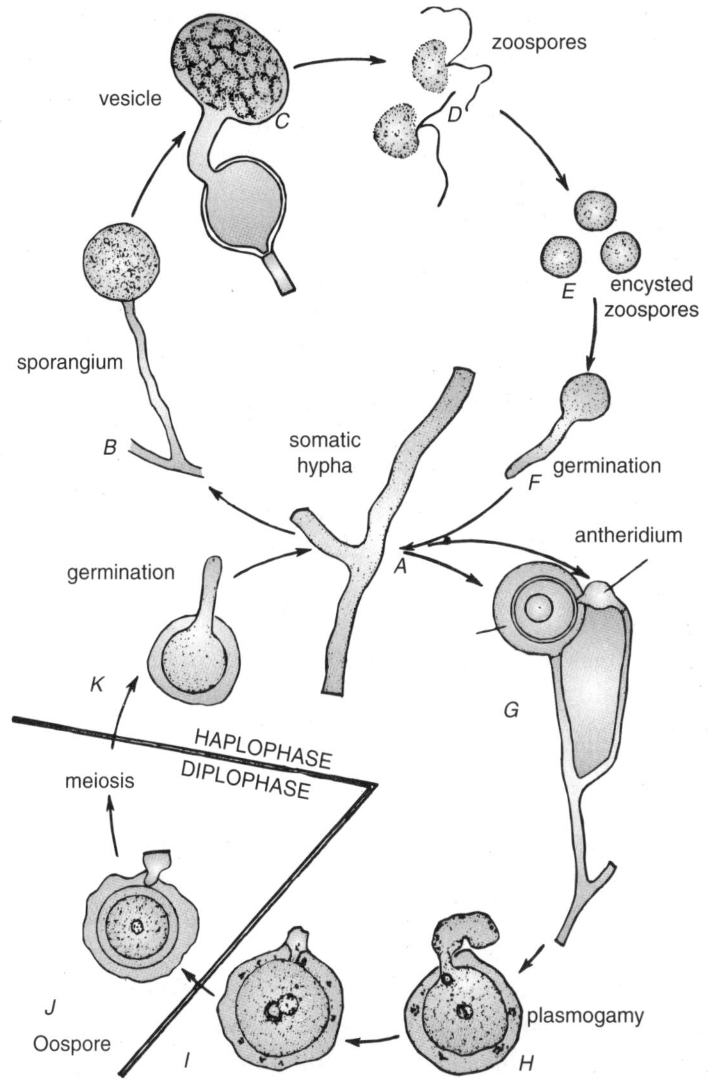

Figure 12.10. Life cycle of Pythium debaryanum.

Sexual Reproduction

Sexual reproduction in the Peronosporales is by means of well-differentiated oogonia and antheridia borne on the same or on different hyphae. The oogonium, which is generally globose, contains, with few exceptions, but a single uninucleate or multinucleate oosphere, surrounded by a layer of periplasm.

The antheridium is uninucleate or multinucleate, depending on the species. When gametangial contact is effected, a fertilization tube is formed by the antheridium, pushes through the oogonial wall and the periplasm, and reaches the oosphere.

The male nucleus or nuclei then pass through the fertilization tube and are shed into the oosphere. If the latter is uninucleate, a single male nucleus fuses with the female nucleus and forms the zygote.

If the oosphere is multinucleate, one or more of its nuclei may be functional, the number of male nuclei that will effect fertilization being regulated accordingly. Thus, either a single zygote nucleus or a number of diploid nuclei may result from a simple or multiple fertilization, respectively.

After fertilization, the oosphere develops a thick wall and changes into an oospore. The periplasm probably serves as nourishment for the developing oospore.

It is also responsible for the external thickenings and ornamentations which it deposits on the oospore walls of some species.

The oospore wall is a triple wall consisting of an outer, a middle, and an inner layer. The outer wall may be smooth or variously sculptured or ornamented; it may be spiny, warty, wavy, ridged, or otherwise marked.

The mature oospore generally lies free within the oogonial wall, but in many species adheres to the latter so closely that it appears to be united with it.

Only in the genus *Sclerospora* is the oogonial wall actually fused with the oospore wall. After overwintering, the oospores germinate in the spring, either by giving rise to zoospores, thus behaving as zoosporangia, or by putting out germ tubes which soon afterwards produce sporangia. The type of germination varies with the species.

Classification

The classification of the Peronosporales is based mostly on the characters of the sporangia and the sporangiophores. The latter are strikingly characteristic of many groups, and the variation among them lends itself to taxonomic treatment. This is in contrast to the sexual (oospore) stage in which the variations are not so obvious.

We divide the order Peronosporales into three families on the basis of sporangiophore characters: the Pythiaceae, the Albuginaceae, and the Peronosporaceae.

The Pythiaceae generally bear their sporangia directly on the somatic hyphae. In some species, the fertile hyphae are no different from the somatic hyphae. The most advanced species of the Pythiaceae produce recognizable sporangiophores, but of indeterminate growth.

This means that the sporangiophore continues growing indefinitely, producing sporangia as it grows. The result is the presence of sporangia of different ages-from some that are mature to others that are just being initiated-on the same sporangiophore at any given time.

The Albuginaceae produce short, club-shaped sporangiop-hores which bear chains of globose sporangia at their tips. As in the Pythiaceae, the sporangiophores are of indeterminate growth. The' Albuginaceae are obligate parasites of flowering plants.

The Peronosporaceae, which are probably closely allied to the higher Pythiaceae, bear their sporangia on unmistakable sporangiophores which are characteristically branched. In contrast to those of the higher Pythiaceae, the sporangiophores of the Peronosporaceae are of determinate growth.

No sporangia are produced until the sporangiophore completes its development and matures. Then a single crop of sporangia is produced, all the sporangia being of approximately the same age. After the sporangia fall off, the sporangiophore withers and dies.

The type of branching of the sporangiophores of the Peronosporaceae serves as the chief distinguishing feature

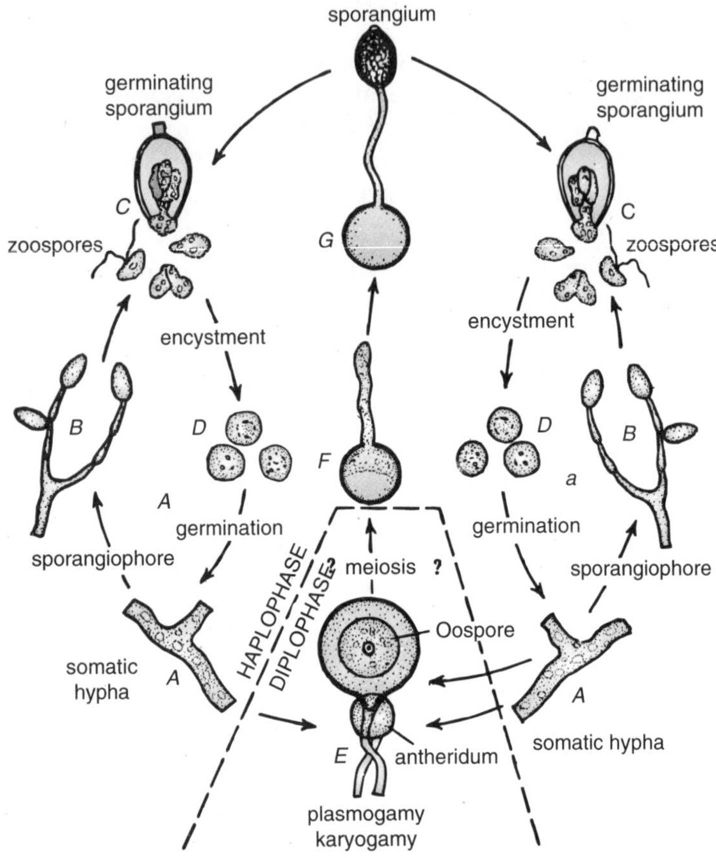

Figure 12.11: Life cycle of Phytophthora infestans.

of the genera in this family. The Peronosporaceae are obligate parasites on plants; no one as yet has succeeded in growing any species on artificial media.

Key to the Families of the Order Peronosporales

A. Sporangiophores similar to the somatic hyphae, or, if different, then of indeterminate growth — *Pythiaceae*

AA. Sporangiophores strikingly different from the somatic hyphae

B. Sporangia in chains at the tips of short, stout, club-shaped sporangiophores *Alhuginaceae*

BB. Sporangia borne singly or in clusters, at the tips of various types of sporangiophores, the latter of determinate growth *Peronosporaceae*

FAMILY PYTHIACEAE

The Pythiaceae include aquatic, amphibious and terrestrial fungi, many of the last causing serious diseases of economic plants. The mycelium is well developed; haustoria are produced in some species. The hyphae which, bear the sporangia are indistinguishable from the mycelium in most species.

In some species, however, definite sporangiophores are formed. In such cases the growth of the sporangiophore is indeterminate. In the most primitive forma-the-sporangia remain art to the hyphae which bear them. Upon maturity they produce and liberate a number of zoospores.

In the most advanced species the sporangia are deciduous, and often germinate each by a germ tube instead of producing zoospores. The type of germination, whether zoosores or germ tube, appears to be governed to a great extent by environmental conditions, especially by temperature.

Sexually the Pythiaceae conform to the general pattern described for the Peronosporales as a whole. Oospores are formed parthenogenetically in some species, but it is probable that fertilization takes place in a large number.

Cytological studies are relatively few. On the other hand, the physiology of growth and reproduction in the Pythiaceae has attracted the attention of a number of investigators. Sexuality appears to be relative in some species and there are indications that a hormonal mechanism, perhaps similar to that in *Achlya,* may be involved in the development of sex organs and oospores.

The Pythiaceae show a considerable degree of advancement over the Saprolegniaceae, but resemble them sufficiently to have caused some authors in the past to include them with the latter in the Saprolegniales rather than in the Peronosporales.

Of interest in this connection are the conclusions of Cantino and Turian (1959) that "nutritional requirements of the Leptomitales and Peronosporales seem to relate these two orders more closely to one another than to the Saprolegniales."

At the other extreme, some writers separate the Pythiaceae from both the Saprolegniales and the Peronosporales, elevating them to ordinal rank under the name of Pythiales.

The most common genera of the Pythiaceae are *Pytthium* and *Ehytophthora.* The first includes some aquatic species parasitic on algae as well as many soil-inhabiting species parasitic on higher plants. The best known of these is *Pythium debaryanum,* the cause of damping-off of seedlings. The genus *Phytophthora* includes many important plant pathogens.

Of these, *Phytophthora infestans,* the cause of late blight of potatoes, is the most infamous. When the weather-is-favorable to the fungus (i.e., when low temperature and high humidity prevail), the disease appears on an epiphytotic scale and, in spite of the control measures ,that have been worked out, causes damage even in modern times.

In former years, the fungus was responsible for the complete destruction of the entire potato crop over large areas. Indeed, the Irish famine of 1845, which was partially responsible for the repeal of the corn laws in England and for a great wave of migration from Ireland to the United States, is directly traceable to *Phytophthora infestans.* The story is related very entertainingly by E. C. Large (1940) in his well-known book,. *The Advance of the Fungi.*

GENUS PYTHIUM

Pythium debaryanum will be used to illustrate the general life history of members of the genus *Pythium.* The mycelium, consisting of rather slender, coenocytic hyphae with cellulose walls lives in the soil saprobically on dead organic matter or parasitically on the young seedlings of a great many susceptible species of seed plants. The hyphae are both intracellular and intercellular.

No haustoria are produced. The sporangia of the organism, constituting the asexual stage, are globose to oval and are either terminal or intercalary on the somatic hyphae. The sporangia remain attached to the hyphae and germinate in place. Germination-is either b zoospores or by germ tube. Production of zoospores is preceded by the formation of a bubble-like vesicle at the tip of a long tube which issues from the sporangium. The sporangial protoplast flows in to t e vesicle through the tube, and differentiation of the zoospores takes place in the vesicle.

The formation and liberation of the zoospores in *Pythium* is a fascinating process to watch under the microscope. The narrow tube which connects the sporangium to the vesicle is well defined, but the vesicular wall is so thin that you need to adjust the microscope mirror very carefully so that the vesicle may be properly illuminated and brought into view.

The sporangial protoplast moves rather rapidly through the tube into the vesicle and appears to remain quiescent while the delimitation of the zoospores is taking place. After some time has elapsed-15 or 20 minutes perhaps-you can detect a slight trembling motion as the crowded zoospores become restless and begin to move.

This motion becomes accelerated, gradually but steadily, until you can see the separate zoospores moving rapidly within the vesicle, bouncing off their neighbors and the wall of the vesicle. Suddenly the vesicular wall bursts like a soap bubble, and the zoospores scatter in all directions, dashing out in a rush.

The zoospore is kidney-shaped and has two lateral flagella attached on the concave side. After a period of swarming in the film of water present in the soil, the zoospore comes to, rest, encysts, and germinates by a germ tube.

Sexual reproduction in *Pythium debaryanum* has been studied by several investigators. Oogonia and antheridia are developed in dose proximity, often on the same hypha, with the antheridium just below the oogonium The oogonium is globose with a multinucleate oosphere surrounded a layer of periplasm.

The antheridia are much smaller, and somewhat elongated or club-shaped. Upon gametangial contact, a fertilization tube develops and penetrates the oogonial wall and the periplasm.

In the meantime, nuclear division has taken place in both gametangia and all but one functional nucleus in each have disintegrated.

The male nucleus now passes through the tube into the oosphere, approaches the female nucleus, unites with it, and forms the zygote. The oosphere develops into a thick-walled, smooth oospore which germinates after first undergoing a rest period.

At high temperatures (28° C.) the oospore germinates by germ tube, which develops a mycelium. At lower temperatures (10-17° C.), however, the germ tube stops growing when it has reached a length of 5-20 μ, and the protoplast of the oospore migrates through the tube, pushes out through the tip, and forms a vesicle in which zoospores develop.

Meiosis probably occurs in the first divisions of the zygote nucleus. A very large number of species of *Pythium* have been described. *Pythium ultimum* and *Pythium aphanidermatum* are other species, besides *Pythium debaryanum,* which cause damping-off.

Pythium aphanidermatum is particularly interesting because of its large, irregularly shaped, branched sporangia. For the taxonomy of the genus *Pythium* see Matthews (1931), Middleton (1943), and Sparrow (1960).

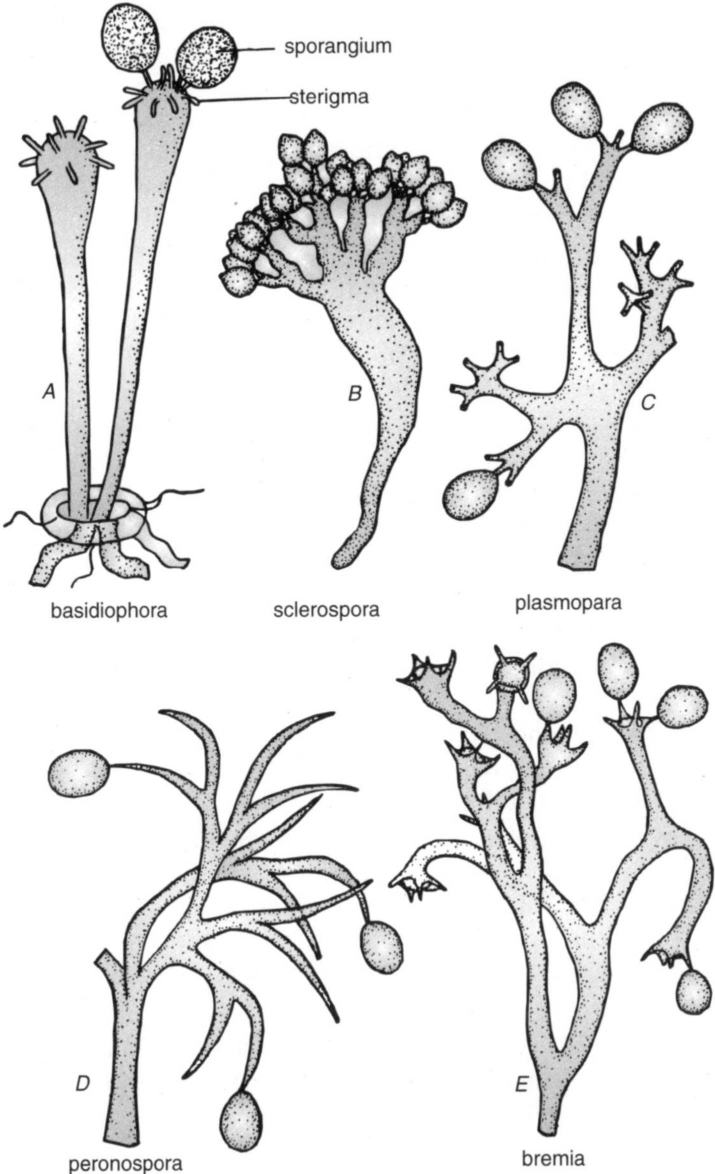

Figure 12.12: Sporangiophors characteristic of five genera of the Peronosporaceae.

GENUS PHYTOPHTHORA

The chief distinction between the genera *Pythium* and *Phytophthora is* the method of sporangial germination. In general, no vesicle is formed in *Phytophthora,* or, if one is formed, the zoospores differentiate in the sporangium proper and pass into the vesicle as mature zoospores; they are liberated by the bursting of the vesicular wall.

Unfortunately, this distinction does not hold all species, and consequently it is very difficult for all but the specialist in the taxonomy of this group of fungi to classify borderline species. Let us look at *Phytophthora infestans,* the notorious cause of potato late blight.

The oospores of *Phytophthora infestans* appear to be very rare in the eastern hemisphere and in the United States and Canada, and may not in fact, play a significant role in the survival of the species. In Mexico, however, oospores have been found in moderate numbers in potato leaves and may be of considerable importance in the survival of the organism.

It is probable that the same situation exists throughout the Central and South American regions where the potato is native. In most parts of the world, then, *Phytophthora infestans* passes the winter, as a general rune, in the form of mycelium in infected potato tubers.

With the arrival of favorable weather in the spring the mycelium grows and production of sporangiophores and sporangia begins. Cultural experiments have shown that 21°C. is the optimum temperature for the growth of the mycelium, but that some growth takes place between 2° and 30°.

Above 26° the hyphae die within a week. Temperature and humidity appear to be the two most important factors determining sporangial production. Abundant sporangial formation takes place in culture between 9° and 22°, but 18-22° is the optimum range. At this range abundant sporangia are produced within 14 hours, whereas at the lower temperatures (9-15°) 48 hours are required. As for

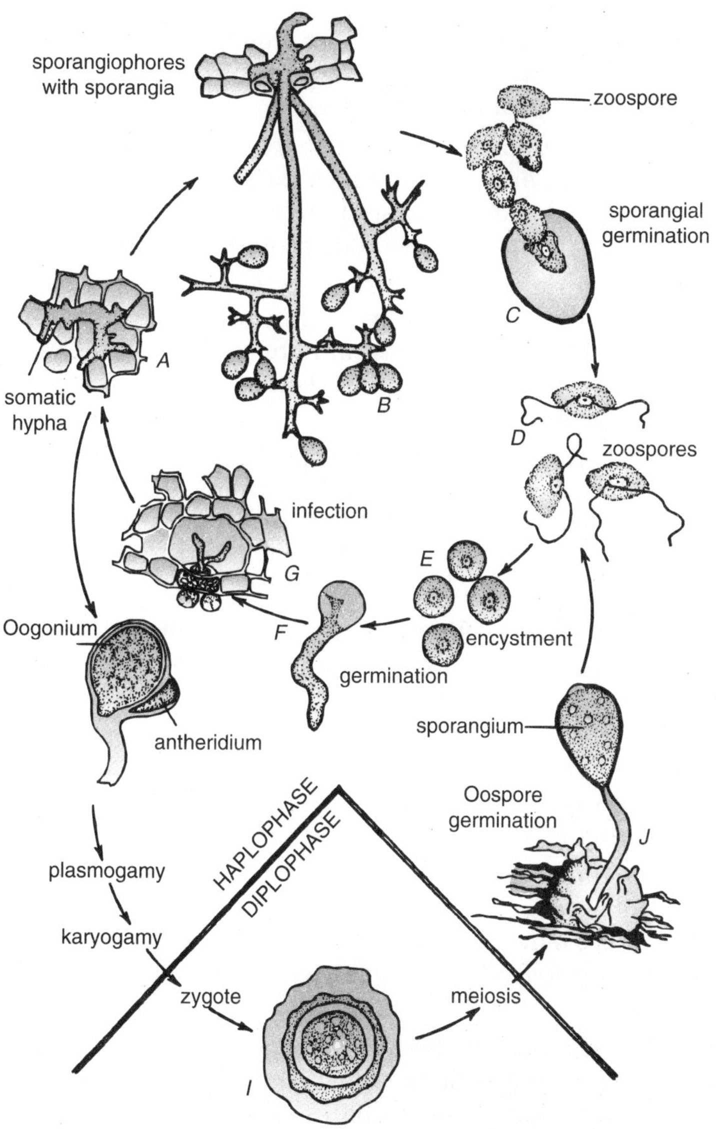

Figure 12.13: Life cycle of Plasmopara viticola.

relative humidity, 100 per cent is optimum and 91 per cent minimum for sporangial production.

Phytophthora infestans differs from many other members of the family Pythiaceae in that it produces sporangiophores distinguishable from the somatic hyphae.

The formation of sporangiophores is an indication of differentiation, and species which possess these structures are considered more advanced than those which produce their sporangia directly on undifferentiated somatic hyphae.

The sporangiophores of *Phytophthora infestans* and of other species in the family Pythiaceae are sympodially branched and are of indeterminate growth. The lemon-shaped, papillate sporangia are borne at - the tips of the sporangiophore branches.

Apical growth of the sporangiophore continues, however, so that the sporangia actually fall off from a lateral position in this species. The sporangiophore forms a sympodium with a more or less zigzag growth and with characteristic swellings at the nodes.

On the potato tuber, the sporangiophores appear in large numbers on cut surfaces, but normally push through the lenticels or injured portions of the skin.

Spring infection of potato plants originates in diseased potato tubers in which the mycelium survives. The fungus grows into the new tissues. *-sprouting-* from the potatoes and sporulates on the aerial parts of plants.

Subsequent infection of potato plants takes place by means of sporangia which are transported by water or are water or are blown by the wind. Sporangia of this and other species of *Phytophthora* are -extremely susceptible to dessication.

When the relative humidity drops much below 100 per cent, the sporangia die in a few hours. In the presence of water the sporangium germinates either directly by a germ tube which enters through a stoma and infects the leaf, orb means of zoospores.

Sporagia are capable of germinating within a wide range

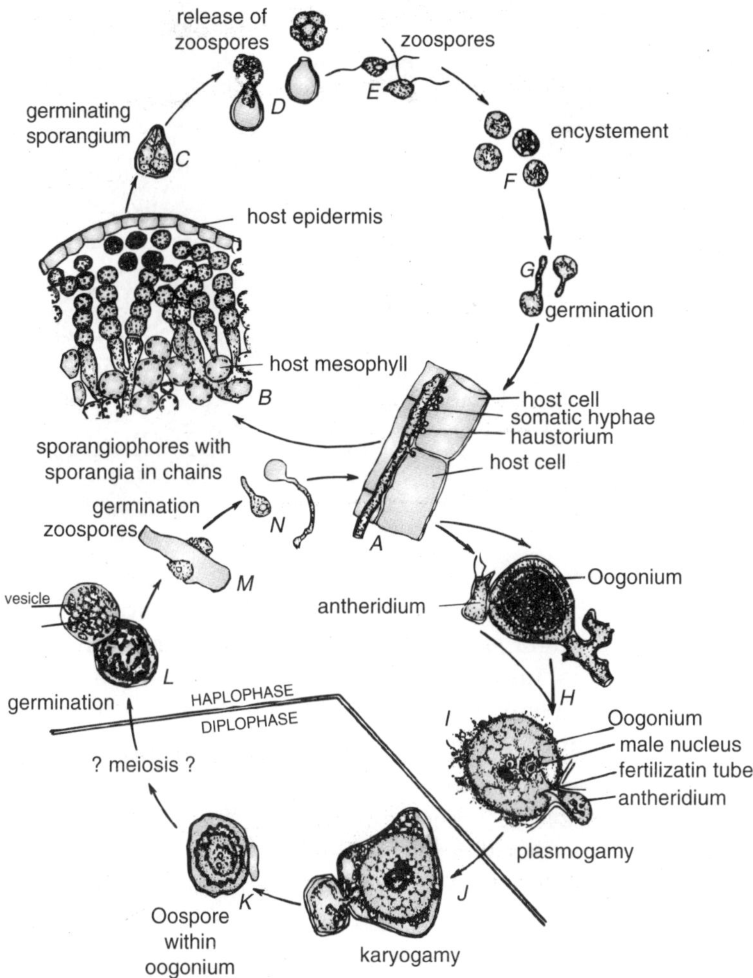

Figure 12.14: Life cycle of Plasmopara viticola.

of temperature from 1.5 to 24° C. However, above 20° the sporangia lose their viability in 1-3 hours in dry air, and in 5-15 hours in moist air. By first exposing sporangia to 40° C., Taylor and his coworkers (1955) greatly increased germination at 20° C.

Without pretreatment, 9 per cent of the sporangia germinated after 12 hours, whereas, after 5 minutes' exposure to 40°, 49 per cent germinated in the same period of time.

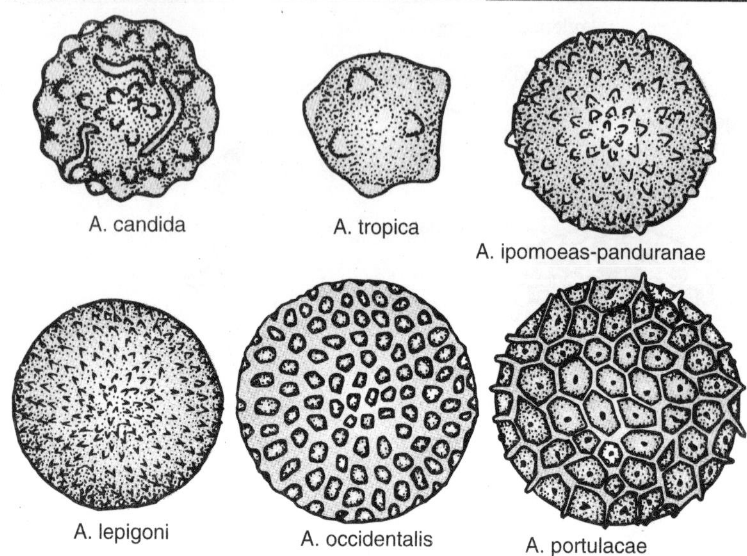

Figure 12.15: Oospores of six species of Albugo.

Other factors besides temperature and moisture such as age of sporangia, also affect germination. The method of germination is largely governed by temperature. Low temperatures favour zoospore production; higher temperatures, germ tube production.

The optimum temperature for direct (germ tile) germination is 24° C., whereas that for indirect germination is 12° C. Zoospores swim in the film of water for 15 minutes at high temperature and up to 24 hours as the temperature decreases.

Eventually they come to rest, encyst, and germinate each tube. The germ tube produces an appresorium (pl. appresoria; *L. apprimere* = to press against), a flattened, hyphal pressing organ, from *which* a minute infection peg grows and enters the epidermal cell of the host. If conditions favorable to penetration of the host last for 10 hours, a high degree of infection may be expected.

After penetrating into the leaf, the term tube develops into a profusely branched mycelium which is intercellular, sending long, curled haustoria into the leaf cells. A few days after infection, if the weather is favorable, numerous spdrangiophores emerge from, the stomata of the potato leaves and give rise to large numbers of sporangia.

These are spread by the wind and infect new plants. A large number of asexual generations are thus produced in one growing season if conditions favor the development of the fungus.

The first authentic report of the discovery of a sexual stage for *Phytophthora infestans* was published by Clinton in 1911. Clinton found the oospores in pure cultures of this organism. Later experimental work has shown that the fungus is heterothallic, i.e., requires two mating types for sexual have explained why oospores are rare in most parts of the world but occur in fair numbers in Mexico.

Whereas both mating types occur in a 1:1 ratio in Mexico, a large number of isolates from the United States, Canada, western Europe, South Africa, and the West Indies all belong to a single mating type. In the absence or rarity of the second mating *type,* oospores are produced very infrequently.

Sexual reproduction takes place by means of antheridia and oogonia of opposite mating types. While still in the, process of development, the antheridium is punctured by the oogonium, which grows through it and develops into a globose structure above the antheridium.

The mature antheridium thus forms a funnel-shaped collar around the base of the mature oogonium. Fertilization has not been observed but is presumed to take place, although it is known that in this species oospores can develop parthenogenetically in the absence. of an antheridium.

Oospores germinate by means of a germ tube which usually tennuiates in a sporangium. At times, however, the germ tube will proceed to produce mycelium.

Where meiosis takes place is not known; but, if the organism follows the regular pattern, meiosis would be expected to take place in the oospore at the time of germination. Mating type should segregate at this point in the life cycle.

FAMILY PERONOSPORACEAE

This is the most highly advanced of the three families of the order Peronosporales. A species in this family y are o. spate parasites of vascular plants causing diseases called downy mildews. Economically they are among the most important fungi. Their hosts include a large number of plant families, many of them widely distributed and widely cultivated commercially.

Diseases caused by the Peronosporaceae include, among many others, the down mildews of grape caused by *Plasmopara viticola,* of onion caused by *Peronvspora destructor,* of lettuse caused by *Bremia lactucae,* of cucurbits caused by *Pseudoperonospora cubensis,* and of various grasses caused by Sclerospora graminicola.

Plasmopara viticola has as interesting a history as *Phytophthora infestans.* The story has been told many times and in various editions, but it always bears repetition for the benefit of those who have not heard it. *Plasmopara viticola* is a fungus native to North America.

It has probably been attacking for thousands of years the grapes native to this continent, during which time natural selection, operating as usual, has produced a balance of power between the parasite and the host so that *Plasmopara viticola* can live on the wild American grape without the latter's being seriously affected by it.

The same balance exists between the American grape and the *Phylloxera,* a root aphid also native to this continent. Somehow, about 1865, *Phylloxera* was introduced into France. The European grape (Vitis *vinifera*), not having had the opportunity to evolve along *anti-Phylloxera* lines, was extremely susceptible.

With millions of Frenchmen depending on the grape industry for a living, this-was no small matter. The problem was eventually solved by the importation of resistant American stock and the grafting of the vini*fera* grape thereon. Now it seems, although no one knows for certain, that some of the American vines imported into France to combat *Phylloxera* carried mycelium or of spores of *Plasmopara viticola,* and, just as the French were beginning to enjoy their wine again, the new pest struck the very susceptible leaves and fruits of the *vinifera* grapes.

In dry years this was not too serious, but in wet years it was disastrous. I have personally seen unsprayed European vineyards in which the crop was *completely* destroyed by this fungus. In the late eighteen seventies, all vineyards were unsprayed because fungicides were unknown. The French grape and wine industry seemed doomed.

One day in 1882, so the story goes, Alexis Millardet, professor at the University, of Bordeaux, was passing by a vineyard, thinking no doubt about his fungi, when he noticed that the vines bordering his path looked much healthier than those beyond them, which showed the now too familiar symptoms of downy mildew.

He noticed further that the outside row appeared to have been sprayed with some substance of poisonous appearance. His curiosity aroused, he made inquiries which revealed that the owner had poisoned the vines along the walk with a mixture of copper sulphate and lime to discourage strangers from picking his grapes.

Millardet returned to his laboratory and started to work on this clue, from which he soon developed Bordeaux mixture the first fungicide to be used in the control of plant disease. The story has a sequel. While the French were worrying about the *Phylloxera* and the mildew, some Mediterranean countries, believing the French grape and wine industries doomed, entered upon an unprecedented program of grape planting.

When the American stocks solved the *Phylloxera* problem and Bordeaux mixture controlled downy mildew effectively, overproduction of grapes created an economic crisis in these countries. The Peronospor-aceae include a number of common genera differentiated chiefly by the branching of their sporangiophores.

Whereas only a few of the Pythiaceae have a differentiated sporangiophore, all the Peronosporaceae bear their sporangia on sporangiophores giophores. In *Basidiophora* the sporangiophore is club-shaped with a swollen head over which the sporangia are borne on minute sterigmata.

In *Sclerospora* the sporangiophore is a long stout hypha, with many upright branches near the end, bearing sporangia at the tips. In *Plasmapara the* branches and their subdivisions occur typically at right angles and are irregularly spaced.

In *Peronospora* and *Pseudoperonospora* the sporangiophores are dichotomously branched at acute angles and taper to gracefully curved pointed tips on which sporangia are borne. *Bremia* is similar to *Peronospora* except that the tips of the branches are expanded into saucer-shaped structures with four sterigmata each along their margin bearing the sporangia.

The sporangiiophores of the Peronosporaceae have a determinate growth as contrasted to the indeterminate-growth of the sporangiophores of the higher Pythiaceae. In the Peronosporaceae, the mycelium produces a sporangiophore which reaches maturity, stops growing, and then produces a crop of sporangia on sterigmata at the apices of its branches. All the sporangia are therefore of approximately the same age.

They are round, oval, or lemon-shaped‘, and, without exception, deciduous and wind-disseminated. In most genera of the Peronosporaceae, the sporangia germinate by zoospores or germ tubes depending on environmental conditions, but the sporangia of *Peronospora* invariably germinate by means’ of germ tubes.

Such sporangia are considered sports in themselves and are often termed conidia. Conidia always germinate by germ tubes. Conidia, which are particularly characteristic of the

Ascomycetes, are also found in some of the lower fungi (Oomycetes, Zygomycetes, Trichomycetes), in which they represent the final stage in the evolution of the sporangia.

Although mycologists generally use the term sporangia to indicate these structures in all the Peronosporales, plant pathologists prefer to apply the term conidia to the deciduous sporangia.

It really does not matter what term you use so long as you understand the development and the function of the structures concerned. Here again we have a question of a man-made definition and a man-created border line which fungal sporangia-or are they conidia?—will continue to defy.

The oospores of the Peronosporaceae as a general rule germinate by germ tubes. Those of *Peronospora tabacina* appear to be an exception. According to Person and Lucas (1953), they produce a sporangial vesicle which releases zoospores.

The life histories of all species in this family follow the same general pattern, which is similar to that of *pythium* and *Phytophthora*, explained in detail a few pages back. The life history of Plasmopara viticola is illustrated in Figure elsewhere in this chapter.

FAMILY ALBUGINACEAE

The Albuginaceae include the fungi known as white rusts. All of them are obligate parasites causing diseases of vascular plants.

There are several species of *Albugo,* the only genus in this family. Of these *Albugo candida,* which attacks crucifers, is the only one causing disease attaining economically significant proportions.

An outbreak of white rust on horse-radish or on cabbage, for example, sometimes causes considerable damage. Some of the other species commonly found are *Albugo ipomoeae-panduranae* on sweet potato and morning glory, *Albugo portulacae* on *Portulaca, Alb go occidentalis* on spinach and *Albugo bliti* on various members of the Amaranthaceae.

Life History

In *Albugo candida* the Mycelium is intercellular and feeds by means of haustoria which penetrate the host cell walls through minute perforations, and expand on the inside of the cells into globose or knob-like structures.

The mycelium grows and ramifies, and, when a certain stage of maturity is reached, produces short, club-shaped sporangiophores from the tips of a large number of hyphhal branches in one locality. The sporangiophores are borne in close proximity to one another in solid layers or beds immediately below the epidermis of the host.

When the sporangiophores reach a certain stage of growth, they begin to cut off a number of sporangia at their tips. Each sporangiophore gives rise to several sporangia which it produces in succession, one below the other, so that a chain of sporangia is formed with the oldest at the tip of the chain and the youngest at the base.

As the sporangia mature, they become detached and are freed—in the space between the porangiophores and the epidermis of the host. Both the growth of the fungus and the production of numerous sporangia exert a pressure from below on the host epidermis, causing it to bulge and eventually to burst over the growing sorus.

Upon the bursting of the epidermis, the sporangia are released and form a white crust on the surface of the host. Individually the sporangia are normally glohose, but pressure during their formation results in flattened sides so that some of them are cuboid or polyhedral

They have rather thin walls and are filled with protoplasm. The sporangia are multinucleate. Disseminated by the wind, by water, and perhaps by other agents as well, a great percentage of them perish, never reaching a susceptible host.

The sporangia of *Albugo* germinate by zoospores or by germ tubes, depending on the temperature. When zoospores are produced, the sporangia extrude four to twelve zoospores in an advanced stage of differentiation, into a sessile vesicle. Subsequent details of the asexual cycle follow the pattern typical of the Peronosporales.

Sexual reproduction in its gross aspects is similar in all species, but the cytological details of fertilization seem to fall into at least three patterns. The following discussion will be confined to only one of these patterns and applies specifically to *Albugo candida.*

Oogonia and antheridia are formed within the tissues of the host. Both organs are multinucleate at the start, but only one nucleus in each is finally functional. The gametangia are formed near each other and are borne terminally on somatic hyphae.

They soon establish contact, the antheridium contacting the oogonium at the side. When mature, the globose oogonium, contains an oosphere surrounded by periplasm. Its functional egg nucleus is drawn near the center of the oosphere while the other nuclei move into the periplasm.

The antheridium now forms a fertilization tube; a single male nucleus passes through it together with some cytoplasm approaches the egg nucleus, and fuses with it.

The resulting zygote nucleus divides several times while the fertilized oosphere is being transformed into an oospore by the development of a thick wall. The oospore wall *of Albugo candida* is warty.

Oospores of some species have a network of ridges over the surface. The character of the oospore is a uselul criterion in distinguishing between species of *Albugo.*

After several divisions of the zygote nucleus, two of which are meiotic, the oospore enters a resting stage. The following, spring the nuclei resume their mitotic activity, and the protoplast of the oospore eventually divides into a large number of uninucleate sections, each of which develops into a biflagellate, reniform zoospore.

An oospore germinates in one of two ways. Either it extrudes its zoospores into a sessile vesicle, or it forms a short exit tube which terminates in a vesicle. Each oospore produces from forty to sixty zoospores. Oospores apparently reedy by germ tubes as do those off *Phytophthora infestans;* for example.

The oospore thus behaves like a resting sporangium. When the vesicle wall bursts, the zoospores are liberated they swarm, encyst, and finally germinate by germ tubes which infect the host.

In species att$_a$ckin$_g$ perennial hosts, the mycelium is capable of overwintering in the infected tissues. Remaining dormant during the winter, it resumes activity in the spring and grows into the new shoots which the host produces. Infection, in such cases, is said to be systemic.

Biological Specialization

We have seen that both the Peronosporaceae and the Albuginaceae are obligate parasites of vascular plants. Species are distinguished on the basis of their morphology, i.e., size of sporangia, sculpturing of oospore wall, etc.

Each species is capable of infecting a certain group of closely related host plants. For example, *Albugo candida* infects members of the family Cruciferae, but no plants outside this family, at least in North America.

Wilson (1907), who examined a great many collections of this fungus, stated that there is a "remarkable stability of essential characters" in this species in spite of the fact that it attacks so many different hosts. *Albugo candida* is therefore a good morphological species.

Within this morphological species, however-and this is important-cross-inoculation from one species of host to another will not always result in infection. This is interpreted to mean that the species *Albugo candida* is composed of a number of biological forms which are morphologically identical, but differ in their ability to infect various crucifers.

These biological forms or strains are, therefore, specialized in their parasitism, and the phenomenon is known as biological special-ization.

Chapter 13 Plasmodiophoromycetes

The Plasmodiophoromycetes are obligate endoparasites of vascular plants, algae and fungi, which usually cause an abnormal enlargement of the host cells, called *hypertrophy* (Gr. *hyper* = over + *trophe* = food). The result is the enlargement of the infected portions of the host and, in higher plants, the disruption of the vascular elements.

In the latter event, the general stunting and premature death of the host occur. The somatic phase of the Plasmodiophoromycetes is a plasmodium which develops within the host cells.

Plasmodia give rise to zoosporangia containing zoospores, or directly to resting spores which are produced by cleavage of the plasmodium into uninucleate portions. No fructifications are formed, but the spores in some genera are united and form spore balls or discs.

Upon germination, each resting spore releases a single swarm cell. Both swarm cells and zoospores bear two unequal, anterior flagella, both of the whiplash type. Work by Kole and Gielink (1961, 1962) on this point is very convincing. The electron micrograph in figure elsewhere in this chapter is theirs.

Nuclear division at some stages of the life cycle of the Plasmodio-phoromycetes is of a type found in no other fungi, but known to occur in the Protozoa. During division, an intranuclear spindle is formed on which the chromosomes are arranged in a ring around the nucleolus. As the chromosomes split, a ring of chromosomes passes to each pole.

The nucleolus elongates, becomes dumbbellshaped, and divides into two portions which form the nucleoli of the two daughter nuclei.

The dumbbell-shaped nucleolus surro-unded by a chromatin ring appears like a cross when viewed from the side, hence the name *cruciform (L. crux* = cross) given to this type of division.

Another interesting phenomenon which has been described as occurring in the Plasmodiophoromycetes is the so-called *akaryote phase* (Gr. *a* = not + *karyon* = nut, nucleus). This is a stage in which the nuclear body seems to disappear, most of the chromatin failing to take the usual stain.

Whether this is a true phase through which the nuclei of these organisms pass or whether it is an artifact due to improper staining is still a matter of considerable controversy.

Occurrence, and Importance to Man

The occurrence and geographic distribution of the Plasmodiophoro-mycetes obviously coincide with those of their hosts. Many species parasitize freshwater algae such as *Vaucheria,* or aquatic fungi such as *Saprolegnia, Achlya,* acid *Pythium.*

Other species parasitize aquatic and marsh vascular plants in the genera *Isoetes, Halophila, Zostera, Juncus,* etc., or land plants, such as *cabbage*, *potato*, *Nasturtium,* and *Veronica.*

There are only two species which are of economic importance: *Plasmodiophora brassicae is* the widespread cause of clubroot or finger-and-toe disease of cabbage and related plants, both cultivated and wild, and *Spongospora subterranea* is the causal agent of powdery scab of potatoes. Its special form *Spongospora subterraneaf.* sp. *nasturtii* causes a serious disease of water cress.

General Life Cycle

In spite of a number of critical studies on various members of this class, no general life cycle pattern for the Plasmodiophoromycetes has emerged as yet. Resting spores, swarm cells, plasmodia, and zoosporangia with zoospores appear to occur in most species.

The great controversy hinges on the occurrence of a sexual stage and the alternation of a haploid with a diploid cycle. A discussion of some points in the general life cycle which need clarification follows.

The resting spores germinate, each releasing a swarm cell. Swarm cells are believed to penetrate into the host cells as uninucleate amoebae and there to develop into

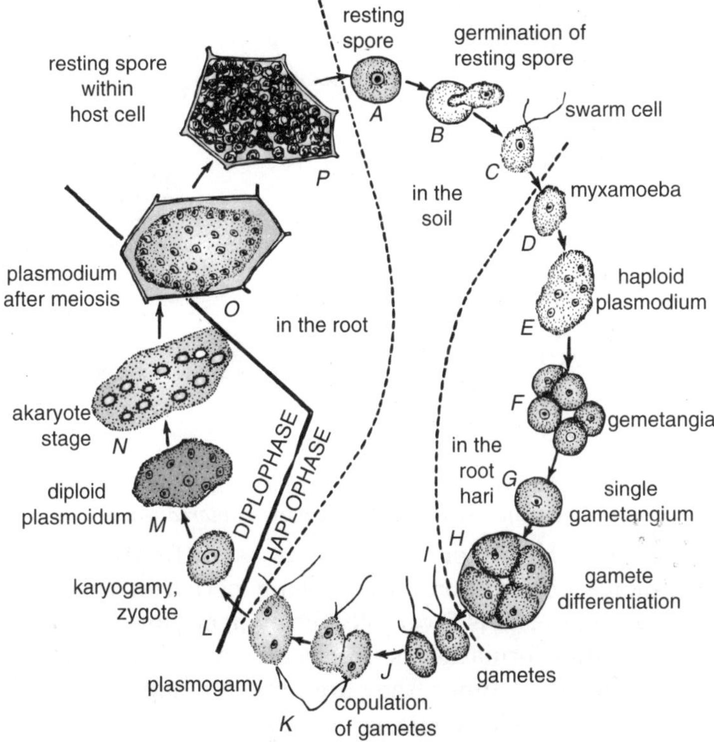

Figure 13.1: Diagrammatic presentation of the possible sequence of events in the life cycle of Plasmodiophora brassicae.

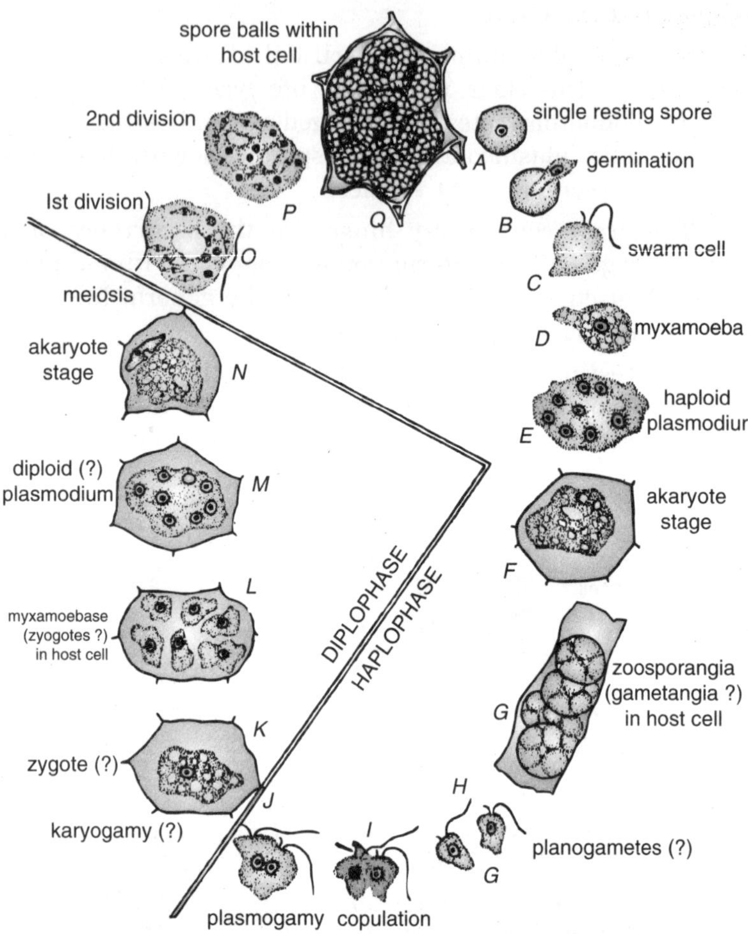

Figure 13.2: Diagrammatic representation of the possible sequence of events in the life cycle of Spongospora subterranea.

plasmodia. However, because it is difficult to make continuous observations over a long period of time, even when the material is favorable, the evidence for this method of plasmodial formation is all circumstantial. If plasmodia develop in this manner, they are probably haploid. Nuclear division in the plasmodia is cruciform.

After the plasmodium reaches a certain size, determined to a great extent by the size of the host cell, it cleaves into usually multinucleate portions, each of which becomes surrounded by a membrane and develops into a zoosporangium.

Zoospores are released outside the host through exit papillae on the sporangia and through pores dissolved in the host wall. What happens next is a matter of controversy. Whether zoospores reinfeet the host and repeat the life cycle, or whether they act as planogametes, fuse in pairs, and infect the host as zygotes, needs to be clarified.

Some plasmodia, instead of developing into zoosporangia, cleave into uninucleate portions which secrete cell walls and become resting spores. These plasmodia are indistinguishable from those which produce zoosporangia until cleavage, occurs.

What is the difference between these two types of plasmodia? Some mycologists believe that plasmodia which develop during early infection produce zoosporangia, whereas those which develop later produce resting spores.

Does the environment then govern the type of structure which the plasmodia will produce? Other mycologists believe that the plasmodia which form zoosporangia are haploid, whereas those which form resting spores are diploid.

If this is true, the diploid plasmodia probably originate by growth and nuclear division of a zygote, as in the Myxomycetes. This presupposes a fusion of cells somewhere in the life cycle. Such fusions have been observed in both *Plasmodiophora brassicae* and *Spongospora subterranea*, but no karyogamy has been seen.

This does not mean that it does not occur! If diploid plasmodia are responsible for the production of the resting spores, it is probable that meiosis occurs before spore formation.

This also has been claimed for *Spongospora subterranea,* but chromosome *counts-the only positive way to prove meiosis*—are so difficult to make in these fungi that no one is sure that meiosis indeed occurs.

Figures elsewhere in this chapter represent our present thinking on the life cycles of *Plasmodiophora brassicae* and *Spongospora subterranea.*

Classification

The Plasmodiophoromycetes comprise a single order, the Plasmodiop-horales, with but a single family, the Plasmodiophoraceae. In possessing a plasmodium, and in their type of motile cells, they resemble the Myxomycetes, with which they have often been grouped.

They differ from the Myxomycetes in their biology, in their zoosporangial stage, in that they form no fruiting bodies when the resting spores are produced, and in that the spore walls apparently contain no cellulose.

If their plasmodia are indeed haploid, this would constitute another important difference. Because of these reasons, many authors have included them in the Phycomycetes, in the wide sense, or in the Archimycetes, a class of lower fungi in which some authors place the nonmycelial, sporangial fungi.

Sparrow (1958/1959), recognizing that the Plasmodiophorales have probably originated independently of the groups with which they were formerly affiliated, separated them from the other classes of fungi and designated them as Plasmodiophoromycetes.

In the present state of our ignorance concerning them, this treatment appears to be justified and has been adopted here. We recognize nine genera in the Plasmodiophoraceae. These are separated currently on the basis of the arrangement of the resting spores, even though serious doubts have been expressed about the reliability of such distinctions.

These genera are *Plasmodiophora, Spongospora, Sorodiscus, Sorosphaera, Ligniera, Tetramyxa, Octomyxa, Polymyxa,* and *Woronina.* A few other genera have also been described, but their validity, or their inclusion in this family is questionable".

Chapter 14 Zygomycetes

In the early days of mycology the large and heterogeneous class Phycomycetes was subdivided into two sub-classes: the Oomycetes, in many of which the resting spore or sporangium develops from the fertilized egg, and the Zygomycetes, in which the resting spore develops from the fusion of two usually equal gametangia.

Whereas the Zygomycetes were recognized as a unified, more or less well-limited group, it became more and more evident as our knowledge of the Oomycetes expanded that this was an artificial conglomeration of unrelated forms.

When Sparrow, in 1943, broke away from the oomycete concept and emphasized flagellation as the important phylogenetic and taxonomic criterion, he placed the fungi formerly called Oomycetes into two large series: the Uniflagellatae and the Biflagellatae, treating the Hyphochyt-riales as a separate order not belonging to either series.

Inasmuch as his book dealt only with aquatic Phycomycetes, he did not include in his classification the Zygomycetes, which are almost strictly terrestrial fungi. Other authors, accepting Sparrow's classification but wishing to deal with all major groups of fungi, divided the Phycomycetes into three series: the Uniflagellatae, the Biflagellatae, and, for the sake of uniformity of concept, the Aplanatae or Aflagellatae.

In his 1958 address to the Mycological Society of America, later published in *Mycologia,* Sparrow recognized four "*galaxies*" of aquatic Phycomycetes and gave them the class names *Chytridiomycetes*, *Hyphochytridiomycetes*, *Plasmodiophoromycetes*, and *Phycomycetes*.

These classes have been the subjects of previous chapters in this book. Logical expansion of this concept elevates the old sub-class Zygomycetes to class rank and retains the old established name.

General Characteristics

The term Zygomycetes refers to the production of a sexual resting spore called a zygospore (Gr. *zygos* = yoke + *sporos* = seed, spore). A zygospore typically results from the complete fusion of two gametangia. It differs from an oospore in that the latter is derived from an oosphere.

The production of a zygospore is, therefore, the chief characteristic of members of this class. Nevertheless, a number of species in which no sexual reproduction has been found are classified in the Zygomycetes with complete confidence because they exhibit other characters which point to such relationships.

Chief among these secondary characters is the production of characteristic sporangia or of conidia, and the complete absence of motile cells. Ecological, physiological, and biological considerations also enter into defining the Zygomycetes, which most mycologists consider as a natural group of fungi.

These are, then, the two main characteristics of the Zygomycetes:

(1) sexual reproduction by means of gametangial copulation, resulting in the formation of a zygospore, and (2) asexual reproduction by means of non-motile spores in the form of sporangiospores or conidia.

Biologically, the Zygomycetes range all the way from saprobes, through facultative, weak parasites of plants, to specialized parasites of animals, and to obligate parasites of other Zygomycetes. Certain groups of Zygomycetes are remarkably specialized in one way or another. Among the most interesting phenomena encountered in this class of fungi are:

(1) certain methods of spore dispersal, as exemplified by the "fungous shotgun" of *Pilobolus* and the repetitional germination and forceful propulsion of the "conidia" of the Entomopht-horales, and (2) the animal-trapping mechanisms of the Zoopagales.

Classification

The class Zygomycetes, as we recognize it here, includes three orders: Mucorales, Entomophthorales, and Zoopagales. These may be distinguished in accordance with the following *key:*

Simple Key to the Orders of the Class Zygomycetes

A.	Chiefly saprobic, some weakly parasitic on plants, a few endoparasitic in vertebrates, including man; asexual reproduction by sporangia containing one to many aplanospores, sometimes by conidia	*Mucorales*
AA.	Chiefly parasitic on lower animals, rarely on plants, sometimes saprobic; asexual reproduction by modified sporangia functioning as conidia, or by true conidia	
B.	Modified sporangia functioning as conidia, forcibly discharged	*Entomophthorales*
BB.	Conidia not forcibly discharged	*Zoopagales*

ORDER MUCORALES

Classification

The Mucorales have been investigated by a large number of workers on both sides of the Atlantic. In the previous century De Bary, Brefeld, Bainier, Coemans, Leger, Schroeter, Van Tieghem, and Vuillemin, among others in Europe, and primarily Thaxter in America laid down the morphological foundations of the classification of these fungi which produced the later monographs of Zycha (1935) and Naumov (1939).

In later years, the cytological and physiological studies of Buller, Cutter, Sjowall, Barnett and Lilly, and many others have extended our knowledge of the Mucorales along lines which had not been greatly explored in the past.

At the present time, the researches of Dr. C. W. Hesseltine of the U. S. Department of Agriculture, and of Dr. R. K. Benjamin of the Santa Ana Botanic Garden, are doing much to clarify the relationships among the Mucorales and to synthesize a modern system of classification from all the knowledge that has accumulated.

According to these workers, the Mucorales have developed along six lines of evolution. The families which represent each line may be grouped as follows:

1. Mucoraceae
2. Thamnidiaceae
   Cunninghamellaceae
3. Choanephoraceae
4. Pilobolaceae
5. Mortierellaceae
   Endogonaceae
6. Syncephalastraceae
   Piptocephalidaceae
   Dimargaritaceae
   Kickxellaceae

In 1958 Boedijn added the family Helicocephalidaceae to accom-modate the genera *Helicocephalum* and *Rhopalomyces*. We can do little more in an introductory discussion than to point out some of the major characteristics of the order Mucorales with an occasional reference to special groups.

Biology

The great majority of the Mucorales are saprobes, living on such substrata as dung and decaying plant or animal matter. Many saprobic species are capable of synthesizing important industrial products and have been utilized by man for his benefit.

Thus, *Rhizopus stolonifer* (*R. nigricans*), the common bread mold, is used commercially for the manufacture of fumaric acid and for some steps in the manufacture of cortisone.

Rhizopus oryzae is capable of producing considerable quantities of alcohol. Various species of *Rhizopus,* like *Rhizopus sinensis, Rhizopus stolonifer, Rhizopus oryzae,* and *Rhizopus nodosus,* are capable of forming large quantities of lactic acid.

Although such lactic acid cannot compete in price with bacterial lactic acid, the mold product is of such great purity that it may find special usage.

Mucorales also produce citric acid, succinic acid, oxalic acid, and other important chemicals. For a complete discussion of the biochemical activities of these and other fungi, see the excellent treatises entitled *Chemical Activities of Fungi,* by Dr. J. W. Foster of the University of Texas (1949), and *The Relation of Fungi to Human Affairs by* Dr. W. D. Gray of Ohio State University (1959).

A few Mucorales are weak parasites growing on fruits and other detached plant parts and causing diseases in transit and in storage. Such a one is *Rhizopus stolonifer,* which causes a serious transit disease of strawberries, designated as leak, and a soft rot of sweet potatoes in storage.

Others are parasitic on fungi, green plants, or animals. *Choanephora cucurbitarum,* for example, attacks squash blossoms and fruits, sometimes causing considerable damage. Still. other species of Mucorales are known to cause human diseases. *Absidia corymbifera* and several species of *Mucor* and *Rhizopus* attack the human internal nervous system with fatal consequences.

Of particular interest to the mycologist are members of the family Piptocephalidaceae, which are obligately parasitic on other fungi, chiefly other Mucorales. These serve as ideal organisms for studies on the physiology of obligate parasitism.

Such studies, now under way at West Virginia, are showing that temperature and nutrition greatly affect the susceptibility of the host to the parasite, and that nutrients provided the host often influence the growth of the parasite even when they do not affect the host itself.

Somatic Structures

Typically, the soma of the Mucorales is a well-developed mycelium. In the few species in which the cytology of the somatic hyphae has been studied critically the nuclei appear to divide directly by constriction without spindle formation or evidence of classical mitotic figures.

In most species the hyphae are coenocytic, producing septa at the bases of the reproductive organs, sporangia, or gametangia, and only occasionally elsewhere when the mycelium ages.

Such septa are solid plates formed by annular growth beginning at the hyphal wall. The more specialized Mucorales, in which the mycelium is septate from the very beginning, have perforate septa, some with tubular extensions projecting forward in the direction of protoplasmic flow, others with special type plugs.

Protoplasmic streaming can easily be seen in vigorously growing hyphae of the Mucorales, and the mycelium of bread mold, so easy to isolate, is frequently used to demonstrate this phenomenon in the classroom.

The mycelium of some species produces rhizoids formed especially at points where the mycelium contacts a hard surface, such as the sides of a glass dish in which the fungus may be growing. The rhizoids adhere to the substratum and anchor the fungus securely.

A hypha which connects two groups of rhizoids ‘is called a stolon, and in function resembles the stolon of the strawberry, which grows out of the parent plant and strikes root at the tip. The similarity, of course, ends here.

ASEXUAL REPRODUCTION

The Sporangiophore

The Mucorales usually reproduce .asexually by means

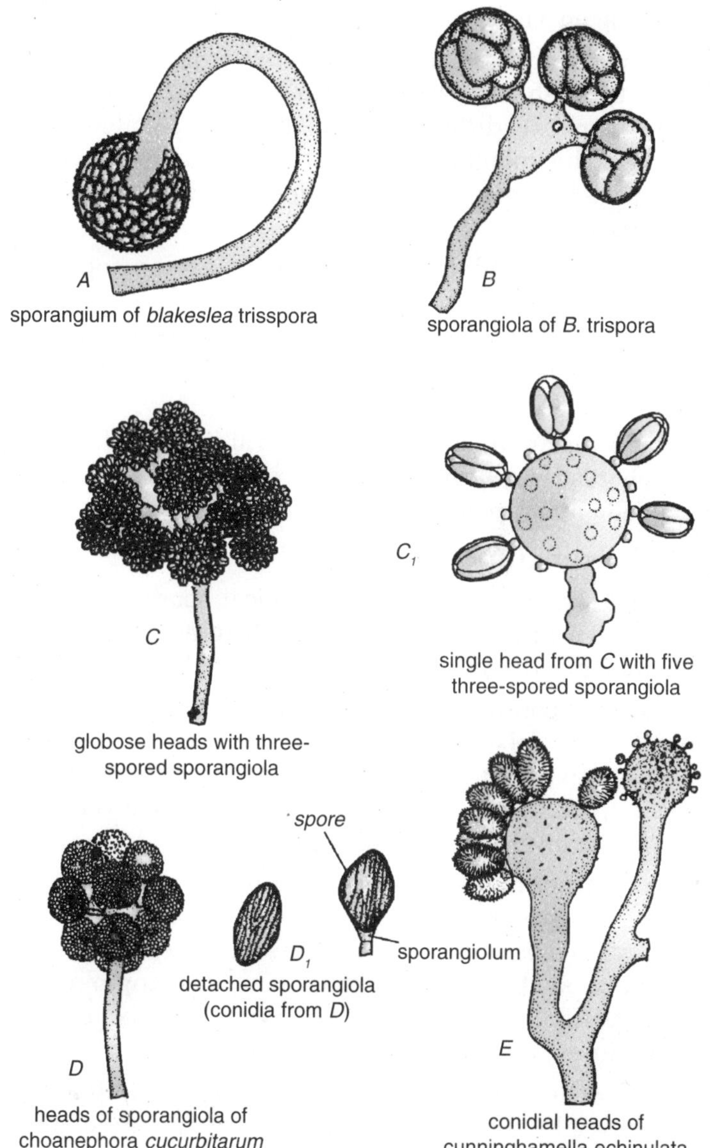

Figure 14.1: Series of drawings showing probable transition stages in the evolution of the sporangium to a conidiuni.

of aplanospores contained in sporangia. They bear their sporangia on simple or branched sporangiophores.

Branching varies from the relatively simple type of *Mucor,* through the whorled arrangement of *Thamnidium,* to the intricate differentiation of special coiled, fertile branches, the sporoladia (sing. *sporocladium*; Gr. *sporos* = seed, spore + *klados* = branch) of *Spirodactylon* in the family *Kickxellaceae*.

The growth and development of the sporangiophores is a complicated process and has been studied extensively in *Phycomyces, blakesleanus,* which has become an extremely important tool for morphogenetic and physiological research.

Particularly intriguing is the spiral growth of the sporangiophores, which appears to be correlated with a spiral arrangement of molecules in their walls.

The Sporangium

What we may regard as the typical sporangium of the Mucorales we find primarily in the Mucoraceae, the largest and probably the most primitive of the eleven families.

Such a sporangium is formed at the tip of a sporangiophore as a globose swelling in which a central columella becomes separated from the outer sporiferous region. The typical sporangium, developed under favorable conditions, contains many thousands of spores.

In contrast to the above, some Mucorales produce small sporangia, with or without columellae, which contain but a few spores each, and in some species are monosporous. We designate such small sporangia as sporangiola (sing. sporangiolum; *sporangium + L. dimin.* suffix *-olum)* or sporangioles.

Both sporangia and sporangiola may be, and frequently are, formed by the same sporangiophore in certain species. Sporangiola which contain but one spore are often regarded as conidia, and are so termed in the literature.

This term applies particularly to structures in which

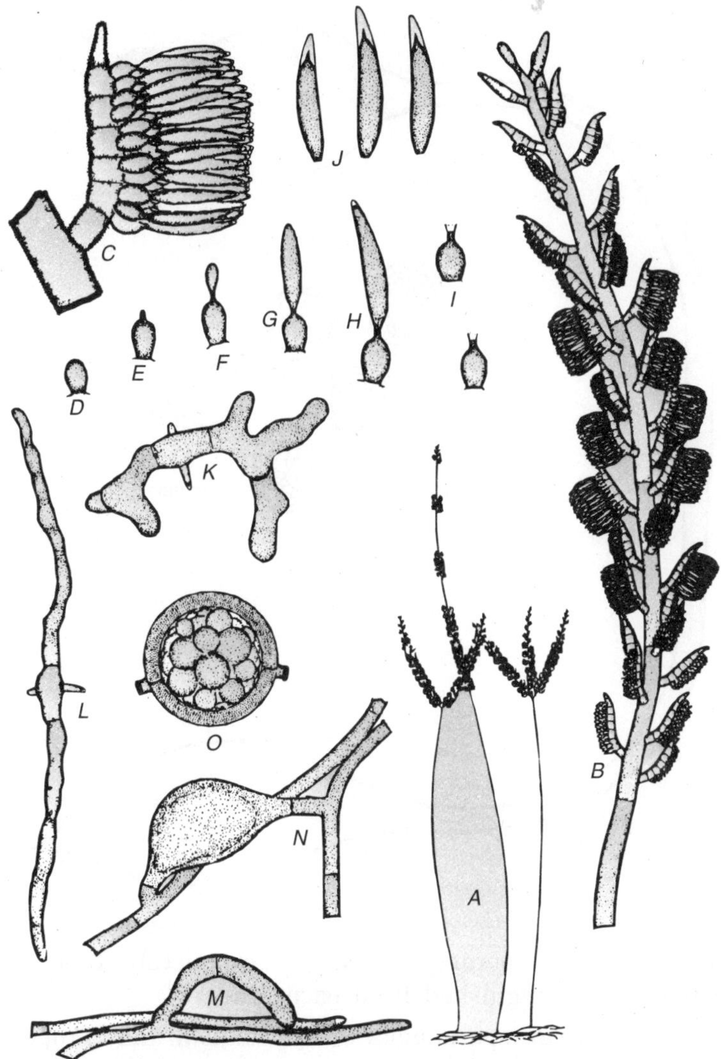

Figure 14.2: Coemansia mojavensis. A. Habit sketch. B. Upper portion of fruiting branch. C. Sporocladium. D-H. Stages in the development of a sporangiolum. I. Collar-like remnant of the basal portion of the sporangiolum wall. J. Mature sporangiola. K-L. Germinating spores. M. Plasmogamy. N. Early stage of zygospore. O. Mature zygospore.

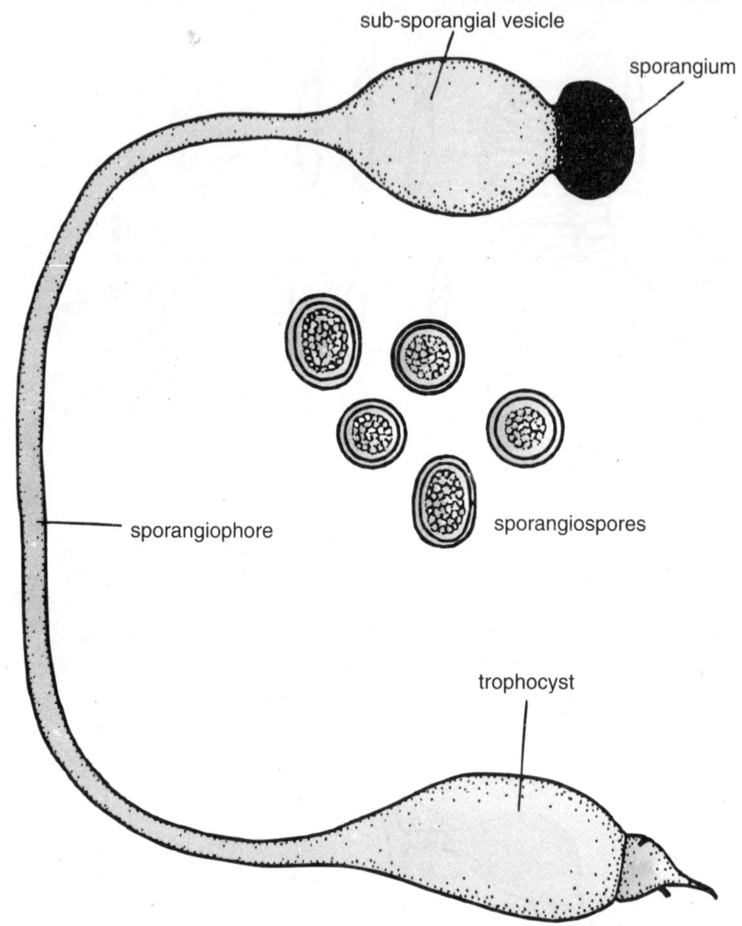

Figure 14.3. Piloholus longipes. Sporangial apparatus.

the sporal and sporangial walls are completely fused and cannot be distinguished from each other.

Either term (sporangiola or sporangiola) may properly be applied to these structures, since, it is probable that the conidia of the Zygomycetes have arisen from sporangia by reduction of the number of spores from many to one and by the subsequent fusion of the wall of the sporangium with that of the single spore within it.

Figure elsewhere in this chapter shows at a glance some

of the structures which suggest to mycologists that the conidium of the Mucorales has been developed from the sporangium.

Look at the drawing (A) of the large sporangium of *Blakeslea trispora.* This may be regarded as a typical sporangium of the Mucorales. Now study the "sporangiola arising from a central head (B). These represent reduced sporangia arising from a branched sporangiophore. Branched sporangiophores are common in the Mucorales.

Next in line (C, C,) are the three-spored sporangiola on small heads at the branched tip of the sporangiophore. The next probable step toward the development of the conidium takes us to the genus *Choanephora (D, D_l).* The inflated heads *(D)* now support sporangiola which contain but a single spore or in which the spore wall appears to be fused with the sporangial wall (Dl).

Once this stage is reached, you can see how *Cunninghamella (E),* which produces conidia on inflated conidiophores, may have developed. The fungi included in the most advanced evolutionary series of the Mucorales produce their spores in cylindrical sporangiola which we call merosporangia (sing. *merosporangium*; Gr. *meros* = portion + *sporangium).*

Merosporangia may be borne on the surface of an inflated sporangiophore tip and radiate out, or they may be formed on sporocladia. In the Syncephalastraceae the merosporangia contain many uniseriate spores; in the Piptocephalidaceae and the Dimargaritaceae, two spores. The Kickxellaceae bear monosporous sporangiola on special cells produced on sporocladia.

Spores and Spore Dissemination

Sporangiospores differ in shape, size, markings, and color. In the majority of species they are globose to ovoid; in some species they are cylindrical. In many forms the spores are longitudinally striate. Some bear long hyaline bristles at each pole.

Sporangiospores are usually formed by the cleavage of

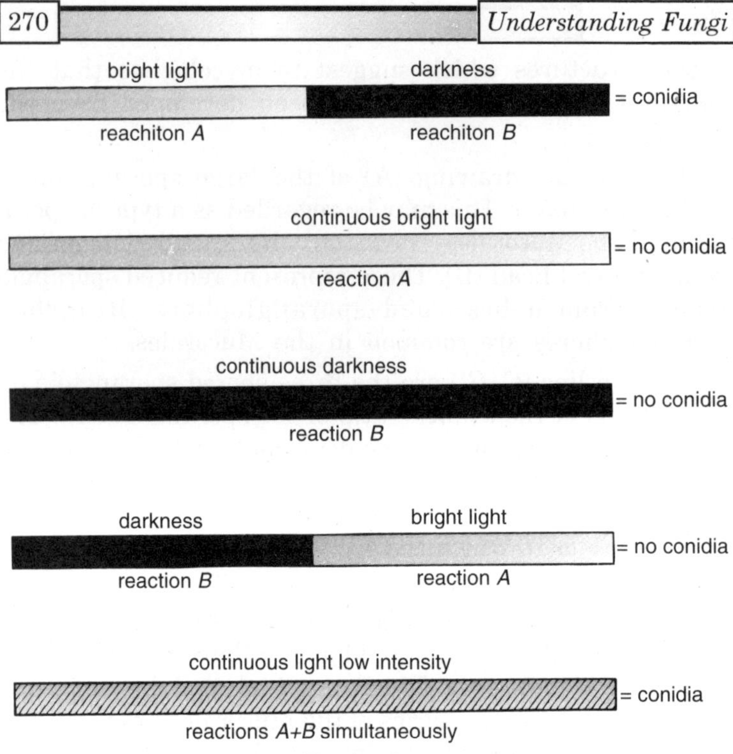

Figure 14.4: Choanephora cucurbitarum. Conidium formation under different light conditions.

the sporangial protoplast into minute uninucleate or multinucleate portions around each of which a wall develops. If the spores are uninucleate at the time of their formation, they often become multinucleate later by nuclear division.

Special methods of spore formation are employed by some members of the more advanced families. The sporangiospores are liberated by the dissolution of the sporangial wall.

In some Mucorales the spores form a dry, powdery mass and are easily dispersed by air currents, but in other species the spore mass is enveloped by a drop of liquid which dries and leaves the spores adhering firmly to each other and to the columella.

Of great interest is the mechanism of spore dispersal developed by *Pilobolus,* a common inhabitant of horse and cow dung. The entire sporangium is violently shot off the sporangiophore and adheres to the first solid object it strikes.

The sporangiophores of *Pilobolus* are positively phototropic and shoot their sporangia toward the light. This is a useful adaptation which helps disseminate the spores. The sporangiophore of *Pilobolus* consists of a swollen trophocyst (Gr. *trophe* = food + *kystis* = bladder), the sporangiophore proper, a swollen sub-sporangial vesicle, and a sporangium whose wall is heavily cutinized.

Buller states that *Pilobolus* can shoot its sporangia

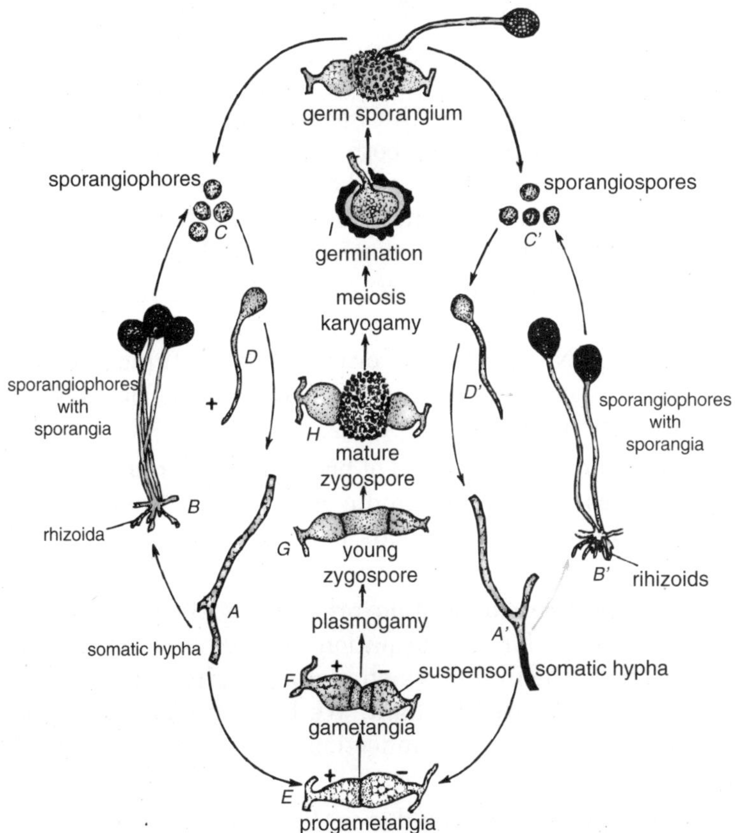

Figure 14.5: Life cycle of Rhizopus stolonifer (R. nigricans).

vertically upward to a height of 6 feet. Thus *Pilobolus* (the hat thrower) deserves its name. Other methods of asexual reproduction in the Mucorales include the formation of chlamydospores-sometimes referred to as gemmae in the hyphae, and the breaking up of the mycelium into yeastlike bodies which reproduce by budding. Yeast-like cells are formed when the mycelium is growing in a liquid medium.

Physiology of Asexual Reproduction

Exactly what triggers the initiation of asexual reproduction in the Mucorales is not known, but considerable progress has been made in the study of conditions which favor or inhibit the formation of asexual reproductive structures.

Of particular interest are the researches of Barnett and Lilly at West Virginia with *Choanephora cucurbitarum,* an organism which produces both multispored sporangia and monospore sporangiola (conidia). High temperature (30-31°C.) and relative humidity (100 per cent) favor sporangial production and inhibit formation of conidia.

Lower temperature (25°C.) and relative humidity favor conidial production. The effect of light is even more spectacular. No conidia are produced in continuous darkness, continuous bright light (60 foot-candles), or darkness followed by bright light.

However, when a period of bright light *precedes* a period of darkness, abundant conidia are formed. Some conidia are also formed in continuous weak light (less than 1 foot-candle).

The possible explanation proposed is that some substance necessary for the formation of conidia is synthesized in two steps, the first of which requires light and the second of which is inhibited by light. We have already mentioned the genus *Pilobolus* in connection with its spore dispersal mechanism.

Until recently, we could grow *Pilobolus* in the laboratory only on media containing dung decoctions. Hesseltine and his coworkers (1952) found in dung a factor which was necessary for the growth of *Pilobolus.* They named this factor coprogen.

That same year Page (1952) announced that he had grown *Pilobolus* on a chemically defined medium with hemin as a substitute for the necessary growth factor in dung. However, even though *Pilobolus* grew well in such a medium, production of sporangia was meager.

Continuing with this work, Page noticed that some plates contaminated with *Mucor plumbeus* produced much larger numbers of sporangia than pure cultures of *Pilobolus.* Further work showed that the stimulatory substance is ammonia and that the fungus uses the ammonium ion in preference to other N sources investigated.

Sexual Reproduction

Sexual reproduction in the Mucorales takes place by the copulation of two multinucleate gametangia which are in the main similar in structure, but which may differ in size.

The gametangia are produced as terminal swellings on the tips of two compatible hyphae or hyphal branches which are attracted one to the other and come in contact. When the gametangia are formed, the walls between them dissolve and the contents mix. The cells of the two gametangia thus actually fuse into one cell, in which karyogamy eventually takes place.

This cell deyelops into a zygospore by the deposition of a thick wall around its protoplast. We shall discuss the details of sexual reproduction and zygospore formation in the next section of this chapter. It was in the Mucorales that Dr. A. F. Blakeslee, the great American geneticist, discovered in 1904 the phenomenon of sexual incompatibility in fungi.

Species which could produce zygospores on, single thalli Blakeslee called homothallic; species which required two compatible thalli to form zygospores he called heterothallic. Since the compatible strains could not be distinguished morphologically, Blakeslee labeled one + and the other.

Twenty years after Blakeslee's discovery of heterothallism, Burgeff (1924), in a series of experiments, demonstrated that a diffusible substance is probably responsible for the initiation of sexual reproduction in the Mucorales.

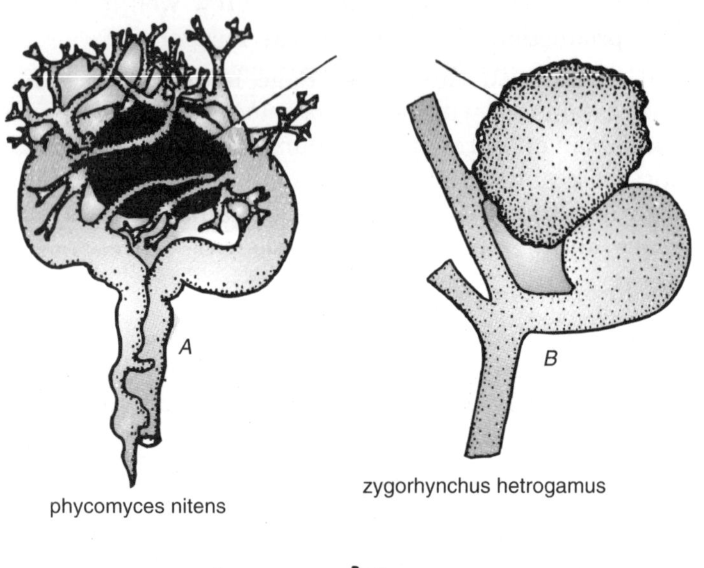

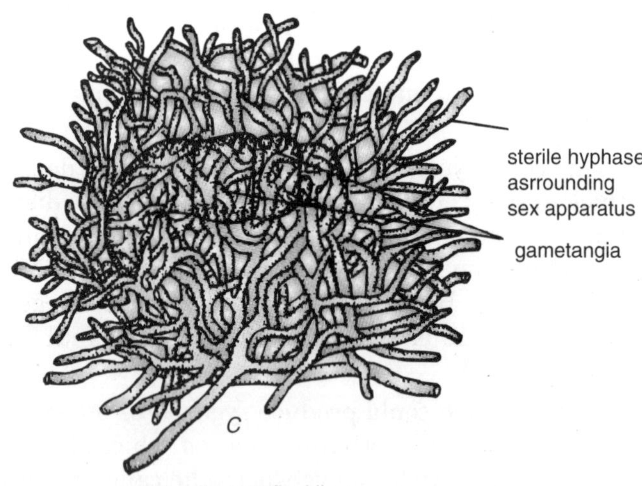

Figure 14.6: Zygospores of Mucorales.

This was the first demonstration of a hormonal sexual mechanism in the fungi. Burgeff, working with a number of species, showed that, when + and - strains were separated by a collodion membrane, hyphae of opposite strains were still attracted toward each other.

Subsequent work by other investigators has expanded upon Burgeff's discovery, and is giving us some knowledge as to the nature of the hormones involved and their method of operation.

As might be expected, sexual reproduction in the Mucorales is influenced by environmental factors, but few studies have been undertaken to determine optimum conditions for zygospore development. Barnett and Lilly (1956) have shown that in *Choanephora cucurbitarum* zygospores form under a much greater range of conditions than asexual spores.

Light has little effect *on* zygospore formation, and the same is true of temperature, pH_2 and CO_2 concentration within very wide limits. Starvation of the mycelium favors production of zygospores.

Life History

The life history of *Rhizopus stolonifer (R. nigricans)* will serve as our example of the general life cycle pattern of the Mucorales. The sporangiospores are released when the wall of the sporangium disintegrates.

The spores are globose to oval and multinucleate. Under favorable conditions a spore germinates by germ tube which develops into a fluffy, manybranched, white, aerial mycelium. The mycelium produces many aerial stolons which develop rhizoids at certain points.

Directly above the rhizoids, one or more sporangiophores are produced. The top of each sporangiophore becomes swollen as the latter reaches maturity, and a sporangium begins to develop.

During its development a great deal of cytoplasm carrying many nuclei flows into the young sporangium and concentrates mainly in its periphery. The central portion

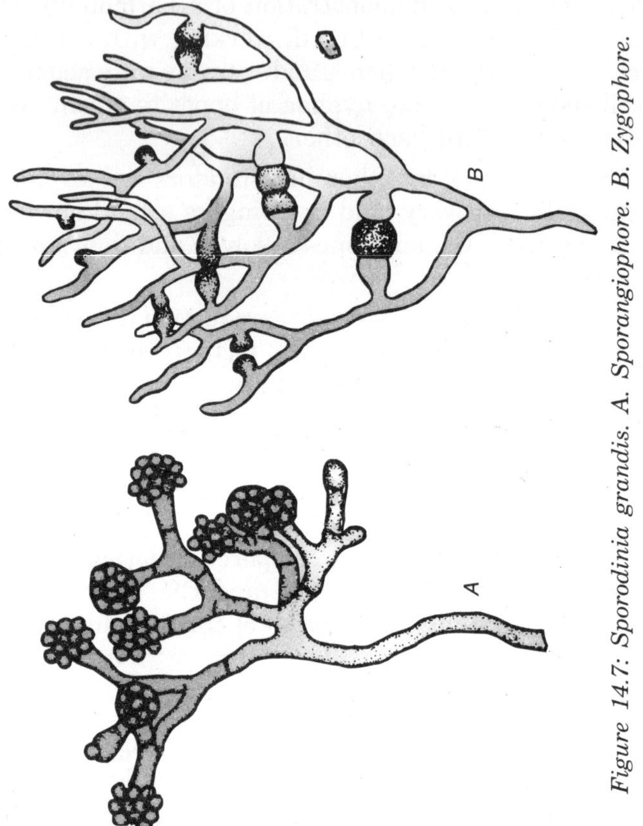

Figure 14.7: Sporodinia grandis. A. Sporangiophore. B. Zygophore.

of the sporangium becomes highly vacuolated and is eventually surrounded by a wall which separates it from the peripheral zone.

This central portion is the columella, and the peripheral zone is the spore-bearing portion of the sporangium. The protoplasm of the peripheral zone soon becomes divided into a large number of multinucleate segments, which eventually round off, become enveloped by walls, and mature into sporangiospores.

With the bursting of the sporangial wall and the liberation of the spores, which fill the air, the asexual cycle of *Rhizopus stolonifer* is completed. Other Mucorales follow the same general pattern, but the structures produced may differ in detail. Thus the majority of the Mucorales do not form stolons or rhizoids; some have no columella differentiated in the sporangium; some have branched sporangiophores; and in some the sporangia may be replaced or accompanied by sporangiola.

Sexual reproduction in *Rhizopus stolonifer* requires the presence of two physiologically distinct and compatible mycelia, + and –, the fungus being heterothallic.

All structures which have originated as a result of the germination of a single sporangiospore are of the same strain as the parent spore. When two opposite strains come in contact with one another, copulating branches called progametangia (sing. progametangium; Gr. *pro* = before + *gametangium)* are formed. Much cytoplasm and many nuclei flow to the contacting tips of these organs, which now begin to enlarge. A septum-then forms near the tip of each progametangium, separating it into two cells: a terminal gametangium and a suspensor cell.

The walls of the two contacting gametangia dissolve at the point of contact, and the two protoplasts mix. The nuclei pair, one + with one, and the two nuclei in each of a number of pairs fuse and form diploid nuclei. Unfused nuclei probably disintegrate.

In the meantime the new cell which has been formed by the copulating gametangia enlarges considerably, its wall thickens, and its surface- becomes black and warty. This heavily walled structure is the zygospore. At 21° C. under laboratory conditions, the zygospores of *Rhizopus stolonifer* germinate in approximately 1-3 months, apparently requiring a rest period before they are activated.

At the time of germination the zygospore cracks open and a sporangiophore emerges and develops a sporangium, called a germ sporangium, at its top. Meiosis takes places during the process of zygospore germination.

Zygospore formation in other Mucorales takes place essentially in the same manner as described for *Rhizopus stolonifer* but differs in detail. Many Mucorales are homothallic, and consequently each thallus is self-fertile. The size and shape of the gametangia may differ considerably.

Thus, in *Phycomyces the* gametangial apparatus resembles calipers holding a zygospore between their tips. The suspensors in this genus are provided with black, hornlike projections which give the zygospore apparatus a chara-

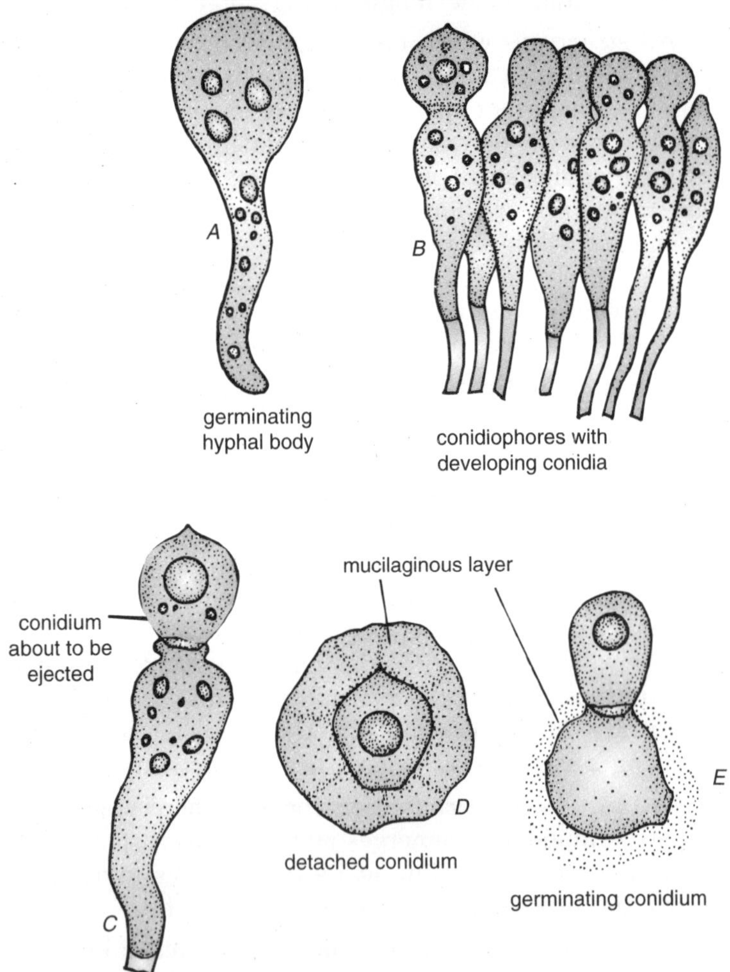

Figure 14.8: Entonophthora nuiscae.

cteristic appearance. In *Zygorhynchus,* another genus of Mucorales, the gametangia as well as the suspensors are unequal in size. Members of this genus are homothallic.

The size and outer sculpturing of the zygospores also differ in different genera. It is particularly interesting to note that in the genus *Mortierella* the zygospore is surrounded by a large number of short hyphae which form a cottony envelope around it. In the genus *Endogone* this tendency is carried further, and a number of closely associated zygospores are enclosed within a hyphal peridium, thus forming a fruiting body.

Such species are believed by some mycologists to represent the ancestral line from which the Ascomycetes have developed. Both homothallic and heterothallic species may and do occur in the same genus of the Mucorales. In the segregation of strains during meiosis, the Mucorales seem to fall into several groups.

The first of these includes the homothallic species in which all sporangiospores in the zygosporangium give rise to homothallic mycelia. In the second group, typified by *Mucor mucedo* and certain other heterothallic species, all the spores in a zygosporangium are of the same mating type, + or –.

In a third group of Mucorales, also composed of heterothallic species, typified by *Phycomyces nitens,* each zygosporangium contains at least three kinds of spores: + , – , and ±.

Finally, *Rhizopus stolonifer,* in accordance with the results obtained by Gauger (1961), is unique among the Mucorales which have been studied in that its germ sporangia contain either one type of sporangiospore (+ or –) or two types of spores: + and –.

Inasmuch as meiosis takes place before the spores of the germ sporangium are formed, we would logically expect all Mucorales to conform to this last pattern of mating type segregation, with half the sporangiospores of the germ sporangium containing + nuclei and the other half nuclei.

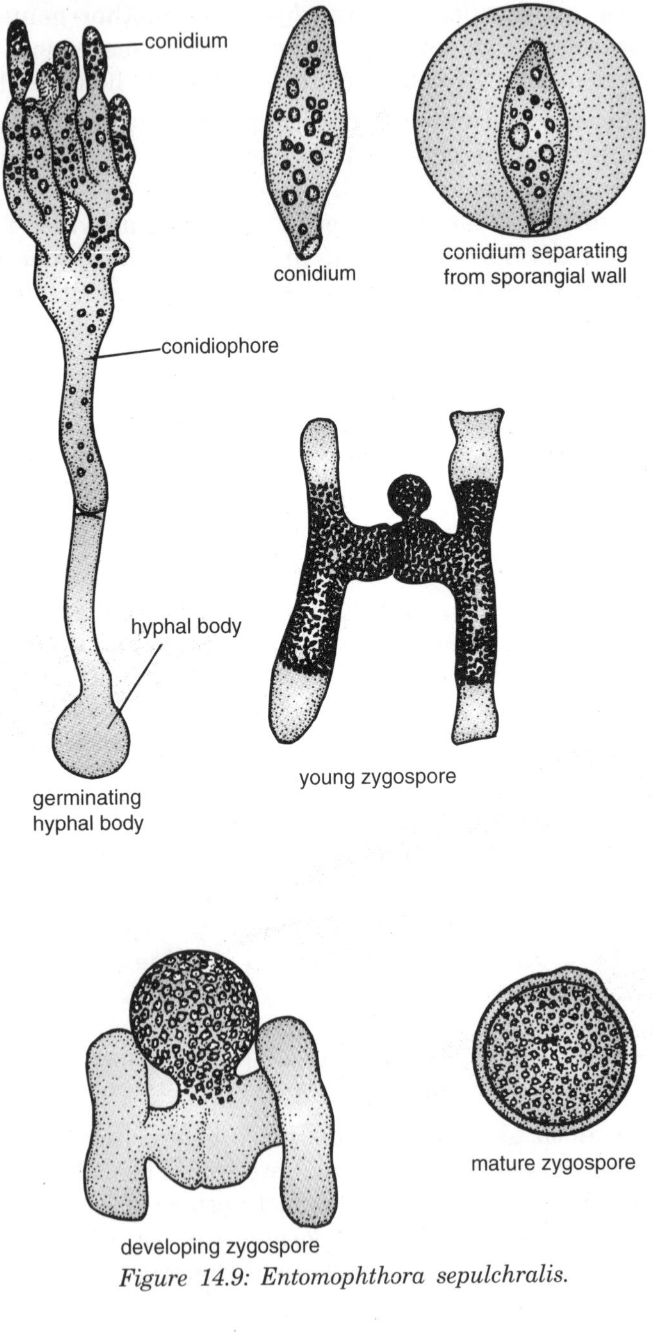

conidium
conidium
conidium separating
from sporangial wall
conidiophore
hyphal body
germinating
hyphal body
young zygospore
mature zygospore
developing zygospore

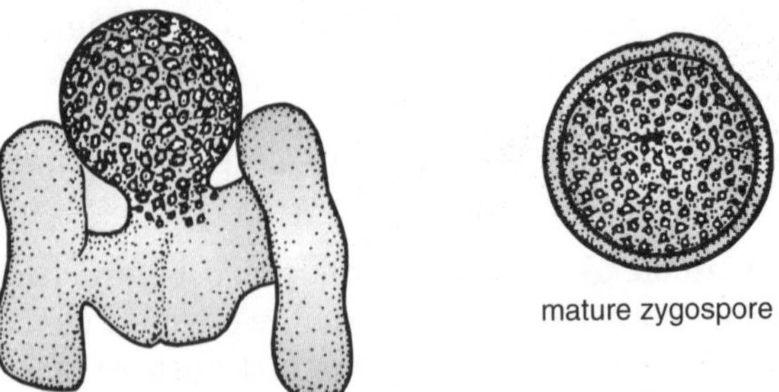

Figure 14.9: Entomophthora sepulchralis.

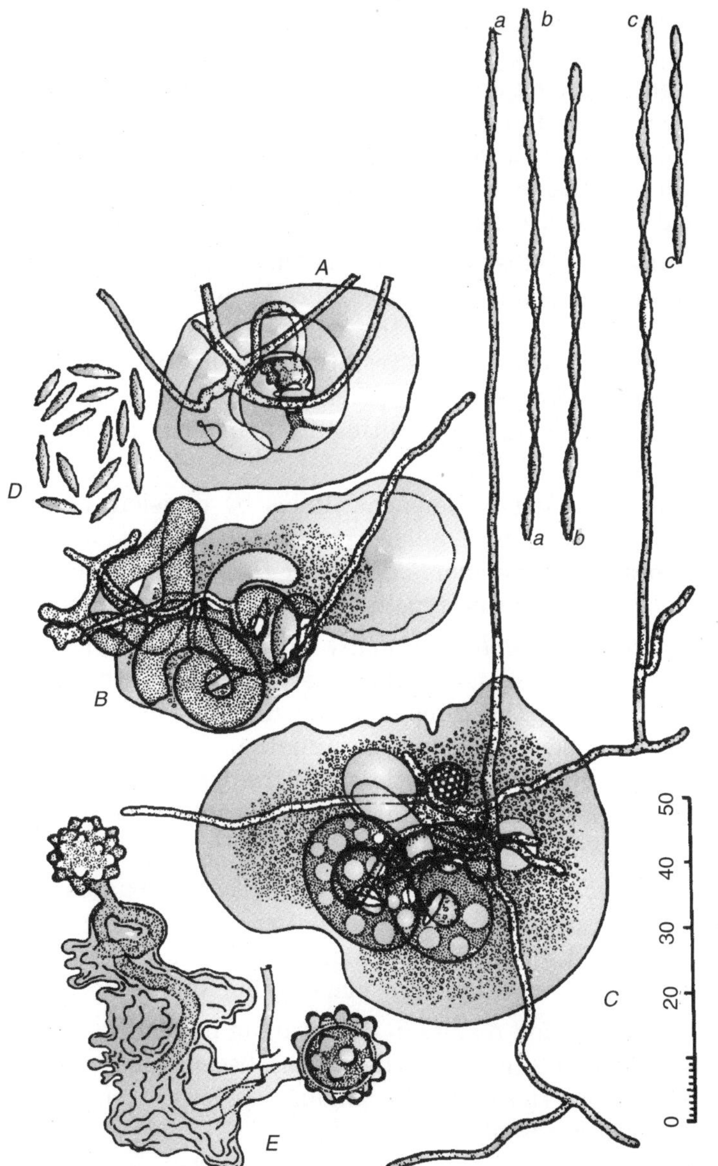

Figure 75. Cochlonema verrucosum. A. Amoeba enveloping a single thallus of the parasitic fungus. B. Dying amoeba with three internal thalli of the parasite. C. Conidial chains shown in sections, whereof a, b, and c represent corresponding points. D. Mature conidia. E. Zygosporangia, one containing a nearly mature zygospore.

Cutter (1942a, b) and Sjowall (1945, 1946) have attempted to give us the cytological explanation for the different segregation patterns. In the homothallic forms, such as *Sporodinia grandis,* there is, of course, no problem. It is interesting, however, to note that, according to Cutter, no nuclear fusion takes place in this species, so that no diploid nuclei are formed.

Cutter's conclusions contradict those of earlier investigators on this point. In *Mucor mucedo,* in which only one mating type survives in the germ sporangium, all the gamete nuclei fuse in pairs resulting in many diploid nuclei, and meiosis occurs before the resting period sets in. All but one of the nuclei resulting from meiosis apparently disintegrate.

The surviving nucleus multiplies by division, and its progeny enter the germ sporangium and become incorporated in the spores. Whether the surviving nucleus is of the + or – mating type is probably a matter of chance.

In *Rhizopus stolonifer* many nuclei fuse in pairs, but some remain unfused. However, the unfused nuclei degenerate and the diploid nuclei undergo meiosis after the rest period, just before germination. Half the haploid nuclei resulting from meiosis are of the + and half of the – mating type. Germ sporangia which contain both spore types receive both + and – nuclei.

In *Phycomyces blakesleeanus* both karyogamy and meiosis are delayed until germination occurs. Some nuclei fuse at this time and some remain unfused. Some of the diploid nuclei then undergo meiosis, but others do not.

This condition results in a mixture of haploid +, haploid –, and diploid ± nuclei. When these become incorporated in the spores, the germ sporangium obviously contains at least three kinds of spores.

The diploid spores give rise to homothallic mycelia; or, if the nuclei are reduced, either in the spore or in the hyphae during division, the spores may give rise to heterokaryotic mycelia which behave as homothallic. The proportion off nuclei diminishes with each asexual generation until no more f spores are formed.

ORDER ENTOMOPHTHORALES

The Entomophthorales include fungi which are chiefly parasitic on insects. *Basidiobolus ranarum is* the cause of a serious human disease. A few species are parasitic on the lower forms of plants, and several are saprobic on animal matter such as the excreta of frogs or lizards.

The most familiar of the Entomophthorales is *Entomophthora muscae,* commonly called the fly fungus, which is often found on the dead bodies of houseflies clinging to long-unwashed windowpanes in attics, garages, and . . . university classrooms. If you examine such a fly on a windowpane, you will find a wide, white, halo-like zone on the glass, surrounding the dead fly.

This white zone consists of innumerable conidia which have been shot off the conidiophores growing out of the body of the fly. This forcible ejection of the conidia is a prominent characteristic of the Entomophthorales. Two families are recognized: Entomophthoraceae and Basidiobolaceae.

Somatic Structures

The mycelium of the Entomophthorales is not so extensive as that of the Mucorales as a rule. In the Entomophthoraceae the mycelium has a definite tendency to form septa and then to fragment into portions which we call hyphal bodies. Such bodies multiply by division or budding, and each eventually produces a conidiophore bearing a conidium at its tip.

In some species, such as *Entomophthora fumosa* and *Entomophthora fresenii,* hyphal bodies copulate and develop zygospores. Some of the saprobic species have a well-developed mycelium which persists as such. The mycelium of the Basidiobolaceae is also septate and persistent. It consists of uninucleate cells.

Few of the Entomophthorales have been grown in

culture. The saprobic species, such as *Conidiobolus brefeldianus,* grow rather easily on artificial media. A few of the entomogenous species have been grown on special media rich in animal proteins.

Wolf (1951) grew *Entomophthora spiculata* and *Entomophthora coronata* on a chemically defined medium with ammonium or amino N. He found that nitrate N cannot be utilized, that only a few sugars (*glucose*, *levulose*, *galactose*, *mannose*, *trehalose*) can serve as a C source for these fungi, and that no external supply of vitamins is required.

Asexual Reproduction

The Entomophthorales reproduce asexually by means of sporangiola, functioning as conidia, which are borne on simple or branched conidiophores. The conidia are forcibly discharged from the conidiophores, and, in most species, germinate by producing germ tubes.

However, in the genus *Basidiobolus,* a common inhabitant of the excreta of frogs and lizards, the "*conidium*" becomes a sporangium at the time of germination, for it produces a number of aplanospores by the segmentation of its protoplast. In some species of *Entomophthora* too, Thaxter showed that the conidium is in reality a one-spored sporangiolum in which the spore can be seen after the "*conidium*" has remained in water for some time.

These examples constitute important evidence of the evolution of the conidium from a sporangiolum in the Entomophthorales. The conidia of the Entomophthorales are covered by a mucilaginous substance which adheres to any object against which the conidium is catapulted.

In *Entomophthora muscae* and other species, if the conidium lands on a substratum suitable for its growth, it germinates and forms mycelium; otherwise it produces a secondary conidium.

This process may be repeated until either a substratum suitable for growth is reached, or the protoplasm is exhausted in the third or fourth conidial generation.

Sexual Reproduction

Zygospores are formed in several species, but their further development is unknown. It is probable that they germinate by means of germ tubes.

In principle, zygospore formation in most Entomophthorales investigated is similar to that in the Mucorales, but the details are somewhat different and characteristic of the group. The copulating garnetangia may be mycelial cells, as in the Mucorales, or hyphal bodies.

The zygospore may be formed by the enlargement of one of the two copulating gametangia or from an outgrowth arising between the two fusing cells or from one of them after fusion. In the genus *Conidiobolus,* zygospore formation differs radically from that in other genera.

Here, two unequal gametangia come in contact and the contents of the smaller one pass into the larger one through a pore. The resting spore then develops within the larger gametangium.

This is somewhat reminiscent of sexual reproduction in the Oomycetes, but no oosphere, periplasm, or fertilization tube ever develops, so that, in spite of the irregularity in its formation, the resting spore is considered a zygospore.

In certain species *(Entomophthora muscae)* zygospores are formed parthenogenetically without gametangial fusion. Such structures are known as *azygospores* (Gr. *a* = not + *zygos* = yoke + *sporos* = spore). In structure they are similar to zygospores and presumably carry on the function of resting spores as well as true zygospores do.

ORDER ZOOPAGALES

Our knowledge of the Zoopagales we owe entirely to the researches of Dr. Charles Drechsler of the U. S. Department of Agriculture, who discovered, these organisms. In 1935 Drechsler proposed that they be recognized as a distinct family and suggested that they may be worthy of ordinal rank.

In 1938 he published a formal description of the family Zoopag-aceae. Bessey treated these organisms as an order in 1950, and we are adopting this view here. Some mycologists, however, consider them closely enough related to the Entomophthorales to include the Zoopagaceae in that order.

The order Zoopagales consists of the single family Zoopagaceae with about ten genera, such as *Endocochlus, Cochlonema, Bdellospora, Zoopage, Stylopage, Euryancale,* and *Cystopage.*

General Characteristics

The Zoopagales are especially adapted for parasitizing small animals such as amoebae, rhizopods, and nematodes. They reproduce asexually by true conidia which are not forcibly discharged, and sexually by the formation of zygospores.

Their gross morphology and general life history have been worked out by Drechsler (1935, etc.), but their cytology and physiology still remain unknown.

Somatic Structures

Three forms of thalli are recognized. In the predaceous species the soma consists of an aseptate, extensive mycelium which branches irregularly and gives rise to variously branched haustoria within the captured animals, which are parasitized.

In the endoparasitic species the soma consists of a short thick hypha which may be spirally wound, forming a coil within the parasitized animal. In ectoparasitic species a swollen conidium, adhering to the host externally, germinates and produces a haustorium which branches inside the host.

Asexual Reproduction

In some forms (*Cystopage*) asexual reproduction is solely by means of chlamydospores. Most species, however, produce aerial, thread-like, spindle-shaped, or globose conidia. These are borne singly, in chains, or in loose heads at the tips or sides of conidia-bearing hyphae or conidiophores.

The conidia break off the hyphae which bear them and germinate, either on the surface of a susceptible host to which they adhere, or inside it if they are ingested.

Sexual Reproduction

Sexual reproduction occurs by the union of two hyphal tips acting as *gametangia*. These usually originate from separate spores, possibly indicating that the fungi are heterothallic.

A zygospore enclosed in a wall (*zygosporangium*) is thus formed. Germination of the zygospore has not been seen, nor, as stated before, has the nuclear cycle been worked out.

Chapter 15 Trichomycetes

Neither the limits nor the taxonomic position of this group of organisms is as yet clear. The chief character which binds them together is, perhaps, their association with the arthropods.

As defined by Martin (1961), the Trichomycetes are fungi with a simple or branched filamentous thallus attached by a basal cell to the digestive tract or the external cuticle of living arthropods. The mycelium is limited in extent and is not immersed in the tissues of the host.

The class Trichomycetes as treated here is probably a heterogeneous group including organisms which may not be related. Miss Manier (1955a) of the zoological laboratory at Montpellier, France, divides the group Tricholnvcetes into two classes, three orders, and ten families.

Martin (1961) accepts Lichtwardt's (1960/1961) classification and considers the Trichomycetes to be a subclass (*Trichomycetidae*) of the class Phycomycetes. consisting of five orders. We shall discuss only one of these, the Eccrinales, and that very briefly.

ORDER ECCRINALES

The Eccrinales are fungi which live inside the bodies of arthropods, usually attached to the intestinal tract of the animal. They do not appear to be parasites but are rather commensals.

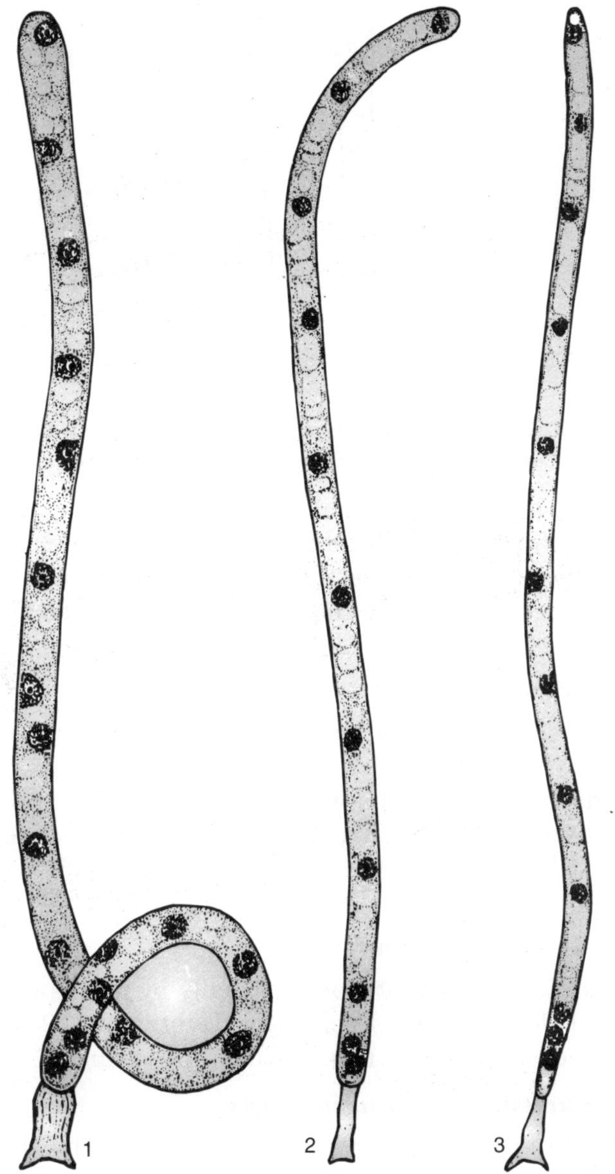

Figure 15.1: Thalli of three species of Eccrinales, showing coenocytic hyphae and holdfasts.

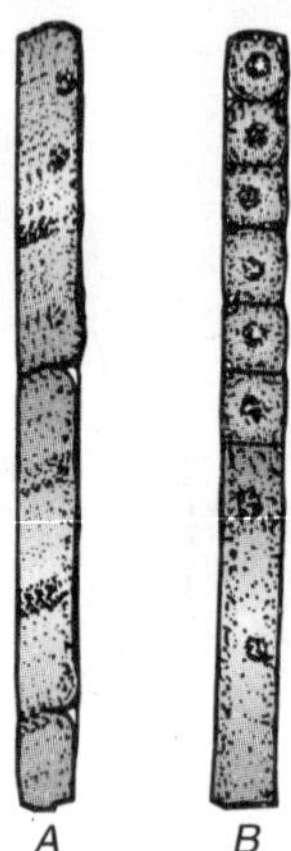

Figure 15.2: Enterobryus borariae. Multinucleate (A), and uninucleate (B) spores within a hyphal tip.

They are probably widely distributed, having been reported from Europe, North and South America, Africa, and some parts of southeast Asia. As more biologists become interested in their study they will undoubtedly be found in all parts of the world.

Somatic Structures

The soma of the Eccrinales is limited in extent. It consists of a long, slender, unbranched, straight or spirally curved, coenocytic hypha with walls that contain cellulose. The basal part of the hypha is in the form of a disc-like holdfast by means of which the fungus is attached to the host.

Asexual Reproduction

The Eccrinales reproduce asexually by means of spores variously formed in the hyphal tips. Lichtwardt (1954, 1958) recognized nine types, two of which are common.

Multinucleate Sporangiospores

These spores are formed singly in linearly arranged sporangia separated by cross-walls. The mature spores are multinucleate (four to eight), and each is discharged through a hole in the sporangial wall. They can germinate within the gut of the host that produced them, thus serving as a means of building up the number of thalli endogenously.

Uninucleate Sporangiospores

Similar in their formation to the multinucleate spores, these are shorter and remain uninucleate. Some produce a heavy wall. These spores pass through the digestive tract and serve to infect other susceptible individuals that ingest them.

Sexual Reproduction

Whether sexual reproduction occurs in the Eccrinales is still a matter of conjecture. Fusion of protoplasts has been reported in some species, resulting in the formation of zygotes which become converted into resting spores.

Fungal Decomposers

Leaves of all manner of types form suitable substrates for many fungi. Long before any leaf fails, the complex process of its decay is initiated. The greater part of this process takes place above ground in the intercovering the sun surface.

In this chapter some facets of this are discussed but particularly the epiphytic leaf surface or phylloplane microflora, the leaf surface as a habitat niche for fungi, colonization by the common primary saprotrophs as leaves senesce and die, the attributes which make these primary saprotrophs such widespread and successful colonizers, and some of the subsequent events occurring in the litter.

The Leaf as a Spore Trap

As any leaf unfolds it is a relatively clean sheet which immediately provides landing sites for air-borne particles such as bacteria, yeast cells and fungal spores but also pollen. Spore trapping by leaves is a natural phenomenon of nature.

Spores may reach leaves in three main ways: wind-borne and deposited by impaction or by sedimentation under gravity; in falling. rain drops ; or in rain splash droplets. Air-brone spores are tally dry and often rough or spiny and readily detachable, from their stalks, excellent examples being the urediospores of rust fungi.

They are readily, washed out of air by falling rain drops.

Rain splashed spores tend to be wet or slimy and borne in a sticky liquid. Adaptations facilitating deposition are far less obvious than in spores of aquatic fungi.

Amongst *dry* spores, a larger size, as seen in the powdery and downy mildews, favours impaction and sedimentation. Rain splashed spores tend to be smaller and spherical.

But these are only generalizations and there are many anomalies. The most ubiquitous and by far the most numerous of the phylloplane fungi are members of the Sporobolomycetaceae, the shadow yeasts. They produce air-borne spores which in relative terms are quite minute.

Leaf surfaces are differential spore traps. Their efficiency as traps depends upon whether they are horizontal or vertical, wet or dry, hairy, or *glabrous*, *glossy* or *mat*, *waxy* or *nonwaxy* and so on. Not all spores that land become securely .attached.

Some are washed off by rain, blown off by wind or .redistributed by dew. Some have **a.** two, phase dispersal system. For example, the large sporangia of pathogenic species of *Phytophthora* and some other Oomycete Peronosporales are wind-borne and normally impacted onto. leaf surfaces.

Under mist conditions the impacted sporangia may germinate directly by a germ tube or indirectly to produce matile *zoospores* which may swim about in moisture or be redispersed further to other leaves in rain. splash, droplets.

Virtually any spare which may become air-borne can be found on leaves. If leaf surfaces are washed and the washings plated out onto nutrient agar, numerous yeast and filamentous conidial Ascomycotina, some Zygomycete Mucorales and the occasional Mastigomycotina and Basidiomycotina develop on the plates.

But microscopic examination of stained leaf surface impressions or peels reveals the presence of not only these but also spores of many other Ascomycotina and Basidiomycotina, including those of agar's, polypores and Gasteromycetes.

They just do not grow or grow too slowly on the culture medium used. These impressions of peels can be made by spraying leaves with cellulose acetate in amyl acetate or painting with nail varnish or molten 1% agar, leaving to dry and then stripping off.

Many of these fungi- and an even larger number of bacteria actively grow on the surface of the: living leaf and have been called resident inhabitants in contrast to '*casual inhabitants*' which are unable to grow in such an environmental because of the lack of essential nutrients, unfavourable physical factors, +competition with or antagonism by others or some combination of these factors.

This rather simple distinction can be extended by dividing the *epiphytic fungi* into three categories : *nonpathogenic epiphytes*; pathogens and exochthonous or casual inhabitants. Exochthonous is a fitting, if somewhat clumsy, term as it is used for fungi found on or in a substrate which is not their habitual one.

PHYLLOPIANE INHABITANTS

Amongst the non-pathogenic epiphytes, two main groups, the phylloplane inhabitants and the common primary saprotrophs, can be recognized.

The phylloplane inhabitants are able to complete their life cycle or a significant part of it on the living leaf without damaging it. *Sporobolomyces roseus* not only is a very good example of such a fungus but is virtually omnipresent, being found on leaves of grasses, dicotyledonous herbs, trees and shrubs, wherever they grow.

Its cells multiply very quickly by budding when conditions are favourable, forming distinct yeast-like colonies on the leaves. Budded cells can be redistributed on an individual leaf or from leaf to leaf by rain splash and are similarly locally dispersed to leaves of other plants.

It also reproduces by ballistospore formation. The ballistospores are very effectively wind dispersed. They are produced under high humidities at night, as are the budded

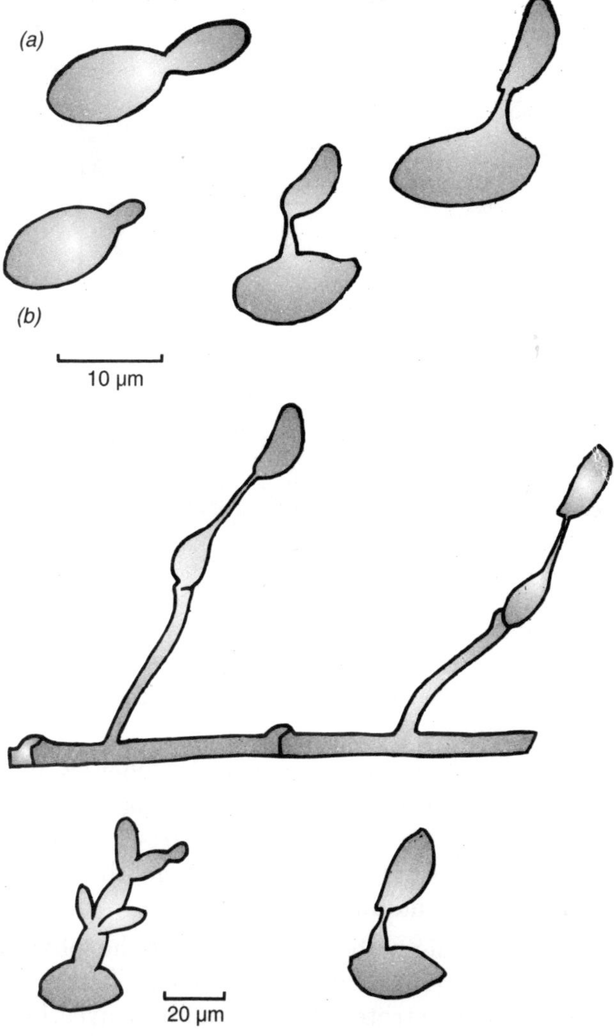

Figure 16.1. (a) Budding and ballistospore formation in porobolomyces roseus. (b) Ballistospore formation in Itersonilia perplexans, ballistospores germinating by budding and ballistospore formation.

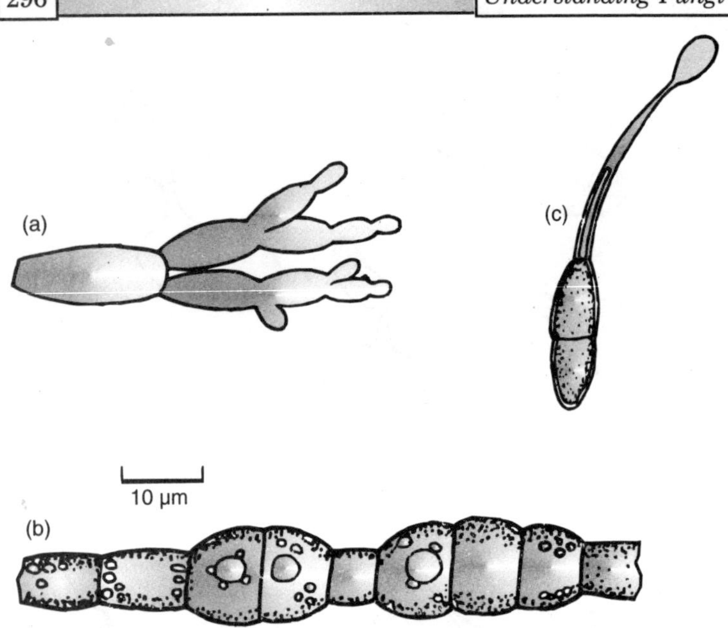

Figure 16.2. (a) Yeast-like budding by Aureobasidium; and (b) chlamydospores of Aureobasidium on a leaf surface. (c) Conidium of Cladosparium germinating to produce a secondary conidium.

cells, and constitute the major component of the air-spora at that time. Other members of the Sporobolomycetaceae are also common.

Species of *Bultera* behave similarly, whereas members of the genera Tilletiopsis and *Itersonilia* produce a sparse mycelium from Which *ballistospores* arise. Other yeasts, especially members of the *Cryptococcaceae*, the non-sporing yeast, exist in the adding phase.

They all complete their life cycle in the phylloplane. Such fungi are often called 'shadow yeasts'. Their presence once can be demonstrated by suspending leaves from dire underside of a Petri dish lid for about 12 h over 2% malt extract agar.

In such a humid and still atmosphere, ballistospores are produced and discharged. They fall vertically onto the agar below and start budding. Tiny colonies, pink in *S. roseus*, become visible after 2-3 days. These form a mirror image of the distribution of the cells of the leaf. Two conidial Ascomycotina also grow in the phylloplane. The conidia of *Aureobasidium pullulans* and several species of *Cladosporium* may germinate after impaction and develop into hyphae forming quite extensive colonies under favourable conditions.

Aureobasidium more often grow by yeast-like budding with minimal hyphal growth. This is a modification of its normal cultural form. The budded cells may again be redistributed in moisture films or by rain splash droplets.

The conidia of *Cladosporium* may germinate and produce secondary conidia from short germ-tubes rather than grow as hyphae. These conidia are dry and become air-borne.

So both reproduce rapidly and complete a signficant part of their *life* cycle in the phylloplane. Both eventually produce ascocarps to complete their *life* cycle. These are found only in the spring on overwintered fallen leaves in temperature climates. Ascospores are discharged from these as new leaves unfold.

Aureobasidium and *Cladosporium* are also both very well-adapted to *survive in* this' rigorous habitat. Their hyphal walls rapidly become thickened and melanized.

This enables them not only to survive exposure to damaging ultra-violet light from the sun but may also help to prevent excessive desiccation and make them more resistant to bacterial lysis. Aureobasidium produces dark, *thick-walled* multicellular chlamydospores in chains of in clumps.

Cladosporium produces more distinct Cladosporium produces more distinct microsclerotia· compact spheres of 10-MO dells-with, an outer layer of thick-varied cells. With heavily melanized walls.

Under favourable conditions, these produce clusters of conidiophores and abundant conidia which, like the ascospores, serve as a source of inoculum as new leaves unfold. In contrast *Sporobolomyces* does not appear to be able to withstand prolonged adverse conditions, such as low relative humidities. At relative humidities of 65% and below, it rapidly disappears but its population equally rapidly expands from reservoirs on more protected less exposed leaves, when favourable conditions return.

In temperate climates with a combination of warm humid weather and aphid infestation producing honeydew on leaves, the so-called sooty moulds appear as black, soot-like coverings over leaves, especially of trees such as limes (*Tilia* spp).

These are the result of the profuse growth of *Aureobasidium* and *Cladosporium* using the trisaccharide melezitose in the honeydew as a carbon-source, together with aphid faeces, sloughed off parts and dead remains. In wet tropical climates, such as in Amazonia, parts of Africa, Australasia and the Caribbean, true sooty moulds occur.

These, like the perfect states of *Aureobasidium* and *Cladosporium*, are also Loculoascomycetes and again grow as saprotrophs associated with honeydew from aphids. A wide range of species from several fungal families, especially the Capno. diaceae and Chaetothyriaceae are involved.

They form distinct dense, dark hyphal networks on leaves often in the form of a thick felt and each fungus produces abundant conidia of often two or even three types as well as ascocarps.

NUTRIENT SOURCES

All the phylloplaue inbabitants to yeasts, the, filamentous fungi and the. bacteria, are chemo-organotrophs requiring organic nutrients for- growth. Some of their nutritional requirements may be met by organic substances absorbed on deposited onto leaves such as detritus trapped in their superficial wefts of hyphen, as also happens with fungi living on paint films or grass.

Most of their nutrients, however, must be derived directly or perhaps indirectly from the host. A great' variety of substances exude or leak out of leaves. These include freesugars, amino acids and inorganic ions which are all essential for fungal and bacterial growth. For example, water droplets placed on leaves exhibit an-increase in conductivity indicating exudation from the leaf; increased" growth of some fungi in these drops shows that certains of these exudates are of nutritional value.

Two sources of added nutrients are from pollens and other spores. Nutrients also leak out of these. Pollen added to leaf surfaces stimulates the development of *Sporobolomyces* and *Cludosporium* and probably accounts for the sudden increase in their population shortly after flowering on leaves of plants such as rye. Conidia of *Botrytis cinerea* placed in droplets on leaves leak out amino acids and sugars in sufficient quantity for phylloplane bacteria to develop in such numbers as to inhibit germina-tion of the conidia themselves.

This all occurs on the intact surfaces of healthy leaves On aphid infested leaves nutrients may be derived indirectly from the host. Host sucrose is converted to melezitose in honeydew and this is used by the phylloplane inhabitants. The number of phyltoplane inhabitants increases with the age of the leaf.

This association between population density and age of the leaf is usually explained by increase in leaf exudates with ageing. It is also assumed that the restricted availability of the nutrients is one of the main causes of the relatively poor development of the phylloplane inhabitants on immature leaves.

There is also evidence that some of these fungi can slowly degrade the surface waxes and cuticle and so :gradually increase the permeability of the epidermis. Their numbers are also far greater on leaves infected by pathogenic fungi, such as rusts and mildews.

Four to five times as many colonies of *Sporobolomyces can* be isolated from mint leaves infected with the rust fungus, *Puccinia menthae*, as from healthy mint leaves.

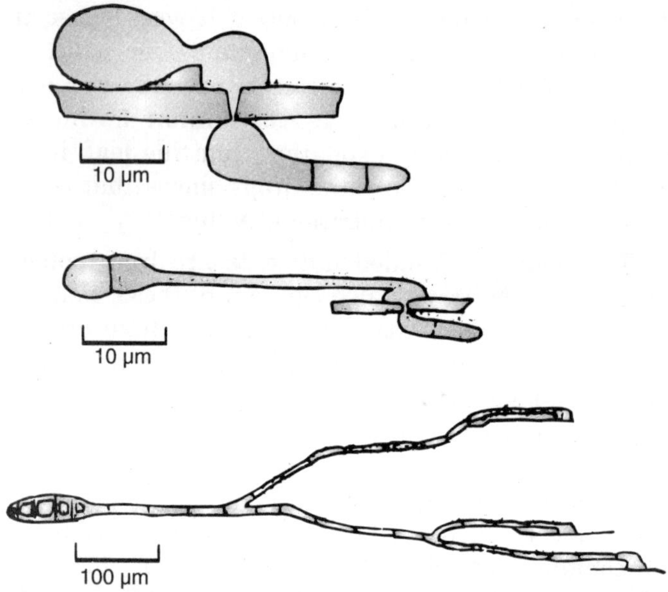

Figure 16.3: Three different types of growth shown by pathogenic leaf—inhabiting fungi on leaf surfaces (a) Botrytis fa& e. (b) Mycosphaerella ligulicola (c) Cochliobolus sativus.

Here the injurious effect of the pathogen, especially perhaps the changes in cell permeability, cause an out-flow of additional nutrients.

The phyllophane inhabitants are also not uniformly distributed over the leaf surface. Most more prevalent on the upper surface and are usually more predominant along the veins, frequently with their cells oriented to lie parallel with the vein axis.

They also tend to align themselves along the anticlinal walls, as with veins there is a slight depression there. They could be washed into these positions but there may also be more exudates released along the veins; also vein sheath cells may bring nutrients nearer the surface and thus facilitate exudation.

Common Primary Saprotrophs

The common primary saprotrophs are unable to grow to their full extent in the phylloplane until the onset of senescence. Their pattern of development is restricted until senescence and several rarely on never grow on the green leaf.

Their spores accumulate on the leaf prior to senescence and remain dormant until the death of the tissues. If they do germinate they do so only to a limited extent. On senescence they *very* quickly take advantage of the changing conditions. Sporing colonies of these fungi are ubiquitous on newly dead leaves of the majority of plants.

The phylloplane inhabitants and the common primary saprotrophs by no deans form distinct groups. *Aureobasidium* and *Cladosporium* have to be included in both groups because, although they grow and reproduce by conidia in the phylloplane, they develop to a much greater extent in the dead leaf.

Other fungi, all conidial Ascomycotina, in this group include *Alternaria alternata, Botrytis cinerea*, *Epicoccum purpurascens* and *Stemphylium botryosum*. In the Tropics the list can be extended to include species of *Curvularia* and *Nigrospora*.

Spores of a great variety of other saprotrophs may also be present on the leaves. They .germinate only on the death of the leaves or sometimes thereafter.

PATHOGENS

Two distinct catagories can be recognized amongst the pathogens found on leaves. There are those from the Plectomycete Erysiphales, the powdery mildews, which are wholly restricted to the phylloplane except for haustoria in the epidermal cells of the host leaf.

All their very extensive mycellium, conidia and ascocarps are borne on the leaf surface. The second category, covering virtually all other pathogens, infect leaves and grow almost entirely within them with only their reproductive structures having access to or being produced on the outside.

These latter exhibit all gradations, from those which

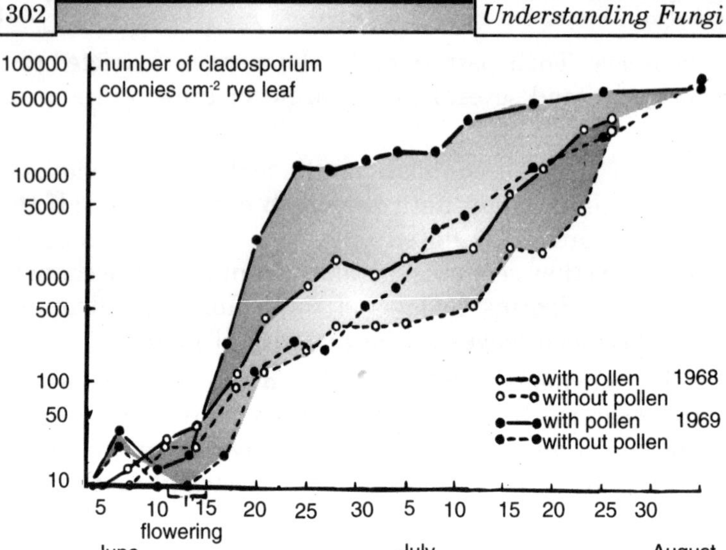

Figure 16.4: The successive changes in the number of Cladosporium *spp colonies per cm' ery leaf during the season. The data are the means of the numbers of colonies from washings of eight penultimate leaves.*

produce an appressorium from their spore and penetrate immediately, to those which have a prolonged and relatively extensive phase of epiphytic non-parasitic hyphal growth on the leaf surface before they penetrate.

The spores of many of these pathogens remain dormant for considerable periods only germinating as host resistance begins to fall prior to senescence or following a suitable change in the weather.

Again no clear distinction can be drawn between pathogens of this latter type and some of the common primary *saprotrophs*.

Botrytis cinerea is one of the latter but is also a necrotrophic parasite of some hosts under particular environmental conditions, such as prolonged very high humidities which favour it but not its host. Its conidia may then germinate on the leaf surface and after a phase of epiphytic growth penetrate and bring about a soft watery rot by means of its pectolytic enzymes.

EXOCHTHONOUS FUNGI

Spores of pathogens which are unable to infact the leaves on which they have landed may also be present. They may remain decimant or they may germinate before they recognize that they are on the wrong host.

They may, contribute, likes-pollen, to the nutrients available on the *leaf* surface. They could be included with the exochthonous or casual fungi as they are found on leaves but do not grow there. The latter are unable to gain any nutritional advantage from the habitat which is clearly a dead end for many but by no means all. Any soil fungi with air-borne spores may be trapped on leaves. and later washed off by rain onto the soil beneath and so they are successfully dispersed.

Spores of many coprophilous fungi on herbivore dung are discharged onto grass leaves surrounding the dung and remain there until the grass is eaten by herbivores. Passage through the gut of a herbivore may be necessary to trigger-off their germination.

Direct dung to dung dispersal is abortive. Thus impaction onto leaf surfaces is important if they are to complete their dispersal and lam= cycle.

The Leaf Surface as a Habitat for Fungi

the leaf surface is a most inhospitable niche in both physical and chemical terms for fungi. Although transpiration may mitigate against extreme low levels of relative humidity, the fungi are repeatedly dried by the sun and wind and re-wetted by rain and dew.

They are not insulated against *temperature* fluctuations and as such are *subjected* to marked and very rapid variations in temperature. Even in temperate climates in relatively still Oil, leaf surfaces may be 10-12°C above ambient in the sun at one moment and in the next 2° below ambient as a cloud passes over the sun.

They are exposed to the harmful ultraviolet component in daylight. Nutrient sources must always be fluctuating and low competition for them must be severe.

Microbial Interactions in the Phylloplane

Interest in the leaf surface as a habitat for fungi has centred mainly on the fact that it is here that any pathogen must spend a critical period of time until it can establish and infect.

During this time it is not only subjected to such environmental stresses but it may also be subjected to antagonism from the phylloplane inhibitants as well as from the host itself.

A great variety of microbial interactions occur in the plylloplane and in the applied field thoughts are turning to consider the possibility of achieving biological control of some leaf pathogens by building up fufficiently large populations of phylloplane inhibitants.

This may be an accordingly difficult objective to achieve but a consideration of some of the research which led to the development of such ideas gives further insight into the *biology* of phylloplane fungi.

Pollen as a Nutrient Source Add Competition for Nutrient

The fact that phylloplane inhabitants such as *Cladosporium and Sporopolomyces* could benefit from nutrients leaked from pollen grains was convincingly demonstrated by Fokkema (1971).

Rye leaves from two separate plots, in one of which the plants had their inflorescences removed or covered, so that no pollen fell onto the leaves below, were taken from plants and washed, twice a week from early June to September, in 1968 and 1969.

The washings were plated out onto nutrient agar and the colonies of *Cladosparium spp.* which developed were counted, the assumption being made that each colony arose from a single spore. In 1969, the number of colonies from leaves with pollen rose from 15 to 13,000 cm^2 two weeks after flowering.

On leaves without pollen the numbers were 10 and 550

respectively. On leaf senescence the colonies recorded from all leaves reached the same levels. The leaves at this stage leaked more nutrients and the stimulating effect of the pollen wore off.

The larger number of colonies of *Cladosporium* recorded in 1969 was shown to be due to more pollen on the leaves, a mean of 3450 cm^{-2} as against 300 cm^{-2}. There was frequent rain after flowering in 1968 so that the pollen was washed off.

Stimulation in the presence of pollen was not restricted to *Cladosporium. Aureobasidium pullulans* and *Sporobolomyces roseus* were also stimulated. For the latter, two weeks after flowering, 33,600 colonies cm^{-2} were recorded from rye leaves with pollen andonly 3800 colonies cm^{-2} from rye leaves without pollen.

The Loculoascomycete *Cochilobolus sativus* is a leaf pathogen of rye which makes a variable amount of epithytic growth before penetration into the leaf. Fokkema inoculated rye leaves with conidia of *Cochliobolus*, together with, pollen and without pollen. The effect of the pollen on successive stages of the infection process and the resultant necrosis is given in Table elsewhere in this chapter.

Table 16.1: Effect of pollen on successive stages of the infection process of rye leaves by Cochliobolus sativus.

		Time after inoculation			
				2-3 days	*7 days*
Experiment	*Pollen addition*	*Mean number of germs tubes/ 100 spores*	*Mean mycelium length in μm mm⁻²*	*Mean number young lesions 10 cm⁻²*	*Mean nectrotie area*
1	—	23	0	17	2
	+	137	3600	113	58
2	—	67	230	22	2
	+	102	3250	56	35

Leaves inoculated with *Cochliobolus* and pollen had a significantly larger percentage of necrotic areas. He attributed this to the pollen leaking out nutrients which greatly stimulated the superficial growth of the mycelium.

The increased the inoculum and so more young lesions unit area were obtained and hence eventual necrosis. In these experiments both the phylloplane inhabitants and the pathogen were relying, in part at least, on the same nutrient source and in nature they might well compete for such a source.

Some degree of biological control could be achieved if the phylloplane inhabitants could markedly neutralize the stimulating effect of the pollen when inoculated with both it and the pathogen. This is exactly the effect that Fokkemà later observed.

The relative inhibitory effect on surface mycelial development of *Cochliobolus* on leaves was depressed by 72% and.; the extent of necrosis by 75% on rye leaves inoculated with *Coehliabolus*, pollen and *Aureobasidlum*, as compared with leaves inoculated with *Cochliobolus* and pollen and *Cochliobolus* and *Aureobasidium only*. Effective competition for nutrients by *Aureobasidium* appears to be an adequate explanation for these reductions.

Antagonistic Reactions

A number of such interactions has been reported but competition for nutrients is not the sole explanation for some of these. In, some cases inhibitory substances produced by the phylloplane inhabitants, may also be involved and normal leaf exudates rather than pollen maybe the nutrient source. Pace and Campbell (1974) found that *Aureobasidium pullulans* and *Epicoccum purpurascens* were common in the phylloplane of *Brassica* spp. and that they were antagonistic to the wound parastic *Alternaria brassicicola* in culture.

Their growing colonies inhibited mycelial growth of *A. brassicicola* and their germinating conidia inhibited the germination of its conidia. They inoculated leaves of cabbage and Brussels sprout after wounding with *Alternaria brassicicola*, *Aureobasium pollulans* and *Epicoccum purpurascens* separately and with brassicicola plus *A. pullulans* and *A. brassicicola* plus *E. purpurascencs.*

There was an 80-100%, infection with *A. brassicicola* alone but none with the two saprotrophs alone. The percentage of successful infections by *A. brassicicola* was reduced where it was, inoculated with either of the two saprotrophs.

The reduction was greater, when the saprotrophs were inoculated 14 h. prior to *A. brassicicola.* Both *A. pullulans* and *E. purpurascens* were capable of active growth on the leaf surface so might compete with the pathogen for nutrients in the form of leaf exudates.

This could explain why they were more effective when inoculated 14 h prior to the pathogen. But they may also produce inhibitory substances. Some evidence for this is that a 50% reduction in successful infection was obtained when conidia of *A. brassicicola* were suspended in a culture, filtrate of *A. pullulans* and used instead of water for inoculation. The culture medium itself enhance infection.

Towards Biological Control

These—sorts of antagonism must obviously be having some -effect in the field but ,the question to be answered in terms of achieving biological control iss how can their effects be maximized ?

One approach is to manipulate the system, to stimulate 'the phylloplane inhabitants. Biological control using the indigenous population, rather than introducing others, would be possible if a sufficiently large population of antagonistic phylloplane inhabitants could be built up.

Bashi and Fokkema (4977) have shown that continuous high humidities and nutrients in excess of those exuded by *leaves* are necessary to maintain a phylloplane population of *Sporobolomyces* dense enough to have sufficient antagonistic potential to control *Cochllobolus.*

Sporobolomyces is particularly sensitive to low relative

humidities. Populations on leaves decreased markedly when maintained at 65% RH. Any added nutrients would have a stimulatory effect on the pathogen as well. To be effective in stimulating only the saprotroph nutrients would have to be added just prior to any significant build up of spores of the, pathogen on the leaf surface.

This would require accurate disease forecasting. But even so it would be almost impossible to maintain in the field the necessary continuous high humidities. However if such control was possible, it would be applicable only to those pathogens which rely on the absorption of exogenous nutrients to enable them to make superficial mycelial growth on the leaf before penetration.

Pathogens which normally penetrate the leaf immediately after germination of which have every restricted superficial mycelial growth are probably less susceptible to competition for nutrients. The alternative approach is to allow the natural control measures to proceed and to avoid the indiscriminate use of fungicides which may affect the phylloplane inhabitants more than the pathogen.

Pace and Campbell (1974) noted that the systemic fungicide Benomyl gave a good control of many diseases but not the leaf spot of brassicas caused by *Alternariabrassicicola*. The pathogen is resistant to it. The two antagonistic saprotrophs which they used. *Aureobasidium pullulans* and *Epicoccum purpurascens* are inhibited by Benomyl.

Therefore use of this fungicide could make the disease worse. Fokkema found that *Cochliobolus* is also relatively resistant to Benomyl, and that inoculation of rye leaves with *Cochliobolus* just after flowering (i.e. with pollen), resulted in 60% less necrosis on water sprayed leaves than on Benomyl-sprayed leaves.

At the time water sprayed leaves had a natural phylloplane population of 10,000 spores cm^{-2} and Benomyl-sprayed leaves only 1200 spores cm^{2}. This implies that the Benomyl had reduced the antagonistic capacity of the phylloplane inhabitants but it also provides direct field, evidence for naturally occurring biological control.

Antagonism via Lysis, Antibiotic Production or pH Changes

Other forms of antagonism are exhibited in the phylloplane. Bacteria may lyse fungal spores. Chitinolytic enzymes are usually involved. Lenne and Parberry (1976) noted clusterss of bacteria surrounding lysed conidia and germs tubes of the pathogen *Colletotrichum gloeosporioldes* on leaf surfaces.

Appressoria are necessary for penetration to occur. The bacteria failed to lyse these. They have melanized walls and there are numerous reports of melanized structures resisting the lyticaction of bacteria. The production of appressoria was enhanced in the presence of bacteria but was reduced by added nutrients, such as 1% glucose peptone solution. The stimulated production of appressoria in the presence of bacteria is a normal response of the fungus to a hostile environment.

Desiccation and starvation also cause appressorial formation. This response serves as an important short term survival role during the infection phase. It should be noted that in this particular case added nutrients increased germ tube growth but fewer appressoria were formed.

Since the latter are necessary for penetration, added nutrients may in this case enhance. disease control. Several phylloplane inhabitants, such as *Aureobasidium* and. *Sporobolomyces* have been shown to produce antibiotics in culture although there is no direct evidence that they play a role *in* vivo.

Although antibiotic production by bacteria on leaf surfaces does not appear to be very widespread, some bacteria have been shown to produce antifungal peptides which, under experimental conditions at least, reduce incidence of disease caused by a number of species of *Colletotrichum*.

Some fungal leaf pathogens are very sensitise to pH

changes. In *Septoria nodorum*, for instance, spore germination is inhibited below pH 6. Conidia of this fungus, placed around the edge of a growing colony of *Botrytis cinerea*, failed to germinate. The pH of the medium fell to below 6 in advance of the hyphal tips of *Botrytis*. Such a mechanism could operate in the phylloplane.

Fungistatic Substances Produced by Leaves

In addition to nutrients, leaves of many plants may exude fungistatic substances which cause inhibition of spore germination or restriction of germ tube growth.

Phenols are the most widely known fungistatic substances produced by leaves. They are responsible for the inhibition of spore germination of the apple scab, fungus *Venturia inaequalis, on* some apple cultivars.

Gallic acid had been identified as an: antifungal component in droplets of dew obtained from sycamore leaves. Apart from substances formed within the leaf cells and exuded onto the surface, some constituents of the cuticular waxes may also be fungistatic.

An acidic ether-soluble fraction from the wax of apple leaves inhibits the growth of the apple mildew fungus, *Podosphaera leucotricha.* The properties of waxes on leaves will also affect the exudation of both nutrients and antifungal substances.

Waxes with high proportions of more hydrophobic constituents will tend to limit the movement of exudates to the surface. Thus at the leaf surface a series of complex interactions occur between pathogen/host/phylloplane inhabitants/environment.

Numerous aspects and the outcome of many of these interactions are still to be discovered, but it is evident that the phylloplane inhabitants act in some sort of buffering capacity ,against some pathogenic fungi at least.

Distribution of the Common Primary Saprotrophs

Eventually the leaf senesces either naturally or prematurely after supporting, in some cases, one or more pathogens. Of the multitude of fungal spores of a vast array of a species which are impacted onto leaf surfaces only relatively few -succeed in colonizing the leaves as they senesce and grow as active saprotrophs within the leaf tissues after death.

These common primary saprotrophs are virtually ubiquitous colonizers. On most leaves such as those of deciduous trees, shrubs, herbs, grasses including cereals and even bracken, most are usually present and exceptions are difficult to find.

Pine need-leaf are a particularly selective substrate and of these fungi only *Aureobasidim pullulans is* ever at all common. In the tropics, *Alternaria alternate* is less common and is replaced by

Nigrospora spp., especially *N. sphaerica*, and *Curvularia spp.*, especially *C. lunata*, as is evident from examining senescent leaves of guinea grass (*Panicum maximum*) and banana (*Musa sapientum*). The differences are also reflected in the comparison of the dry air-spora of tropical and temperate climates.

The association of these particular fungi has been noted on other substrates, such as cereal stubble and cotton fabrics exposed to the weather. The blackening of the ears of cereals in a damp season is caused mainly by *Alternaria*, *Cladosporium* and *Epicoccum.*

Christensen and Kaufmann (1965), in their studies on the deterioration of grain, designated these and others, such as *Chaetomium*, *Fusarium* and *Rhizopus* spp., as 'field fungi'. This is an appropriate term as they are almost always and constantly associated with exposed freshly decaying green parts of plants.

On leaves they are usually associated with one or more other saprotrophs which are more restricted in the range of leaves which they colonize. These restricted primary saprotrophs may be confined to a particular host genus or a related group of plants.

Table 16.2: Mycelial growth rate, latent period for germination, growth rate of germ tubes at 100% RH and lowest RH at which spores germinated.

Primary colonizers	*Mycelia growth rate (mm day^{-1})*	*Latent period (h)*	*Germ tube growth rate (gm $^{-1}$)*	*Lowest RH at which Germination occurs*
Cladosporium herbarum	2.96	6-12	4.2	89%
Alternaria alternata	6.41	3-6	29.1	89%
Epicoccum puepurascens	645	0-3	31.6	92%
Secondary colonizers				
Torula herbarum	1.41	12-18	0	Water
tetraploa aristata	3.34	12-18	2.4	98%

Readeriella mirabilis and *Piggotia stellata* appear to be restricted to *Eucalyptus*. Several species of *Leptosphaeria*, such as *L. microscopica*, are restricted to the Gramineae and *Fusicoccum bacillare* and *Sclerophoma pithiophila* are both very common on pine needles but the latter, at least, is also found on other coniferous leaves.

In many of these substrate specificity might be synonymous with and explained by, host specificity. Many of these, although very active saprotrophs, may have an additional advantage in that they can gain access as parasites, *S. pithiophila*, for instance, has been associated with the defoliation of the current year's needles of *Pinus sylvestris*.

As a group these common primary saprotrophs may be -well-established in leaves long before leaf-fall. For example *Cladosporium herbarum* often colonizes and produces conidia on damaged necrotic parts of beech leaves in June, within two months of their unfolding.

The duration of their persistence on leaves once they are in the litter is dependent upon many variables, one of which is the texture and another the composition of the leaves.

In general, free leaves, such as those of ash and sycamore, which decompose and disappear rapidly from the litter, support a more substantial growth of these common primary saprotrophs for a shorter time than do leaves of beech and oak which persist much longer in the litter.

On beech leaves, for example, *C. herbarum* persists in high frequency through the winter after leaf-fall until the following -June and disappears after September. Similar sequences can be found on other substrates. Primary saprotrophs are the first fungi to appear on flowering stems of cocksfoot, *Dactylis glomerata.*

They are present on the basal leaves in early summer and progress up the stems as successive leaves senesce. They are well-established by July and August on the upper leaf sheaths and intermodes of stems which flowered in late May and June and they persist there until the following summer.

On nettles, *Urtica dioica,*primary saprotrophs colonize the upper leaves in August or September of the year of flowering at the onset of basipetal senescence. They again persist throughout the winter until the following spring and summer.

Attributes of the Common Primary Saprotrophs

The intriguing aspect of this particular fact of fungal ecology is to ponder why so few of all the fungi use equipped to assume this role of primary saprotrophic colonizers of such exuberantly plentiful substrates.

NUTRIENTS

In the well-known scheme for fungal successions proposed by Garrett (1963), the primary saprotrophs to invade are 'sugar fungi'. They are not-cellulolytic and rely upon readily such as available sugars, hexoses and pentoses, and other carbon sources simpler than cellulose such as pectins and starch.

These fungi also normally possess a high mycelial growth rate and a capacity for rapid spore germination.

The classic example of such fungi is the Zygomycete Mucorales, common on herbivore dung. Primary saprotrophic sugar fungi are usually very ephemeral because of the transient nature of their substrate.

The persistence of the common primary saprotrophs for months on leaves would suggest that they are not confined to such ephemeral substrates. The ability to utilize cellulose is often regarded as essential for saprotrophic fungi and the majority, except most Zygomycotina and Mastigomycotina, can do this.

Of this particular group of leaf saprotrophs only *Aureobasidium pullulans* is non-cellulolytic. It probably relies on pectic substances for *its* carbon sources and this ability is often used, to explain its role as a primary colonizer. None of the others is markedly cellulolytic when compared with some of the Basidiomycotina which later colonize leaves in the litter layer.

For instance, Hering (1967) inoculated oak leaves sterilized by y irradiation with *A. pullulans*,*Cladosporium herbarum* and *Mycena galopus*,a Hymenomycete agaric from the leaf litter, and measured loss in mass after six months at 9-15°C. The two former brought about a loss of 2 and 4% respectively and the latter 15-20%.

Not all the loss in mass was of cellulose but in the latter case the loss corresponded with the utilization of about one sixth of the total cellulose present. On filter paper cellulose, various isolates of *Alternaria alternata* brought about losses of 4-8% in 14 days and *Epicoccum purpurascens* about 4%.

For comparison, under the same conditions the vigorously cellulolytic *Chaetomium globosum* brought about a 10% loss. It must be remembered that mass loss methods measure only the amount of substrate, in this case cellulose, respired and lost as carbon dioxide and water and not the amount incorporated into fungal material.

The cellulytic ability of these fungi thus varies and they all probably use simpler carbohydrates, such as sugars and starch, as long as they last and then go on to utilize cellulose even if to a limited extent and slowly. Thus they persist. This maybe placing undue emphasis on their carbohydrate nutrition to the neglect of their nitrogen requirements.

The nitrogen supply might be extremely critical in determining their distribution. In culture they can all use nitrate, ammonia or amino acids as their sole nitrogen source but nothing is precisely know as to what sources are available to them within the leaf.

Indications of the over-riding limitations of their nitrogen supply are seen when leaves are amended with an available source. Foliar applications of 5% urea solution, after harvest but before leaf fall prevent ascocarp development in the apple scab fungus, *Venturia inaequ-dlis*,on the overwintering leaves and is used as a control measure to limit the ascospore inoculum available to infect the newly emerging leaves in the following spring.

Birchill and Cook (1971) in studying the mode of action of the urea demonstrated that "both chemical and microbial changes occurred in the leaves after treatment. Marked alterations occurred in the composition and density of fungal and bacterial populations present on treated leaves.

The urea in particular enormously increased the relative abundance, as assessed by the number of conidia produced, of both *Cladosporium* spp. and *Alternaria* app. So marked was the development of the conidia and conidiophores of *Cladosporium* that they could be seen with the naked eye as olive green lawns.

Many times more conidia were produced overall on the treated leaves suggesting that the added nitrogen enabled them to utilize more carbon sources and thus outcompete *Venturia* for substrate. Application of urea to fallen pine needles also dramatically changes the fungal succession.

Cladosporium herbarum,rather than being an occasio-nal inhabitant, is again stimulated to develop to such any extent that its conidiophores may cover the needles as a denser felt and other common primary saprotrophs, such as *Epfcoccum purpuruscens*,which does not normally occur on pine needles, are stimulated to develop by the urea. The mode of action of the urea is not known in this case out is complex ; its property of acting as an alkali may be one important aspect of its effect. For example, several agarics which have not been recorded from pine litter appear when plots are treated with urea or alkalis.

An example is *Myxomphalia maura* which is characteristically found on the alkaline ash of bonfire sites on acid soils in coniferous woods._it is not found on woods on alkaline soils so is not a calcicole.

M. maura is markedly encouraged by the addition of lime to pine litter. Pine needles treated with sodium carbonate are also colonized by *C. herbarum* and *E. purpurascens*. Urea and alkalis both produce similar effects on the litter.

They both cause it to darken, become water-soaked and raise the pH from about 3.5-4.0 to 5.5-6.0. They both bring about the release of ammonia from the litter and its use as a nitrogen source may be another important factor inducing these changes.

These saprotrophs are not primary colonizers solely because they grow faster than any other would-be colonizers. Their only attribute with regard to growth rate is their great variability.

Aureobasidium pullulans produces its slimy conidia very rapidly, but its yeast-like colonies are relatively slow growing. *C. herbarum* also sporulates rapidly but its growth rate is even slower. *Botrytis cinerea* grows very rapidly and *Alternaria alternaia* and *E. purpurascens* not so rapidly but faster than *C. herbarum*.

TOLERANCE TO DESICCATION

Senescing leaves on the tree and recently fallen leaves are very prone to drying out and also subject to strong sunlight. Webster and Dix (1960) compared the growth rates, latent period forger mination, germ tube growth rate at 100% RH and the lowest RH which spore germination occurred in three primary colonizers with two later secondary colonizers. *Torula herbarum* and *Tetraploa arlctata*.

They found that there was (little difference between the capacity of the mycelium of the various colonizers two grow at low humidities and the primary colonizers did not make better growth at low humidities.

But it can be seen from Table elsewhere in this chapter that under favourable humidities (100% RED, *A. alternata* and *E. purpurascens* not only grew faster than the secondary colonizers but also had a shorter latent period before germination and their germ tubes grew faster.

These features, coupled with the fact that their conidia can germinate at lower relative humidities, would give their an advantage over the others in that their conidia would germinate udder less ideal conditions of humidity and they would quickly exploit, by virtue of their more rapid growth rate, any changes to more humid conditions.

Because of the rapidly fluctuating conditions on the leaf surface, germinating conidia may rapidly dry out before penetrating into the leaf. Diem (1971) has investigated the survival at low humidities of germinating conidia of *C. herbarum,A. alternata* and some casual inhabitants of the phylloplane. He found that germinating pigmented conidia, such as those of *Cladosporium* and *Alternaria*, were more resistant than germinating colourless conidia of *Aspergillus* and *Penicillium.*

The germ tubes of *Cladosportum* were remarkedly resistant. Some 90% grew on at 100% RH after 8 h in a desiccator over hydrous calcium chloride and 99% did so after being kept at 40% RH for 8 h. This would indicate that if they germinated in the more humid conditions of the night. and had not penetrated into the leaf by the morning they could survive the drier conditions of the day.

Germ tubes of the conidia of *Alternaria* were equally resistant but some failed to grow on after periods at relative humidities below 65% but the conidia either germinated again from another cell or from a lateral branch from below the damaged part of the germ tube. In contrast, the germ tubes of the conidia of *Aspergillus* and *Penicillium* were no longer viable after periods at 85% RH.

Species with coloured conidia are thus more likely to be successful in the phylloplane and as subsequent primary colonizers of the leaves. But it should be noted that the conidia of *Aureobasidium* and tis are not pigmented.

The biotrophic Erysiphales which produce their mycelium on leaf surfaces also have colourless r hyphae and conidia. Thus pigmentation is a useful but not an essential attribute to possess. Primary saprotrophs also show an equally remarkable tolerance to desiccation in their hyphal tips as distinct from germ tubes.

Hyphal tips are very delicate structures but in these fungi they survive periods of extreme desiccation, some as long as three weeks, above a saturated solution of potassium nitrate (a_w 0.45).

Thus they can rapidly exploit the return to favourable conditions of humidity with no apparent loss of previously synthesized biomass. Other fungi do not show this ability. This attribute may be critical in enabling such fungi to tolerate cycles of wetting and drying.

SURVIVAL STRUCTURES

Once established on the leaf surface, most of the common primary saprotrophs produce some form of pigmented survival structure *Cladospo-rium herbarum* minute microsclerotia; *Botrytis cinerea* and *Epicoccum purpurascens* sclerotia and *Aureobasidium pullulans* aggregates of chlamydospores.

All have a pigmented mycellium. Such structures and pigmentation protect against desiccation, ultra-violet light and microbial lysis. It is thus clear that the common primary saprotrophs Possess a multiplicity of attributes by which they have become successfully adapted to this relatively inhospitably niche with each fungus possessing its own particular complex of attributes, not all necessarily the same. As suggested, in temperate climates some of the common primary saprotrophs produce ascocarp initials in the late autumn in the year of leaf-fall as do a number of leaf pathogens, such as *Apiognomonia errabunda* on beech and *Venturia inaequalis* on apple.

Ascospores are discharged from these over the period early April to early June. This is the time when the next crop of leaves is. unfolding. The initially spore-free leaves become impaction sites for air-born ascospores and under favourable conditions infection occurs.

Such a life history is of particular significance in leaf pathogens with restricted periods of spore formation and release and where the host virtually frees itself of infection by shedding all its leaves prior to its dormant season.

The requirement for an overwintering phase, a period of low temperature (5-8°C), before ascocarp initials mature is very common in these fungi. The maturation and release of the ascospores thus coincide with the breaking of bud dormancy of the host.

Thus telemorphic states of *Aureobasidium pullulans* (*Guignardia fagi*) and *Cladosporium herbarum* (*Mycorsphaerella tassiana*),which are common on fallen leaves, may be regarded as additional survival structures adding an ascospore inoculuim to the conidial inoculum available in the spring.

Subsequent Colonizers and Leaf Decay

These initial colonizers gradually disappear, being replace& by other leaf-inhabiting saprotrophs which begin to reproduce in the late summer of the year after leaf-fall, reach a maximum in the autumn and persist over the winter, until the spring.

These include a very wide variety of conidial fungi, such as. *Polyscytalum fecundissimum* and *Chalara cylindrospora*,*Ascomycotina* such as *Microthyrium fagi*,and *Helotium caudatum*, and Basidiomycotina with minute basidiocarps, such as *Lachnella villosa* and *Plstillaria pusilla* on beech leaves.

With fragmentation in the final stages of decomposition, the fungal flora becomes dominated by typical soil-inhabiting fungi, mainly Zygomycete Mucorales, especially species of *Mucor* and *Mortierella*, and conidial fungi, such as species of *Penicillium*, and *Trichoderma*, together with litter-decomposing Hymenomycete Agaricales, such as species of *Collybia* and *Mycena.*

The soil-inhabiting fungi grow up from the soil *via* the con-tinuum of organic debris. The role which they play in the decomposition process has not been fully elucidated. At this stage the Mucorales are certainly not using any simple carbohydrates initially present in the leaves as these would have been utilized already.

They could be living in association with the cellulolytic Agaricales as commensals by taking a share of the hydrolytic products of cellulose and thus acting as secondary saprotrophic sugar fungi rather than primary ones.

Alternatively, they could be primary colonizers of the wealth of faecal pellets produced by the micro-fauna, especially mites, as they are on pellets of *Glomeris*. The H layer of the soil is particularly rich in chitin in the form of hyphal wall fragments, and exoskeletons of insects or other chitinized remains of the micro-fauna.

Species from several common genera of soil inhabiting fungi, including *Mortierella*, *Penicillium* and *Trichoderma*, have the ability to break down this very resistant substrate and their activity may well represent one of the final stages of the mineralization of primary and secondary organic materials in the soil.

Decomposition of Pine Needles

The time period between leaf-fall and the final decomposition of a leaf varies enormously. In cool North temperate pine forests it may be 10 years or more, in ash and sycamore under 1 year and in tropical forests mere weeks. Pine needles are extremely durable and decay very slowly. Their decomposition most often results in the formation of a mor type of soil.

The needles are shed mainly in August and September and there is an accumulation of considerable bulk of leaf litter, each successive leaf-fall burying the previous one so that a stratified litter layer is produced. The animals in the litter are sufficiently small not to disturb this stratification and such a litter layer well illustrates the diversity of organisms, fungi and, animals, involved in the decomposition process.

A very considerable *amount* of potential energy is available for microorganisms in this litter. In *Pinus sylvestris*, production of needles accounts for about one third of the total productivity and accounts for about 60-80% of the total litter. Although the decay process is a continuous, if fluctuating; one, it *is* convenient to recognize a number of stages.

The A horizon may thus be divided into L, F_1, F_2 and H layers. The L layer consists of freshly fallen, undecomposed needles, light brown to buff *in* colour and others somewhat darker in colour, which have fallen earlier. Needles remain in this layer for about six months.

They all have a high tensile strength, a relatively low but fluctuating moisture content and form a loose, uncompacted layer on the litter surface. In this layer the needles are very susceptible to drying out and conditions are unfavourable for continuous fungal growth.

In the tipper parts of the F_I layer, the needles are grey, becoming dark brown with depth but recognizable as needles. Their tissues become softened and they have a low tensile strength and a high moisture content. They remain in this layer for about two years.

Below, in the F_2 layer the character of the needles again changes. They are greyish, fragmented and compressed, but again still recognizable as needles. The mesophyll collapses and most bear dark amorphous faecal masses of the microfauna.

Eventually the remains of the needles enter the H layer which consists of an amorphous mass of faeces and the remains of both the micro-fauna and fungi, the needles having undergone complete physical reduction.

Below this layer is an intimate mixture of humus and mineral soil. Two factors that may greatly influence the sequence of decomposer fungi on the needles are the time at which they fall and their previous history.

Pine needles are far from being a homogeneous entity and at needle fall vary in age, physical structure, nutrient content and the presence or absence of fungal colonizers in or *on* the needles. The needles have a very thick, waxy cuticle and support a much sparser population of phylloplane inhabitants.

Sporobolomyces roseus, although present on most attached needles, occurs in very low frequencies *only*. This contrasts markedly with its abundance on leaves of deciduous trees and herbaceous plants. It decreases rapidly on needle fall, whereas some other yeasts, such as *Bullera spp.*, increase in frequency and persist.

A number of other mycelial fungi such as the conidial *Sclerophoma pithiophlla* may grow and sporulate on the leaf surface. Vigorous ones, such as *Lophodermella sulcigena*, an apothecial Ascomycete, and *Coleosporium senectonis*, a rust, cause premature needle cast, either directly or by predisposing first year needles to infection by secondary pathogens.

For example, *L. sulcigena* infects young first year needles and predisposes them to infection by *Hendersonia acicola or Lophodermium pinastri* and finally *Naemocyclus niveus*, which cause the needles to fall in their first summer.

Such weak pathogens may colonize the needles directly but spread very little until senescence. They may also gain access via tissues damaged by insect pests. Living needles may also be colonized by *Fusicoccum bacillare* or *Sclerophoma pithiophila*.

Needles infected by either of these two conidial fungi soon die and turn brown but remain attached to the tree. Such needles again fall in the summer. *S. pithiophila is* also a frequent colonizer of needles containing high nutrient levels, such as first year needles, shed while still green and of needles of felled pines.

Clearly pine needles can fall at varying times of the year and may already be colonized by a variety of fungi which have already initiated the process of decomposition *Lophodermella sulcigena* actively decomposes the mesophyll tissue and *Hendersonia acicola* may remove much of the cellulose, reducing the needle to a skeleton of epidermal waxes and lignified tissues.

Lophodermium pinastri produces. pigmented diaphragms across the needles delimiting the extent of its colonization). Such parts later escape extensive internal attack by saprotrophic needle-inhabiting fungi.

This is often attributed to their inability to penetrate the melanized diaphragms but in culture at least *Lophodermium* produces powerful antifungal antibiotics and they may also play a part in restricting saprotrophic colonization. Such parts of the needles decay more slowly than uninfected parts and as a consequence accumulate in lower layers of the litter.

The saprotrophic colonization of naturally fallen needles and needles shed after parasitic attack may thus be distinct. Most needles, the bulk being second and third year ones, falling in August and September, are colonized by *L. pinastri* and somewhat fewer by *S. pithiophila.*

Soon after needle-fall, a dark brown to black hyphal network develops on the surface of the needles. A number of fungi may be involved, including the conidial *Sympodiella acicola* and *Helicoma monospora* and, in drier situations, the ascocarpic *Kriegeriella mirabilis* there is no apparent penetration of the needles by the surface hyphae although erosion of the needle surface does occur.

The hyphal network shows marked linearity with the hyphae growing longitudinally along the call boundaries. Internally the needles become colonized by *Desmazierella acicola*, which produces its conidial state from compacted, pigmented, hyphal cushions. formed over the stomata. In spite of intensive grazing of the fungi by the micro-fauna, including mites, springtails and enchytraeid worms, all become more frequent as the needles become incorporated into the more moist regime of the F_1 layer.

They persist for two years in the F_1 layer, that is for up to 2 years after needle-fall. *D. acicola* produces crops of conidiophores in both the first and second summers after needle-fall. *L. pinastri* produces its ascocarps in the L layer over the period January to May, providing the inoculum to infect further needles on the trees. After about 10 months in the L and F_1 layers, it too disappears.

In the F_1 layer, which the needles enter in the third year after needle-fall, the micro-fauna assume more importance. The external feeders continue to graze upon the fungal hyphae and reproductive structures whilst the internal feeders rapidly comminute needles attacked by *L. pinastri* and *D. acicola.*

Any needle fragments which escape extensive internal colonization become colonized by more general litter inhabitants such as species of *Penicillium* and *Trichoderina* and by pine litter-inhabiting agarics. Needles remain in this layer for about 7 years, by which time the fungi and fauna reduce them to an amorphous mass, typical of the humus layer.

The role of agarics in the decomposition of pine needle litter has not been extensively investigated. It is usually assumed that they colonize the litter when it is in a relatively late stage of decay. This is not always so. The tiny agaric, *Marasmius androsaceus*, is very common in pine needle litter. It is often, called the 'Horse hair fungus' because its stalk is shiny black,. like horse hair and is of about the same diameter.

M. androsaceus colonizes the needles very shortly after needle-fall. Its. delicate black, cotton-like rhizomorphs grow up from previously colonized needles below, binding them together in a loose tangle. Dense masses of basidiocaxps may appear on, the needles in the litter, any time from May to November.

It is both strongly cellulolytic and ligninolytic and causes very extensive internal decomposition. The role of such Basidiomycotina should not be underestimated. Their mycelium is often prolific in both the L and F layers.

Long, lists of agarics have been recorded from pine woods. Richardson has estimated the total productivity of these in a. woodland of *Pinus sylvestris* in Scotland, to be between 0.25-0.5 million basidiocarps 10^4 may 1.

The majority are produced. from August to September. However, because of our inability to distinguish species of Basidiomyc-otina from their mycelium. and because we know insufficient about the biology of some of these, the problem into assess the relative contributions of the litter decomposers and the mycorrhizal fungi.

Since many, agar's in the litter decompose both cellulose and lignin, it is, probably delignification that reduces the needles to a greyish colour in the F_2 layer.

The Role of the Litter Micro-fauna

As in other litter systems, the micro-fauna are important agents in the decomposition process. Mites and springtails cause considerable comminution of the needles and in so doing, convert them to faecal pellets.

It has been estimated that a pine needle with a surface area of 180 mm^2 would have a surface area of 1.80 m^2 after comminution to faecal pellets by micro-arthropods. Such comminution would present a much, larger surface area to microbial enzymes and thus be erected, to increase the decomposition rate.

This may not ways be so. Orobatid mite pellets persist longer than the source from which they are derived. This may be due to the nature of the: substances cementing the particles of the pellets together and, digestion by the animal of the more easily decomposable components of, the litter.

It is clear, however, that the water holding capacity of

the pellets is higher and the rate of evaporation from the pellets decreased. This creates a higher and more stable moisture regime which again should favour microbial activity.

The enehytraeid worms, which are very abundant is podsols in northern coniferous forests, in addition to their grazing activities, play a vital role in the absence of earthworms in this mor type litter, in mixing the amorphous remains with the Mineral soil.

The major group of animals involved in the decomposition of pine needle litter are mites, many of which are strictly mycophagous, with some showing marked preferences for particular fungi.

They are most abundant in the moister F layers where fungi are also more active. Protozoa and nematodes also occur in pine litter and feed on the contents of living fungal hyphae.

There is no clear evidence to -support or refute the hypothesis that mycophagy by the microfauna stimulate the growth of fungal mycelia. Perhaps the most important effect of the micro-fauna is that they act as a reservoir of plant nutrients as they do in decaying wood, gradually making available the minerals which have become immobilized in the fungal hyphae.

The large number of -different species involved and their varying life spans mean that the nutrients contained in their tissues are only gradually mineralized.

FUNGI AS DEOCOMPOSERS OF WOOD

Perennial woody plants are the predominant vegetation on earth. Forests form the climax vegetation of all parts of the world except where temperature and moisture extremes limit plant growth. Forests also contain the greatest biomass varyring from 500 his 10^4 m^{-2} in tropical rain forests to 100-300 Mg 10 m^{-2} in northern temperate coniferous forests.

Perennial woody pmts above ground make up about three-quarters of this biomass. Woody tissues thus provide the bulk source of organic carbon for decomposer heterotrophs. Fungi are the Major group of organisms responsible for wood decay and a number of groups of fungi are solely wood-inhabitants.

They exist entirely on the components of wood. A detailed consider-ation of these fungi will further illustrate the versatility of fungi as saprotrophs.

The Structure and Components of Wood

Technically, wood is the xylem cylinder inside the break of trees. In many trees it consists of an outer, light coloured sapwood and an inner, darker heartwood. The bulk of the wood consists of dead and empty lignified vessels and/or tracheids and fibres but it also contains xylem parenchyma.

Much of the parenchyma in the sapwood remains alive and unlignified and acts as a food store, mainly for starch but soluble sugars, proteins, peptides, and amino acids, lipids, nucleic acids and vitamins, such as thiamine, are also present.

Once the tree is dead, these afford substrates for a wide variety of fungi but are all relatively minor and ephemeral components. Wood consists of three major components-40-60% cellulose, 10-30% hemicellu-loses and 15-30% lignin.

Although the biological decomposition of lignin is of critical import-ance in the continuous cycling of carbon, its degradation is incompletely understood.

This can be attributed to many facts not least of these are our lack of understanding of its precise chemical structure, the diversity of its structure in different woods, our inability to produce a pure form of lignin for cultural studies and a suitable assay for lignin degradation, the availability of a very potent lignin degrader, and the general cellular and chemical complexity of wood.

Lignin, in addition to making up about one-quarter dry mass of wood, is undoubtedly the structurally most complex of all the polymers and the most resistant of all to microbe decomposition. It is a three dimensionally branched aromatic cpolymer, formed by the oxidative polymerization of three different building blocks, not! just one as in cellulose.

The building blocks are the phenyl prpanes coumaryl, coniferyl and sinapyl alcohol. The lignin of different plants may contain different proportions of the three building blocks. Conifer lignin consists of mostly coniferyl alcohol, with small amounts of coumaryl alcohol and minor amounts of sinapyl alcohol.

In angiosperm lignin there are approximately equal amounts of coniferyl and sinapyl alcohol and minor amounts of coumaryl alcohol. These phenyl propane units are built up into a branched polymer by covalent bonding involving three major linkage types.

By far the commonest, making up 40-60% of the total and most important structures form 10-20% of the linkage types and biphenyl structures another 10-25%. Thus in lignin there are three functional monomers, varying in proportions in the various lignins, and three major linkage types, but also other minor ones.

There is no regular repeating unit as there is in starch or cellulose, nor are there bonds which are easily hydrolysed. Because of this structural complexity, decomposition must necessarily differ from that of most natural polymers where there is usually straight cleavage, often. by hydrolysis, to produce the monomers.

There is also the possibility of microbial enzymes bringing about a variety of limited changes to the intact molecule and only partially degrading it to substances which pass with little further change into humic materials. It appears that only the so-called white-hot fungi can completely decompose lignin to carbon dioxide and water.

Lignin imparts rigidity and resistance to mechanical stress in woody plants and also resistance to microbial attack. Nevertheless it degraded in natural environments but degradation is a. very slow process.

Types of Wood Decay-White, Brown and Soft Rots

As with other decomposing substrates, the form in which wood is presented to micro-organism and the environment in which it occurs have a major influence on the path that degradation takes. The degradation of wood in the form of trunk and large branches of trees above the soil may be very different from that of the woody tissues of leaves and small roots in the soil.

This may be quite different again from logs submerged in the sea. The fungi which cause the decay of large masses of wood such as tree turnks above ground, have been most thoroughly investigated because such wood is the natural material utilized in greatest quantity by man and any fungi which attack it are of potential economic importance.

Three types of wood decay have been recognized-white, brown and soft rots. In white rots, the wall polysaccharides, such as cellulose and hemicelluloses, are attacked more or less simultaneously with the lignin and the wood becomes markedly paler and fibrous as the pigmented amorphous lignin is removed.

There is a general progressive thinning of the secondary cell walls of the xylem outwards from the cell cavity, the enzymes responsible acting in the near vicinity of the hyphae. Decomposition occurs-uniformly in the region of attack.

Fungi causing such rots preferentially attack hardwoods and simultaneously decompose all the components of the lignified cell walls. This type of rot has sometimes been called simultaneous rot and the term white rot used in a more restricted sense for rots in which the lignin: is removed much more rapidly than the carbohydrates.

The cellulose microfibrils in this latter case are unmasked and the-cellulose utilized later. Brown-rot fungi preferentially attack. softwoods. In these rots the wall polysaccharides are principally utilized.

Very little, if any, of the lignin is used, although it may

be altered structurally as, for instance, by the removal of methoxyl groups. With decay the wood becomes darker brown.

There is no thinning of the walls. The enzymes responsible diffuse away from the hypha and act on the entire cell wall, often at some distance from the hyphae. The structural polymers are removed, leaving a framework of lignin to maintain the general cell shape so that there is little apparent damage until the cell walls collapse.

Decomposition occurs in irregular patches in the attacked wood. This leads to the cubically cracked appearance of brown-rotted wood. It also crumbles readily to a powder when rubbed between the fingers. In both white and brown rots, the hyphae grow and branch in:, the cell cavities and penetrate the walls mechanically via pits or the surfaces in general, by coupling penetration with enzymic erosion, producing bore holes somewhat wider than the hyphae.

In both, they penetrate deeply into the wood. Soft rots, on other hand, are more conspicuous near the surface, advancing inwards after destroying the outer layers of the wood. They occur only in wood of unusually high moisture content, suck as water-logged river and marine timbers.

The soft-rot fungi again principally utilize the cellulose and the hemicelluloses of the walls, but their hyphae penetrate and grow within the secondary cell walls here they enzymatically create chains of typically rhomboidal or elongated cylindrical cavities, with conically tapering ends.

Decomposition is restricted to the immediate neighbourhood of the hyphae. Whereas soft rots are caused by Ascomycotina, such as species of *Chaetomium* and *Ceratocystis*, and anamorphic states such as *Alternaria* and *Phialophora*, white and brown rots are caused mainly by Basidiomycotina.

Two good examples of these are *Coriolus versicolour* and *Piptoporus betulines* respectively. The former is one of the commonest polypores and is found on a great variety of hardwoods whereas the latter is a facultative wound parasite restricted to birch (*Betula* spp.).

Coriolus can degrade over 90% of the lignin in wood. Several hundred species in the Hymenomycete Agaricales, but more so in the Aphyllophorales, an order almostentirely confined to wood, cause white rots. But apart from these, only a very few Ascomycotina, including *Xylaria polymorpha* and *Ustulina deusta*, can cause a white rot. Somewhat fewer Basidiomycotina cause brown rots. Thus even in the fungi, the ability to degrade lignin completely is limited to the relative few.

Lignin Degradation

It is still not at all clear how these fungi act on lignin, in spite of the fact that many studies have been made on the effects of white-rot fungi on lignin model compounds consisting of two phenyl propane units, such as the dilignol pinoresinol, or extracted lignin in liquid culture and the changes that occur in wood as it rots.

Extracted lignins have been of little use in laboratory studies simply because of the physical and chemical changes brought about in its structure on extraction.

Two extracted lignins, Kraft lignin and lignosulphate, have been widely studied because they are produced in such vast amounts as waste products *of* the paper industry. The compound which has been most widely used is a synthetic lignin designated DHP (dehydrogenative polymerizate).

Like lignin, it is produced by condensation and it is chemically very similar but has a much lower molecular weight. ^{14}C labelled DHP is usually used. The amount of $^{14}CO_2$ evolved is the most sensitive measure of ligninolytic activity.

ROLE OF EXTRACELLULAR PHENOLASES

When cultured on agar containing phenolics, such as gallic **or** tannic acid, most-over 90%-of the white-rot fungi produce extracellular phenolases, such as lactase, peroxidase and tyrosinase, which oxidize these acids a brown coloured diffusion ring appears around the colony margin. These catalyse the removal of electrons from phenols.

They have long been considered as being involved in lignin degradation because lignin is a phenolic and so a substrate for these and lignin degradation is certainly an oxidation.

Lignin is resistant to decomposition in anaerobic conditions. Also white-rot fungi produce these enzymes but the closely related brown-rot fungi, which do not decompose lignin, do not. Thus there is the apparent correlation between the ability to degrade lignin and the production of extracellular phenolases.

The ability to degrade implies the formation of smaller compounds, yet it is usually considered that these oxidases act by coupling and polymerization to form compounds of higher molecular weight.

There is, however, some scant evidence from experiments using whiterot fungi and model compounds that these enzymes can bring about limited depolymerization.

It has also been shown that the continued action of these enzymes on wood itself lead to some degradation of the lignin.

It is doubtful, however, whether they play significant part in lignin degradation. In any case they can only be part of the enzyme complex which attacks lignin.

It has been suggested that they have an indirect role in polymerizing and so detoxifying any toxic phenolics released during degradation—that is to suggest that they act after the monomers have been cleaved off.

Simple phenolics are often toxic to fungal growth and they may have an important function in coupling these. This would be comparable to depside and depsidone formation from monocarboxylic acids in lichens.

CLEAVAGE OF MAJOR LINKAGE GROUPS

One obvious step towards decomposition would be to cleave any of the major linkage groups between the phenyl propane units to release the C_6—C_3 monomers. *Coriolus verstcolour* and a number of other white-rot fungi can cleave lignin models bonded by the arylglycerol-β-aryl ether bond.

Although oxidative cleavage of the β-ether linkage occurs, there is again no convincing evidence that any great part of the lignin molecule is cleaved by white-rot fungi to produce the single monomers. There is also evidence that the monomers may be attacked while still bonded in the polymer, not by breaking the bonds between them but by directly attacking the aromatic rings, by either ring cleavage and/or demethylation of the methoxyl groups to hydroxyl ones.

Demethylation may also be coupled with side chain oxidation. These are oxidized by the loss of two carbon atoms and the formation of new carboxyl groups. Both these, the formation of-OH and-COOH groups, wouldlead to increased solubility.

Support for demethylation and side chain oxidation comes from two sources. Lignin degraded by white-rot fungi contains less carbon, slightly less hydrogen, fewer methoxyl groups but more oxygen and carboxyl and hydroxyl groups. Culture filtrates from white-rot fungi grown on extracted lignin contain small amounts of vanillin, vanillin acid and syringaldehyde.

There is also slightly less vanillin in rotted wood compared with sound wood. This is taken to indicate that some phenyl propane units, either in the lignin or after cleavage, have their side chains oxidized with the loss of two carbon atoms.

Alternatively, it has been argued that vanillin and vanillic acid are attached as side groups along the main polymer and are released on hydrolysis.

A Hypothetical Scheme for Lignin Degradatlon

Although white-rot fungi unquestionable can use lignin as a sole carbon source and completely decompose it, we are by no means certain as to how lignin is degraded. A number of very hypothentical schemes have been put forward.

These usually assume intial cleavage of the arylglycerol-b-aryl ether bounds between the monomers. This is followed by oxidative cleavage of the side chain with the loss of two carbon atoms and the formation of a carboxyl group to give vanillic acid is demethylated to protocatecbuic acid.

Ring cleavage then occurs to keto-adipic acid and this is used in the tricarboxylic acid cycle. It is most likely that these reactions occur simultaneously over the surface of the polymer with the - oxidative cleavage of the side chains being centrally significant for fragmentation of the polymer.

Role of Agents other than Enzymes

Evidence is accumulating that agents other than enzymes such as the hydroxyl radical (OH), may be involved in lignin, degradation. In cultures of *Phanerochaete chrysosporlum*, one of the most widely used white-rot fungi, hydroxyl dependent formation of ethylene coincides with ligninolytic activity.

The radical is probably formed from hydrogen peroxide in the so-called Haber-Weiss reaction which is catalysed by iron and requires the superoxide radical (O_2^-)

$$O_2^- + Fe^{+++} \rightarrow Fe^{++} + O_2$$

$$F^{++} + H_2O_2 \rightarrow Fe^{+++} + OH^- + OH$$

The dependence of ligninolytic activity on the radical is verified by the fact that specific OH quenchers, such as mannitol, inhibit it. Wood rotting fungi produce sufficient hydrogen peroxide, by the actlon of a variety of oxidases, from the components of wood.

Such oxidases are synthesized most rapidly when readily available carbon and nitrogen containing nutrients are low, when ligninolytic activity is at its peak. Sufficient amounts of Fe^{++} are also present in wood. Cultural conditions are critical for ligninolytic activity.

For example, to convert some 40% of DHP to carbon dioxide and water with *P. chrysosporium*, the culture must be maintained in the stationary phase at pH 4-5, with very low levels of metabolizable carbon compounds, low available nitrogen and high oxygen concentrations.

The oxygen supply is a very critical variable as can be shown from the fact that incubation in pure oxygen increases lignin degradation 10-fold over incubation in air. The rate of degradation also increases if very thin mycelial mats are used rather than thick ones, diffusive supply being important.

Cultures have also to be starved of carbon sources, such as glucose, sucrose and cellobiose, as well as nitrogen sources, such as ammonia, if high rates are to be maintained. Kirk and Fenn (1982) thus argue that lignin degradation is a strictly secondary metabolic function in that the products, as opposed to primary metabolites such as amino acids and simple sugars, are not essential for growth.

But the process of degradation itself is of a selective value to the fungi. It gives such fungi a competitive ecological advantage in providing access to the cellulose and hemicelluloses masked by the lignin.

White-rot fungi clearly produce a very elaborate and complex ligninolytic system, in part enzymatic and in part associated with the hydroxyl radical, to be able to degrade lignin completely to carbon dioxide and water.

Brown-rot fungi lack the complete system. The most that many of these can do is to bring about a limited attack on the lignin molecule and cause such effects as demethylation.

Lignin as a Physical Barrler to Cellulase

Both the brown-rot and soft-rot fungi decompose the carbohydrates, especially the cellulose of the wood. In the soft rots, the characteristic cavities are caused by decay being restricted to the immediate neighbo-urhood of the hyphae.

The diffusion of their cellulase is definitely restricted. This situation contrasts markedly with the brown-rot fungi where the cellulase diffuses freely into the walls, hydrolysing the cellulose throughout and leaving a skeleton of predominantly lignin.

It has often been suggested that the cellulolytic enzymes of the two groups differ in size and shape and that the lower diffusibility of the cellulase produced by the soft-rot fungi indicates larger molecular dimensions but this is not so.

The cellulases produced by the two groups have similar dimensions and properties. Many actively cellulolytic fungi may be restricted in their ability to utilize cellulose in wood by virtue of the intimate nature of the association between the cellulose and the lignin.

A particularly good example is *Chaetomium globosum* which rapidly degrades cotton and filter paper cellulose completely, but only attacks wood of high moisture content and merely produces soft rot cavities in the cell walls.

Lignin appears to act as a physical barrier that prevents thecellulase from reaching sufficient glycosidic bonds in the cellulose to permit any large scale hydrolysis. Thus the accesdsibility of the cellulose to the degrading enzymes is a most important factor.

The evidence for this comes from a number of sources. Increased accessibility can be achieved by breaking down the wood to much finer particles before adding cellulase. This exposes larger surface area of the cellulose free of its association with lignin. For example, in experiments using sawdust and ball-milled sawdust, increased hydrolysis occurred in the latter when cellulase was added.

It thus appears that brown-rot fungi possess some systems-a pre-cellulolytic phase—which enables the cellulase to get at cellulose in wood. In the cell walls of wood, the cellulose microfibrils are encrusted with and surrounded by lignin and hemicelluloses.

One suggestion that has been made is that brown-rot fungi produce enzymes which the soft-rot fungi lack. Some of these degrade—the hemicelluloses and others disrupt the links between the cellulose and the lignin.

There is also some evidence that one does not necessarily have to postulate enzymic dissociation of the lignin from the cellulose. Brown-rot fungi growing in wood develop and maintain their own pH of between 2-4, whereas soft-rot faux develop best in near neutral conditions.

It may well be just that acidic conditions are necessary to disrupt the association between the lignin and the cellulose. If wood is treated initially with acid and, after removing the acid, softrot fungi-allowed to attack it, the fungi bring about a greater loss than in untreated wood.

NATURAL RESISTANCE OF WOOD TO FUNGAL DECAY

Lignification

Ligaification of the cell walls is obviously a very important :factor that contributes to the natural resistance of wood to fungal decay. This is more important in soft rots. Softwoods -are more resistant to these than hardwoods.

This is usually attributed to the higher degree of lignification and the higher density of cell walls in conifers. It seems unlikely that mere abundance of lignin can account solely for the difference in resistance.

The different proportions of the various phenyl propane units in the lignin, the degree of cross linkage with the cellulose and the nature of the hemicelluloses must also be important. Nevertheless lignification must act as some sort of physical barrier.

Many very actively cellulolytic fungi and -bacteria cannot attack wood because the lignin prevents their cellulase from reaching sufficient glycosidic bonds to permit hydrolysis on such a scale that they can grow on the proceeds.

Refractlvity of Cellulose

Many other factors contribute to decay resistance. The -cellulose in wood tends to have a higher degree of refractivity or crystallinity than in the cell walls of herbaceous plants.

The microfibrils are more highly ordered and there are corresponddingly less amorphous or more randomly organized areas. The higher the refractivity, the smaller the surface immediately accessible to the components of cellulase.

NITROGEN CONTENT

In addition to being distinguished by its high lignin content, wood can also be distinguished from other plant materials by its very low nitrogen content. This also increases its resistance to decay. Woody tissues contain 0.03-1.0% nitrogen as compared to 1.0-5.0% in herbaceous tissues.

The carbon nitrogen ratio in most woody tissues is thus high, in the order of 350-500: 1 and may exceed 10(0: 1. For most fungi a substrate with such a high carbon : nitrogen ratio would be nitrogen difficient and growth limiting.

Wood-decay fungi are unusual in that they can grow in such substrates. They metabolize large amounts of carbohydrates (and lignin in white rots) in the presence of very small amounts of nitrogen. The mycelium of most fungi, grown on nutrient media, contains about 5.0% nitrogen and has a carbon nitrogen ratio of about 10 : 1.

The nitrogen content of the medium may fall, under starvation conditions, to around 1.0% before growth stops. The white-rot fungus *Coriolus versicolour* is unusual in that on high carbon : nitrogen containing media, the total nitrogen in the mycelium may fall as low as 0.2% before growth rapidly declines.

The ability to grow under such conditions suggests a greater efficiency in its nitrogen metabolism. This may be achieved in a number of ways. Mycelial nitrogen may be re-used either by internal translocation from old to young byphae or by autolysis and reduse. Extracellular lytic enzymes may be secreted which break down the old hyphal walls making the constituents, especially the nitrogen in the chitin, available for re-assimilation.

Preferential allocation of available nitrogen to nucleic acids and enzymes may occur. For example, when growth of C. *versicolour* on media containing low and high carbon-nitrogen ratios was compared, the total nitrogen, expressed as percentage dry mass of the mycelium, fell from 4.4 to 0.2 but the percentage nitrogen in nucleic acids rose from 4 to 25 and the amount of cellulase produced per unit of mycelium was comparable in each.

In fungi in general, cellulolysis diminishes with increase In the carbon-nitrogen ratio. White-rot fungi are unique in being able to produce cellulase at a carbon : nitrogen ratio of 2000 : 1 whereas in most other fungi this ability is negligible at a ratio of about 200 : 1.

MOISTURE CONTENT

Wood-decay fungi have higher moisture requirements for growth than fungi which attack most other plant materials. Their growth rate is very sensitive to changes in the water activity (a_w) of the medium. Whereas cotton is susceptible to fungal attack when it has a moisture content of more than 10% on a dry mass basis and cereal grains more than 13%, wood decay can be initiated only at moisture levels of about 26-32%.

In standing trees and freshly felled timber, most of the cell cavities in the wood are water-filled. Such wood may have a moisture content of well over 100%. Such completely saturated wood is quite immune to fungal attack, presumably because the oxygen tension is too low to support active hyphal growth and the carbon dioxide content raised considerably above atmospheric levels.

Many wood-decay fungi are very tolerant of high carbon

dioxide concentrations. Whereas litter-inhabiting Basidiomycotina may be inhibited from growth by a partial pressure of 10 kPa, wood-decay species still grow at 30 kPa and some, including *Piptoporus betulinus*, still grow at 70 kPa.

It appears that air equivalent to something more than 20% by volume of the wood is necessary for actual decay to take place. The existence of intact wooden galleys, submerged since Roman times, is adequate proof that completely waterlogged wood does not decay.

The point at which all the free water has disappeared, but the cell walls are still fully saturated, is known as the fibre saturation point. For most woods this is around 26-32% (c. 0.3 gg^{-1}, equivalent to an a,. of 0.97).

Wooddecay fungi begin to grow at around this level and make optimum growth at about 40%. Tresner and Hayes (1971) tested just over 100 species of Basidiomycotina and found that 94 were unable to grow at an a_w of 0.97 and below and only one species grew down to 0.94.

Other evidence suggests that the lower limit for growth of wooddecay fungi is about 0.97, with the linear growth rate reduced to about half normal even at 0.989. Worked wood that has been thoroughly air-seasoned contains 15-18% moisture, which is far too low to support any fungal growth.

Requirements for such high moisture contents, and thus water activities, obviously contribute to the resistance of wood decay. Dry rot, caused by *Serpula lacrimans*, is an exception. Wood with a moisture content as low as 20-24% becomes liable to attack by *S. lacrimans*.

Furtherdmore, as a brown-rot fungus, it produces metabolic water during cellulose degradation which considerably raises the moisture content of the wood on which it is growing.

Once established on a small pocket of damp wood it can continue to colonize dry wood in this way. The exact relationship between water activity and wood decay is difficult to obtain because all, like *S. lacrimans*, degrade the cellulose in the cell walls. The complete degradation of 1.0 g cellulose liberates 0.56 g metabolic water. This is sufficient to alter the a_W of the wood significantly.

Toxic Substances

All these factors contribute to decay resistance but the principal sources of such resistance in wood are toxic substances deposited during the formation of the heartwood. These are synthesized in the senescing parenchyma cells and diffuse out into the walls of the adjacent xylem elements.

The distribution of decay resistance within a tree has been correlated with both the distribution and the nature of these toxic substances. They have been studied most in Gymnosperms,. Most are phenolics. They fall into four main chemical groups, terpenoids, tropolones, flavonoids and stilbenes. Of these the thujaplicins (tropolones) are the most inhibitory. They all provide protection from decay for many years but with time they may become lost by leaching or become inactivated.

In spite of their toxicity, it is well-known that several fungi are able to destroy the heartwood, even in living trees, and also timber impregnated with similar phenols, such .as pentachlorophenol and 2, 4-dinitrophenol, which are used to protect less durable timbers and the sapwood of conifers.

Such heartwood rotters are not insensitive to these toxins. They use their phenolases to oxidize them and polymerize the products to non-toxic melanins. Tannins are very common in the heartwood of *Angiosperms* and they play a similar role in decay resistance there.

They inhibit fungal phenolases but decreased toxicity of the heartwood occurs with time by autod-oxidative polymerization of the tannins. Sapwood is ordinarily very susceptible to decay but the resistance of different heartw-oods is very variable.

Trees with very resistant heartwoods include many oaks, cedars and the redwoods and those with non-resistant or only slightly resistant heartwoods include alders, beech, elms and poplars. A durable heartwood may be of survival value to the tree itself. Cedars live 2000 years or more whereas any of those in the slightly resistant category rarely live as long as 500 years.

OTHER WOOD-INHABITING FUNGI

Other fungi which inhabit wood occur chiefly in the sapd-wood where they obtain their food supply from the contents of the dead xylem parenchyma cells. These are the so-called moulds and stain fungi.

Mould fungi are mainly conidial Ascomycotina. They discolour the wood by producing pigmented conidia on the surface. Their hyphae accumulate within the ray parenchyma -cells but may also be present in the cell cavities of most of the surface xylem elements, spreading from cell to cell via pits.

This causes shallow discolouration and surface staining of the wood. For instance, surface blue-stain occurs most frequently on sawn timbers and on any wood surface exposed to the rain.

It is caused by the surface growth of common airborne fungi, but especially *Cladosporium* spp., with dark brown hyphae and coloured conidia. Such staining is easily removed during planing treatments.

Blue-stain Fungi

Typical blue-staining is caused by pigmented hyphae that grow in the wood, whereas other stains, such as brown ones, are caused by chromogenic substances actually excreted by the byphae into the wood. At least one fungal stain has been used commercially.

The mycelium of the Ascomycete *Chlorosplenium aeruginascens* permeates the dead wood of oak and beech on the woodland floor and colours it a brilliant green.

Such 'green oak' has been used for inlays and decoratively as Tunbridge Ware. The wood is unaltered in texture and resists decay. Blue-stain fungi are common in coniferous sapwood, especially pines, but are also found in hardwoods.

They are non-cellulolytic 'sugar' fungi, in that they utilize only the more readily assimilable carbon compounds, such as sugars and starches, which occur in the ray parenchyma cells of freshly killed wood. They do no structural damage to the wood as they move across it mainly through the pits.

Blue-stain is thus not the first stage of a form of rot, but its occurrence does indicate the wood has been kept moist and exposed to conditions favourable to the development of decay fungi. Although the structural properties of the wood are unaltered, blue staining of coniferous sapwood is responsible for large financial losses to the timber producer.

The mere discolouration of the wood makes architects disinclined to use it and it is less acceptable to the manufacturers of packing cases and paper. In vigorously growing pine trees, the moisture content of the sapwood is too high to permit growth of blue-stain fungi.

The low oxygen tension again appears to be the major limiting factor in the growth of these fungi in wood with a very high moisture content. In nature they may colonize standing pine trees which have been killed either by root-rot caused by *Heterobasidion annosum*, or some other disease, or by suppression.

They are much more common on felled pine logs and will soon appear on these if they are left on the forest floor for any length of time. However they are rapidly replaced by wood-decay fungi.

Both death and felling cause the Wood to dry but progressively and such wood will support the, growth of blue-stain fungi unless the moisture content falls below about 27% Blue stain fungi are Ascomycotina, mainly of the genus *Ceratocystis*, most of which have been perithecial and conidial states.

The majority present their spores for dispersal in the form of stalked spore drops, the spores, in this case being insect dispersed. The perithecia of *Ceratocystis* have a swollen base and a very long, slender neck, some often 1 mm or more in length.

The ascospores are not violently discharged but the asci break down within the ascocarp and the ascospores are forced up the neck; they are extruded in a mucilaginous drop at the apex where they are held in place by a fringe of hair-like hyphae lining a pore.

A variety of conidial states are produced. The *Graphium* state has a thick sheath of dark hyphae forming the stalk. The component hyphae branch at their tips and produce masses of sticky conidia, whereas, in the stalked spore drop of the *Leptographium* state, the stalk is a deeply pigmented and very wide single hypha which branches profusely at the apex.

Blue-staining is usually associated with attack by *bark* beetles. Species of *Hylastes*, *Myelophilus* and others introduce spores in making their brood chambers at the interface of sapwood and bark. The spores germinate and grow radially and longitudinally in the sapwood forming wedges of bluestained timber and then produce their conidia projecting into the brood chambers.

These adhere to the young beetles as they emerge and are dispersed to other logs as they in turn make brood chambers. Blue staining becomes a problem where felled pine logs are left in piles on the forest floor for 2-3 months before being removed to timber depots.

There are a number of ways of treating the problem, such as the use of insecticides and fungicides, but the most successful method o•· control, widely used in Europe, is to remove the bark immediately on felling. This not only prevents beetle attack but assists rapid drying out to moisture contents below those which will support fungal growth.

Depletion of the food reserves of the xylem parenchyma

cells during ageing is one nutritional factor that tends to limit the susceptibility of sapwood to staining fungi. During ageing and the transition from sapwood to heartwood the parenchyma cells gradually die and become depleted of reserves, especially starch, and become less capable of supporting growth of blue stain fungi.

Similarly, during air-seasoning of wood, the parenchyma cells continue to respire reducing their food reserves and thus moulds and stain fungi are less common on seasoned than on unseasoned timber. From the above, wood-inhabiting fungi can be conveniently divided in those which can live only on the cell contents, such as the moulds and the stain fungi, and those which in addition can degrade or partially degrade the cell walls,. such as the white-, brown-and soft-rot fungi. Many are saprotrophs and can colonise only when the host tree has died. or has been killed.

Some such as *Piptoporus betulinus* and *Ceratocystis ulmi* are would parasites, gaining entry at sites where the xylem is exposed. Still others, such as *Heterobasidion annosum* and *Armillaria, mellea*, are necrotrophic parasites. They invaded and kill the living root tissues and then degrade the cell walls of the xylem.

Dutch Elm Disease

Ceratocystis ulmi causes Dutch elm disease it is spread in a similar manner to the blue-stain fungi by bark beetles, especially *Scolytus scolytus* and *S. multistriatus.*

The beetles bore and breed within the bark of weakened, dying and dead elms, including those which are suffering from the disease. In infected trees, the fungus grows within the breeding galleries and produces either stalked spore drops of the *Graphium* state or rather smaller droplets of its *Cephalosporium* state.

Perithecia are less easily found but in damp conditions develop on the surfaces of wood chips or partially immersed in fissures in the bark. The young adults emerge in May to October and the sticky conidia may adhere to their bodies.

They fly immediately too feed on young, healthy, elm

twigs, and in doing so may introduce the conidia into the xylem in, wounds made as they feed. Beetles thus spread the fungus from branch to branch and tree to tree.

The fungus enters the xylem and grows in a yeast-like form. It can be carried up in the xylem in the traspiration stream as such or as conidia. Infected trees soon show signs of wilting and yellowing or drying out of the foliage. Fungitoxins may be involve& but part of the symptoms may be explained by the occlusion of the xylem of the current year's growth by gums and tyloses.

Environmental Factors and the Decomposition of Wood

The decomposition of wood under natural conditions is an exceedingly protracted process. Whereas leaves of the majority of northern temperate deciduous trees may decompose in one, two or three years, a tree trunk under the same conditions may take a decade or even two to do so.

The low level of available nitrogen may be the overriding factor contributing to its slow rate of decay. The addition of organic nitrogen to wood blocks inoculated with various Basidiomycotina has been shown to increase their decay rate by over 60%. Other minerals, especially phosphorus and potassium, may also be limiting.

The relatively high demand for such mineral nutrients, combined with their relatively low availabilily places a limitation on the amount of fungal mycelium such a substrate can produce. Fluctuations, both diurnal and annual, in temperature content must also be important.

However, in aseptic laboratory experiments decomposition of wood by a single' species of decay fungus may be relatively rapid. The whiterot fungi *Lenzites betulina*, *Coriolus hirsutus* and *C. verstcolour*, inoculated onto small blocks (20 mm^3) of birch wood kept in sterile moist oil at 22°C, caused more than a 75% loss in dry mass in three months.

Piptoporus betulinus and a number of other brown-rot

fungi caused mass losses of 50-70% over the same period. These are substantial losses, the more so when it is borne in mind that birch wood contains some 20% lignin which is not available to brown-rot fungi.

These facts may be contrasted with the observation that *P. betulinus*, which had killed birch trees in East Angila, was still producing basidiocarps on these at least five years after they had fallen. The time period from infection to falling was not known but it may have been at least another five years.

Even if the variable temperature and moisture regimes are taken into account, the decomposition of one of the least durable woods is very much slower in nature than in laboratory tests.

Most wood-decay fungi are mesophiles in terms of their temperature requirements, although some come into the category of cold-tolerant ones. The optimum temperature for the growth of most lies between 25 and 30°C. *P. bitulinus* has an optimum at 25°C and its growth falls off very rapidly above and ceases at 30°C.

Its minimum temperature for growth, it must often experience in the field, lies between 7 and 9°C. For many others, the minimum lies below freezing point but decay at such temperatures would be very slow. The geographical distribution of a number of species is related to their temperature requirements. *Serpula lacrimans* has a low maximum of 25-26°C.

It is absent from the tropics and other parts of the world with high summer temperatures. In bulk wood, temperature is probably a more important variable than moisture content. With reference again to *P. betulinus*, it is able to decompose birch wood with a moisture content within the range 35-100% on a dry mass basis, although near maximum decomposition rates only occurred between 60 and 120% in laboratory experiments.

Birch logs, stored outside in Central Sweden, had a moisture content of 85-91 % on felling and after three years the moisture content was still 51-67%. Fluctuations did occur, with some drying in the summer and some water uptake in the winter, but over the whole period the moisture content was somewhere near the optimum for decay.

However, if the bark peels off the position is quite different. In summer, rapid drying out may occur to moisture contents below those which will support growth and equally rapid soaking will occur in rain. A thick, highly suberized outer bark is not only a structural deterrent to fungi, but because of its high content of tannins, phenols and the like, also a chemical one.

However, given this, if it remains intact after death of the tree, it helps to maintain a more equitable moisture regime within the wood and this will favour any decay fungi.

Habitat relations and specificity of wood-inhabiting fungi.The habitants of wood-inhabiting fungi vary from minute twigs, small and large branches to the most massive of tree trunks and stumps and from minute rootlets to major roots and include such man-made habitats as fencing post, house timbers, sawdust and chip piles.

Any one of these substrates is particularly complex in more ways than one. The trunk of any one tree will have varying proportions of bark, sapwood and heartwood along its length. The proportions will differ from those in the trunk of another species.

The wood from different tree species differs structurally as can be seen by contrasting ring-porous with diffuse-porous types. Further marked differences occurs between softwoods and hardwoods. Over and above these differences as already indicated the composition of the lignin varies in different wood.

This complexity and heterogeneity make it difficult to generalize about the decomposition process. A number of successional studies have been made on woody substrates but these have to be interpreted with caution. A succession can be defined as the appearance of different fungi in seque-nce on the same part of the substrate.

The fact that one fungus appears on one part of a log at one time and another fungus on another part, even an adjacent part, at another time does not necessarily prove a succession. Their habitat niches may be quite different, one growing on the sapwood and one on the heartwood or the latter may be colonizing a part of the heartwood not colonized by the former. For example, basidiocarps of *Daedaleopsis confragosa* or of *Hypholoma fasciculare* may appear on a birch trunk which has, for a number of years, supported basidiocarps of *Piptoporus betulinus*, but the mycelia of these would almost certainly be growing on parts of the wood not colonized by *P. betulinus.*

The latter is specific to birches and is a wound parasite gaining entry where a branch has been fractured. Infected trees are usually killed by the fungus and the trunks of these often break off remarkably cleanly and transdversely at a height of about 3 m in high winds.

The structural polysaccharides in the walls are rapidly and completely removed leaving a cellular framework of amorphous lignin which has insufficient tensile strength to withstand to bending strains incurred.

The fungus then continues to grow and to produce its characteristic kidney-or hoof-shaped basidiocarps on the fallen and standing parts of the tree. As with many woody substrates, *P. betulinus* is the primary and sole colonizer.

It may completely permeate the wood of the whole trunk and, persist there, virtually in pure culture, for several years, by which time the wood is in a very late stage of decay and extremely friable. In such a state the wood is unlikely to be capable of supporting fungi such as *D. confragosa* and *H. fasciculare.* They would not succeed *P. betulinus* but would be growing on parts not colonized by it.

Wood-decays fungi exhibit all degrees of specificity. Considering the white-rot and the brown-rot fungi as two groups, there are many more of the former than the latter. Those of the write-rot group primarily attack hardwoods and those of the brown-rot group softwoods. Some of these may be restricted to a single host genus. *P. betulinus* is a good example. *Fistulina hepatica* which causes a serious decay of the heartwood of oaks is another. The causes of such marked specificity are obscure.

Other fungi may be restricted to the wood of a relatively small number of trees *Polyporus squamosus* is, like *P. bitulinus*, a wound parasite, in this case of elm in particular but it is often found on other trees, such as ash and sycamore.

It causes a white-rot of the heartwood and may persist for a number of years on fallen trees which it has killed or which have been wind-blown, as a consequence of the rot. On elm trunks.

P. squamosus is replaced, but only in a temporal sense by a number of other wood-decay fungi. Two in particular, *Auricularia mesenterica* and *Pleurotus cornucopiae* are rarely found on other wood. Basidiocarps of the former soon., appear on any felled elms and production of these continues. for up to eight years.

Spatially it utilizes the bark and surface layers of the sapwood so it does not succeeded *P. squamosus.* Basidiocarps of *P. cornucopiae* appear on elm trunks only some 3-10 years after they have fallen. The fungus then:., fungus then persists until the wood is well-decayed.

Its mycelium appears to be confined to the sapwood not utilized by *P. squamosus* and again it does not actually succeed the latter. Where as *P. cornucopiae* is most common on fallen elm trunks, *Flammulina velutipes* is most often found on standing dead elms, especially those killed by *Ceratocystis* ulmi and which have lost their bark.

Still other fungi, such as *Cariolus versicolour* and *Stereum hirsutum*, are much less discriminating and grow on a wide-range of hardwoods. The former is entirely saprotrophic and is one of the commonest fungi found on fallen twigs, branches, trunks and dead stumps of hardwoods where it produces the most rapid of white rots but,

Stereum, is confined to the sapwood. It can actually replace, and therefore succeed, other established and less aggressive white-rot fungi. *Xylaria hypoxylon* and *Daldinia concentrica*, two Ascomycotina, produce black lines, zone lines, in the sapwood of ash delimiting. areas which they have colonized.

The hyphae of *C. versicolour* will penetrate these and grow on to replace them. Other fungi show a preference for coniferous wood.

Heterobasidion annosum, *Paxillus atrotomentosus* and *Tricholomopsis rutilans* are character-istic of conifer stumps, *Hirschoporus abietinus* and *Stereum sanguinole-ntum* of coniferous twigs and branches and *Auriscalplum vulgare* of pine cones.

These are all Basidiomycotina but similar examples can be found in the Ascomycotina. For example, *Daldinia concentrica* is very common on ash but is occasionally found on other hosts, especially beech and birch *D. vernicosa* occurs on gorse, especially bushes which have been burnt and subsequently weathered.

Ustulina deusta causes a white-rot of lime and beech, whereas *Xylaria polymorpha* and *X. hypoxylon* are very common on a wide variety of dead hardwoods. Each tree species thus may have, within limits, its own particular wood-decay fungi.

A number of these may enter as necrotrophic parasites at wounds above ground or along roots below ground and then persist as active saprotrophs after death.

They would thus have a competitive advantage over purely saprotrophic fungi in being established first. As parasites they may only be overcome the host resistance of one or a few species of trees.

This might account for some of the specificity noted. It may well be that the different naturally occurring tannins, terpenoids, etc., present in the different-u heartwoods further help to determine specificity. Only fungi: which can tolerate or degrade these are able to become established.

Ecologlcal Studies on Decaying Wood

Numerous ecological studies have been made of fungi - colonizing specific woody substrates including wounded living tree trunks and fallen dead ones, tree trunks after insect attack, fire-killed trees, branches and slash on the ground, tree stamps, fence posts, beech capules, etc.

Changes with time in the fungal communities on these have been recorded and described, accurately or inaccurately, as successions. As might be expected, the sequences of fungi observed on these considerable variation depending upon the *species of wood*, the type of substrate and, in addition, the environment in which decomposition is occurring.

But fungi are not the only organisms found in decaying wood. A very wide variety of invertebrates and bacteria also occur and they, too, may play an important role in its decomposition. Swift (1977) recognized three stages in the decay process—the pioneer colonization stage, the major decomposition stage and the incorporation stage, in which the products of decay are incorporated into the soil.

Pioneer Colonization Stage

Patterns of colonization may vary. In some cases, the Basidiomycotina which are going to dominate the decomposition stage are the primary and sole colonizers. In others, their colonization is preceded or accompanied by a variety of decay or non-decay fungi or bacteria.

This may be illustrated with some specific examples. *Heterobasidion annosum* is a white-rot fungus causing butt- and root-rot of conifers. It may colonize via roots or the surfaces of freshly cut stumps.

Infection of a healthy living root almost invariably occurs as a result of mycelial transfer from another infected root coming into contact with it. From the root the fungus grows up to the base of the stem and colonizes and kills the combaium, thus effectively girdling and so killing the tree.

It then progressively rots the roots and the stem base.

Rapid desiccation of the wood after death usually prevents extensive spread up the stem. In this case it is the sole colonizer. Alternatively it may colonize the surfaces of freshly cut stumps via its air-borne basidiospores. These stump surfaces are highly selective substrates and are initially colonized by a relatively small number but, nevertheless, a variety of fungi.

These include, in addition to *H. annosum*, non-cellulolytic blue-stain fungi utilizing the contents of the parenchyma cells, cellulolytic fungi, such as *Phialophora* and *Trichoderma spp.*, utilizing cell, contents and may easily accessible cellulose, and other wooddecay fungi such as the white-rot fungus *Peniophora gigantea.*

This is a much more competitive situation whether or not it emerges as the major decomposer will depend upon a multiplicity of factors, including its ability to compute with these for the more readily available nutrients which are necessary if it is to become established.

Similarly patterns of colonization, can be seen in the initiation of decay in trunks following, woudings, such as by the branches breaking off in high wind. This. applies to most species of *Sterium.* They invade only freshly exposed tissues and are inhibited by the presence of other pioneer micro-fungi and bacteria.

In other cases, such as with. *Phellinus igniarius* invading wounds on poplars and other hardwoods, prior colonization by bacteria and micro-fungi such, as the stain, mould and soft-rot fungi generally occurs and may even be a prerequisite if it is to attack and cause of progressive rot of the heartwood.

Insects, especially members of the Ipidae and Scolytidae, may attack living trees and introduce bacteria, yeasts, blue-stain or ambrosia fungi below the protective bark.

The combined activities of the insects and the fungi may weaken or kill the tree. The wood-decay Basidiomycotina then follow. The attack of *Scolytus scolytus* on elms introducing *ulmi*, followed by *Flammu-lina velutipes*, is a case in point.

DECOMPOSITION PHASE

The decomposition phase is dominated by the white-and· brown-rot fungi but wooe-boring beetles (Coleoptera) and wood-eating termites (Isoptera) may also contribute to decay.

In many woody substrates only one fungus may be involved in the decomposition phase examples of *Piptoporus betulinus* on birch, *Heierobasidion annosum* on pines and *Coriolus versicolour* on hardwoods in general, have already been given.

In others, a number, but usually a very limited number of fungi are involved. Each of these occupies discrete volumes of wood which are often clearly demarcated from each other by distinct dark lines. These colonies may intricately interlock but their mycelia do not intermix.

They remain isolated by zone lines into virtually pure cultures. This balanced state may persist for a number of years, but, depending upon the relative competitive ability of adjacent mycelia, there may be eventually some replacement of one fungus by another, or aggressive saprotropbs, such as *Hypholoma fasciculare*, *Phallus impudicus* and *Phlebia merismodes*, may colonize from the surrounding litter and replace them.

For example, both *C. versicolour* and *Stereum hirsutum* are susceptible to replacement by any of these three in hardwood trunks and branches and *Heterobasidium annosum* by *Peniophora gigantea* in pine stumps. *H. annosum* is particularly sensitive to hyphal interference caused by the latter and this may be one factor involved in its replacement.

The Role of Animals in Degradation

Many wood-boring beetles and their larvae and termites are wood feeders depending upon microbial symbionts in their guts to semi-digest the wood. Some feed on sound wood, others on decaying and well-rotted wood.

In the latter case, the fungi growing in the wood may

be an important component of their food. Many termites are polyphagous. When *Kalotermes flavicallis* is fed on wood, it decomposes 94-95% of the cellulose, 60-70% of the hemicelluloses and 3-4% of the lignin.

Thus large populations of these wood-boring beetles would almost certainly contribute substantially to wood decay. Another important aspect of their degradative activity is the comminution of the wood as they attack it.

As the whited and brown-rot fungi exploit the wood, it softens and becomes friable and as such is more attractive to animals as a food source, as somewhere to live and as a breeding ground. Their access to it, if it is bulky, may be dependent upon the prior activity of wood-boring animals, such as the beetles.

Their bore holes afford ports of entry for—a very great variety of animals generally common in litter and—soil. These include micro-arthropods, such as Acari and Collembola, and macro-arthropods, such as Diptera and Isopoda, as well as Oligochaetes, such as Enchytraeid and Lumbricid worms.

Many of these, such as the Mycetophilid dipterous larvae feed mainly on the mycelia of the fungi. They all accelerate the process of comminution and carry spores from the surrounding litter and soil into the wood and thus inoculate it with common soil fungi.

Many Zygomycete Mucorales appear for the first time on the decaying wood, along with a variety of conidial fungi including species of *Penicillium*, *Scytalidium* and *Trichoderma*. These now have a -quite wide choice of substrates on which to grow.

They may utilize the partly degraded wood, the dead hyphae of the wood-decay fungi, dead fauna or their faecal remains. Some may live as commensals sharing the hydrolytic products of the enzyme systems of the major decomposers.

This is the incorporation stage. As the wood becomes more extensively decayed, the activity of the wood-decay fungi may decline and they are eventually replaced by such soil-inhabiting fungi. With time, the wood disintegrates and as it does so it is incorporated into the soil.

Wood Decay and the Cycling of Mineral Nutrients

Wood decay is important in regulating the cycling of mineral nutrients in the woodland ecosystem and contributes to the process of soil development there.

Over the period of fungal decay, virtually all the important minerals, but in particular nitrogen and phosphorus, become immobilized in an organic form in the fungal hyphae and their reproductive structures, such as basidiocarps.

Although the mineral content is low per unit volume, the sheer volume of decomposing wood means that it forms a very substantial part of the total minerals in the woodland ecosystem. Comminution of the decaying wood by the animal invaders leads to a release of some minerals.

The small particulate form of the frass or faecal materials means that they are more effectively leached. As with the fungi the animals themselves act as a further reservoir of plant nutrients in a considerably more concentrated form than in the wood itself.

Their wanderings, after feeding, lead to some redistribution of minerals but by far the more major redistribution and export from the wood occurs when adult stages emerge from the broods reared in and on the decaying wood.

But this is essentially only a redistribution. The adults eventually die and their tissues are mineralized elsewhere in the ecosystem, while any fungal remains are mineralized *in situ.*

DECOMPOSITION OF LIGNIN AND HUMUS IN THE SOIL

The white- and brown-rot fungi are, more often than not, associated with relatively large masses of wood, such as the dead tree trunk and decaying stump. This may be because only these contain enough energy resources for these fungi to amass sufficient to produce their relatively massive and conspicuous basidiocarps.

Vast quantities of lignin are incorporated into the soil in the vascular network of the leaves, fine rootlets and so on. These are very different substrates for fungi and other micro-organisms and they are in a vastly different environment.

The substrate is richer in terms of associated readily available carbon and nitrogen sources, as tissues other than the highly lignified xylem are present in relatively larger proportions than in bulk wood. It is also presented to a much more varied population of micro-organisms.

As such it would support a more diverse micro-flora and any lignin decomposers would be competing for, not necessarily lignin, but other more generally assimilable components, which are necessary for establishment, and would also be exposed to antagonism by others.

This situation is markedly different from the decaying tree trunk with its one or few decomposer fungi in isolation. Further large quantities of lignin may be introduced into the soil in the form of organic residues from wood decay, especially from brown rotted wood.

The process of lignin degradation in the soil may be quite different from that occurring in a tree trunk. There is very little direct evidence that any Basidiomycotina degrade such lignin in the soil. This may be because we are ignorant of the facts.

In studies on soil fungi, Basidiomycotina are only rarely recorded. They tend to be slower growing and so are easily overgrown on most widely used culture media. They are often very sensitive to antagonism by others and so suppressed.

Most do not produce spores or possess any other readily recognizable feature so could easily be overlooked. Nevertheless, they may be equally important as lignin decomposers in the soil itself as they are in the litter and decaying wood. The number of soil-inhabiting micro-organisms which have been reported as being able to utilize lignin is very small. These include a few aerobic, Gram positive, non-sporing, red-shaped bacteria, in the genera *Bacillus* and *Flavobacterium*, and a few conidial fungi, in genera, such as *Humicola* and *Phialophora.* The evidence for their ability to utilize lignin has again been obtained from the use of extracted lignin and lignin model compounds.

These have been used incorportated in Kaolin pellets to enrich soil and fungi subsequently isolated from them and tested for their ability to utilize such compounds as vanillic acid and syringaldehyde. The ability to grow on and utilize these should not be taken as an ability to utilize lignin itself just as the ability to utilize carboxymethylcellulose is not taken as an ability to utilize native cellulose.

They are partial degradation product and these fungi should be regarded as occupying a similar niche with regard to lignin as secondary sugar fungi do to cellulose. The latter do not possess the whole enzyme system necessary to hydrolyse cellulose.

They lack the C_1 component but possess the C_1 component and. P-glucosidase so that they can utilize the hydrolytic products. Some also lack the C_x component as well. Similarly with lignin, the fact that a fungus lacks one component of the multi-enzyme system does no necessarily debar it from participating in lignin degradation.

Fungi may co-operate, sometimes synergistically, in the degradation of both cellulose and lignin. For example, it has been shown in experimental: systems that a mixture of the C_1 component from one fungus and the C_x component of another is as efficient at cellulolysis as when both components are derived from the same fungus.

It has also been shown using lignin preparations in culture tests that, in many cases, when two wood-decay fungi are grown together in mixed culture, degradation is more pronounced than when both fungi are grown apart. Lignin in the soil decomposes very slowly and its degradadtion there is more of a joint effort.

There may well be a pooling of enzymes from a variety of fungi and perhaps bacteria and actinomycetes—some enzymes capable of cleaving bonds between monomers, others of demethylation and still others of side chain oxidation and so on until the final products enter the respiratory pathways of one organism or another.

THE NATURE OF HUMUS

With this breakdown there is a gradual accumulation of dark, amorphous, organic humus. The chemistry of humus has by no means been fully elucidated.

It is very heterogeneous and. can be separated into a number of molecular categories using extraction techniques. It forms a very dark solution in dilute NaOH and a black precipitate called humin. Acidifi-cation of the solution with HCl to between pH 1-2 precipitates out a fraction called humic acid, leaving fulvic acid.

The *humic acid* fraction is the major molecular category and forms from between 50 to 80% of the soil humus. It "Usually contains about 5% nitrogen, mainly in the form- of bound amino acids but also in amino sugars and heterocyclic purine or pyrimidine derivatives.

The most favoured idea is that humic acid has a heterogeneous aromatic core with carbohydrates, peptides and proteins, phenolics and metals attached peripherally.

In some soils, especially under lands the humic acid may originate from lignin residues, possibly the end products of the brown-rot fungi, which have been considerably modified by microbial action.

Syringic and vanillic residues can often be detected in the degradation products of humic acid and the distribution of these residues is consistent with the-composition of the lignin found in the vegetation above, Work with-tracers has shown that as much as one third-of the humic acid in the so l is derived from lignin and only fit one twentieth Prom cellulose.

Reductive cleavage of most humic acid fractions shows that they also contain units—b sad on phloroglucinol. This suggests that seed, plant flavonoids also contribute to humus. Flavonoids are phenolics with two aromatic rings and include pigments, such as anthocyanins.

The phenolics are degraded to simple phenols which become polymerized into the humic acid traction. But humus is not solely a product of degradation of the more resistant parts of seed plants. It is also in substantial part a product of microbial synthesis.

When ^{14}C labelled glucose is added to the soil, 40-80% of the carbon is lost as carbon dioxide within a few days, but even after two years, about 5-10% is still present in the soil humus. Intracellular transformation of carbohydrates and other simple organic organic substances occurs to produce phenols, quinones and other aromatic substances.

These are oxidatively polymerized and combined with peptides and other cell constituents to form humic-like pigments, melanins, inside or outside the cell. These serve several functions. They may be deposited in the walls of hyphae, spores or ascocarps, to protect against excessive ultra-violet light or as a water-proofing to prevent water loss.

Eventually, on the death of these structures and with time, they become variously transformed and incorporated into the humus fraction. The existence of significant amounts of amino sugars and non-protein amino acids, such as diaminopimelic acid, also suggests that residues of bacterial cell walls may form part of the humus.

Turnover of Humus in Soil

Humus is extremely resistant to microbial degradation but nevertheless there is a very slow turnover with the rate depending upon the soil type. A sample from a chernozem soil from the USA was ^{14}C dated as 990±60 y old. In other soils, humus is less stable *e.g.* humus from a coniferous forest soil in Sweden was dated as 370±100 y.

A number of fungi have been found to decompose humic acid in, laboratory test. Humic acid was extracted from a Canadian soil. It contained 26% of the total soil carbon and was dated as 785±50 y old. It was supplied as the sole carbon and nitrogen source as a 0.2% solution to a number of microorganisms, isolated by direct plating of the soil onto humic acid· containing media.

Four bacteria, in the genera *Bacillus* and *Pseudomonas*, and two conidial fungi, *Penicium frequentans* and *Aspergillus versicolour*, could utilize the humic acid as a sole-carbon and nitrogen source but no actinomycetes could Op. *frequentans* made the best growth and it appeared to utilize the humic acid by initially reducing carboxylic groups to aldehydes, and then alcohols.

Salicylaldehyde and salicyl alcohol appeared in culture filtrates. A number of Basidiomycotina, including *Coriodus versicolour; Hypholoma fasciculare* and *Trametes auaveolens*, all active white-rot fungi, can also utilize humic acid and this ability is always associated with the reduction of carboxylic acids to alcohols.

This suggests that one of the first steps in the degradative process is an aerobic reductive one. Subsequent steps have as yet to be elucidated. Very little can be concluded from such studies about the process of degradation in soils.

Resistance to degradation may not be so much that it is not susceptible to microbial enzymes but that its multidimensional complex structure physically restricts the access of such enzymes.

Index

A

B

C

D

E

F

G

H

I

J

K

L

M

P

Q

R

S

T

U

V